THE THEORY PRIMER

For Joan
— my greatest treasure —

In memoriam Kurt Paul Schneider

THE THEORY PRIMER
A Sociological Guide

Mark A. Schneider

ROWMAN & LITTLEFIELD PUBLISHERS, INC.
Lanham • Boulder • New York • Toronto • Oxford

ROWMAN & LITTLEFIELD PUBLISHERS, INC.

Published in the United States of America
by Rowman & Littlefield Publishers, Inc.
A wholly owned subsidiary of The Rowman & Littlefield Publishing Group, Inc.
4501 Forbes Boulevard, Suite 200, Lanham, Maryland 20706
www.rowmanlittlefield.com

PO Box 317
Oxford
OX2 9RU, UK

British Library Cataloguing in Publication Information Available

Library of Congress Cataloging-in-Publication Data

Schneider, Mark A.
   The theory primer : a sociological guide / Mark Schneider.
      p.   cm.
   Includes bibliographical references and index.
   ISBN-10: 0-7425-1891-4 (cloth : alk. paper)
   ISBN-10: 0-7425-1892-2 (pbk. : alk. paper)
   ISBN-13: 978-0-7425-1891-9 (cloth : alk. paper)
   ISBN-13: 978-0-7425-1892-6 (pbk. : alk. paper)
   1. Sociology.   I. Title.
   HM585.S38   2006
   301.01—dc22   2005031268

Printed in the United States of America

∞ ™ The paper used in this publication meets the minimum requirements of American
National Standard for Information Sciences—Permanence of Paper for Printed Library
Materials, ANSI/NISO Z39.48-1992.

Contents

Figures and Tables

Preface: Toward Theorizing as a Skill

THIS BOOK INTRODUCES sociology majors, as well as graduate students without much prior background, to sociological theory. It is a primer, or elementary guide, and it has three goals: (1) to familiarize students with the classics of sociological theory, (2) to show how the classics connect with current theorizing in sociology, and (3) to do this in a way that teaches students how to theorize. Of these goals, the third really dominates the book and most differentiates it from other theory texts. I take theorizing to be a *skill*, and a signally important one. Theorizing, after all, is a major component of the critical thinking we'd like all students—really all citizens—to make a routine part of their lives. But it's not something we spend much time teaching people to do.

While most methods and statistics courses in sociology are skills oriented, the theory course usually is not. It is taught as intellectual history, which is to say that exemplary classical or contemporary texts are described and analyzed in relation to their historical and cultural settings. This approach assumes that students will easily gather, simply from presentations of theories and their origins, what a theory *is* and how theorizing is *done*.

In my experience, they won't, and for several perfectly good reasons. The first is that sociologists don't agree on what a theory is. Indeed, someone visiting us from another discipline would find it hard to decide, when presented with the array of works included in the more comprehensive theory anthologies, just what we consider a theory to be. Though theoretical writings all surely give us "insight" into social life, they do so in such various ways that an outsider would have to see theorizing as incoherent. Little wonder, then, that students have difficulty figuring out what sociologists mean by it, much less how to do it themselves.

Second, existing texts usually present material discursively, in lengthy descriptions that fail to highlight a theory's logical or argumentative structure. This poses little hindrance where the logic of the theory is relatively simple, as perhaps it is with Émile Durkheim's explanation of variations in suicide rates, but throws up real barriers where matters are more complex, as they are with Karl Marx's explanation of capitalism's dynamics. Exactly how a student is to *see* the theory in the oceans of description is not clear, and seeing theories is no mean feat to begin with. I appreciate this all the more from having struggled to see them better in order to write this text. So sobering has my own experience been that I now see my past practice in teaching theory as the pedagogical equivalent of throwing students into very deep water and watching as they sank or swam. Those who sank I was ill equipped to save, while those who swam never needed my help to begin with (Indeed, I did not really understand how I swam myself, at least well enough to teach others.)

Third, so varied are the theories that standard texts present that students get scant opportunity to reinforce hard-won generalizations about theories and their construction. Each theory seems to have a novel structure and to grow out of a novel sociohistorical circumstance. Theorizing, it would seem, is never the same thing twice, and, yet, unless there is *some* routine involved, the *aptitude* to theorize cannot be developed into a *habit of mind*, although it is precisely a habit of mind that a theory course should instill. Research suggests, after all, that students do not long retain the informational content of their courses. If this is so, however, the more time we can steal from conveying information and devote to developing and reinforcing skills, the better. But to do so, we must present our material so that it does, in fact, *reinforce* the skills we want to impart.

Teachers of theory easily forget that their own spontaneous facility at abstract reflection is not shared by the majority of their students. That students perhaps lack spontaneous facility in this regard, however, doesn't mean they can't develop the habit. Undergraduates come to higher education handicapped by an ambient culture that is profoundly hostile to abstract reflection and complex explanation. Indeed, prior to college, most students have had little opportunity to learn of and to practice sophisticated explanatory strategies. Obviously, our courses will not provide such an opportunity unless we can actually articulate what these strategies *are*, coach students through their initial efforts to grasp them, and then give them repeated opportunities to practice what they've learned.

To do this means, first, that we need a very explicit conception of sociological theory. Mine is the standard scientific one in which *a theory explains patterned variation* in the world around us. This view is narrow, but a broader one can easily be developed later, after the explicit conception has been mastered. Next, it means that we must routinize as much of the practice of theorizing as its creative character will allow. Otherwise, students will be unable to discern the actual steps involved in creating a theory or to detect any pattern in the process after which to model their own efforts to theorize. And, finally, it means that, to the extent possible, we must show how this routine is evident in the logical development of each of the theories we teach so that it will be reinforced as the student proceeds from one theory to another. At the same time, we can build outward from this routine to show how forms of theorizing that don't employ it strictly nevertheless utilize some of its elements.

In what follows, then, I mold the classical theories as much as possible into a standard format, introduced in the first chapter and then followed throughout, from which students can learn to theorize. In doing so, I remain sufficiently faithful to the originals to place students firmly in the ongoing conversation with the classics that knits sociologists together as a community. Indeed, it is the ongoing vitality of this conversation that caused me to focus on the classics in the first place and to stress consistently their relevance to contemporary theories.

Throughout, I rely extensively upon figures to present the logical structure of theories and theorizing. In part as a result of writing this book, I'm inclined to believe that when we can't present the relationships among concepts in a theory visually, there's good reason to suspect that we don't understand them well or to worry that the theory wasn't well thought out to begin with. Visualization, in other words, is a strong antidote to fuzzy thinking, be it someone else's or our own.

Finally, I've almost completely ignored biographical information about the theorists discussed. Not only is such information soon forgotten, but it steals attention from the theories themselves. In a sense, I am more interested in the biographies of the *theories*, as they have given rise to traditions that revise and refine them, than I am in biographies of the *theorists*. Karl Marx, Max Weber, Émile Durkheim, and George Herbert Mead were indeed fascinating people, but learning about them doesn't help us acquire the habit of theorizing, whereas anatomizing and reflecting on their theories does. The theories remain very much alive for us today, sometimes in cautionary ways and sometimes as progenitors of more acute and effective contemporary theories. Throughout, I stress this contemporary connection in order to show that the conceptual strategies of the classics remain vital. The men themselves may be dead, but their habits of mind are very much alive. We *can* do sociology without the men (or their colleague Charlotte Perkins Gilman, 1860–1935), but we can't without their habits of mind, their very real and ever-relevant intellectual skills. A theory text that fails to impart these skills, I've come to feel, shortchanges its readers.

My aim, then, is to teach about theory and theorizing primarily by means of the classics, and to do so in a way accessible to the typical student. My emphasis on skills connects the practice of theorizing, as much as possible, with the habits and skills that statistics and methods courses teach so that the triad of theory-methods-statistics takes on a pedagogically unified aspect. Understanding variables is obviously critical here. More than any other habit of mind, coming to view the world around us as revealing patterned variation is crucial to theorizing. A facility with registering variation increases spontaneously as we broaden our experience with the world, whether on our own or through books. But it can also be stimulated by becoming familiar with existing datasets. In this regard, workbooks like Rodney Stark's *Doing Sociology: A Global Perspective* (Wadsworth 2002), which leads students through the analysis of six different datasets, can be an invaluable adjunct to a theory course. Stark provides a multitude of empirical generalizations that beg for theoretical explanation. He also provides an accessible introduction to basic statistical concepts that will give students a better sense of how the behavior of one variable can be used to explain the behavior of another.

I've found *Doing Sociology* of great help in devising exercises to clarify and reinforce the strategy of theory construction I present in this text. Adding these exercises here would make this book cumbersome and would intrude too much upon the instructional strategies adopters will likely develop on their own, but a website containing my preliminary efforts will accompany this text. I hope over time to expand on these as part of a collective project that engages students and professors who share my interest in theorizing as a skill. After all, there's no reason why theory courses shouldn't have labs in which students actually practice what we preach to them about theory, and a website is the proper place to stockpile resources in this regard.

I remain convinced that no skill more appropriately culminates a liberal education in the social sciences than the ability to theorize. Theorizing is the highest and most important practice in the sciences. To engage in it is to participate in the very activity that has made our world so profoundly different, at least in its material aspects, from the worlds of the past. No other skill could connect us more firmly with the tradition of sociology and the social sciences in general. No other could entail such intellectual adventure in its acquisition. No other, therefore, is more worthwhile *to teach*, or more pedagogically challenging. I offer this book as a step toward meeting this challenge . . . and as restitution to innumerable students I've thrown into deep water.

Note: throughout the text I have used *italics* for emphasis and **boldface** to indicate terms included in the glossary at the end of the book.

Acknowledgments

I WOULD LIKE TO THANK my colleague Professor Thomas Burger for the care he took in reading the entire manuscript and making many helpful suggestions as to matters of substance. In addition to benefiting from his counsel, I received help from anonymous reviewers, who convinced me to add two sections, namely, the appendix on the dialectic and the interlude on the social and historical setting of classical sociology. I appreciate their thoughtfulness in trying to make this a better book. Professor Richard Nisbett was kind enough to answer questions I put to him about the theory discussed in the first chapter. I hope I've put his work to good use. Professor Joan Friedenberg read the entire manuscript and gave me guidance in unraveling numerous unnecessarily complex sentences, as well as in making the referents of my pronouns unambiguous. (Her sufferance of my ill humor when I believed the referents were already unambiguous was especially remarkable.) Further and substantial help in this regard came from my copyeditor, Ms. Jen Kelland. For the execution of the figures, I need to thank Mr. Shannon Wimberly. Special appreciation for his support is due my colleague and sometime collaborator, Professor Lewellyn Hendrix. I'd like also to acknowledge the training I received by my theory teachers, professors Daniel Bell, Peter Blau, George Huaco, Morris Janowitz, and Donald Levine. Finally, two consecutive Rowman & Littlefield editors, Dean Birkenkamp and Alan McClare, have shown great enthusiasm for the project and great patience in awaiting its completion. None of those from whom I received aid should be held accountable for flaws in the final product.

1

Theories and Theorizing

IN THIS INTRODUCTORY CHAPTER, I'll first define what I mean by a **theory**. Throughout the book, I'll be using the term in a sense that's narrower and more specific than in everyday speech (as well as in some sociological writing), and we need to be clear about what it means here. Since the primary purpose of theories is to explain how the world around us works, I'll also spend some time clarifying what it means to explain in the social sciences. The longest section of the chapter then introduces you to a specific theory. Though the theory is interesting in itself, my purpose in discussing it in detail is to break down and illustrate the steps we must go through to create a theory. The remainder of the chapter will differentiate theories from some neighboring concepts, helping to clarify what we mean by the term.

A Definition of *Theory*

To understand sociological theories, as well as how we create them, we need first to develop a good sense of what a theory is. While there's some disagreement over this among sociologists,[1] for the purposes of this text, I'll define a theory as an integrated set of **concepts**, formed into **propositions**, that explains particular conditions or events in the world around us.

Let's unpack this definition a bit. Its key terms are *concepts* that are *integrated into propositions* and that *explain*. First, concepts are abstract terms by which we group together specific concrete phenomena in the world around us. They denote the entities of which the world is composed and define them in terms of their properties. The concept "women," for instance, groups together all female humans and defines them as having particular properties. As a concept, "women" is clearly more general than any specific woman or group of them. At the same time, "women" is less general than the concept of "females," which includes not just women but the female versions of all animals. Thus, "females" is much more general than "women," and we can see that while all concepts are general (or abstract), some are more general than others. It's because concepts are abstract that explanations using them can apply to many concrete cases; for instance, if women have some specific property, then each and every woman should have that property.

It is especially important in the sciences that our concepts be clearly defined so that we know whether they apply to specific concrete cases or not. When I use the word "women" casually, for instance, it's not clear whether I mean to include all female humans or to include only adult female humans and exclude the juveniles as "girls." This is something I'd have to clear up if I wanted to use the concept sociologically.

Second, our definition of a theory says that it *integrates* a set of concepts by forming them into propositions. The equations that are familiar to us from the natural sciences, such as $E = mc^2$, are models of what I mean by a proposition that integrates concepts. In Albert Einstein's equation, you can see, in the simplest form, how a theory involves abstract ideas (energy, mass, speed of light) and indicates their relations to one another (equivalence, multiplication, squaring). This relation among concepts (along with many additional ideas) is used to explain the relation between mass and energy that allows for their conversion. Thus, the general (abstract) theory explains the behavior of particular, concrete material—as in an atom bomb. Similarly, a proposition from Émile Durkheim's theory of suicide, which we'll discuss several chapters hence, states that suicide rates are influenced by **social integration** (i.e., how connected people are to one another), according to a specific pattern. Durkheim proposed that suicide rates are high whenever integration is either too high or too low, whereas they are low when integration is moderate. Further, he believed that too much or too little integration actually caused the elevation in suicide rates. His theory allows us to infer that these rates will be higher among people who are socially isolated from their surroundings (that is, who are too little integrated), and we can use this abstract relation among concepts to explain the suicidal behavior of real, concrete individuals. We can also use the theory to explain occasional mass suicides among members of cults who have very broad and deep ties to one another (that is, who are too much integrated).

Note, however, that Durkheim doesn't state the relations among his concepts as precisely as does Einstein. His propositions don't give us an equation that indicates just how much of a decline (or rise) in social integration would produce a given rise in the suicide rate. This lack of precision causes problems when we try to test his theory, and (unfortunately, but perhaps unavoidably) it's characteristic of theories in the social sciences. For instance, political scientists have found that our tendency to vote increases as our age and socioeconomic status rise, but just how much it increases varies from one community or one election to another. Of course, knowing this is better than only knowing that age and socioeconomic status "influence" voting behavior (does this mean positively or negatively?) or knowing nothing at all, but the more precise theories are about the specific character of the relations among their concepts, the better for us all.

To summarize: theories make general, but explicit, statements about what the world is composed of and how it works. They do this by developing abstract concepts and stating relationships among them in terms of propositions. We can use these propositions to "model" the nature and behavior of phenomena in the world around us—to form abstract pictures of what things consist of and how they work. Such models abstract from (or summarize the properties of) particular phenomena. Like maps, they simplify the world by focusing on only a few of its aspects and properties. They isolate crucial features of phenomena and depict the relationships among them. And they cover all specific, concrete examples of the phenomena they model because their concepts are general—as are the ideas of mass, or of suicide rates, or of social integration. Further, the more clearly defined the concepts and the more precisely stated their relations to one another, all other things being equal, the better the theory can explain what the world is composed of and how it works.

Let's note that this definition of "theory" is much narrower than common usage. In everyday speech, we often say, "I have a theory that . . ." when we merely want to indicate our belief about a particular state of affairs. For instance, we might be convinced (or just have a hunch) that Martin Luther

King Jr.'s assassin did not act alone, or that people are basically good, or that there are more people in gambling casinos on Sundays than there are in church, and we might call each of these a "theory." But none of them is a theory in the sense we are using the term here. They don't state relations among abstract concepts so as to explain the nature or behavior of the world around us. Instead, they describe particular states of affairs that we assume exist. They're what we call **descriptive hypotheses**, and although we sometimes casually use the word "theory" for such hypotheses, they don't qualify as theories in the sense we want here. To take another example, we often say things like, "My theory is that marijuana use precedes heroin use." Now, though we might do research to show that this is (or is not) the case—that is, do research to show that our hypothesis is *descriptively accurate* or not—a theory in our sense would have to show not just that marijuana use did precede heroine use, which is a factual issue, but why it did so, which is a theoretical one. This is what separates a descriptive hypothesis from a theory, and it's an important distinction, which we'll return to in a moment. In any event, just note that when we're dealing with matters of fact (e.g., there are not actually more people in casinos than in church on Sundays), we're not dealing with a theory.

Thus far, we've managed to unpack only two parts of our definition: concepts and their integration through propositions. In our definition of a theory, we use integrated concepts to explain what the world consists of and how it behaves. We now need to tackle the difficult topic of explanation.

Theory and Explanation

I've indicated that theories are used to explain, but this word has many meanings. Let's think about three of them: **analysis**, **explication**, and **causal accounting**.

Analysis

One mode of explanation involves **analysis**, which means taking something to pieces conceptually and showing how its parts relate to one another. Across Western history, for instance, people have wondered what the physical world was composed of. In Greece and Rome, it was thought to be built out of four basic elements: air, earth, fire, and water. We've since come to understand that there are many more elements and that these are related to one another in terms of their relative numbers of electrons, neutrons, and protons, which themselves are composed of more elementary particles, whose relations we do not yet fully understand. Similarly, sociologists have argued that complex societies comprise various "institutions" that organize basic social processes, such as reproduction and socialization (the family); the manufacture of food, clothing, and housing (the economy); the defense of the group (the military); and the articulation of ultimate purposes (religion).

Analysis thus explains what something consists of. Consider another example: suppose you attended an American football game with someone from abroad who has never seen one before. Your companion would be very confused by what was happening on the field. To dispel this confusion, you'd have to describe the rules of the game and its general objectives and show how, taken together, they make sense of what's happening on the field. This would take a very long time to do. You have to analyze the game, explaining the positions of the players, the different running and passing plays, and the rules that govern players' behavior. Only then would it become intelligible to someone who didn't understand it.

This breaking down of a game like football is called analysis, just as the separation of a chemical compound into its component parts is called analytical chemistry. We learn something quite helpful about water, for instance, when we learn that it is composed of one part oxygen and two parts hydrogen. Later, we'll see Max Weber analyze the abstract concept of **authority** into its component types. This is a fundamental way of explaining what authority is: Weber provides us with lower-level concepts that categorize real-life instances of authority into different "species," each of which has different properties, but all of which involve the voluntary subordination of one person to another, which is what defines authority. In this way, analysis often provides us with the concepts that we use to group phenomena together. It tells us what the world is composed of, and without this knowledge, we can't begin to explain its behavior.

Explication

A second mode of explanation is called **explication**, which identifies the meaning of an act or expression. Suppose a student from abroad were to ask you why American students sometimes greet one another by asking, "What's up?" (often contracted to "'Sup?"). You would answer by translating the meaning of "What's up" into terms more familiar to the student. You'd say, "This is a form of greeting, like saying 'Hi' or 'How are you?'" In a sense, we're translating for the student, providing familiar synonyms for the unfamiliar phrases.

But explication normally does more than provide synonyms. It doesn't just translate; it enlightens us about a person's motives for using a phrase like

"What's up?" For instance, " 'Sup?" may be used intentionally to reinforce a sense of common identity among African American students, and knowledge of this motive adds something quite important to our sense of its meaning. Much the same can be said for almost any custom with which we are unfamiliar: we only really come to understand it when the motives behind it are explained to us. Often this is done through analogies to customs with which we are more familiar.

Explication is very important in the social sciences and in the humanities. When we don't understand a poem or a novel, for instance, we need someone to provide an explication of its meaning for us. Often explication relies on uncovering the possible motives the author might have had for writing what she did since, when we understand these, we can often resolve difficulties we've had in understanding a text. And when we don't understand why people cheat on their taxes, commit hate crimes, or torture animals, we'd like to develop some sense of their motives. A lot of research in the social sciences, and particularly in cultural anthropology, investigates people's motives in this way, hoping to make their behavior intelligible to us. Often we can't comprehend motives without doing some investigation, which perhaps means no more than asking people about them.[2]

This form of explanation is not much used in the natural sciences, of course, because nonhuman agents or forces don't normally have motives, or, in the case of animals, don't have motives we can understand with any confidence. But this is also sometimes true of humans: people may not have motives for, and thus may not be able to explicate, their own behavior. Do people who torture animals, for instance, really understand why they do it?[3] Behavior of this sort often cannot be explicated, at least not in a way that satisfactorily explains it. So explication has its limits, which are reached when behavior does not appear to have intelligible motives.

Causal Accounting

A third form of explanation is **causal accounting** (or **causal modeling**). Actually, unless they remain simple translations, explications themselves are causal accounts. They simply use motives as causes. But, as was just indicated, people sometimes don't have motives, or they don't understand where their motives have come from. Thus, social scientists often try to get beyond or behind motives (as the immediate causes of behavior) to find their ultimate origins. For this, they need a broader form of causal account, one that can explain behavior when motives prove of limited value or otherwise unsatisfying.

In contrast to analysis, which explains *what* something is composed of, causal accounts (including explications involving motives) tell us *why* something happened, and they do so by piecing together the chain of causes that brought that event about. If you want to know why water freezes, for instance, a causal account would explain that, as the surrounding temperature declines, the movement of water molecules slows to a point where a solid lattice automatically forms among water molecules. Here, the basic cause of the water freezing is the decline in temperature, but our causal account will only be complete when we fully understand the **mechanisms** by which cooled water automatically forms a solid lattice structure, how the salt content of the water can interfere with this, and so on. When an explanation can fully detail all of the mechanisms involved, it is sometimes called mechanistic.

Consider once again Durkheim's explanation of suicide. Although suicides clearly have motives, Durkheim was convinced that these could not explain the significant variations we find in suicide rates from one place or time to another. To explain these variations, he invoked variables like social integration, which affected people beneath their awareness and, thus, could not factor into their motives. Just as drops in temperature can cause water to freeze (or rises can cause it to boil), Durkheim proposed that drops (or rises) in social integration could cause suicide rates to rise. If true, this is very good to know since it gives us some sense of how we might lower suicide rates: we could make sure everyone is moderately integrated into society. But Durkheim wasn't clear about the mechanisms by which the condition of being too isolated (or too deeply involved) produced the acts by which people took their lives, and a better knowledge of this would give us much better control over suicide. As I will show later, investigating this mechanism is one of the most fascinating areas of research in the social sciences today, and it points out that sciences often progress by trying to become clearer about the mechanisms by which more distant causes produce the effects of interest to us, often quite apart from our immediate motives. It also points out that the causes of an event can be linked backwards in chains from the most proximate (like suicidal motives) to the most distant (like social integration). And, of course, we can always step back further to ask what causes increases or declines in social integration. Thus, how far we go back in seeking causes is somewhat arbitrary, but we generally stop when further inquiry seems to change the focus of our initial concern, which was to explain some particular condition or phenomenon.

Satisfying causal accounts have been harder to produce in the social sciences than in the natural sciences, in part because of the difficulty of bringing social life into the laboratory and treating people the same way we might treat bacteria. But the difficulty may also be that social life is less mechanistic than our bodies or the organisms that attack them. For instance, it is very interesting to note that while the United States experienced a dramatic rise in crime rates in the 1960s and an equally dramatic decline in the 1990s, sociologists have been unable to reach much consensus on the causal mechanisms involved (see Blumstein and Wallman 2000; also Rosenfeld 2004). There are many candidate causes, but it's difficult to demonstrate convincingly which of them actually caused the rise and then the decline or how much each may have contributed to the pattern. It remains unclear whether this is because our research hasn't been good enough or because crime rates vary for such complicated reasons that we may never be able to develop convincing causal accounts of them.[4]

We've now looked at three forms of explanation: analysis, explication, and causal accounts. (Note that each of these terms is itself a concept and that I've used them to divide up, that is to analyze, the more general concept of explanation.) All three can be involved as we develop theories to account for human behavior, but we can also use them separately. Analysis tells us what things are composed of, while explications or causal accounts tell us why they happen. Explication helps us understand the immediate cause of someone's behavior in terms of his or her motives, which is particularly useful when we don't initially understand them. It probes the meaning of events and informs us about what people take themselves to be doing. So, explication and causal accounting are not really two different forms of explanation. It's just that causal accounts often emphasize causes that precede the immediate motivations themselves. Because of this, and because we only call upon explication where we don't originally understand motives, it seems best to have separate names for the two strategies of explanation.

We've talked about theories for too long in the abstract, however, and it's time now to turn to an actual theory so that we can understand how it was built. Theorizing is a complicated practice, but in its most elemental form, it can be broken down into simple steps that are easy to understand. Of course, creativity is also involved: some of the steps require imagination, and imagination isn't something we can reduce to simple steps. But to exercise imagination, you first have to understand where it's called for, and that is something we can be quite clear about.

Theorizing as a Process

How do we develop theories? In this section, I break the process down into three phases—developing a problem, creating a theory to solve it, and evaluating the theory—then subdivide each phase into steps. I exemplify all of these by introducing you to a theory developed by Richard Nisbett and Dov Cohen in a marvelous book called *Culture of Honor* (1996). Because this section contains the most important ideas we'll be using, I've made it quite detailed and explicit, establishing steps for each phase and reviewing them as we go along.[5] And I've presented the example in detail too, first because it's so interesting, and then because it's good for you to be aware of how involved forging and evaluating a good theory actually is.

Phase 1: Developing a Problem

In order to develop a theory, we first need to have a *problem*, which our theory will "solve" by explaining. Indeed, setting up the problem properly is crucial to solving it. For practicing sociologists, many problems have already been developed in the literature, and so are more or less ready-made for solving. But other problems occur to us all in daily life, and these often need to be transformed a bit before they can be solved by a sociological theory.

Problems occur to us whenever we are curious about the world around us and wonder why it operates the way it does. Often a problem presents itself to us when we observe something that puzzles us. Indeed, observation is the seedbed of most problems: we note some incident occurring in the world around us and then wonder why it happens. It's by this wondering that we begin to develop the problem we'll use the theory to solve. Let's consider an imaginary (and quite drastic) example. Suppose that while attending college, you go to a party off campus at which two male students get into an argument over a woman, the girlfriend of one of them. The student with the girlfriend leaves, returns with a gun, and fatally shoots the man he was arguing with. This is a case of homicide, and you are almost certain to wonder why it happened, especially because you yourself can't imagine shooting another student under such circumstances. What would cause a person to respond so violently in an argument over a woman? Sociological theorizing begins in wonder of this sort.

Satisfying our wonder might take us down any of several, very different, avenues of investigation, some of them not sociological at all. Indeed, it's not immediately clear that this is a problem we want to address sociologically. It might ultimately turn out, for instance, that the perpetrator of this homicide was afflicted with a brain tumor that made him subject to uncontrollable rages and that the shooting you witnessed resulted from one of these. Here, we would be providing a biomedical explanation of the event and not a sociological one. Along a different avenue, it might turn out that the shooter was a "sociopath" for whom a human life meant little more than a mosquito's and who thus had no compunction about "blowing away" an annoying male competitor. Here, we would explain the event by a complex and little understood psychological disposition we call sociopathy.

For our purposes, however, let's assume that neither of these possibilities is true: let's suppose there's nothing biomedically or psychologically wrong with the perpetrator.[6] How can we understand the behavior sociologically? It seems clear that satisfying our wonder is going to involve *explication*. We need to understand the motive of the shooter, and we need to understand it in a particular way. We can't just say, "Well, one guy got angry when another guy made a pass at his girl, so he got a gun and shot him." This isn't a good explication: after all, we get angry ourselves, but we usually don't shoot people because of it. (If we did, we'd be sociopaths.) So, why did the shooter resort to lethal violence when another person might just have gotten mad?

Explicating this demands that we develop a sense of the wider motivational context in which our shooter was operating, a context that's initially hard to understand because it is so different from ours. Here, we have to try out some motivational scenarios, seeing if any of them make sense.[7] For example, suppose the shooter believed it a rule of good conduct for men to respond violently to trespasses on their "sexual property" (for instance, when other men make passes at a girlfriend or a wife). Further, the greater the violence (or so the shooter might believe), the less apt a man will be to face such trespassing in the future. If the shooter believed this, then the shooting "makes sense," even though we remain convinced that it was wrong. We now have a plausible explication of our shooter's behavior, and we can state, as a descriptive hypothesis, that this was in fact his motivation. If our hypothesis is right, then we have the very last step in a causal account of the shooting, a step that's an explication. But we're left with the question of where the shooter got the idea that lethal violence is a good response to a trespass on sexual property in the first place. Why does the shooter have a different sense of the proper rules of conduct from ours? This is the sociological problem, and when we're able to answer it, we'll have a theory that will explain more than just this single instance of violence.

Our observation of a homicide caused us to wonder about its cause, and we used explication to argue that the perpetrator subscribed to rules of conduct very different from ours. But we don't yet know why. One approach open to us now might simply be to ask him, but he's very unlikely to have an answer that would be sociologically helpful. He could perhaps confirm our explication, but this leaves unanswered the sociological question of why anyone believes as he does in the first place. In other words, what causes people to believe such things or to behave like this?

To answer this, we can't just look at the particular instance of homicide before us. We have to understand whether there are particular conditions that cause people to resort to violence under these circumstances, and to arrive at that understanding, we need to see whether there are patterns to doing so, for instance, places where this behavior is comparatively common and places where it is rare. Comparing these places and noting what makes them different from each other may allow us to understand why the belief behind the behavior occurs. Another way of phrasing this is to say that we have to turn our singular incident into a **variable**. *A variable is merely a phenomenon or property that varies from one circumstance or instance to another.* Individuals differ from one another in height and weight, for instance, so height and weight are variables. Sex takes on the varied forms of male and female, and personal income takes on different dollar values for different people. Each is a variable. Similarly, our assailant varies from us in his willingness to use lethal violence to protect his "property." The only way we can begin to answer why is to see some pattern in the differences between us, and to do this, we need more data. We need to get beyond our single case of homicide and look at others like it, properly setting up our problem.

> **Step 1: Wonder about an incident or property.**

Nisbett and Cohen do this in their book. Before we look at the data they gather, however, let's reflect that, if the first step in setting up our problem is to wonder about an observed incident or property, the second step is to turn incidents into variables.[8] To do this, we have to conceptualize the incident, deciding about the general category of behavior to which it belongs. For Nisbett and Cohen, a shooting like ours would belong to the category of *argument-related homicides*. These have a pattern quite distinct from homicides committed in the course of crimes like robbery or theft (*felony-related homicides*). For instance, Nisbett and Cohen note that rates of argument-related homicide have an interesting geographical pattern in the United States. Consider figure 1.1, derived from *Culture of Honor*. It indicates that homicides of the sort you've observed at the party occur more frequently in the U.S. South than elsewhere. The difference is especially strong when we look at small towns and rural areas. In fact, murders of this sort are about three to four times more frequent in the rural South than elsewhere, as you can see in the figure.

> **Step 2: Conceptualize the incident or property as a variable.**

This is what we call an **empirical generalization**. *An empirical generalization states a relation between two variables developed by observing many cases and generalizing about them.*[9] In other words, it summarizes the pattern we discover (and can show to exist) by examining many actual cases similar to ours. In the present instance, the variables are (1) geographical location (South/Southwest versus the rest of the country) and (2) argument-related homicide rates. Our

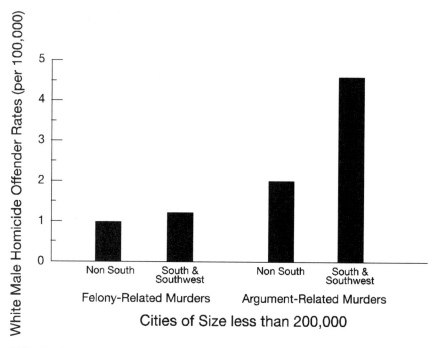

FIGURE 1.1
White Male Homicide Offender Rates for Cities of Size Less Than 200,000

From figure 2.3 of *Culture of Honor* by Richard Nisbett and Dov Cohen. Copyright © 1996 by Westview Press, Inc. Reprinted with permission of Westview Press, a member of Perseus Books, L.L.C.

empirical generalization is that argument-related homicide rates are significantly higher in the (rural and small-town) South than elsewhere.[10] (You will recognize this form of proposition as a descriptive hypothesis. It's something that could be shown to be true or not by empirical investigation.)

> Step 3: *Form an empirical generalization by relating your first variable to another variable that shows a pattern in its occurrence.*

Now we have a third step in setting up our problem: *form an empirical generalization by relating your first variable to another variable that shows a pattern in its occurrence.* This third step firmly sets up our problem and gets us ready to theorize. But, let us note again that our empirical generalization is not itself a theory. Although it states a relation between abstract concepts (like a theory), it does so as a matter of fact that can't explain any behavior. (It's just a descriptive hypothesis that happens to be true.) As we'll see, the fact that argument-related homicides are more frequent in the South than elsewhere is an important clue to how we can explain some of them, but it doesn't explain anything by itself. In fact, it's initially just as puzzling as the violence at our party. Why, after all, should argument-related homicides be more frequent in the South? In a sense, having an empirical generalization just makes our initial wonder more general and abstract. Hopefully, as in this instance, it does so in a way that points us in the direction of a theory that will satisfy our curiosity. It does this because it shows a pattern to the occurrence of events like ours.

Let's pause here for a moment to consider what we've done. First, we've taken an incident (someone getting shot) and conceptualized it as belonging to a category of incidents (argument-related homicides) that varies across time or from one social location to another. Therefore, argument-related homicide becomes a variable, and we refer to it as our **dependent variable** (DV) because we're going to seek the cause upon which it depends. *The dependent variable is what we want to explain.* We might occasionally have a good idea about this on hand, but normally we're left wondering just as much about what causes our dependent variable to increase or decrease from one place or time to another as we are about what caused our initial incident. So, we have to seek out clues. We do this by looking for variables that are associated with our dependent variable. Let's call these clue variables (CVs). In our case, we've found that argument-related homicide rates vary geographically (a pattern!), so we can form an empirical generalization that links our dependent variable to a clue variable: argument-related homicide (DV) is higher in the rural South than elsewhere (CV). It might help to picture this as we do in figure 1.2. The figure makes it visually apparent that empirical generalizations relate two variables, which we designate here as the dependent and the clue variables. Rates of argument-related homicide change from low to high as we shift locations from the rest of the country to the rural South and Southwest.

Let's review this first stage of setting up our problem: we go from our ini-

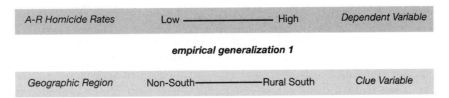

FIGURE 1.2
Empirical Generalization 1: The Geographic Distribution of Argument-Related Homicide

tial *wondering*, to *conceptualizing* the phenomenon we're concerned with as a *variable* (the DV), to forming an *empirical generalization* about it by relating it to another variable (the CV). As we do so, the phenomenon of concern to us becomes more general and related to other phenomena: we go from the particular shooting we witnessed, to the category of crimes to which it belongs, to relating this category to another variable that shows it to have a pattern. (Recall that an empirical generalization states a relation between at least two variables.)

Of course, this conceptualizing and generalizing doesn't happen automatically: there are numerous places where our creative input is essential. First, we have to decide whether it makes sense to investigate our attempted homicide as a biomedical, psychological, or sociological phenomenon. And once we've opted for a sociological approach, we have to call on background knowledge to conceptualize our incident as properly belonging to the category of argument-related homicides. In the course of doing this, we develop some hunches about what might cause a person to resort to lethal violence. In this case, our hunch is that our student believes lethal violence to be an appropriate response to another's trespassing on his sexual property. Our hunch makes sense of, or explicates, the behavior. In other words, we're providing a motive for the behavior where one was previously lacking, and it was lacking because the behavior initially seemed so foreign to us. (Here, we're in a position similar to that of an international student who doesn't immediately understand "'Sup?") Our hunch may point us in a particular direction as we look for a clue variable to form an empirical generalization about the behavior of interest to us.

Once we've done this, we again have to use our background knowledge, or look at some data to see whether we can form an empirical generalization about the behavior (or about the type of behavior to which it belongs), or both. Here, we're interested in seeing whether we can find a pattern to the distribution of the behavior. Does it vary from one time or place to another? If it does, this may give us a clue about where the motive comes from. Any pattern we find to the distribution of argument-related homicides across space or time can serve as a clue that may help us explain the behavior.

Through this process, let me emphasize once again, the question of interest to us has risen in its level of generality and changed in form somewhat: this is what we mean by setting up the problem. We're no longer interested in a specific shooting that happened at our party. That's an appropriate subject for a journalistic, historical, or biographical treatment. We're interested in differences between rates of argument-related murders in the South of the United States as opposed to elsewhere. (That we frame the problem this way identifies us as sociologists!) We now have a more general question, and there's an important principle involved. We set up our problem by examining *patterns of variation* in the phenomena of interest to us. (We might just happen across these patterns as we gather data, or we might already have some ideas about them, perhaps acquired from background reading or from our observations of the world, before we begin to do research.[11]) The next question is, why does this pattern exist? Why should the North and South vary in argument-related murders? In sociological terms, this question is actually much more interesting than our initial question about why a particular shooting occurred, and it's more interesting because an answer to it promises to tell us much more about how society, or at least an aspect of it, works. When we arrive at our question, we've successfully prepared our problem to be solved by a theory.

We are now at the doorstep of our second phase in constructing a theory, but let me point out before proceeding that it's here, in the first phase of setting up our problem, that sociological imagination (Mills 1959) is particularly called for. It is what guides our search for clue variables, providing us with hunches that some variables will prove more fruitful than others. To put this another way, sociologists wonder in a particular manner, guided by a sense of how the incidents or features of the surrounding world that we want to explain are best conceptualized and of where we are apt to find clues that will help us explain them. In particular, sociologists look to the character and structure of the groups to which people belong in seeking possible explanations for their behavior. It follows that a good sense of the general ways in which the character and structure of groups vary is crucial to developing a sociological imagination. This sense informs and actually stimulates the wonder that sociologists experience as they contemplate events or properties in the world around them, and it is nurtured and made more sophisticated by familiarity with exemplary instances of sociological explanation. The more we possess this sense, the easier it is to turn our wonder into productive theorizing. To that phase we now proceed.

Phase 2: Creating a Theory

Knowing now that there's a difference between the North and the South in argument-related homicide rates, we can begin to look for a *cause*, which we also call an **independent variable** (IV). The cause will also vary, in this case between the North and South, which serves as our clue. This is the point at which *theorizing* begins.

> **Step 4: Find another empirical generalization with a matching pattern.**

Think for a moment: in what ways does the South differ from the North that might explain variation in argument-related homicide rates? We have to find a second empirical generalization that will explain this variation in rates between North and South. Thus, the second empirical generalization will link our clue variable to our independent variable, which we can propose as the social cause of the phenomenon in question. This constitutes our fourth step.

When Nisbett and Cohen developed their initial empirical generalization that argument-related homicide rates were higher in the South than elsewhere, they had no clear idea about the cause of this variation. While on sabbatical abroad, however, a possible explanation occurred to Nisbett.[12] The South retained features of a *culture of honor* brought to it originally by early Scots-Irish settlers. In a culture of honor, one's social rank is directly related to one's honorability and to the honorability of one's family. Honor is a form of respect, and it's something one tries to accumulate and that others try to challenge and take away. In a culture of honor, when people challenge you, for instance with an insult, you have to respond with force or be seen as a coward, a deeply dishonoring quality. One form of insult is to make a pass at, or to make crude comments about, one's girlfriend (or sister or mother). Such a pass or comment challenges you to defend your "female property," and if you're not ready to respond violently, you are only inviting more, and more serious, challenges. Indeed, you can expect to be dishonored in the community at large if you fail to take action. You will be seen as less than a man.

Nisbett and Cohen present a good deal of evidence to show that remnants of a culture of honor are still to be found among residents of the rural South. So, we now have a second empirical generalization, depicted in figure 1.3. This is just a simple way of representing the generalization that a culture of honor is more prevalent in the rural South than elsewhere. Nisbett and Cohen believe this explains the tendency of Southerners to resort to violence rather than walk away from an argument. And they believe that the higher argument-related homicide rate of the South can be explained by this tendency.

Let's call this the *culture-of-honor theory of argument-related homicide*. It might, or it might not, explain the particular observation with which we

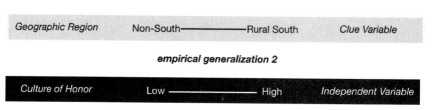

FIGURE 1.3
Empirical Generalization 2: The Geographic Distribution of a Culture of Honor

began. It will if we find, upon further investigation, that the student who used the gun was raised in the rural South (or any other place where a culture of honor is important) and saw the pass at his girlfriend as a challenge that could not be ignored without damage to his honor.

We'll see in a moment that there's a good deal more to this theory, but we need to stop again and be clear about what we've done. We began with the empirical generalization that argument-related homicide rates are higher in the rural South than elsewhere. This generalization linked our dependent variable to a clue variable. To develop a theory explaining argument-related homicide rates, we needed to find a matching empirical generalization that linked the clue variable to an independent variable that could stand as a cause of the variation in our original empirical generalization. Once we developed this second generalization, we could drop the clue variable to state our theory directly. Thus, we went from figure 1.4 to figure 1.5. This is our theory, and stating it constitutes our fifth step.

The theory has the same form as an empirical generalization in that it relates two variables, but it differs in that it asserts that variation in the independent variable causes change in the dependent one. This sort of assertion

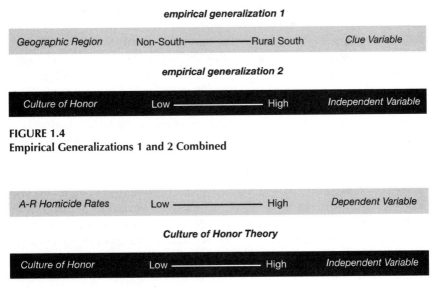

FIGURE 1.4
Empirical Generalizations 1 and 2 Combined

FIGURE 1.5
The Culture of Honor Theory Stated Directly

cannot be directly tested in the same way that an empirical generalization can. It makes a statement not about the facts of the matter (e.g., there are more argument-related homicides in the

> Step 5: State the relation between independent and dependent variable directly as a theory.

South), but about how the world works. In relation to our original definition, we can see that it states a relation among abstract concepts as a proposition that explains events in the world around us, and we can apply it to the particular instance of homicide that caused us to wonder in the first place. Essentially, we've used our clue variable to identify the causal culprit: it's the prevalence of a culture of honor that causes high rates of argument-related homicide in the South. Knowing that rates are higher in the South allowed us to narrow the candidates for our independent variable down to those with the same pattern of variation: high in the rural South and low elsewhere. Hence, we arrived at a fourth step in theorizing, namely, *finding another empirical generalization whose matching pattern indicates it might be a cause of the empirical generalization to be explained.* By "matching pattern," we mean that the independent and dependent variables must change in step with each other.

While we can analyze the process of theorizing into these simple steps, each one of them obviously requires creativity. Settling first upon a good clue variable and then upon a good independent variable requires the instincts of a detective. If you think of variation in argument-related homicide rates as a sort of "crime," you're looking for "who did it," which will be another variable: in this case, it is the culture of honor, which is prevalent in some places and not in others. In this sense, creating theories is like solving a sociological whodunit. You have to round up likely suspects and see if you can figure out which of them might be responsible for the crime. The likely suspects will all vary in conjunction with our dependent variable. That is to say, each change in the measured value of our candidate explanatory variable (the independent one) should be associated with a change in the variable we're trying to explain (our dependent variable).

A graphic representation of this may help. In figure 1.6, we see that the difference in argument-related homicide rates between the South and elsewhere parallels differences in the percentage who agree that "a man has the right to kill to defend his house," one of the survey questions Nisbett and Cohen use to show that rural Southerners continue to espouse elements of a culture of honor. This paralleling is what we mean when we say the independent and dependent variables must change in conjunction with one another. Sometimes this paralleling is direct (an increase in one is accompanied by an increase in the other), and sometimes it is inverse (an increase in one is

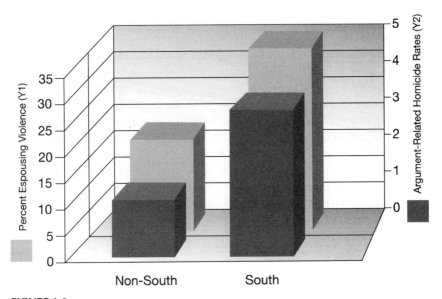

FIGURE 1.6
Matching Patterns to Develop a Theory
Source: Data drawn from figure 1 above as well as from figure 3.1 of *Culture of Honor*

accompanied by a decrease in the other), but it must exist if we are to have a viable theory. Indeed, it's the existence of the parallel that allows us to speculate that change in the independent variable causes change in the dependent variable so that we're on our way to a causal account.

We now have a preliminary answer to the question of where our shooter's motives might come from: a culture of honor. But this answer only stimulates further wonder: where do cultures of honor themselves come from, and why is violence so much a part of them? To answer these questions, we have to turn cultures into a dependent variable and look for further patterns of variation that might explain where cultures of honor occur and where they do not. In this way, we can build a thorough causal accounting of our particular shooting, tracing it back to its ultimate causal origins.

This is what Nisbett and Cohen do. They explain how and why the South developed a culture of honor while the North did not. They do this with a **functional** theory: the economy of the south was originally based significantly on herding, and the herders were Scots-Irish immigrants who had herded in Ireland and Scotland. In herding economies, a culture of honor frequently develops because responding to threats or challenges with violence helps men protect their livelihoods. In other words, your reputation for readiness to use violence keeps other people from stealing your cattle or pigs. Thus, a culture of honor develops because it proves economically adaptive, especially where government is too weak to provide for the protection of property, and it survives when herding has ceased to be important because honor becomes built into masculine patterns of socialization. In other words, a willingness to use violence in response to challenges gets built into what it means to be a man, and once lodged in the concept of masculinity, it is relatively resistant to change. Thus, even though the economy of the South today is no longer importantly based upon herding, and although its original Scots-Irish immigrants have become largely indistinguishable from the rest of the population, their legacy of a culture of honor retains enough currency to elevate Southern rates for argument-related homicide significantly above those for other parts of the country.[13]

We've now arrived at an interesting sociological theory that can explain our shooting, finally satisfying our curiosity. It explains (1) the motivational context of the shooting in terms of behavior mandated by a culture of honor, (2) differences in the frequency of such shootings by the geographical distribution of this culture, (3) the distribution as a consequence of migration to the South by Scots-Irish who initially lived by herding, and, ultimately, (4) their culture as a functional adaptation to the precariousness of property—the ease with which pigs and cattle can be stolen—in herding economies that lack strong governments. Our case will be clinched, as indicated before, if we find that our shooter subscribes to the norms of a culture of honor. In developing this theory, we've seen that explication, analysis, and causal accounting can all be involved, and we've seen how they combine to afford us a better understanding of how the social world works. We now know that elevated argument-related homicide rates (to which our shooting may contribute) are a predictable consequence of cultures of honor and that cultures of honor are themselves predictable consequences of herding economies lacking strong governments.[14]

Phase 3: Evaluating the Theory

Having created an interesting theory, our next concern is to evaluate it. Just being interesting, after all, is no guarantee of being right, as the psychoanalytic theories of Sigmund Freud classically demonstrate. Perhaps the first step in evaluating a theory is see whether it provides **mechanisms** by which change in the independent variable causes change in the dependent one. I noted earlier that Durkheim really offered no clear picture of how a decline or increase in social integration could increase suicide rates. Theories without mechanisms leave us scratching our heads, wondering why the independent variable has the effect it does. Without a good mechanism, it's always possible that the relation between independent and dependent variable is **spurious**, that is, caused by their common link to a third variable that is really the cause. Really good mechanisms have the causal necessity of mechanical gears: turning up or down the independent variable entails changes in the dependent variable as if the two were linked together by gears whose teeth mesh. Turning one mechanically forces the other to turn as well. Of course, social variables rarely work as neatly as gears in this regard, but as I indicated earlier, a major feature of the sciences is their interest in improving our understanding of causal mechanisms. Although even without viable mechanisms we can use theories to predict behavior, it is still a deficiency not to know just how they work.

Whether a theory provides mechanisms or not, there are three additional ways of evaluating it: checking it for **robustness**, drawing out and testing its **substantive implications**, and using its **logical implications** to test it against competing theories. A first indication of a theory's being right is that it is *robust*, which is to say that *we can repeatedly test it in different circumstances and still find that it holds*. In our case, this means that we expect to find elevated rates of argument-related homicide repeatedly wherever we find cultures of honor prevalent. This amounts to finding new clue variables to substitute for our original one. For instance, if a culture of honor elevates argument-related homicide rates in the U.S. South versus the North, and if this is explained by the herding background of the South, we would expect to find the same elevated rates when we compared herding to agricultural regions of other countries, say using Sicily (herding) in comparison to Veneto (the agricultural region around Venice) in Italy, perhaps in the nineteenth century. If the relation holds across time and place in this way, it will be robust enough to warrant our confidence in it. Finding that it holds in many different locations and eras is just like finding that an experiment *replicates*, which is to say that it can be repeated over and over, using new subjects, with the same result. If we find the culture-of-honor theory to be robust, we become convinced that the apparent dependence of elevated homicide rates on such a culture in the U.S. South isn't simply an accident but, instead, can be interpreted as causally determined.

A second way to establish confidence in a theory is to draw out and test its substantive implications. **Implications** *are consequences that would flow from a theory if it were true*, and they can be either substantive or logical. We develop substantive implications by drawing upon knowledge from other disciplines to devise tests of our theory. For example, Nisbett and Cohen argue that one component of a culture of honor is a readiness to respond aggressively to insults. They had learned from the field of physiology that our

bodies react to stress with increased levels of the hormone cortisol and prepare for aggression by increasing levels of testosterone. On the assumption
that preparing to fight is stressful, they thus drew out the implication that
Southern students, as more likely socialized into a culture of honor, would
show measurably higher levels of these hormones in response to an insult
than would Northern students, indicating that Southern students were more
stressed by the insult and preparing physiologically to respond with violence.
This prediction could not have been made without substantive knowledge
drawn from physiology.

They then devised an ingenious experiment to test their hypothesis. They
knew that changes in levels of cortisol and testosterone quickly show up in
one's saliva, so they orchestrated a situation (explained to subjects as an
experiment testing blood-sugar levels through saliva) in which male students
were asked to spit into a paper cup, traverse a narrow corridor filled with
filing cabinets on their way to another room where they would drop off a
questionnaire, then pass back up the corridor to once again spit in a paper
cup. In the corridor was an associate of the experimenters, a student who
pretended to be filing material in the cabinets. As the naive subject initially
passed down the corridor, the associate pretended to be very inconvenienced
and closed the filing drawer he was working over. When the naive subject
returned, the associate, now appearing to be exasperated, slammed the
drawer shut, bumped the subject with his shoulder, and called him an "ass-
hole." This constituted the insult.

Nisbett and Cohen found that subjects from the South, when insulted in
this manner, showed on average much greater increases in both cortisol and
testosterone levels than did subjects from the North. They were thus able to
infer that the culture of honor has the sort of hormonal consequences that
studies from physiology would lead us to anticipate. In fact, this is striking
evidence of one of the mechanisms by which a culture of honor produces
violence. The Southern norms of honor actually condition men's bodies to
respond differently to insult, preparing the individual to fight in response.
This is not something we could have deduced logically from the theory, however. It's an implication that would occur to us only on the basis of substantive physiological knowledge. Just the same, this substantive implication
allows a further test of the theory, and each test the theory passes increases
our confidence in it. (After all, if we found that Northern students responded
to insults with higher levels of cortisol and testosterone than Southern students, rather than vice versa, we'd suspect there was something wrong with
our theory since a mechanism that it substantively implied would be working
backwards.)[15]

A third guarantee that our theory is correct is the ability to use its logical implications to test it against competing theories. A culture of honor, for instance, is not the only variable that has been proposed to explain why argument-related homicide rates in the South are higher than elsewhere. As Nisbett and Cohen note, the higher temperatures and higher rates of gun ownership in the South have also been used to account for these differences. These theories were formulated as propositions in the same way as ours. Schematically, they look respectively like figures 1.7 and 1.8.

I have retained the clue variable in both theories to make clear their relation to the culture-of-honor theory and to point out how similarly they are constructed. In terms of our whodunit metaphor, higher temperatures and higher gun-ownership rates are among the likely suspects that sociological detectives have rounded up to interrogate about what causes elevated argument-related homicide rates in the South. As the three theories stand

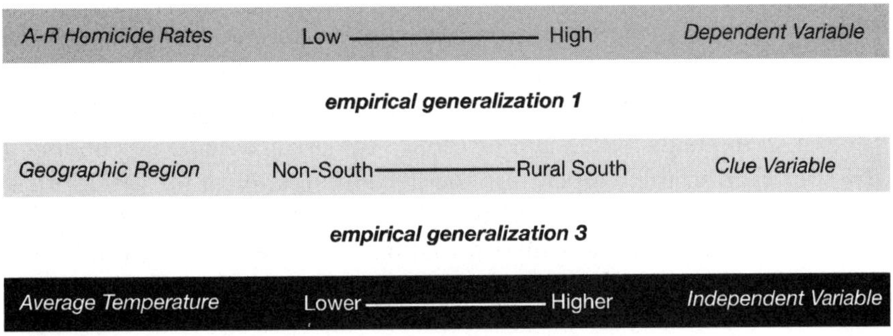

A-R Homicide Rates	Low ———————— High	Dependent Variable

empirical generalization 1

Geographic Region	Non-South————Rural South	Clue Variable

empirical generalization 3

Average Temperature	Lower ———————— Higher	Independent Variable

FIGURE 1.7
The Temperature Theory of Argument-Related Homicide

A-R Homicide Rates	Low ———————— High	Dependent Variable

empirical generalization 1

Geographic Region	Non-South————Rural South	Clue Variable

empirical generalization 4

Gun Ownership Rates	Low ———————— High	Independent Variable

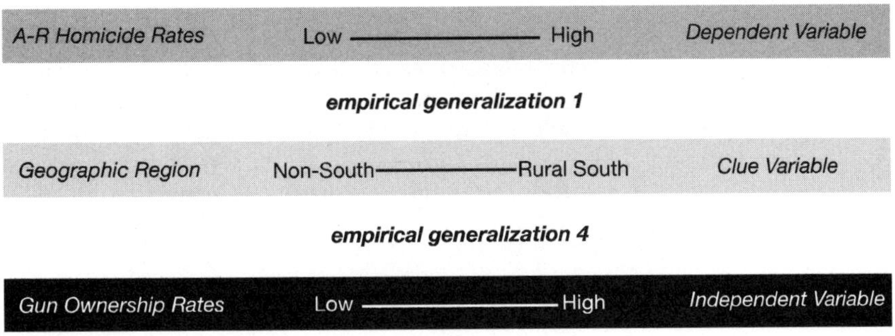

FIGURE 1.8
The Gun Ownership Theory of Argument-Related Homicide

initially, they are equally plausible. They all respond to the same clue: higher temperatures and higher gun-ownership rates, as empirical generalizations, match up equally well with our generalization about the geographical distribution of argument-related homicide rates. And they are humanly plausible as well: higher temperatures might cause more homicides by making people "edgy" and, thus, quicker to anger, while higher gun ownership might make disputes more likely to end in homicides rather than in mere fist fights.

To decide which of these competing theories is most satisfactory, we need to develop their logical implications and see how these agree with further data. There is some evidence that, as Nisbett and Cohen admit, "violent crimes are more likely when temperatures are higher" (1996:83). Perhaps, then, the higher argument-related homicide rates of the rural South can be explained by the higher temperatures of these regions in comparison with the rest of the country. If so, they might have nothing to do with a culture of honor, making our argument spurious. Yet, when we compare regions within the South, separating the hotter lowland areas from the cooler Piedmont or highland regions, we find that the cooler regions have the higher argument-related homicide rates! (Logically, the temperature theory must predict the reverse, mustn't it?) Interestingly, it was just in these cooler regions that Scots-Irish migrants settled and developed the original herding economy of the South. Thus, the temperature theory cannot account for variations in homicide rates within the South as well as the culture-of-honor theory can. The latter logically implies these variations, while the former implies the reverse. (We see again here how important it is to observe patterns of variation, both to create and to assess theories.) Thus, we can evaluate the culture-of-honor theory as superior to the temperature theory.

Similarly, rates of gun ownership are higher in the South than elsewhere in the United States, which causes us to wonder whether ready access to guns accounts for the elevated rate of argument-related homicide there. However, as Nisbett and Cohen write,

> Even where gun ownership rates are equal, there are huge discrepancies between southern and northern homicide rates. As we found in a survey of rural counties of the South and Midwest, residents of both regions were equally (and overwhelmingly) likely to own guns. But . . . in this sort of rural county, there is a difference in homicide rate of three or four to one between South and North. (1996:20–21)

In this case, the "access to guns" explanation of heightened homicide rates in the rural South implies equally high homicide rates in rural areas of the Midwest since, in these areas, men have equivalent access to guns. This implication flows logically out of the theory, and finding evidence that disagrees with it casts the theory into doubt. Once again, we evaluate the culture-of-honor theory as superior to the access-to-guns theory.

In the above cases involving temperatures and guns, we draw out the implications of the competing theories logically. The process can take the form of a syllogism[16]: if homicide is higher where it is hotter, and if it's hotter in the lowland South, then homicide rates should be higher in the lowlands. By contrast, if homicide is higher where a culture of honor is more prevalent, and if this culture is more prevalent in the highland South, then rates should be higher in the highlands. Given that we find the latter to be true, this implication of the culture-of-honor theory better accords with the data than does the temperature theory. We can do the same with the gun-ownership theory.

Logical and substantive implications, then, are used to make predictions about how the world will behave if our theory is right. Thus, the richer a theory is in implications, the easier it is to test. And the more tests a theory stands up to, the greater our confidence in it. Good theories can never be shown to be true in the way that factual matters can, however. The best they can do is fare well in competition with other theories, always pending the development of a theory that fares even better. And they fare well by explaining as many patterns of variation in the world as possible, patterns that the logical and substantive implications of theories cause us to see as connected to them. When they do this, we adopt them provisionally as the best way of satisfying our curiosity—the curiosity that caused us to theorize in the first place.

> *Step 6: Attend to mechanisms, and then check the theory for robustness and draw out its logical and substantive implications, so as to test it by further observations.*

In testing the implications of our theory or examining its robustness, we're back again to making observations, which is where the whole process started when we observed a shooting. Our initial curiosity about this shooting caused us to develop a theory to explain it, and testing this theory to see whether it is good or not requires that we make many further observations—for instance, of the cortisol and testosterone levels in the saliva of insulted Southern students! (One of the fascinating aspects of theorizing, and of science in general, is how often we are led in directions we would never have anticipated when we originally formulated our theory.) If our initial observation was casual, however, our final, evaluative observations are systematic and guided by the theory we've developed. They require that we gather a good deal of data through the procedures we study in methods courses, then analyze them with statistical methods when appropriate. In any event, we can conclude with a sixth step of theorizing, seen in the box above.

Let us now review and amplify a bit our discussion of how to evaluate theories. First, we look for mechanisms. Theories without them are less trustworthy. Then, we can assess the theory's robustness by finding new circumstances in which to test it. This amounts to finding new clue variables to substitute for our original ones. The logical structure of such tests is represented in figure 1.9. In this figure, Sicily substitutes for the South as a clue, and Veneto, for the non-South. We then test to see whether our causal account works as well in Italy as it does in the United States. Perhaps we should say our Italian clue variable here is serving less as a clue to than as a confirmation of our theory. The more places we can find to apply the theory in this way, and the more it succeeds when we apply it, the greater our confidence in it will be. The diagram makes clear why theories are so helpful: they apply to many instances of the same phenomenon, allowing us to make predictions about how the world will behave (when we look to the future) or did behave (when we look to the past).

The logical structure of tests against competing theories by means of logical implications is different, as we see in figure 1.10. In this case, the new clue variable must be selected carefully so that the competing theories make opposite predictions about the behavior of our dependent variable, as we have seen they do above. This is the logical structure of what are sometimes called *crucial experiments.* They are considered crucial because the data we gather have the opportunity to support one or the other of the two competing theories clearly, hopefully allowing us to discount one while increasing our confidence in the other.

Finally, consider the logical structure of tests of substantive implications, as represented in figure 1.11. In this case, the notion that we should test the

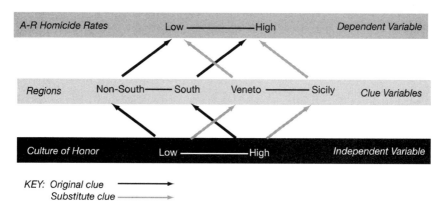

FIGURE 1.9
Evaluating a Theory for Robustness

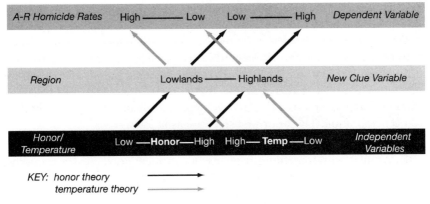

FIGURE 1.10
Evaluating a Theory through Logical Implications

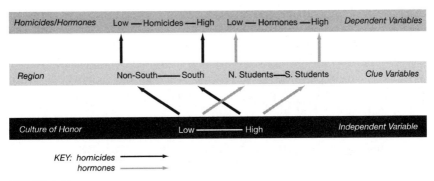

FIGURE 1.11
Evaluating a Theory through Substantive Implications

variable levels of cortisol and testosterone in insulted students from both North and South is suggested to us by substantive knowledge imported from the discipline of physiology. To be aware of such implications, researchers obviously need to monitor developments in other sciences. Their usefulness in increasing the warrant for sociological theories reminds us that the sciences are collective enterprises in which knowledge advances in part by strategic borrowing from one's neighbors.

A Brief Review

We are now prepared to review the entire process of theorizing. As indicated, we can divide it into three phases: formulating our problem, creating a theory to solve it, and evaluating our theory. Each of the phases can be further broken down into steps.

Formulating our problem requires that we first wonder about some incident or property in the world around us. We then have to conceptualize this property or incident as something that varies, making it a variable. Next, we must seek patterns to this variation that connect our variable to a second variable that will serve as a clue in developing our theory, giving us an empirical generalization. Thus, our first steps are as follows:

1. Wonder why something happens (an incident) or exists (a property) (Why did one student shoot another?).
2. Turn the incident or property into a variable (DV) (Conceptualize the shooting as argument-related homicide).
3. Develop an empirical generalization about the variable (DV + CV) (Argument-related homicides [DV] are more common in the rural South than elsewhere [CV]).

The empirical generalization is important because it tells us where to begin looking for a matching empirical generalization, one that will link the clue variable to an independent variable. Once we find this matching empirical generalization, we can drop the clue variable and state the theory directly. Thus, we have our next rules:

4. Find a second empirical generalization whose pattern matches our first one (CV + IV) (A culture of honor [IV] is more prevalent in the rural South than elsewhere [CV]).
5. State the theory directly (DV + IV) (The more prevalent a culture of honor [IV], the more common are argument-related homicides [DV]).

Once we have the theory, we need to determine whether we should place any confidence in it. We do this by seeing whether it provides mechanisms (or, instead, leaves us without reasons for the link between IV and DV) and, then, by assessing its robustness and drawing out its testable implications. We are particularly interested in comparing it with competing explanations of our dependent variable. Thus, our final rule states,

6. Look for mechanisms, and then evaluate the theory for its robustness and test its logical and substantive implications. (The culture-of-honor theory substantively implies a physiological mechanism, has logical implications permitting crucial tests against the temperature and

access-to-guns theories, and can be assessed for robustness in different locations, such as the Italian states of the nineteenth century.)

These "easy" steps all require creative input, however. Hunches, intuitions, background knowledge, and knowledge from other disciplines all have to be brought into play as we move from one step to the next. Because these inputs are creative, there's no formula to follow for them. Once again, we have to call on the combination of our background knowledge and our sense of how the world works, both of which are part of our sociological imagination.[17] One thing's for sure, however: if you don't think about the problem long and hard, you won't have prepared the seedbed in which background knowledge and intuitions can be expected to sprout. It's sometimes hard for students to realize that *thinking is hard work*. Results don't come easily, even to people you might consider very smart. For instance, most of us wonder about things only very briefly, and when we can't come up with a good answer, we just stop wondering. But scientific curiosity involves systematically returning to the phenomenon that excited our initial wonder and wondering about it again. Good detectives don't quit until they've solved the crime, even if this means going back to the evidence year after year and reviewing it to the point of weariness. Similarly, good theories won't just somehow occur to us as soon as we wonder. They require patient and recurrent curiosity—and then some inspiration. And to prepare yourself to be inspired, you have to read widely about society, as well as observe and ponder the behavior of people around you.

You should now have a good idea of what we mean by a theory. Theories use general concepts, related to one another in propositions, to explain patterns of variation in behavior, whether of individuals or institutions. They arise out of the detective work we employ to discover what social phenomena are composed of and what causes them. And they yield implications that allow us slowly to develop (or, indeed, lose) confidence in them. Only a few of the theories we will look at in subsequent chapters have the same exact form as Nisbett and Cohen's culture-of-honor explanation of argument-related homicide, but we want to keep this picture of theorizing in front of us as we proceed. It is the most common form used in sociology.

The two preceding sections of this chapter have defined theories and given an example of how they are formed. We'll conclude with some reflections that will help you separate theories from other things that look like them, as well as give you more information about where the sociological intuitions that we use to formulate theories come from. You'll see that theories tend to fall into families that I'll call **paradigms** and that these paradigms may be called upon for models when we want to develop a theory.

Theories, Causal Narratives, and Descriptive Narratives

I have just argued that sociological theories explain regular variations in human social behavior and institutions. Among the classical theorists, Karl Marx and Émile Durkheim expected that a good deal of people's behavior, as well as the behavior of social institutions, could be explained in this way. Max Weber and George Herbert Mead, in contrast, believed that fewer social phenomena could be causally modeled and explained by theories, although this didn't necessarily mean that they couldn't be explained at all. Understanding Weber's point of view, in particular, will help us better understand what theories are and what properties social phenomena must have to be explainable theoretically.

To introduce the problem, I need first to discuss the idea of **contingency**.[18] Let's take an example of something that's contingent. Think about how we came to drive on the right side of the road, and recall that in Britain people drive on the left. Driving on the right is a convention (or custom) that was instituted early in the history of U.S. overland transport, when wagons were drawn by horses. However the convention came about, there's nothing to be preferred about driving on the right as opposed to the left. Nevertheless, once you opt for the right, everyone has to conform to the rule. The choice between right and left is initially optional, or contingent (here meaning incidental): it doesn't matter which you choose, as long as a choice is made. So, we can say that the choice itself is "free" between right and left. This usually means that there's no way to point to a good reason, to a *cause*, for the choice. The initial choice could properly have been made by flipping a coin, which would have made it the result of pure chance.

Choices of this sort are not things we look for theories to explain. There is no regular pattern of variation to the choice of right versus left, which is to say that the choice isn't caused in a way that's important to us as sociologists. The issue of driving on the right versus the left isn't any more interesting sociologically than the question of why, on a particular toss, a coin comes up heads instead of tails. You can describe and record events like this, but you don't seek explanations for them, and because we're not looking for explanations, there's no point in proposing a theory. All that we can do is provide a narrative that recounts the contingent events: this happened, and then this happened, and then something else occurred, as a result of which we drive on the right, say. I'll call accounts like this **descriptive narratives**. They tell us what happened, but not why, and this isn't a fault of theirs because why questions simply aren't appropriate here.

Consider an example of a descriptive narrative about driving on the right. William Richter writes,

Driving on the right came from the habit that Conestoga-wagon drivers, and later army mule skinners, had of sitting on the near-wheel animal, and the swampers' left-side seat on following wagons in a caravan. The custom was enshrined in early road laws on the Lancaster Pike and in New York State, which flowed over to other pikes. Peasants in Europe had traditionally kept to the right as a matter of deference—the French Revolution sanctified this "democratic rule" and Napoleon I spread it to the rest of Europe. Of course, his sworn enemies in England did the opposite (which probably clinched the use of the right lane among doubters in still-anti-British America. (1995:69)

Of course, descriptions like this often enshrine myths, but if we take this one at face value, it does no more than say that an early custom associated with wagon transport was continued in early (wagon) turnpikes and then on motor roads. This can seem to explain why we drive on the right, but all it really tells us is that an unexplained custom was carried over in succeeding forms of transport. In consequence, we have more historical information, but not an explanation.

Now take a different example. It comes from a nursery rhyme, but it has figured in some very sophisticated analyses of causation.[19] It goes like this:

For want of a nail the shoe was lost,
For want of a shoe the horse was lost,
For want of a horse the rider was lost,
For want of a rider the battle was lost,
For want of a battle the kingdom was lost,
All for the want of a horseshoe nail.

If we play this little story backwards, it tells us why a kingdom collapsed. The kingdom collapsed because a significant battle was lost, and the battle was lost because—let us add some detail here—a rider failed to deliver a crucial message. The rider failed to deliver the message because his horse went lame, and the horse went lame because it lost a shoe. The shoe came off, finally, because a nail fell out (or was never put in). Thus, the kingdom fell (a dramatic event affecting many people) because of something as incidental as the lack of a horseshoe nail.

Notice that this story (unlike a descriptive narrative) provides an explanation. If the story is correct, the true cause of the kingdom's fall was indeed the absence of a nail in a particular horse's shoe. Had the shoe stayed on, the battle would have been won and the kingdom remained viable. In common usage, we're thus apt to speak of the "horseshoe-nail theory of why Kingdom M fell," but as we're using the concept here, this loose usage isn't permissible. Our explanation doesn't involve a theory; instead, it's a **causal narrative**. A causal narrative tells us how and why something came to be but will only be applicable to the single instance at hand. It's not generalizable. We can't argue that when a horse loses a shoe (even a military horse), kingdoms generally fall. By way of contrast to this, theories are general. They cover many instances of the same phenomenon: argument-related homicides will be higher whenever cultures of honor hold sway, for example. Conversely, we use causal narratives to explain singular happenings. With regard to our example, it wouldn't make much sense to argue something like "the more nails lost from horses' shoes, the more kingdoms are lost." This chain of events happened only once and is unlikely to recur: thus, we don't want to generalize on its basis.[20]

Usually, the best we can do with contingent events is to explain them in a narrative—how the failure to deliver a message was crucial to losing a battle that was crucial to losing the kingdom. In common usage, we might say we had a theory about this, but what we really have is a *descriptive hypothesis.* In other words, we're saying, "My research on why kingdom M was lost shows that *x* happened, and because of this, *y* happened, and *z* resulted from this, which caused the kingdom to fall." There's nothing wrong with this. Causal narratives are perfectly good explanations—they're just what we want to answer the question of why kingdom M fell—but they are not theories! This is because theories involve generalized models that will always apply, not just apply to the case at hand. Thus, causal narratives always explain a particular event that occurred at a particular point in time, whereas causal models are, in principle, independent of place and time. They apply generally, while causal narratives do not.

Let me enter one reservation here: If we can suggest a deterministic mechanism whereby antecedent causes are linked to their consequences with a high degree of certainty, we can claim to have a theory explaining even a single instance of a phenomenon. For all we know, after all, our universe has happened only once, evolving gradually but deterministically out of the Big Bang. Although this may be a singular occurrence, we can claim to have a theory of it because the prior events in it *necessarily* yield the later ones, on the basis of physical principles we understand very well and see evidence in the world around us today. This is very different from our horseshoe story, where the links between events remain very chancy. Thus, although theories normally apply to many instances of a phenomenon, they may be used to apply to a single instance when they remove chance from its development. We will see a particularly important instance of this principle when we turn to Marx.

Figure 1.12 summarizes the argument thus far. It gives us a convenient way of recalling the differences among descriptive narratives, causal narratives, and theories (or causal models). Descriptive narratives and causal nar-

Type of Treatment	Relations among events	Explanation?	Theory?
Descriptive narrative or historical chronicle	X, then Y, then Z	✗	✗
Causal narative (historical explantaion)	X causes Y, which cause Z	✓	✗
Causal model/theory	More of X causes more of Z (or X mechanically produces Z)	✓	✓

FIGURE 1.12
Theories, Causal Narratives, and Descriptive Narratives

ratives are normally the business of the discipline of history. They apply to unique events (why *this* kingdom was lost). Descriptive narratives just chronicle a specific sequence of events, while a causal narrative of the same events would explain why they are linked together to lead to a particular outcome. Whenever chains of events involve a lot of chance, a causal narrative is the best explanation we can expect to achieve.

Now we must confront the question Weber felt was important: *just how much is chance or contingency involved in the events that interest sociologists?* This is a good question to ponder in your spare time. Weber believed that chance and contingency so affect human institutions and behavior that it often isn't possible to develop causal models for them, thus, to theorize about them. Their behavior is something we can describe or, perhaps, develop causal narratives about, but it isn't something about which we can develop a theory. This is one reason why Weber had modest theoretical ambitions for sociology in comparison to Marx and Durkheim. Both of the latter expected that the important events in society might be explained through causal models.

Because this problem of contingency is so important, let's consider it in greater depth. Let me quote from Randall Collins about explaining the chance event of a rock falling off a building and hitting you on the head:

Chance . . . does not mean the absence of causality. It means the absence of causality that we know about, from the point of view of what we are looking at.

More generally, it also means that different orders of causality are essentially unconnected. The fact that you are walking beneath the building when the rock fell off the roof is also the product of a series of causes: your intention to go to a certain place, to see a certain person, say, which can be further analyzed into such factors as your social class culture which made this person attractive to you as a friend, and so forth. There need be nothing uncaused about any aspect of the situation, either in the social motivation that made you walk by or in the physics which carried the rock down onto your head. But the two causal orders are unconnected. There is no relationship . . . between your walking that way at that time and the rock falling when it did. *It is the unconnectedness of different causal orders in the universe that gives rise to the phenomenon of chance.* (1988:497, emphasis in original)

When we think back to our example of the thrown shoe/lame horse's causing the loss of the kingdom, we see the same unconnectedness. Normally, throwing shoes and losing battles belong to different **causal orders**; therefore, their connection seems incidental, chancy, and contingent. Because this is so, we can't develop a causal model, which depends upon regular, persistent relations between cause and effect.

A final example may drive this point home. We now believe that a meteor struck the Yucatan peninsula around 65 million years ago, changing dramatically the course of evolution. Prior to the cataclysm caused by that meteor's impact, dinosaurs ruled the earth, and mammals were a trivial order of animals. The disappearance of the dinosaurs allowed mammals to flourish and radiate to occupy many of the niches dinosaurs previously held. The eventual evolution of humans was thus causally dependent upon this cataclysm. In all likelihood, we wouldn't have evolved if the meteor hadn't struck the earth. But the two orders of events are normally causally independent, and their relations are thus incidental. The meteor striking the earth is like a rock falling off a building onto your head or a horse throwing a shoe. Further, evolution itself is so "chancy" that we would never say that the disappearance of the dinosaurs *caused* the evolution of humans. (It may have been a **necessary condition** for this to happen, but it wasn't a **sufficient condition** for it to happen.) Humans just happened this way . . . *this time.* Were there a next time, something completely different might happen.

This example shows how important chance events can be in the course of history. It also makes clear why we don't develop theories about chance events. Theories are about regular relations among events of the same causal order—about the regular relation between social integration and suicide, for instance, or about cultures of honor and rates of argument-related homicide, not about why a rock fell off a building and hit *you* on the head yesterday.

It's a bit too pat to say that causal narratives are the business of history and causal models, the business of sociology, since the two fields share so many interests. But thinking about the relation between history and causal narratives on the one hand and sociology and causal models on the other helps us clarify what is distinctively sociological and why theory is so important to it.

Theories and Paradigms

To conclude this introductory chapter, we need to consider just one more critical distinction. It will help us better understand what a theory is, as well as where sociologists get their sense of how the world works that guides them in formulating their theories.

Many introductory textbooks view sociology as composed of three theories that compete with one another: **conflict theory, functional theory**, and **symbolic interactionism**. Theory textbooks themselves often discuss these viewpoints—as well as feminism, rational actor theory, ethnomethodology, and many more—as "theories." Without wishing to diminish the importance of such viewpoints, these are not theories as we're using the term here. Just as causal narratives are too specific to be theories, these viewpoints are too general. They offer us models we can use to create theories, and they make general suggestions that can guide us in the detective work that goes into forming a theory, but they don't qualify as theories themselves. They don't explain any specific regularities in human social behavior.

Such viewpoints can be called orienting strategies, sensitizing frameworks, theoretical families, metatheories, or paradigms, among other terms. With some misgivings, I'm using **paradigm** here. David Wagner, who calls them "orienting strategies," has this to say about them:

> The claims of an orienting strategy are of several different kinds. First, orienting strategies make assertions about the subject matter of sociology, about the nature of social reality, and about the goals of sociological inquiry. Such statements identify what is to be treated as distinctive about sociological phenomena: they tell us what can safely be ignored in dealing with such phenomena; and they specify how one should go about dealing with the critical features that remain. (1984:26)

He points out that a statement like, "The history of all hitherto existing society is the history of class struggles," which we owe to the original conflict theorist, Karl Marx, in his *Communist Manifesto*, cannot be taken literally.[21] It is not meant as part of a theory that explains variation in the intensity or extent of class struggle, for instance, but instead as a recommendation that if you want to know where the historical "action" is, you should look to class struggle. In other words, it's a dramatic way of telling us how important Marx believed class struggle was to understanding the development of societies across time. More broadly, it alerts us to how central conflict is to the formation of social structures and the relations of groups within them. Thinking back to our image of theorizing as being like detective work, Marx's statement serves as a tip from a trusted source about where we might find some important evidence, but it doesn't solve the crime itself.

Earlier in this chapter, I noted that Nisbett and Cohen used a "functional" theory to explain why cultures of honor develop in herding societies. Functional theories are used in many disciplines to explain why certain practices (e.g., incest avoidance) or attributes (e.g., bipedalism, the ability to walk upright) spread throughout populations. Specifically, Nisbett and Cohen suggest that a willingness to use violence, when publicly recognized as part of one's reputation, discourages would-be poachers from targeting one's property. In economically precarious circumstances, where loss of property can mean destitution and death, such a reputation will put one at an advantage against potential predators, particularly in comparison with less violence-prone individuals. (It's they who will more likely suffer losses.) Thus, a reputation for being tough and touchy can be functional in these circumstances, particularly when there aren't police around to protect us. More generally, the spread of the attribute (being tough and touchy) throughout the population (as part of a culture of honor) is explained by the competitive advantage it confers on those who possess it. This is the general form that functional explanations take.

We will discuss the conflict and functional paradigms in much greater detail in subsequent chapters. It is important to recognize about them now that they are part of the tool kit that sociologists bring to the task of theorizing. Initially, they inform and stimulate our wonder, insisting that we ask the question, why? Having stimulated this, they offer rough guides to explanation, showing us ways of conceptualizing causes that have proven effective in the past or in other circumstances. They're available to try out as we look for explanations of the variation in the social world around us. At the same time, once again, they're not theories themselves. Theories explain; paradigms do not.

Conclusion

You should now have a good sense of what a theory is and what it does. Theories relate abstract concepts to one another in propositions so as to explain the nature or behavior of the world. In forming them, it's crucial to explore ways the world around us varies: in fact, many sociological theories focus explicitly on explaining variation. Theories are different from descriptive hypotheses (e.g., marijuana usage precedes heroin usage), descriptive narratives (e.g., the history of driving on the right), and paradigms (e.g., **functionalism**). Each of these is useful, but none can satisfy the specific curiosity that starts us theorizing. A causal narrative ("for want of a nail") can satisfy this wonder and may sometimes be the best explanation we can come up with, but it lacks the generality that qualifies it as a theory.

For ease of exposition, I've emphasized explication and causal modeling at the expense of analysis in this chapter. Analysis will come to center stage only as we take up Max Weber's theorizing, and as it does, we'll see that theories take somewhat more varied forms than this initial chapter has been able to encompass. Nevertheless, the specific example we looked at, the culture-of-honor theory of argument-related homicide, illustrates the most common form that theories take. They explain a particular incident or phenomenon by first transforming it into a variable (by means of conceptualization), looking for empirical generalizations that involve it, and then seeking another empirical generalization that varies with it to serve as its cause. Theories are comprehensive and thorough when they can explain variation in terms of a fundamental cause and specify the mechanisms that link this fundamental cause to the behavior of interest to us. Often, as a last step, this string of causes or mechanisms will involve actors' motives, thus explicating the behavior in question.

The culture-of-honor theory we've used as our example is particularly interesting because it shows us that we only get a little help in explaining people's behavior from an understanding of their motives. Explication usually only gets us so far. The real sociological question is why people's motives vary (from one person, group, or time to another) in the first place. People themselves almost never understand this. In fact, the only way they can understand why motives vary is to become social scientists. The ability to see larger social forces at work in the motives of individuals requires what C. Wright Mills (1959) called the **sociological imagination**. In Nisbett and Cohen's work, you've been exposed to one of the finest examples of the sociological imagination in the contemporary social science literature. Their book is an adventure in theorizing and is particularly useful in demonstrating that it is by comparing the implications of theories with the evidence that we gradually judge them worthy of our trust.

Over the next seven chapters, you will encounter many more theories, and I'll be using the terminology developed in this chapter to present and analyze them. Each one is an adventure in its own right, and all certainly exemplify the sociological imagination.

Notes

1. For an interesting discussion of the various uses of the term *theory* in sociology, see M. Francis Abraham (1982:1–18). While the National Academy of Sciences defines a theory as a "*well-substantiated* explanation of some aspect of the natural world that can incorporate facts, *laws*, inferences, and *tested* hypotheses" (1998, emphasis mine), this definition seems to place too much emphasis on the theory's being accepted on the strength of existing evidence. In this book, theories will qualify as theories even when not well substantiated.

2. Note that explication is often used when we try to justify our actions. When you were young, if your mother caught you doing something wrong and asked you to "explain yourself," she'd be asking you to offer a justification for your behavior. You'd say, "I punched Jimmy (your brother) because he tripped me." In other words, you're saying that Jimmy's tripping you excuses your punching him and, thus, your mother shouldn't punish you. Now, sometimes justifications of this sort reflect the person's real motives, but other times people simply invent justifications because they don't know their real motives or don't find them flattering. We always want to look good in the eyes of others (and especially in our own eyes), and so we often invent justifications that are bogus but make us look good. But these are *bad* explanations. We lie about our motives to make us look good rather than to explicate our behavior accurately. This is one reason that we don't always trust people's reports about their motives. For instance, asking people to tell us why they cheat on their income taxes may not provide us with a good explanation since the answers we get may be self-serving rather than accurate.

3. In the past, as among children today, animals were sometimes tortured as a form of recreation (see, e.g., Darnton 1984). We can presume that people participating in such a practice would initially explicate their behavior as simply being "fun," but this only defers a satisfying explication because we want to know why they see as fun something that horrifies us. It is unlikely that we can explain either torture-as-fun or torture-as-horror through individual motives. People commonly do not have good reasons for viewing animal torture either way.

4. For a fuller analysis of causal accounting, see Little (1991:13–38).

5. My discussion of the process of theorizing has been influenced by Wallace (1971) and Stinchcombe (1968).

6. Of course, there are other questions we might pursue here, such as why men seem more prone to homicidal behavior than women (see Daly and Wilson 1988; Courtwright 1996) and whether jealousy is perhaps a particularly powerful stimulus to homicide (see Buss 2000). These questions are often addressed today by the controversial subdiscipline of evolutionary psychology.

7. Where do we get a stock of stories to try out? From talking to other people about what drives them and from reading broadly in anthropology, sociology, and

literature so that we're acquainted with alternative ways of viewing the world and the motivations that these views produce.

8. While I've chosen to speak of "incidents" here, the same strategy would apply to a puzzling property of the social world, for instance, to why some social groups have emblems, such as flags or mascots, that symbolize them. It's not just what happens in the social world, but what it is composed of, that interests us.

9. If you think back to Einstein's proposition $E = mc^2$, you'll note that it's only an empirical generalization itself. You need to add a lot more concepts if you're going to explain why the amount of energy an object contains is proportional to its mass times the speed of light squared.

10. This same generalization would not be true for felony-related homicides, which are nearly the same in the South as elsewhere.

11. As to where his own idea came from, Nisbett reports (personal communication) that he grew up in El Paso, Texas, and had a relative involved in an argument-related homicide. After living in the East for a while, it struck him that such events were rarer there, especially in middle-class circumstances. This was the initial observation that guided his empirical generalization.

12. He writes (personal communication), "Then by chance I took a semester's sabbatical in the south of France, living in Aix-en-Provence. The university there houses the world's major center of Mediterranean studies. The Mediterranean region is more violent than more northerly regions of Europe, so I went to the center to talk to people. One person listened to my descriptions of the U.S. South and said it was a clear culture of honor. He pointed me in the direction of several excellent sources, which quickly convinced me he was right."

13. This legacy, in being passed from white Southerners to black, may also help account for elevated inner-city homicide rates today (Courtwright 1996). For a particularly gripping case study, see Butterfield (1995).

14. It might be interesting to apply this knowledge to your image of the Wild West as depicted in Hollywood films.

15. In contrast, competing theories that we will introduce in a moment, involving temperature or access to guns, lack this substantive implication and the confidence-building tests it allows. For this reason, we evaluate them as less satisfactory than the culture-of-honor theory.

16. A syllogism contains three statements: a major premise, a minor premise, and a conclusion. Usually, the major premise makes a very general statement, and the minor premise a more specific one from which the conclusion flows logically. Thus, if all men are mortal (major premise), and if Socrates is a man (minor premise), it follows logically that Socrates is mortal (conclusion).

17. The example I've chosen is interesting in this regard. Most of you probably suspect, from reading American history and seeing films like *Gone with the Wind*, that Southern culture differed somewhat from Northern culture in the past. Further, you may be aware that an appreciation of honor caused violent disputes in the past, such as the duel between Alexander Hamilton and Aaron Burr. When I originally asked you to consider in what ways the South differs from other parts of the country that might be relevant to explaining its higher rate of argument-related homicide, these images may have occurred to you. But you probably dismissed them as

"ancient" conditions that would hardly be relevant now. Further, you probably didn't connect them with the concept of a culture of honor. To do so, you need your sociological imagination to be in action!

18. *Contingent* is one of those unfortunate words with two meanings that are opposite to one another. The first meaning is something that happens by chance or accident or is incidental, meaning that it doesn't matter much one way or the other. The second meaning is "dependent," so that something is "contingent upon" another thing when it depends upon the occurrence of that second thing. We're using the word in the first sense here, as something that happens by chance or is incidental.

19. Philosopher Norwood Hanson introduces it in *Patterns of Discovery* (1961:50). It is also discussed by David Owens in *Causes and Coincidences* (1992:15), from whom I quote the ditty. These are among numerous discussions.

20. It is unlikely to recur because the probability of each event actually causing the following one in the story is very low. Shoeless horses don't always go lame; when they do, substitute horses are often available; loss of a rider only very occasionally causes loss of a battle; and so forth. Such chains of unlikely events yield outcomes (the kingdom falling) of vanishingly low probability; yet, when each link in the chain is the true cause of the next, they also provide a good explanation of the outcome. Just because they're not theories doesn't mean they're not good explanations.

21. The only way that all of history could be characterized as class struggle would be to broaden the notion of class struggle so far as to make the statement true by definition and, thus, untestable.

Interlude: The Context of Classical Theory

WHILE SIGNIFICANT PORTIONS of this book discuss contemporary developments arising out of classical theory, the classics remain its core. Experience suggests that the classics can be difficult for students to appreciate. They are conceptually complex, and their subject matter initially seems foreign to our everyday life. Certainly, the phenomena the classical theorists tried to explain aren't things we talk about every day. Further, the examples and data they used are, well, somewhat dated. So, it takes at least modest effort to grow comfortable with them. We can reduce the effort needed somewhat, however, by placing their work in a wider context that, first, makes their interests more understandable and, then, gives us a sense of their relevance for our world today. That is the purpose of this interlude.

Classical sociology is rooted in the intellectual development we call the Enlightenment. Prior to the Enlightenment, many educated people believed that our ability to understand the world had not much improved since the time of Aristotle. Further, what was really important to know, they believed, could be found in texts like the Bible and in the discipline of theology, both of which were thought to *reveal* (rather than to *discover*) truths about existence, truths assumed to be eternal. Many would have rejected the notion that we might accumulate a better understanding of the world around us by studying it scientifically as misguided or as impious (not adequately pious because men usurped the role of God in doing so).

The Enlightenment changed these attitudes. Revolutionary thinkers such as René Descartes rejected the notion that the whole truth about the world was contained in ancient texts. They introduced the idea that new truths could be discovered through the power of reason, the human faculty of disciplined thought and investigation. It was the duty of educated people to assess the beliefs of the past and reject those that did not stand up to reasoned evaluation. This scrutiny, it was believed, would show that much accepted truth was actually unexamined superstition, that is, had somehow acquired a hold on people without warrant. Thus, all our notions, Descartes argued, needed to be scrutinized relentlessly and, when necessary, rejected and replaced with others that were either logically indubitable (not capable of being doubted) or securely and publicly grounded in experience, having been witnessed and agreed upon by numerous individuals.

In the late seventeenth and early eighteenth centuries, the new attitudes of the Enlightenment allowed early modern science to take hold. Numerous discoveries and inventions—consider William Harvey's discovery of the circulation of the blood and the inventions of the microscope and telescope—gave people a sense that new frontiers of understanding were opening up. Thinkers like Francis Bacon popularized this attitude, while organizations like the Royal Society of London, led by illustrious scientists like Isaac Newton, gave it an institutional foundation with political protection.

By the middle of the eighteenth century, the Enlightenment's new scientific attitude came to be directed toward society and social institutions. The idea that the pattern of society had been ordained by God as something eternal slowly gave way to the idea that society could be improved through rational analysis and social engineering guided by reason. Many social institutions came to be seen as repressive, that is, as hindering the development of human abilities. A group of French thinkers, called the *philosophes*, were particularly critical of existing social institutions and aimed to replace them with new and more reasonable ones.

Two social revolutions accompanied this intellectual ferment: the political revolutions in America and France and the economic and industrial revolution that began in England and Holland and spread slowly across Europe. These revolutions led to profound disruptions of traditional society: people's customary expectation that they would live from birth to death in the same community, doing the same thing from one day to the next (and the same thing that their fathers and mothers had done before them), under the very weak supervision of some distant political authority over which they had no say, gave way to an expectation of change. People now anticipated, over the course of their lives, both geographical movement (perhaps from countryside to town, for instance) and social change (perhaps switching occupations from farmer to machine operator, for instance). And they began to consider demanding a say in their governance.

From the standpoint of the average citizen, not all of these changes were necessarily for the better. Sometimes people did not choose to move but, rather, were thrown off their ancestral lands and driven into industrial employment in towns. Further, this new industrial work could be unrelenting and boring, so people sometimes had to be forced to accept it, either from hunger or through coercion by political authorities. At the same time, many conservative thinkers worried that attempts to transform society through intentional social engineering could easily go astray, as could democracy. Figures like Edmund Burke in England and Louis de Bonald and Joseph de Maistre in France looked at the consequences of the French Revolution and decided that human reason, left to its own devices, produced completely unrealistic pictures of society—utopian visions, so to speak—and that the pursuit of these visions often led people into catastrophic eruptions of violence, of which the Terror of the French Revolution was a prime example. (The Third Reich, as well as regimes like the Khmer Rouge in Kampuchea [Cambodia], which saw mass murder as an instrument of utopian policy, continued this trend in the twentieth century.) Thus, the conservative reaction saw unfettered human reason and its hope for change as apt to run amok. Conservative thinkers emphasized the need for tradition, for religion, and for repressive force to hold reason in check. According to this view, people were neither intelligent nor mature enough to devise and implement exclusively beneficial changes. In comparison to utopian enthusiasms, the old patterns of social organization had at least withstood the test of time and, perhaps, served hidden functions of which reformers were unaware—or so it was claimed. The new institutions invented by the reformers often overlooked these functions, argued the conservatives, with results that could be catastrophic.

It was in this context of Enlightenment optimism and conservative pessimism about "progress" that the classical sociologists developed explanations of the changes they saw going on around them—some of which were theories in the strict sense set out in chapter 1. Developing these theories required that they go beyond evaluating changes as good or bad to ask why they were occurring. Why had Europe, seemingly alone among the civilizational centers of the world, developed an innovative economic and industrial system, which soon came to be called capitalism? Why did it produce the particular pattern of stratification—of social inequality—that it did, and how did this pattern differ from previous patterns of inequality? What would be the immediate and long-term effects of breaking down the old rural, agrarian patterns of association that had largely constituted society in the past and building up new ones in an urban and industrial milieu? What would be the fate of religion in this process? What organizations could be devised to manage the increasing complexity of industrial social and economic systems?

As these questions indicate, the classical theorists were interested in explaining large-scale social changes across quite lengthy time spans. This makes them somewhat hard for students to appreciate. After all, most of us don't spend our time wondering about issues like where capitalism came from and how it changed our world. But the issues of interest to the classical theorists are really not that different from issues of concern to us. We may wonder, for instance, about how the Internet originated and whether it is going to change our lives. On a grander scale, we may also wonder whether the global society that seems to be in the making, in part as a result of the Internet, will be culturally and socially distinct from societies of the past. Along the way to this global society, for instance, can the extreme inequalities we find in the world today be sustained, especially across national boundaries, or will they have to be reduced? If they are reduced, will this be done by raising the incomes of the world's poor, or by lowering those of the rich? If the former, how will we manage the potential environmental impact of bringing to all of the world's inhabitants the standards of living of the developed societies? If the latter, how will citizens of the advanced economies be made to accept lower standards of living? In responding to these changes, what role will religion play?

These are very big questions, and they link us directly to the classical sociologists both because of their large scope and because they have to be answered by the strategies of inquiry originating in the classics. These strategies constitute paradigms to guide investigation, as we discussed in chapter 1, and they remain as relevant today as when they were created since they define the ways in which we can answer important questions about social change in our own day.

Thus, there's a very real sense in which the broader interests of the classical sociologists are not unfamiliar to us at all. Indeed, they also connect directly to us in a more personal way. Although Karl Marx's notion of **alienation** and the pattern by which it developed across history can at first seem somewhat foreign, for example, it's really not. Most students are in college, after all, precisely because they hope to escape alienating work, and they need the credential of a college degree, they believe, to do so. Thus, their daily lives in college classrooms are very much embroiled in the historical changes and social conflicts that Marx was among the first to describe in a systematic way. Some students enjoy their classes very much and actually enjoy studying, while others don't. The former are likely to come from, or aspire to, **status groups** for whom learning "for its own sake" is a badge of prestige; the latter likely don't. Max Weber developed the concept of status groups and discussed the use of learning for its own sake as a badge of prestige among the Chinese literati (1958:416–44). Indeed, understanding status groups can help us explain why students react so differently to the college work they do. Those who enjoy their course work identify with the role of student, while those who don't experience "role distance," a noninvolvement that Erving Goffman conceptualized in the tradition of George Herbert Mead. Émile Durkheim worried in general about the ability of modern societies to elicit people's commitment and saw failure to do so as a pathology evidenced by rising suicide rates, which are a problem among college students today.

Thus, we can bring Marx, Weber, Mead, and Durkheim together in a none-too-fanciful association that points directly at us and what we are doing in the classroom. The classics are very much to the point, then, although, to see this, we must get beyond the somewhat old-fashioned dress in which they quite naturally appear. When we do, we can take up their ideas as tools as we work to understand better the world around us and our situation in it. Thus, we learn most profitably from them the skills involved in sociological explanation. These are ageless and can be used everywhere.[1]

Note

1. For further discussion of the intellectual and social context of classical theory, see Nisbet (1966) and Levine (1995).

2

Karl Marx and Capitalism

THE THEORISTS WE WILL TAKE UP in later chapters were each responsible for several theories. In contrast, Karl Marx (1818–1883) created one big theory. Its specific goal was to explain the character, origins, and fate of a particular form of economic organization called capitalism. Its wider goal was to establish a paradigm that could help us create theories to explain important social changes across history. In this chapter, I will describe important aspects of the specific theory in terms of the framework established in the first chapter. In the next chapter, I'll discuss the paradigm Marx developed and then present and illustrate two modern paradigms that owe a good deal of their inspiration to Marx.

But let me first note that presenting Marx's theory and paradigm in an easily digestible form poses certain practical challenges. To begin with, Marx, like many other nineteenth-century social scientists, sought to understand social change across all of history, and this means that many of the social institutions of concern to him, such as those of feudalism, will probably be unfamiliar to you. Second, Marx borrowed certain strategies of analysis, especially his dialectical method, from the German philosopher G. W. F. Hegel. The dialectic is difficult to describe, in part because it's quite foreign to the way we think today. No discussion of Marx can dispense with it, but rather than make it an integral part this chapter, I've chosen to mention it in passing and then treat it more systematically in appendix 2A. Throughout this chapter, I've sometimes ignored complexities so as to give Marx's theory the utmost clarity and usefulness for my goal of presenting theorizing as a skill (rather than presenting theorists as figures in intellectual history).[1] But even with some simplification, the theory remains more complex than the one we looked at in the first chapter, so I'll be stopping every once in a while during the presentation to connect us back to the analysis of theories outlined there.

Finally, I should note that focusing so much on Marx diminishes the importance of his frequent collaborator, Friedrich Engels. Randall Collins (1994:56–62) argues that Engels was actually the better sociologist of the two and, in many respects, the more interesting thinker. Be this as it may, making sure always to give Engels the credit he is due would distract us from the central goal of presenting the theory he and Marx together created in the simplest manner possible. Be aware, then, that I'm often using "Marx" as shorthand for "Marx and Engels."

Capitalism as a Problem

The first stage of theorizing, as I argued in chapter 1, is to set up a problem. This involves first observing and wondering about a phenomenon, then conceptualizing it, and finally forming an empirical generalization about it. Since Marx was born in 1818 and Engels in 1820 (both in Germany), the world they observed looked quite different from the world of today. When they were college students in the late 1830s, it was clear to them, as it was to many people in Europe, that the world was undergoing a significant transformation, a transformation we characterize as the industrial revolution. Jobs that had previously been done by hand and often in one's home, such as weaving cloth for sale, were increasingly done by machines that were driven by inanimate power (e.g., water or steam) and situated in large buildings, called *factories*, to which workers went each day as paid laborers. This development marked the transition from a system of economic production based on handicrafts to a system based on manufacturing, and it entailed numerous other social and economic changes. Where craftsmen had generally owned their own tools, worked alone or in small groups under a master craftsman (often in his home), and joined together in associations called *guilds* to share markets and set prices at a level to their benefit, as well as to regulate the apprenticeship system whereby new craftsmen were trained, the system of manufacturing was organized by factory owners who bought machinery and hired workers to run it. The workers, rather than forming guilds to control their own production and pricing, were now subject to labor markets in which they competed with one another to be hired by factory owners, who often sought to pay them the lowest wage possible. In fact, under the guidance of such early economists as Adam Smith, the idea of creating competitive markets to exchange goods and services, free of interference from guilds or governments, grew more popular.[2] Such free markets were assumed to work best (and for the good of all) when *entrepreneurs* (people willing to venture their own money or borrow from others to create a business enterprise) competed with one another to produce goods for sale, buying labor and materials at the lowest cost possible and selling the finished product for as much as they could get. Competition among entrepreneurs for increased sales in the market, it was felt, would drive down prices and give entrepreneurs incentives to look relentlessly for ways to produce goods even more cheaply, thereby gaining an edge on their competitors. The reward to entrepreneurs was the profit they made in the process, a profit that allowed the more successful among them to become wealthy, and the most successful to become fabulously opulent. The reward to everyone else was less expensive goods, since the pricing policies of the guilds had kept the cost of goods artificially high. This new system, where entrepreneurs used capital (their own money or what they could borrow) to create competitive enterprises in pursuit of private profit, was called *capitalism*, and it had existed before, but developed much more dramatically during, the industrial revolution.[3] It meant that the lives of people came to be coordinated through and dominated by *markets*, and Marx wondered what the outcome of this new way of organizing societies would be.

Capitalism Observed

Engels's family were entrepreneurs. They owned several factories, with one in Manchester, England, an early center of the industrial revolution, that Engels himself helped manage for a period between 1842 and 1844, as well as at other times throughout his life. Before moving to Manchester, Engels had already written a treatise critical of capitalism, and he used his stay in England partly to gather information about the effects of the industrial revolution and capitalism on workers. He published his results in 1845 in a book titled *The Condition of the Working Class in England*. It is filled with observations of the effects of capitalism, some by Engels himself and others by British investigators whose works Engels cited.

Engels was interested in the living and working conditions of laborers across a variety of industries, as well as in how their health was affected. Very long hours tending machines, sometimes spent in awkward postures, seemed to him (and other observers) to increase rates of physical deformity among the workers. For instance, he wrote,

> I have seldom walked through Manchester without seeing three or four cripples whose deformities of the spine and legs [were due to their work]. I have had ample opportunity of observing these cripples closely. I know of one cripple personally. . . . This operative [i.e., worker] got into his condition through working in Mr. Douglas's mill in Pendleton. This factory has a very bad reputation among the workers because of the long hours of night work which are customary there. It is easy to identify such cripples at a glance, because their deformities are all exactly the same. They are knock-kneed and deformed and the spinal column is bent either forwards or sideways. (1958:172–73)

Such deformities were only one health problem the workers faced. As Engels pointed out later, working conditions and living conditions were so poor that "men grow old before their time. Most are no longer fit for work at 40," with only a few lasting until they were fifty years of age (1958:180). Further, industrial accidents, often leading to the worker's death, were common, as was death due to illnesses not directly caused by work. Engels used data gathered by others to show that mortality rates increased dramatically as the quality of the housing in which workers lived declined (1958:120). The poorer the housing, the shorter the life, with one's chances of dying in any given year (which were already very high) being roughly doubled in the poorest circumstances.

In the same section of the book, Engels described the rules under which the factory operative worked:

> He must arrive at the factory by half-past five in the morning. He is fined if he arrives a few minutes late. If he is ten minutes late he is locked out until after

breakfast and loses a quarter of a day's pay, although he has only actually missed 2½ hours work out of twelve. He is forced to eat, drink and sleep to a fixed routine. He is allowed only the minimum time to satisfy the most urgent demands of nature. The manufacturer does not worry if the worker lives half an hour's walk or even a full hour's walk away from the factory. The tyrannical bell calls the wretched worker from his bed and summons him to breakfast and to lunch. (1958:200–201)

The "he" in this quotation obscures the fact that many workers, especially in the textile industry, were women and children, with the latter sometimes starting work as early as age five.

The Condition of the Working Class in England makes for sober reading today. It reminds us of how difficult, depressing, and, indeed, dangerous were the circumstances in which people labored to earn a living in the early years of the industrial revolution. On the other hand, these qualities did not necessarily distinguish industrial employment since much labor, even prior to the industrial revolution, had been difficult, dangerous, and depressing. To understand and explain the plight of workers in the new industrial order, Marx and Engels needed to conceptualize it in terms of variables that would reveal its distinctive features in relation to other modes of economic production. They were driven to do so by a deep sense of wonder at how capitalism had arisen and what might become of it.

The Workers' Condition Conceptualized as a Variable

We know that the second step in setting up our problem is to conceptualize the phenomenon of concern to us as a variable. We can't develop explanations of things until we can see patterns to their occurrence, noting where they are more common and less common, and this means seeing them as variables. Indeed, it's only by attending to where and when a phenomenon occurs (versus when and where it doesn't) that we can narrow down its possible causes to factors that vary according to a similar pattern. In order to take the first step in this direction, however, Marx and Engels needed to decide which aspects of the workers' condition to focus on in characterizing it. For instance, I noted above that work increasingly was done outside the home as a result of the industrial revolution. Would this change in the location of labor (in the home versus out of the home) perhaps be the best variable to focus on if we want to understand capitalism's effects? Or would it be the workers' ill health? Or something else?

There's no formula we can use to answer such questions. As noted in chapter 1, conceptualizing the phenomenon of interest to us involves creative intuitions or hunches. We have to review the possibilities open to us and decide which "feels best," that is, which intuitively seems most likely to illuminate the phenomenon. The shooting we discussed in chapter 1 could have resulted from a brain tumor or been the act of a sociopath, but our hunch was to conceptualize it as an argument-related homicide whose motives were neither sociopathic nor tumor driven. Similarly, Marx had the option to see the out-of-the-home character of industrial work as the crucial variable but rejected it as not very illuminating. Instead, he believed the workers' condition could best be conceptualized in terms of two variables: **alienation** and **exploitation**. As you will see, each variable initially involves quite complicated ideas, but we should be able to make them manageable. That we must put so much effort into sorting matters out, however, means that Marx's work leaves something to be desired when it comes to conceptualizing variables.[4]

Alienation

To see what Marx meant by this concept, we need some anthropological background. People living in the most technologically primitive societies today (as in the earliest human societies) need to develop and use a wide variety of skills in order to feed, clothe, and house themselves. While there is generally some **division of labor** in such societies, with men doing the hunting and women the gathering of food (as well as carrying the primary responsibility for child care), by and large each person is able to do all the tasks required for survival. In a sense, such people are free in a very fundamental way: they are autonomous producers of their own means of livelihood and, thus, are not dependent upon any one. Although usually living socially, they have all the knowledge and skills necessary to produce the requisite food, clothing, and shelter without help from anyone else. Indeed, even the tools they use to make a living, such as blowguns or baskets, they can produce for themselves. Individuals in such societies have little wealth (in the sense of accumulated possessions), in part because possessions would impede their capacity to move frequently in search of game. Despite their relative poverty, however, modern research (see Sahlins 1972) suggests they are rich in leisure: in normal circumstances **hunters and gatherers** probably spend about half as much time working as do people in industrial societies today.

Marx's believed that in such societies, the work people did must have been very satisfying because it called on such a diverse set of skills, in each of which a person had to become competent. You made your own arrows, made your clothes, built your "house," carved your religious artifacts, made your musical instruments and entertained with them, searched your environment for intoxicants and prepared them, made up stories for the group's entertain-

ment, and so on. And you did each of these tasks at your own bidding, auton-
omously, free of the control of other people. Thus, each day called for, or
allowed, the exercise of the most varied capacities, each at the individual's
discretion (as long as food was gotten and prepared).

The development of agriculture began to change this. **Agrarian societies**
could produce more food by planting and harvesting crops (and domesticat-
ing livestock) than hunters and gatherers could, and this allowed them to
support specialists in various activities, such as religion, warfare, and craft
production (weaving, basket making, metalwork, pottery, and so on). While
working in such specialized areas was still satisfying, it did not call upon quite
as varied a range of talents and skills as had daily life in hunting-and-
gathering societies. The same was true of farming, the occupation of the great
majority of people in agrarian societies, in comparison with hunting and
gathering. At the same time, the division of labor among craft specialists, as
well as between these groups and farmers, increased both the total **productivity** of society and the store of human inventions. Hunting-and-gathering
societies, after all, lacked the wonders of metals and ceramics that agrarian
specialists produced, albeit at the sacrifice of variety (as well as leisure) in
daily life. The irony that increased productivity and expanded human inven-
tiveness for the society as a whole came at the cost of variety, autonomy, and
leisure to the individuals in the society, Marx tried to capture in his concept
of alienation.

As societies developed still further economically, and especially with the
advent of the industrial revolution, this irony only increased. Driving it was
the division of labor. Adam Smith, in *The Wealth of Nations* (1776), had
argued that dividing up the labor involved in some craft process, say, making
cloth, so that each individual specialized in a particular portion of the productive process, say, spinning the yarn, would lead to greater and greater productivity. That is, the same number of workers could make more cloth in the
same time if they divided up the labor into distinct components and worked
together, rather than working independently to make the entire product
from start to finish. Smith felt this was a good thing since it would allow
societies to produce more goods and grow wealthier collectively, if not necessarily as individuals.

Marx felt it was good in one sense and bad in another. It was good because
it allowed for greater productivity, but it was bad because, as labor became
more and more divided, the tasks performed by each individual worker grew
simpler and more repetitive. And as the tasks grew simpler and more repetitive, they demanded less competence from the worker. When Marx surveyed
history, he thus felt that work had "progressed" from requiring the broad
range of skills and talents we find in hunter-gatherer societies to the very

restricted competencies of the industrial factory worker in his day. As the process of production evolved from craft work to manufacturing, the work force became deskilled, no longer needing the variety of abilities that had previously made work both challenging and satisfying. Further, whereas craft workers had owned their tools and joined together in guilds to regulate the production and sale of the goods they produced, industrial workers owned only their *labor power*, or their ability to work. In order to work, they had to be hired by someone else, someone who owned the machine workers would now have to operate and who would control the development and sale of their output. Thus, they lost autonomy and control. Further, in order to be hired, they had to compete with other workers in the labor market, replacing the cooperation of the guilds with competition among workers.

Marx tried to weave all these developments together in his concept of alienation. Workers under industrial capitalism, he felt, were alienated in four distinct ways. In the *Economic and Philosophic Manuscripts of 1844* (not published until 1932), he analyzed alienation into four separate forms: (1) alienation from the product of labor, (2) alienation from the process of labor, (3) alienation from the **species-being**, and (4) alienation of man from man. The first and fourth forms of alienation are less important and will be ignored here; the second and third capture the central irony referred to above: that the enormously expanded productivity of the human species under industrial capitalism entailed stultifying (boring and repetitive) work, under the control of others, for individual members of the species. This, he believed, was a crucial aspect of what Engels observed in Manchester.

Alienation from the species-being sounds strange initially, but it's only Marx's way of indicating that industrialization both expressed heightened collective human capacities and prevented the majority of individuals from utilizing these capacities in their work. Marx felt that as industrial society progressed, the capitalist system was producing goods that demonstrated extraordinary human abilities. As a society, we were thus better expressing our capacities as a species than could people in hunter-gatherer or in agrarian societies. After all, they couldn't make steel bridges or steam engines, while nineteenth-century capitalism could. In this sense, capitalist society better expressed the species-being (as human capacities) than did earlier societies. It was transforming nature in more inventive and impressive ways so as to reveal what humans were capable of. But, at the same time, individual workers were less and less able to express their potentials because their work required so few skills. This meant that individual workers were more and more alienated from the potentials of the species, or the species-being, even as industrial society as a whole was better at achieving these potentials. This was because individuals were more alienated from the process of labor, even as the society as a whole was less alienated from the species-being.

Marx captured the stultifying character of industrial labor in the concept of alienation from the process of labor. (As you consider this concept, you should reflect on the worst job you've ever had and try to analyze which of its aspects made it so bad.) Even today, much of the physical labor in industrial societies is extremely boring ("mind-numbing" is an apt phrase) and repetitive, and it is often done in environments, such as on assembly lines, that give individual workers little control over their work or room for initiative. In a sense, men and women assist machines, doing the tasks the machines cannot do, and doing them over and over again as quickly as can reasonably be expected. (Such work presumably led to the physical deformities Engels observed in Manchester workers.) This situation contrasts deeply with that of hunters and gatherers, and only somewhat less deeply with that of craft workers or farmers. Since Marx believed that it was through work, through transforming the world through labor, that men and women come to know who they are (in the sense of what their capacities and talents are), he believed they could only be repelled by a work process that gave them no real opportunity to test themselves. Thus, they would be individually alienated from the process of labor, even though the overall outcome of their work (in cloth, in steel bridges, and in steam engines, say) might collectively better express the human species-being.

To avoid terminological awkwardness henceforward, I want to combine alienation from the process of labor (which is akin to what we today call "job satisfaction") with the individual component of alienation from the species-being (whereby those unable to express their human potentials find little satisfaction in their jobs) and simply refer to both together as alienation. (After all, the two seem necessarily to vary together because they only represent different aspects of the same phenomenon.) In Marx's view, alienation increases as society's productive powers increase. On the other hand, the collective component of alienation from the species-being declines as society progresses. As simplistic as it may seem, this development is better expressed for us today in a measure like productivity per capita, that is, the aggregate of goods and services a society produces divided by its population. Where productivity per capita is very low (as in hunting-and-gathering societies), alienation from the species-being is high, and vice versa. U.S. society today is so productive that less than 4 percent of the population can feed the rest of us, who are thus freed to create communications satellites and symphonies. (In the past, around 95 percent of the population were farmers working to feed themselves and the remaining 5 percent were **aristocrats**, religious specialists,

and craft workers.) Our immense productivity per capita makes us, collectively, less alienated from the species-being than our predecessors.

Thus, Marx conceptualized as very alienated the workers whom Engels had
observed, even as he recognized that capitalist society was dramatically
increasing, through industrialization, its productivity per capita and, thus,
decreasing alienation from the species-being. In *The Communist Manifesto,*
Marx actually celebrated the latter phenomenon even as he argued that it was
accompanied by alienation:

> [Capitalism] has created more massive and more colossal productive forces
> than have all preceding generations together. Subjection of Nature's forces to
> man, machinery, applications of chemistry to industry and agriculture, steam-
> navigation, railways, electric telegraphs, clearing of whole continents for culti-
> vation, canalisation of rivers . . . what earlier century had even a presentiment
> that such productive forces slumbered in the lap of social labour? (Tucker
> 1972:339)

But alienation and rising productivity per capita do not encompass all the
important aspects of Engels's observations of industrial labor in England, a
primary feature of which was workers' poverty. To conceptualize this additional aspect, Marx developed his notion of exploitation.

Exploitation

Worker poverty and capitalist wealth both resulted, Marx believed, from
exploitation. Like alienation, the concept of exploitation evaluates the workers' circumstances at the same time as it describes them. Not unlike the word
"torture," the words "alienation" and "exploitation" carry seemingly automatic negative connotations. (One should enjoy being alienated and
exploited only somewhat less than being tortured.) As Marx's thinking developed across time, exploitation became a technical concept, as well as a moral
one, defined in terms of numerous notions specific to his economics. I will
give only the barest outline of them here, especially since one of the concepts
involved, the labor theory of value, although widely accepted in Marx's time,
has since fallen out of fashion. Instead, I turn to a current definition of the
concept for a more acceptable characterization.

By and large, Marx believed, the value of goods that we exchange in markets is determined by the amount of labor necessary to produce them. This
seems clearest when we consider systems of barter, where one item is directly
exchanged for another, as when a shoemaker might trade a pair of shoes with
a farmer for several chickens and some corn. In these circumstances, the
amount of labor necessary to produce the several chickens and some corn

should be about the same as the amount of labor necessary to produce the shoes. Indeed, if you always traded a day's worth of shoe making for ten minutes worth of farming, either you'd starve, or the farmers would quickly grow very rich. Because this does not occur in barter systems, the items exchanged must be roughly equivalent in the amount of labor needed to produce them. So, the price of every object should reflect the cost in labor of producing it, and Marx believed this to be true of every commodity, except labor itself, in a capitalist system. When someone hires a worker and puts her to work, the result is a given product in a certain amount of time. This product can be taken by the employer and sold for a price on the market. But the employer need only pay the worker a wage sufficient to keep her and her family alive, compensation much lower than what a person would receive if she bartered her work or sold it herself on the market.

The idea that labor was worth more to capitalists than they had to pay for it was central to Marx's analysis of capitalism. The difference between what workers were paid and what their labor was worth to capitalists he referred to as **surplus value**. By appropriating surplus value (when goods were sold) as profit, employers always got more value out of laborers than they paid them. Furthermore, there was no other place for them to get profit, according to Marx. It always came from paying workers less than the value of their work, and this difference amounted to exploitation. The more capitalists exploited workers, in this view, the richer they got.

Modern considerations of exploitation (e.g., Wright 1997:9–13) generally define it as occurring where several conditions are met: the benefits to one of two (or more) economically interdependent people or groups must depend upon deprivations to the other, the deprived person or group must have no effective way of leaving the situation, and the well-being of the exploiting person or group must depend upon the accomplishments of the exploited. Consider a hypothetical (if rather unlikely) example: imagine a software firm owned by a person who contributes nothing herself to a new product. It is entirely the creation of a group of very poorly paid programmers, who would quit were it not for a high unemployment rate across the economy as a whole, and who would start their own business (cutting out the owner) were they not too poor to qualify for a bank loan to capitalize this business. Imagine, then, that the new product is wildly successful and makes the owner rich beyond her imagination. Her riches would result exclusively from exploitation, according to the definition above.

For Marx, exploitation was making the capitalists of Manchester rich and the workers, poor. Only their poorly paid jobs stood between them and starvation, and the industrial revolution itself was destroying alternative employment, for instance in traditional crafts. In other words, they had few options but to work for low pay in factories. On the other side of the equation, factory owners were dependent upon these workers, who, although their contribution may not have been as "creative" as those of the programmers in our example above, provided surplus value and, thus, profits for the owners. The fictional example of programmers and the real example of Manchester factory workers together show us that exploitation and alienation are separate variables, which can vary independently. Programmers might have quite enjoyable work that allows for expression of at least a few aspects of the species-being but still be exploited by an entrepreneur. By contrast, the factory workers were both alienated and exploited.

We now have all the tools we need to conceptualize our dependent variable, the condition of workers. Marx sees it as a composite of three variables: productivity per capita (the reverse of collective alienation from the species-being), alienation (which for us adds the individual component of alienation from the species-being to alienation from the process of labor), and exploitation. Figure 2.1 illustrates the relations among these three variables. At the lower left foreground of this figure, individuals are neither alienated nor exploited, but their productivity per capita is very low. As the arrow ascends

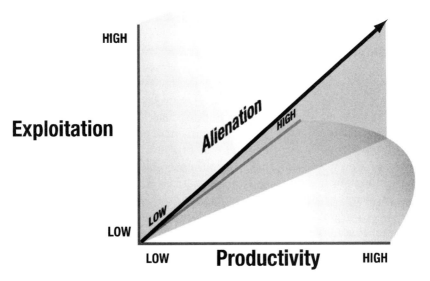

FIGURE 2.1
Relations among Alienation, Exploitation, and Productivity

to the upper right rear, productivity increases, but at the cost of alienation and exploitation. The path that the arrow takes, combining values for all three variables, describes possible conditions for workers.

This path itself became Marx's dependent variable. Unlike our example in the first chapter, where our dependent variable was the relatively simple one of rates of argument-related homicide, this dependent variable is complex, resulting from the contributions of three separate variables. This means that our dependent variable is already an empirical generalization. What we need now is a clue variable that will lead us to an explanation of why our dependent variable follows just this path. From this, we can form a second empirical generalization that will hopefully point in the direction of an explanation.

Changes in Working Conditions: An Empirical Generalization

In chapter 1, we saw that the final stage of setting up our problem is to form an empirical generalization about our variable. We do this by observing that it varies in relation to another variable, our clue variable. In the case of argument-related homicide, we saw that our dependent variable varied geographically, with rates being higher in the rural South than elsewhere. This led us to believe that there must be something about the rural South, something in addition to its mere geographical location, that would cause argument-related homicides there to be high. We used the clue of "Southness" to direct us to the culture of honor as our independent variable. So, we use clue variables as guides to focus our thinking about what might cause changes in our dependent variable.

In the present case, we've already given away our clue variable in the process of conceptualizing our dependent variable. We've seen that the condition of workers varies according to how people earn a living, whether by hunting and gathering, by agriculture and crafts, or by industrial labor. If we hadn't used these particular examples but, instead, had merely talked about alienation and exploitation abstractly as they affected workers in Manchester, then cast about for clues as to where these vary, we'd have said something like, "Well, the conditions of work seem to be a good deal better in hunting-and-gathering societies." In other words, just as we found argument-related homicide to be high in the South and low in the North, we'd find working conditions poor in Manchester and better in hunting-and-gathering societies (ignoring productivity). Having linked variation in working conditions (our dependent variable) to the clue offered by the variable of industrial versus agrarian or hunting-and-gathering societies, we'd be ready to probe deeper, looking for the independent variable or variables that will explain why the condition of workers varies.

Our three different ways of earning a living—hunting and gathering, agriculture, and industry—can be considered a **nominal variable**, like male and female, differences that can't easily be ranked or explicitly measured. If we map this variable onto figure 2.1, it looks like figure 2.2. This figure summarizes our empirical generalization: as ways of making a living change from hunting and gathering, through agriculture and crafts, to industry (our clue variable), productivity per capita, alienation, and exploitation all increase (our dependent variable). The question now becomes, why?

Creating a Theory to Explain the Change

As we saw in chapter 1, creating a theory requires that we discover an independent variable or variables that will link up with our clue variable in the same way our dependent variable does. When we're satisfied that the changes in our independent variable can reasonably cause change in our dependent variable, we can drop the clue and state our theory directly. As we will see in chapter 3, Marx developed a paradigm, called *historical materialism*, that

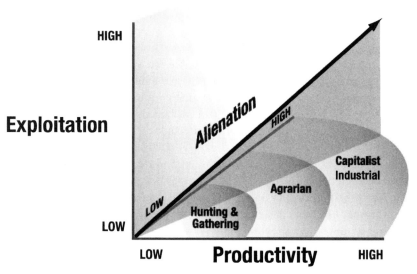

FIGURE 2.2
An Empirical Generalization Relating the Condition of Workers to Modes of Production

guided his selection of likely candidates for his independent variables. But even without this paradigm to help us, it seems evident that candidates for our independent variable or variables here must be able to explain why ways of making a living, what Marx called **modes of production**, change across time and why this causes the condition of workers to worsen as it does. Let us first concentrate on changes in working conditions and then turn to the more complicated issue of why modes of production themselves change across time.

Working Conditions and Concentration of Power

It seems clear that for alienation and exploitation to exist, we need two things: stultifying, poorly paid jobs and people to work at them. While the jobs may appear to be the important thing here, and the people filling them may seem secondary (since specific people come and go, while the jobs remain relatively stable), in reality, there wouldn't be alienating and exploiting jobs in the first place if there weren't people to take them, and there wouldn't be people to take them if they had the power to do otherwise. (The once sizable occupation of servant, for instance, almost completely disappeared over the course of the twentieth century because people weren't willing to serve others when alternative ways of earning a living were available to them.) This means that comparatively powerless people must exist if alienating and exploiting jobs are ever to develop. Why? Marx believed that people are by their very nature strongly attracted to challenging work. Given the alternative of a satisfying job as opposed to a stultifying one, humans will always choose the former. This means that in a competitive market where labor is in demand, you'd generally have to pay people more to do the stultifying jobs than to do the satisfying ones! In other words, people would want extra (not less) compensation to put up with the dreariness and dangerousness of alienating work, at least when more stimulating work was open to them. This means that it should be very hard to exploit workers in the most alienating jobs because you'd have to pay them good money to get them to work for you. But Engels observed the reverse circumstance in Manchester: there, the stultifying and dangerous jobs paid poorly. Because this could happen only where people were comparatively powerless, explaining alienation and exploitation first required Marx to explain why some people were powerless.

His key insight here was that power and social-class position were importantly related. In fact, powerlessness itself was a result of social stratification, or the division of society into ranked classes, where those highly ranked had more power than those below them. It was stratification that left people at the bottom of the class hierarchy unable to avoid alienating and exploited labor, which is only somewhat less true today than it was in Marx's time.[5]

For Marx, one's class was determined by one's *relation to the means of production*. This complex idea is easier to illustrate than it is to define in a few words. Recall that in hunter-gatherer societies, people feed, clothe, and house themselves using their own tools at their own discretion. Such people own the means of production (the tools, land, and so forth necessary to produce a living) and employ their own labor in the process. An interesting consequence of this is that power is relatively equally distributed among them since no one can easily coerce anyone else. Such people, Marx argued, live in a **classless society**. At the other extreme, consider slaves: their labor power and the tools with which they work are both owned by another person. This means that slaves and slave owners have very different relations to the means of production. For Marx, they formed antagonistic social classes, with slave owners being powerful and slaves largely powerless. Industrial workers, on the other hand, are not owned by anyone; nor do they own the means of production: they own only their labor power. Capitalists purchase this labor power and put it to work with tools they own in processes they direct. Thus, capitalists and workers have different relations to the means of production, relations themselves different from those of slaves and slave owners. But these relations still give capitalists much more power than workers, leaving the latter powerless to avoid alienating jobs. Thus, the **mode of production** determines class relations, and class relations insure the powerlessness of some people.

Marx's analysis of class is quite complex, too much so to allow us easily to transform class relations directly into a variable suited to our needs at this moment. But, as the preceding analysis begins to suggest, we can capture what is important about Marx's use of social class to explain alienation in the variable concentration of power.[6] In hunting-and-gathering societies, power is spread nearly equally among all members of the group and, thus, is not concentrated in the hands of a few. In contrast, slaveholders in agrarian societies may constitute only a small segment of the population in a social system where much of the work is done by slaves, and yet hold almost all the power. In such a society, power is highly concentrated. Indeed, if we can imagine the amount of power over others in a society as some fixed amount, then its concentration increases as more of it is possessed by fewer people. Thus, the more concentrated power is, the larger the proportion of the population that will be unable to avoid alienating work where it exists. Although this way of putting it is a bit too simple, we can say that the more concentrated power is, the greater will be the average alienation from the process of labor (which is to say, the lower will be the average job satisfaction) and the greater the prospect of exploitation. Thus, we've found one good candidate for an independent variable that partially explains why workers become more alienated and exploited as ways of making a living (modes of production) change. Suppose we summarize this as in figure 2.3.

In this figure, I've had to collapse alienation and exploitation into one dimension in order to represent everything in just three dimensions. This figure solves the puzzle of why people are available to fill alienating jobs in which they are exploited: rising concentrations of power give them no alternative, and power concentrates as modes of production are transformed across time. (It also gives us a good sense of why we needed to look for further variables on the basis of the clue we have developed.) But we still need to understand why the modes of production change since this is key to the whole theory.[7]

Mode of Production, Technological Innovation, and Class Struggle

You may have realized that Adam Smith already provided a simple answer to the question of why modes of production change over time: when new

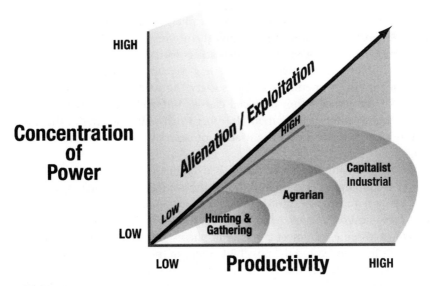

FIGURE 2.3
Marx's Theory in Linear Form: Concentration of Power and Mode of Production Explain Alienation, Exploitation, and Productivity

technologies or ways of organizing labor are invented that produce more goods with the same amount of labor, they tend to be adopted and to spread because it is human nature to want more goods from less work. But this functional answer works only if we ignore the stultifying working conditions that result: we might want more for less (increased productivity), but not at the cost of alienation and exploitation.

Marx's proposed a more complex explanation. To appreciate it fully, we'd have to call in the dialectic (see appendix 2A), but we can do passably well without it. We need to understand how Marx believed modes of production developed across time, since he viewed them as dynamic. In the first place, modes of production should be viewed as integrated systems that in practice tend to exclude one another. Hunting and gathering was replaced by agriculture as the dominant way of earning a living, which itself was replaced by industrial capitalism. Although industrial capitalism of course still needed to produce food through farming and hunting—we still hunt for fish on the seas, after all—it was no longer significantly organized around these activities.[8] In essence, later modes of production drive earlier ones out of existence. Agrarian and industrial societies, as we know, have gradually driven the hunter-gatherer way of life to the verge of extinction, and agrarian societies themselves are rapidly succumbing to industrial ones, where even food is often produced by large corporations rather than small farms.

Further, each such system has technological and social components, which are closely connected. For instance, hunters and gatherers use bows and arrows or spears to hunt and baskets to gather food, and they have specific ways of constructing housing, clothing themselves, and cooking food. Since all members of the society have equal access to these means of production, their technology determines their "classless" social relations, that is, the relative equality of all members of the society. Agriculture and industry both allow for the introduction of social classes, but each for a different set of classes and relations among them. In other words, the character of the mode of production affects the concentration of power as this is reflected in class stratification.

Finally, each mode of production is dynamic: it develops across time as minor technological and organizational innovations "fine-tune" the system and allow it to become more productive (see appendix 2A for examples). Like biological organisms, Marx believed, modes of production have something like juvenile, adolescent, and adult phases, through which they proceed as people learn to exploit the possibilities within them to achieve greater productivity. Here his key insight was that this process of development *changes the concentration of power, first increasing and then decreasing it.* The decreasing concentration of power allows for previously exploited classes to challenge those above them, as well as to *introduce fundamentally new technologies* that might inaugurate a new mode of production. Such changes always involve political conflict between classes, or what Marx called *class struggle*. In fact, class struggles, which Marx saw as inevitably being won by the original underdogs (to whom a new technology has given increased power), are critical to the process of societal development as a whole.

If we were to present Marx's theory graphically, it would look like figure 2.4. While this figure looks a good deal like figure 2.3, it adds the critical difference that working conditions, concentration of power, and productivity do not develop together **linearly** (in a straight line); instead, concentration increases and decreases cyclically (while rising overall) as productivity increases, and working conditions worsen. With each dip, conflict between classes increases (which is only another way of saying that the concentration of power is decreasing), and this allows a previously subordinate class to implement a new technology or way of organizing labor that solidifies its power.

This theory is considerably more complicated than Richard Nisbett and

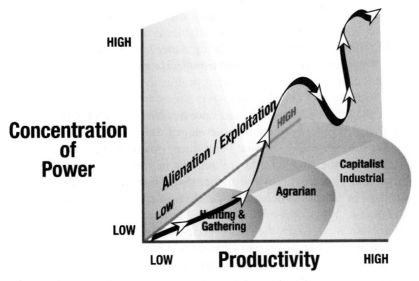

FIGURE 2.4
Marx's Theory in Nonlinear Form: Concentration of Power and Mode of Production Explain Alienation, Exploitation, and Productivity

Dov Cohen's, presented in the first chapter, and we haven't actually completed outlining it. It depicts a relation among five factors (alienation, exploitation, productivity, concentration of power [or class conflict], and mode of production) so as to explain our initial empirical generalization that working conditions worsen as we pass from one mode of production to the next. Marx's theory argues that this generalization would not hold at all without the concentration of power that leaves workers no choice but to accept alienating work; that the concentration of power is directly determined by the mode of production and its effect on class relations; that modes of production are **dynamic systems** that change across time first to concentrate and then to diffuse power; and that diffusion of power (or class struggle) allows for the introduction of new modes of production. (Now we better understand why Marx viewed all history as the history of class struggle!) In this complex relation, the most important factors, Marx believed, are the changes in technology and in the organization of labor that cause the concentration of power to ebb and flow.

Mechanisms of Change

We will return in a moment to complete the theory but need to stop here for a moment, not just to catch our breath but to reflect on a problem Marx had in identifying the mechanism that caused change. We noted in the first chapter that pursuing the *mechanisms* by which changes in our independent variables cause change in our dependent variables is one of the main strategies by which sciences progress. But outlining a mechanism was the part of the theory with which Marx had the most trouble. He argued that concentrations of power wax and wane as each mode of production is fine-tuned to become more productive and that this cycle gives rise to new modes of production. He saw a dialectical pattern here, and since he believed, with the philosopher Hegel, that nature and society both developed dialectically, he was inclined to see the mechanism as "natural" and, thus, not really in need of further explanation. At the same time, he realized that he was under some obligation to indicate why such patterns exist rather than simply asserting that they do.

But here he faced a problem. Mode of production is a very general and crude concept. When we look around the globe and across history, we find the same basic mode—say, the agrarian one—exemplified in distinctive ways in particular societies. (Agrarian China, for instance, would differ at least somewhat in its class relations from agrarian Europe.[9]) Thus, while Marx very much wanted to develop a theory that applied to all societies at all times and firmly believed that societies change and develop across time according to a necessary and inevitable pattern, differences among them (of which he was well aware) made such a theory hard to develop. A "one-size" theory did not easily fit all the concrete cases Marx hoped to explain.[10] In fact, he was never able to explain the shift from hunting and gathering to agriculture,[11] and the best he could do for the shift from agrarian to industrial society in Europe was to offer a causal narrative as opposed to a theory.[12] This provides an explanation, as we argued in the first chapter, but not a theoretical one. Yet, because my presentation thus far has been very abstract, it would probably be good to review the causal narrative he offered and see how it embodies many of the concepts introduced above, before resuming the main line of argument. The version I give here somewhat modifies Marx's thinking in light of more recent scholarship.

A Causal Narrative Explaining the Transition from Handicrafts to Manufacturing in Europe

Recall that in early modern times in Europe, most nonagricultural goods were produced by artisans who acted together, in guilds, to set prices and control entry into their trades through an apprentice system. As we've seen, a system of industrial manufacturing developed out of, and in conflict with, this craft mode of production. In order for this to happen, it was necessary for possessors of capital (whom Marx referred to as the **bourgeoisie**) to attract and retain workers (whom he referred to as the **proletariat**) for their factories and then to penetrate urban markets, where buyers for mass-produced goods were concentrated. Both prospects were denied them, however, by a series of codes and practices written into legislation by the craft guilds as a result of their dominance of medieval town politics. These codes and practices had to be challenged and destroyed if manufacturing was ever to get off the ground. Capitalists attacked the codes by establishing alliances with rural aristocrats, who sold the capitalists land for factories and allowed them to hire workers from rural areas who were not subject to the guilds of the towns. Thus, capitalists were able to develop zones of "free labor" beyond control of the guild system. The threat this posed to the guilds was immediately apparent but not necessarily devastating. The guilds originally managed to restrict the sale of manufactured goods to *foreign markets* (you could make cloth outside a town, but you couldn't sell it there) and, hence, preserved their control over local markets: thus, they could live with the system of manufacturing. The system of capitalist manufacturing, however, could not long live with the guilds, at least if it was to develop fully, since, to do this, it needed to sell in local urban markets as well. Thus, a lengthy political struggle ensued, won eventually by an alliance of capitalists and pro-change state administrators, who saw in the growth potential of new industries a source of tax revenues with which to fight wars. By state dictate, the restriction on selling in local markets was removed, and the collapse of many craft guilds soon followed since they could not compete on a price basis with the output of the factories. The wealth that then flowed to the capitalist manufacturers increased their power in relation to the aristocrats, whom they were soon able to supplant as the dominant social class, concentrating power in the hands of the bourgeoisie. The whole process was "lubricated" by the growth in global trade following the European discovery of the Americas and a sea route to the Far East, as well as by the influx of gold from the Americas, which caused an inflation that was primarily detrimental to aristocrats.[13]

Of course, this brief narrative only sketches what was a much more complex process, but it goes some way to explaining how a struggle between classes (bourgeoisie versus aristocrats and guildsmen) caused the transition from handicrafts as a mode of production within an agrarian system to the new system of capitalist manufacturing. Through it, you get a better idea of what Marx meant by suggesting that a mode of production was a *system*, since it entailed not just a particular way of producing goods but a set of rules and laws that governed production and distribution of goods, as well as the relationships among different social classes. The narrative begins with power concentrated in the hands of aristocrats and, to a lesser degree, the guilds, then shows how capitalist manufacturers attacked this system as the concentration of power declined and how they used this "opening" to spread their new and antagonistic mode of production, and finally shows the consequences of this as capitalist manufacturers were able to supplant aristocrats and guilds to concentrate power once again. The process was facilitated by some events that did not flow from the system itself, such as the discovery of gold in the Americas, that can be thought of as contingent.[14]

I have thus far presented only the first segment of Marx's theory and am reserving very important features of it for the next section, where we will proceed to evaluate it. The theory is already complex enough, however, that it is not easy to keep in mind all at once. Just remember here that we first conceptualized our dependent variable, the conditions of workers, as defined by productivity, alienation, and exploitation. We then formed an empirical generalization that linked the worsening of working conditions to different ways of making a living (hunting and gathering versus industrial work, for instance). These served as a clue forcing us to look much more deeply into modes of production to see how they changed in ways that first concentrated and then diffused power. Specific productive technologies underlie modes of production, and specific relations among social classes arise from them. Viewing modes of production as dynamic systems allowed us to see them as developing in ways that cause specific classes to form, then allow once subordinate classes, as power diffuses, to supplant previously dominant classes and to inaugurate a new mode of production. We've seen this summarized, as best so complicated a theory can be, in figure 2.4.

I am sure that the theory, especially in its focus on conditions of labor in the nineteenth century, initially seems quite remote from our own daily lives, but it is crucial to realize that Marx is addressing matters that remain very relevant to us today. Not only do many students learn about Marx's explanation of alienation, for instance, on the way to a college degree by which they hope to avoid alienating work (thereby forcing it upon others who have less power), but throughout the world today, comparatively powerless people must still work in circumstances similar to those of early industrial Manchester. In fact, the distribution of alienating labor today is perhaps developing more importantly *across* national boundaries than it is *within* advanced economies, like that of the United States, which have lately been busy exporting their most alienating work to underdeveloped countries where people have less power to avoid it (or to be relatively well paid when they can't).[15] Thus, what Marx was attempting to explain is very much of continuing concern to us.

Evaluating Marx's Theory

As we noted in chapter 1, we don't spin out theories for the pleasure of doing so and then just contemplate them for their elegance: we want them to be both intellectually stimulating and right, and we become convinced they are right only by determining whether they are robust and then drawing out their implications and testing these in the light of additional observations. The focus of Marx's theory on capitalism makes it difficult to test for robustness because, unless we view the Japanese development of a form of capitalism as a second instance, we are faced with a singular phenomenon. On the other hand, Marx's theory is rich in implications, and by developing some of these, we can test it, as well as become better acquainted with it. In what follows, I will add some elements to the theory, elements that could have been introduced in the previous section but have a clearer purpose in relation to the major prediction Marx used his theory to make: that the capitalist industrial mode of production would give way to a new, communist mode. Since this prediction seems clearly to have been wrong—industrial capitalism is still with us well after Marx anticipated that it would disappear, and the communist mode as Marx envisaged it was never developed, even by so-called communist regimes[16]—we can safely conclude that something must have been wrong either with his theory or with the way he used it to make his prediction. But to arrive at this conclusion responsibly, we need first to examine his prediction, understand the theory of capitalist development that was involved in it, and then consider what should count as evidence (that is, as relevant observations) for or against the prediction. I will take these topics up in turn.

Predicting the Transition from Capitalism to Communism

Predictions result from developing the implications of a theory as they apply to events in the future. The ability to make predictions is a major attraction of scientific theories, and for very obvious reasons: knowing what will happen in the future allows us to prepare for it, and knowing why it will happen gives us, at least in principle, a way to intervene if we're not happy with the predicted future. By the same token, predictions allow us to test theories since, when a predicted event does not occur, we can conclude either that the theory is wrong or that some factor intervened so as to void the theory's application in this instance.[17]

To see how Marx developed his prediction, we need first to reflect on a property of alienation and exploitation as variables. In the preceding figures, I've presented them as dimensions with low and high values. The way I've drawn the figures implies that there is a lower limit to alienation (where the axes of the figure meet) but not a higher one. (If we imagine extending the dimensions indefinitely higher, alienation and exploitation would just go on, gradually getting worse.) But, we noted some time ago that people don't like alienation and exploitation, and it is hard to imagine that they would put up with them if they increased indefinitely. In other words, there must be some upper limit, in practice, to the alienation and exploitation people are willing to endure since, at some point, their work would become so repetitive, so boring, and so poorly paid as to drive them to suicide or revolt. Thus, both these variables must have built-in upper limits, although my figures haven't included them, and we don't, in practice, know just where they lie.

Marx used the self-limiting nature of alienation and exploitation to make his prediction. As alienation and exploitation worsened, he believed, workers would have more incentive to revolt. But revolt is never simply against something: it also looks forward to better circumstances, and the circumstances to which alienated workers would look forward, Marx believed, would entail a mode of production that dramatically reduced their alienation and exploitation. What would this mode look like? Although, in principle, workers could destroy the industrial system and return to crafts and farming or to hunting and gathering, this would mean dramatically reducing productivity and thus realienating themselves from the species-being.[18] Because this meant destroying great human accomplishments, Marx believed they would opt for a new mode of production that eliminated exploitation by transferring ownership of all property to the people as a whole and that reduced alienation from the process of labor by *socializing* work so as to divide up and rotate jobs among individuals in ways that would allow them to express all their talents and potentials. This new mode of production would be a *communist* form of industrial organization, and it would decrease alienation (and eliminate exploitation) while allowing for further increases in productivity.

Before we explore further what Marx meant by a communist mode of production, it would be good to visualize his prediction in the framework of our previous figures. In fact, this will give us a much fuller sense of Marx's actual theory. We'll do this first in a simple form and add some complexity later. In figure 2.5, I've added a limit to alienation and exploitation, signifying a point at which people simply will no longer put up with the conditions under which they must work. When this built-in limit is reached, Marx argued, the path of societal development will reverse itself dramatically so as to lower the amount of alienation. In a sense, we could say that the worsening of workers' conditions "hits the wall" by becoming truly unbearable and then rebounds as far as it can in the opposite direction (just the sort of zig-zag pattern Marx felt exemplified the dialectic: see the appendix 2A).

Suppose now we make the picture more complex by making necessary

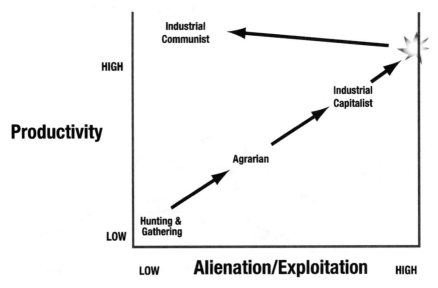

FIGURE 2.5
The Transition to Communism in Reduced Form

changes to figure 2.5. The pattern of development will now look like it does in figure 2.6. In this figure, I have added the necessary limits to figure 2.4, indicating that our variables cannot increase indefinitely into regions where people simply will not go. The arrow describing the path of working conditions extends to this limit and reverses itself, as in figure 2.5, but now also in relation to the dimension of concentration of power. The figure remains open to the right, however, because productivity per capita can, in principle, increase indefinitely, and Marx expected that under the new mode of communism, it would far outstrip the productivity of nineteenth-century capitalism.

Figure 2.6 summarizes Marx's theory in a form that makes it relatively easy to remember. The arrows describe the complex path of working conditions from one mode of production to the next, a path so involved that it would take many paragraphs to describe, but which is easily grasped by means of the figure itself. To understand the final part of this path, however, we need to look a little more closely at what Marx expected the communist mode of production to do.

Interestingly, Marx wrote very little about the nature of the communist society his theory placed on the immediate historical horizon. Its two most central features, however, flowed from the need to overcome exploitation and alienation. It would eliminate exploitation entirely by having the society as a whole take over ownership of the means of production and return to each individual the full value of his or her work contribution (minus a

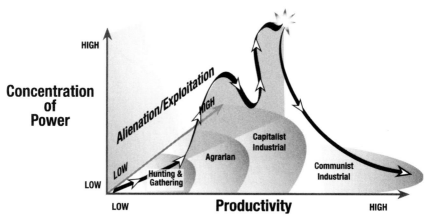

FIGURE 2.6
The Transition to Communism

deduction to support public goods like roads and public libraries). This meant that the surplus value that had been going to capitalists would now be going to the workers themselves. And communism would dramatically reduce alienation by allocating and rotating jobs so as to allow people variety in their work and more of a chance to develop their human potentials. About how to do this, Marx gave us no exact plan; yet, in an early book titled *The German Ideology* he wrote,

> In communist society, where nobody has one exclusive sphere of activity but each can be accomplished in any branch he wishes, society regulates the general production and thus makes it possible for one to do one thing today and another tomorrow, to hunt in the morning, fish in the afternoon, rear cattle in the evening, criticize after dinner, just as I have a mind, without ever becoming hunter, fisherman, shepherd or critic. (Tucker 1971:124)

While this passage is somewhat whimsical, Marx meant that, in a communist society, people would be able to trade and rotate jobs to such a degree that no individual would ever be defined by a single occupation. Thus, his objective was not necessarily to reduce the division of labor as it affected specific jobs but to allow a given individual the opportunity to work at enough such jobs to express a range of potentials and to develop a broad set of skills. Further, he anticipated that as productivity increased, machines would come to do the most repetitive and boring jobs for which humans were needed in the nineteenth century. Thus, technological advances and a new way of distributing work would dramatically reduce alienation. This explains why the arrow in figure 2.6 takes the path it does with the transition to communism. Alienation and exploitation decline as jobs are shared and workers are paid the full value of their labor, and the concentration of power declines as political and economic equality increase.

The Mechanism of Transition

As I noted before, Marx needed not just to assert that modes of production changed over time but to explain why they did. Further, though he believed that such changes flowed "naturally" from the dialectic of history, he needed to outline the mechanisms by which they took place. In the case of the transition from the mode of agrarian-handicraft production to the capitalist industrial, as we saw, he gave a causal narrative account that includes too many contingencies to qualify as a mechanism. In the case of the transition from capitalism to communism, though, he did provide a mechanism. It takes the form of an *analysis* of capitalism—breaking it down into its components and showing their dynamic relations with one another, relations in which he saw a *necessary* developmental pattern leading to capitalism's destruction and replacement by communism. For Marx, once you understood the dynamics of capitalism, you would see why it had to disappear as a mode of production. (As I indicated in chapter 1, the necessity in this mechanism qualifies it as a theory rather than as a causal narrative.) At the same time, these dynamics did not yield a date certain for its disappearance but, instead, outlined a set of conditions whose gradual worsening would make the overthrow of capitalism increasingly likely. In what follows, I will give only a sketch of the mechanism since each of its components is in fact quite complicated.

We have seen that capitalist employers always got more value out of laborers than they paid them in wages, and that they appropriated the difference, or the surplus value, as profit. Furthermore, there was no other place for employers to get profits: according to Marx, they always came from paying workers less than the value of their work. This claim took on great significance as Marx analyzed the apparent consequences of capitalist competition for profits. Competition for profits among capitalists led to the further **mechanization** of work, and mechanization in turn had the ironic consequence of causing profits to decline, ownership of industries to grow concentrated (and thus power to become more concentrated), and unemployment to increase. These effects, Marx believed, especially when coupled with the cycles of boom and bust to which capitalism was prey, would lead large segments of society to see the system as profoundly irrational and, thus, to overthrow it in favor of a less alienating, less exploitative, and more rational mode of production, namely, communism. Let us briefly sketch this mechanism.

Marx believed that capitalists *must* further mechanize the production of goods. Machines were unavoidable precisely because they were "labor saving": they could produce more goods in less time than could human workers. Capitalists who introduced new machines to perform work previously done by humans could thus produce more goods, less expensively, than could their competitors, and this allowed them to acquire an edge in the market. Unless and until competitors also introduced the new machines, the innovating capitalist would be able to pile up profits (producing goods more cheaply but selling them at the old price) or drive the competition out of business (by offering the product at a price others couldn't match). Further, the less expensive goods allowed by machine production fueled mass consumption, as items that were previously too expensive to be purchased broadly came within the means of average citizens. Yet, mechanization had two further consequences, Marx believed: it threw people out of work and into what Marx called the *reserve army* of the unemployed, and it slowly caused profits to fall since machines did not give rise to the surplus value from which profits could alone be derived.

These two features of mechanization worked against each other. Because more and more people would be thrown out of work by the machines that replaced them, the wages of those who still worked could be kept very low or driven down, potentially affording capitalists more profits. Yet, only so much surplus value could be gotten from the smaller workforce that mechanization caused. As the overall human labor involved in production declined, the only way to maintain profits would be to employ a greater percentage of the remaining workers, which led to industrial concentration as one or a few firms attempted to buy up all the others as a way of expanding market share. Seeking profit in the face of decreased surplus value, capitalists would be forced to expand the scope of their businesses constantly, first coming to dominate the production of a particular good and then seeking to dominate the production of additional goods. In a sense, the logical conclusion of the capitalist system, for Marx, was one immense business producing everything and run by one inconceivably rich capitalist, who employed everyone else as workers whose wages were kept low by the threat of being forced to join the reserve army of the unemployed.

The closer this logical conclusion of capitalism was approximated by actual conditions, Marx felt, the less happy people would be with the system, especially as it depended upon their alienation and exploitation. Further, their perception that capitalism was not just unfair but irrational would increase during periods of recession or depression as more and more people were thrown out of work. Marx pointed out that industrial capitalism, in constantly mechanizing the labor process and, thus, lowering the unit cost of production, tended to overproduce goods, making more than the market could absorb. This meant that capitalism was prone to **crises of overproduction** in which goods flooded the market but found no buyers. The people who produced these goods then had to be let go, which meant they had to curtail their own purchasing, which in turn caused other people to be let go and forced them to curtail consumption, until the economy spiraled into a depression. The catastrophic downturns that had occurred under capitalism roughly every fifty years seemed to everyone a very real problem with the system: its inability to fit supply to demand meant that the economy performed like a roller coaster, with busts consistently following booms. Busts, Marx felt, would destroy the confidence of the populace in the system. Further, communication would become easier among the workers as industry became concentrated, making organization for change easier among them. Joined by failed capitalists forced to enter the ranks of workers as their businesses collapsed, and facing a smaller and smaller class of very wealthy capitalists on one side and a larger and larger group of impoverished, unemployed people on the other, the working class would become fully conscious of its situation and rise up to expropriate the capitalists, socializing the process of production. In this way, the dynamics of capitalism would lead to revolution and the destruction of the system itself, a standard dialectical outcome.

After the workers rose up to expropriate the capitalists, the process of production could be organized so as to dealienate labor and allow men and women to achieve their full human potential through varied forms of work. Furthermore, the economy would become so powerful, thanks to the innovations of capitalism, that a decent level of general well-being could be provided for all. This would mean an end to alienation, exploitation, and the consequent struggle among classes that had previously driven history forward. Power would cease to be concentrated in the hands of a few. Although productivity would continue to increase with scientific advances and technological innovations, the communist mode of production would be with us forever since it had solved all the problems that had led to changes in the mode of production in the past.

From the above, we can see how Marx's prediction flowed from and expanded upon his basic theory. Indeed, the theory is incomplete without the forecast it makes about the transition to communism and the mechanism Marx used to make this forecast. The way he explained this transition is different from the way he explained the transition from the handicraft-agrarian mode to the capitalist, however. There, he employed a causal narrative to show how capitalist manufacturers gained the upper hand over the previously dominant aristocrats and guilds. He did not picture the agrarian-craft mode as having a mechanism whose internal workings necessarily produced its own downfall: instead, the downfall was aided significantly by events, like the European discovery of the Americas and theft of their gold, that cannot be predicted based on a knowledge of the agrarian-handicraft system itself. In contrast, Marx's analysis of capitalism stands as a theory (rather than as a causal narrative) because it relies solely upon what Marx believed were necessary, internal processes fundamental to capitalism itself. Just as pressing $2 \times 2 \times 2 \times 2 \ldots$ indefinitely on my hand calculator causes it soon to overload and cease functioning, Marx believed that mechanization, falling profit, industrial concentration, and economic crises would eventually cause capitalism to cease functioning. The outcome is entirely predictable once you understand how the system works, and your understanding comes from a theory of the system rather than from a causal narrative. There is no chance or contingency involved.[19]

Evidence for and against the Theory

I have already suggested that Marx's theory must have been wrong since the events he used to predict it have not occurred. We might be tempted because of this to simply dismiss it as not worth further scrutiny. (After all, if you were told by a prophet that the world would end at midnight tonight, and yet you lived through the night quite normally, you wouldn't spend much time pondering this prophet's theory to figure out what was wrong with it.) But since industrial capitalism underwent significant transformations after Marx wrote, and since these transformations were geared to address some of the problems he predicted would cause capitalism's demise, it could also be claimed that his theory was "right" in a very loose way. By analyzing where it was most wrong and where most right, we can determine whether some modified form of it might be useful today.

One obvious problem with Marx's analysis of capitalism was that rates of profit did not fall as predicted. His assertion that all profit derives from surplus value, which was the basis for this prediction, was simply wrong. While Marx had to modify this notion even in his own day to explain why profits to specific industries did not necessarily decline as they mechanized (see Giddens, 1971:50–51, for a discussion), it seems clear today that a firm's ability to generate profits simply has nothing to do with the amount of human labor it has available to exploit.[20] Marx's mistaken supposition to the contrary was a key flaw in his mechanism for the transition from capitalism to communism.

A second problem is that mechanization doesn't necessarily cause unemployment since service jobs can replace manufacturing ones. In fact, to the extent that we have seen a major change in mode of production since Marx's day, it has been in the development of a service-information economy to replace the old industrial manufacturing mode. The expansion of services, itself allowed by increased industrial and, especially, agricultural productivity, has kept unemployment relatively low, while unionized workers have been able to force wages up despite the presence of a certain percentage of unemployed people. The supposition that mechanization will consistently increase the unemployment rate was thus a second key flaw in Marx's mechanism since the widespread and dire poverty that he expected to result, and then to undermine the legitimacy of capitalism and encourage its revolutionary overthrow, simply did not occur.[21]

These two very specific problems with Marx's mechanism, I would argue, are accompanied by a third serious problem that arises out of vagueness in his concept of mode of production. In chapter 1, I argued that the concepts we use in theories must be very clearly defined so that we know what constitutes an instance of them. "Mode of production" does not quite satisfy this criterion. Indeed, when we think about it, it is not clear that Marx's vision of a communist industrial order qualifies as a new mode of production rather than simply being the old industrial order modified by public ownership and job rotation. At issue is how important new technologies are to defining new modes of production, in comparison, say, to features like ownership of the means of production and the social distribution of job assignments. Some modes seem to be defined primarily by their technological base. For instance, farming employs technologies not present in hunting-and-gathering societies, and industrial production employs technologies not present in agrarian-handicraft economies. This might lead us to conclude that the mode of production that replaces capitalism must rest on some novel technology, and, yet, Marx did not see communism as dependent on a fundamental technological innovation. But what exactly are, then, the criteria defining a new mode of production?

To put the problem somewhat differently, the vagueness in Marx's concept of mode of production raises the question of whether we should view our mode today as distinct from the capitalist industrial mode Marx described. After all, we are seeing a major shift from an industrial order to a service-information economy, facilitated by new communications technologies. Is this a new mode of production, run by a new elite of highly educated professionals, or is it simply the same old capitalism? Unless we can decide questions like this, we can't even begin predicting or explaining transitions between modes of production. Indeed, Marx did not define the concept clearly enough for us to decide when transitions have occurred.[22]

With such serious problems, it makes little sense to give much credence to Marx's theory in the specific form I have outlined. At the same time, we might argue that his prediction of a transition to communism was derailed not just by his mistaken assumptions and conceptual vagueness, but by reforms within capitalism that obviated some of the specific problems with it that Marx identified. In particular, the new economic theories of J. M. Keynes and the development of government regulation of consumption by deficit spending and control of the money supply have significantly dampened the cycle of boom and bust to which capitalism was prey and which Marx saw as precipitating its downfall. At the same time, worker organization and government regulation of labor conditions have significantly reduced the severest manifestations of alienation involved in industrial production (at least in the most developed economies). As a result, the capitalism of today looks quite different from the capitalism of Marx's day (at least in the most developed economies), and the change in its character seems very much in the direction Marx's theory might have predicted, were it a theory of gradual, rather than of revolutionary, change. This gives us some confidence that Marx's theory can be modified, eliminating its mistaken assumptions and conceptual fuzziness so as to yield a theory that would still be useful today. Indeed, a vigorous program of theorizing and research led by sociologist Erik

Olin Wright (e.g., 1992, 1997) attempts to do just this. It also encourages us to explore the general paradigm Marx developed to guide his theorizing, which remains largely unaffected by the mistaken assumptions included in his theory of capitalism.

Conclusion

This chapter has dealt with a theory that's quite a bit more complex than the culture-of-honor theory we discussed in the first chapter. We saw, to begin with, that the initial conceptualization of variables in Marx's theory, by means of which the condition of the workers is characterized in terms of the abstract concepts of productivity, alienation, and exploitation, is more complicated than was viewing a particular murder as belonging to the category of argument-related homicides. We saw also that Marx had options here, but he chose productivity, alienation, and exploitation as conceptually efficient means of characterizing specific aspects of a complicated situation so that it would be generalizable across history. All work, after all, can be situated in relation to these variables. Further, the influential philosopher Hegel had made the term *alienation* central to his philosophy of history, and so it was natural for Marx to appropriate it and then give it his own twist. Still, we've found that defining our variables is a complicated process, and this is often true of concepts used in the social sciences. For instance, we often talk of "developed" or "underdeveloped" societies without thinking much about how difficult it would be to specify all of the societal differences that could be bundled together in these omnibus concepts. We can't successfully incorporate such concepts into theories without first clarifying them.

Next, we saw that Marx had discovered an empirical generalization, linking changes in alienation and exploitation to the clue variable of mode of production, as he worked on his conceptualization of the dependent variables. This set up his problem: he now had to explain why changes in modes of production increase the three factors characterizing work. Here, both the division of labor and changes in technology explain variation in productivity, while changes in the concentration of power explain why people have no choice but to work in alienating and exploitative jobs. We brought all of these variables together to define a complex, three-dimensional space, through which societies pass as they develop across history, proceeding roller-coaster fashion through levels of power concentration, moving gradually upward and away from their starting points toward a moment when they "hit the wall" and then reverse course with regard to two of the variables (alienation and exploitation), but continue forward with regard to a third (productivity).

This pattern is so complex that it is much easier to recall by means of an illustration than in words. After taking some time to catch our breath, we looked in detail at how Marx explained two of the transitions between modes of production, using a causal narrative for the transition from agrarian to capitalist modes and then a thoroughly worked-out mechanism to predict the transition from capitalism to communism. The causal narrative and mechanism add further complications to the theory. They provide the engines, so to speak, by which societies are pulled along the path described in figure 2.6.

In reflecting upon the failure of Marx's prediction that capitalism must collapse, we speculated that systems like modern economies may be too complex and too sensitive to chance events (such as the presence of massive quantities of gold in the Americas, there for the looting) to be always explicable through causal models. This issue returned us to the contrast between Marx and Max Weber that we discussed in the first chapter. Recall that Weber believed important events in world history were likely to be too "chancy" to be easily modeled in terms of causal mechanisms. Perhaps it is easier to understand what he was getting at now that we've looked at a concrete case.

In addition to seeing an illustration of principles and processes discussed in the first chapter, we've also been reinforced in our conviction that building theories depends crucially on perceiving patterned variation in the social world around us. It was easy for Engels to see that the sort of work he did as a manager in a factory was different from that of his workers. Most of us take differences like this as facts of life and don't even think to question why they occur. Yet, as soon as we've asked this question, we launch ourselves on a quest for additional patterns of variation that can explain the one of interest to us. Marx and Engels saw variation in modes of production and in power differences (linked to social class) as the most likely causal culprits in their whodunit. Their investigation turned in the direction of these particular variables because they were guided by a paradigm, that of historical materialism, to which we turn in our next chapter.

Appendix 2A: The Dialectic

Marx viewed social change as a *dialectical process*. This presents a barrier to understanding him because the dialectical pattern is both complicated and somewhat alien to our current ways of thinking. Arguably, you don't need to be familiar with it to understand "the essential Marx," but on the other hand, it certainly helps us see why Marx thought that the changes his theory predicted were inevitable. Thus, I'm taking time here to discuss what a dialectical pattern of change looks like and why Marx was so attracted to it.

As a way of orienting ourselves to such a complicated and alien idea, let's first consider some other ways in which we might characterize processes of change. For instance, consider how organisms grow to maturity. Organisms begin as single cells, which then divide and multiply. The divided and multiplied cells are at first relatively homogeneous (all the same), but soon they begin to differentiate and specialize in their functions. This differentiation occurs for reasons that are still somewhat obscure, but the process is governed by a particular set of genes included in our DNA. The pattern of cell division and differentiation proceeds to the point where a highly complex, multicellular entity results, with specialized organs contributing to the common good. DNA guides this differentiation so that it takes a particular form: what starts out as a dog doesn't wind up as a cat. The overall process is one of internally regulated growth and transformation: the original tiny cell gradually turns into an amazingly complex and large adult organism. Organismic maturation thus instances a particular type of change process.

Another type of change process is evolution. Darwin argued that species evolved as differences among individuals, some produced through random mutations, led them to cope with their environments with greater or lesser effectiveness, or, in the case of sexual selection, to prove more attractive to mates. The measure of success in both cases is reproduction, with some differences leading to more descendants than others. As these differences become established in the population, the pattern by which they ramify and succeed one another over time is viewed as evolution. When differences become large enough, a new species may emerge. This overall pattern is another form of change, quite different from organismic growth. The process of growth and differentiation is very directed (governed by genes), but evolution is not. As far as we are aware, it doesn't have any direction, at least once a certain degree of differentiation is achieved. (It certainly needn't lead to intelligent creatures such as ourselves.)

Consider now a third pattern of change that I'll introduce with an example. When automobiles were first introduced, they were slow and relatively uncomfortable, as were the roads they drove on. Improvements to both resulted in faster and more comfortable travel by automobile. At least, they did so as long as there weren't too many autos. Where there were, you got traffic jams that slowed travel. Further, highway planners couldn't fix this problem by building more roads, because the new roads soon became just as clogged as the old ones. In this pattern of change, the very success and popularity of some innovation leads to eventual problems with it, problems that can't be solved by "more of the same." Thus, there's pressure to come up with a new solution.

Consider one of these: since many traffic jams result from commuting to work, we can get beyond them by creating a "virtual office" at home via communications technologies so that office workers, at least, may no longer have to commute. If they can work at home nearly as well as they could in the office, travel to and from the office becomes unnecessary. To put this another way, new communications technologies allow offices to disperse spatially. As the advantages of this become apparent, more and more development occurs in the new technology (communications) and less and less in the old (highways). Traffic ceases to be as much of a hassle because we've solved the old problem by developing an entirely new system, one that may eventually turn out to have its own problems.

This pattern of change, in which a new technology arises to address the problems created by the very success of the old technology, is roughly dialectical in character. In dialectical change, the process of enlarging or perfecting some way of doing things reveals problems within it—we can call these its *contradictions*—that eventually become so disabling that a new way of doing things must take its place. The contradiction in automobiles is that they are large and independently operated vehicles—both great advantages, but only until there are so many of them that their very largeness and independence actually slows down the transport of large numbers of people.

We need only add to this that, in truly dialectical change, the new way already exists within the old in juvenile form and grows and develops along with the contradictions. Further, the old and the new are in an antagonistic relation, which can only be resolved by a significant transformation in which the new way displaces the old by leaping over its contradictions in a novel and unanticipated way, whereupon the process begins all over again: as the new way develops, contradictions within it are revealed that energize the development of a still newer way already existing within it, that will eventually take its place. This pattern is fully dialectical.

Marx was introduced to the idea of dialectical change through the work of the philosopher G. W. F. Hegel. Hegel believed he had found in the dialectic the key to understanding all of human history. For Hegel, history showed a zig-zag pattern of development, as an initial stage matured to reveal contradictions, contradictions that were "leapt over" by an innovative resolution. The innovative resolution retained certain properties of previous stages (just as the "office" doesn't disappear as a concept when it is spatially dispersed) but embodied them in novel ways that could not easily have been predicted at earlier stages.

The basic unit of this process includes an initial stage, or *thesis*, which, as it develops, generates its own *antithesis* internally. As contradictions with this antithesis deepen, the process enters its second stage, out of which arises a third, the *synthesis*, which resolves the contradictions between the first two stages.

An example will make this more concrete. Early human societies, Hegel said, consisted of free individuals in roughly equal circumstances. A contradiction was revealed, however, in that humans by their very nature sought to dominate one another as a way to increase their personal freedom. The success of the strongest and most talented individuals in contests for domination led to a new social institution: slavery. This institution gave maximal freedom to slaveholders precisely by denying it to slaves, who did the hard work that allowed slaveholders their freedom. The relation of master and slave thus stood as the antithesis of the original condition of equality and freedom and precisely as a result of a contradiction within it. But a new contradiction soon arose in the institution of slavery itself.

Little did masters realize, Hegel argued, that their very freedom incapacitated them and spelled their doom. As slaves worked for their owners, they learned more and more about the world and how to transform it through labor, while, as slaveholders enjoyed their freedom, they became increasingly disconnected from the practical aspects of life and the knowledge acquired through working. It was precisely the slaves' engagement with the world that gave them the understanding and power eventually to overthrow their masters and to set up political institutions (such as parliaments) in which freedom became more widespread. These new political institutions allowed some play to the natural tendency to domination while guaranteeing individuals much more extensive freedoms than slave societies had afforded. They represented a synthesis of the original state of freedom (thesis) and the lopsided freedoms of slave societies (antithesis).

We can think of the dialectical pattern of change as a zig-zag that also includes an element of progress. Responding to contradictions within the original condition of human equality, slavery zigs away from it in a quite radical direction, molding society around very dramatic inequalities. We then zag back from this to societies that guarantee individual freedoms, but now at a much more advanced level of social organization than in the original circumstances of freedom and equality. Thus, history zig-zags upward according to a dialectical pattern of change. This pattern was filled with irony and misdirection: slaveholders never realized, for instance, that their own style of life, for which slavery was necessary, carried within it the seeds of its destruction.

History, Hegel believed, was filled with such ironies. It often misled us with appearances while hiding fundamental directions of change. Hegel viewed this as history's "cunning"; it was leading us forward (toward increasing freedom), but often by misdirection (such as the institution of slavery, which for most was the antithesis of freedom). Thus, dialectical patterns of development got us to places we never would have imagined, but, at the same time, they did so by a very regular, if often wildly innovative, process, one whose workings were inevitable. Understanding the dialectical character of the process gave us the key to understanding and explaining all of history, Hegel believed. Marx was only one of many early-nineteenth-century thinkers who found Hegel's vision almost breathtakingly insightful (if in need of some modifications, which Marx felt called upon to provide). To get a brief taste of Hegel and see what all the fuss was about, you should read his essay *Reason in History* (1987).

Like organismic maturation or evolution, the dialectic identifies a specific *formal pattern* of change. For human society, Marx followed Hegel in believing, the same general pattern could be seen in instance after instance. And once you understood that history behaved dialectically, it was difficult to resist analyzing its cunning to see what the future held. The promise of insight into our future was what made the dialectic so compelling to early-nineteenth-century thinkers, just as the frequency with which this promise has been betrayed has caused it gradually to fall out of fashion. In fact, it's fallen so far out of fashion today that it seems almost as odd and foreign as the idea of men wearing powdered wigs. But the example I gave of the dialectical development of commuting should indicate that this pattern of change, at least in very rough outline, is one we should have in our repertoire as we try to understand the forces at work in society around us. Of course, there are many further such patterns, entropy being among them. Familiarity with these formal patterns helps us think about the ways things change.

Notes

1. Integrating the dialectic stood between us and these goals: hence, the appendix. In other words, while I'm interested in fidelity to Marx, I'm just as concerned to show how his theory and paradigm illustrate the process of theorizing and address issues of relevance to us today. Students might compare my approach with that of Giddens (1971), which offers one of the best brief intellectual-historical introductions to Marx and to which I am indebted in my own presentation.

2. An interesting book on this topic is Karl Polanyi's *The Great Transformation* (1957). Polanyi points out just how limited and regulated the exchange of goods and services had been prior to the inauguration of capitalism. In particular, there was little market for land or money. Most people were forbidden to sell land (since by law it had to be handed down to their heirs), and there were few banks that marketed money (in the forms of loans, by which one buys the use of money for a period of

time through interest payments). For Polanyi, the "great transformation" occurred when land, labor, and capital (money) all become more or less freely available for purchase in markets. Other scholars (e.g., Macfarlane 1989) view this transformation as much less dramatic and consequential than does Polanyi.

3. The question of when and where capitalism actually originated is a topic of much scholarly controversy. It is possible to view the Italian city-states (e.g., Venice and Genoa) as already "capitalist" in the fourteenth and fifteenth centuries or to argue that European markets were so restricted by guilds and governments that capitalism was not a critical social factor until the eighteenth century. In either case, capitalism clearly existed before the industrial revolution.

4. As you read through my discussion of the concepts of alienation and exploitation, you should ask yourself which is better conceptualized. I'd argue that, although both are quite complex, the problems with alienation are more severe because its component properties don't necessarily vary together.

5. Ironically, many people go to college today not because they find studying enjoyable and their course work a means to display their human potential but because they believe that a college degree is a ticket to more satisfying work. This belief overlooks the fact that craft work today often provides greater job satisfaction than does work requiring a college degree. On what motivates college attendance, see Labaree (1997), and on work satisfaction, see Terkel (1974).

6. I borrow inspiration here from the analysis of Tilly (1992), who separates the concentration of power into the concentration of force, on the one hand, and the concentration of capital (or wealth), on the other.

7. For a much fuller discussion of modes of production, see Lenski (1995).

8. Further, both hunting and farming are increasingly organized industrially. Family farms, for instance, are being supplanted by large corporate farms that employ farm laborers in ways similar to industrial workers.

9. In fact, Marx distinguished three separate forms of agrarian modes of production: the ancient (which employed slaves), the Asiatic (which had a strongly centralized government that conscripted labor), and the feudal (which used serfs obligated to warrior aristocrats).

10. Max Weber, as I suggested in the last chapter, would have argued that Marx's ambition to theorize here was mistaken since societal development is too prey to chance and contingency to be theorizable in the first place. In his view, the best we can hope for is causal narratives.

11. We should not much fault Marx on this score since the topic remains controversial to this day. See MacNeish (1992) on the origins of agriculture and Harris (1977:67–82) for an interesting explanation of how stratification develops in primitive horticultural societies using primitive agricultural technologies.

12. You should recall here that causal narratives can offer us perfectly satisfactory explanations without constituting theories and that they should not be faulted for not being theories.

13. I have modified Marx here somewhat in light of Walker's (1971) interesting analysis of the German case. An early version of Marx and Engel's treatment is in the section of *The German Ideology* titled "Intercourse and Productive Forces" (Tucker 1971:140–50).

14. As you ponder this causal narrative, you should relate it to the present and

consider how a company like Wal-Mart, using new inventory and distributing technologies, has formed an alliance with government officials favoring "free trade" to transform the U.S. economy substantially, shifting manufacturing jobs to low-wage countries like China.

15. For an accessible discussion of this development, see Ehrenreich and Fuentes (1981).

16. Certain reservations to this generalization would have to be entered if we considered small cooperative communities such as the kibbutzim of Israel (see Spiro 1963[1956]).

17. Because it is impossible in a single instance to decide between the two alternatives, namely, bad theory or intervening factors, the failure of a prediction does not conclusively refute a theory. Indeed, when a theory works well in most circumstances, then fails in a particular prediction, we are much wiser to look for intervening factors than to discard the theory. For example, if some water does not freeze when lowered to 32 degrees, we are better off suspecting that it contains salts (an intervening factor) than to question the theoretical relation between freezing and temperature decline.

18. There were, in fact, many efforts to prevent the introduction of machines that did the work of craftsmen and, thus, threw people out of work (see Hobsbawm and Rudé 1968). Marx acknowledged this impulse to turn back the clock but believed it was unlikely to carry the day.

19. We might want to exempt from this strong statement of necessity the revolutionary organization of the working class and the moment it chooses to initiate revolutionary class struggle, factors that depend upon contingent events that Marx was unable to systematize fully.

20. Further, profits have no direct relation to capitalists' acquisition of wealth since unprofitable companies can nevertheless be seen as (or made by accountants to seem) very valuable, particularly as sources for looting by management.

21. Because these two errors in Marx's analysis of capitalism are both very serious and, in hindsight, rather obvious, we might imagine he should have known better than to make them. Yet, understanding social systems, particularly, predicting their future behavior, requires that we make certain conceptual gambles, informed by our best current understanding, then see if they prove right or wrong. When I went to graduate school in the 1960s, demographers studying the growth of human populations routinely predicted widespread famine by the century's end. Using the best evidence then available, they made assumptions about how food supplies and populations would grow—and were proved wrong. Their understanding of the population system and the factors that would slow birth rates was mistaken, as we now can see, but it's not clear how they could have known this at the time of their predictions or how they could have anticipated the "green revolution" that increased agricultural output. We should view Marx's errors with the same generosity.

22. We could carry this further to ask whether modes of production should be seen as discrete systems between which relatively abrupt changes occur or whether it would be better to view the economy as one continuously evolving system, where change is more gradual. In other words, while it is clear that every society must have a mode of production, it doesn't necessarily follow that modes of production are distinct from one another in the way that, say, chemical compounds are.

3

Historical Materialism and Its Legacy

IN INTRODUCING CHAPTER 2, I indicated that Karl Marx's ambition was not simply to explain the development (and predict the collapse) of capitalism as a mode of production but to outline a paradigm that would help us formulate theories to explain major social changes across history. His model in this regard was G. W. F. Hegel, who made understanding historical change the centerpiece of his philosophical system. Like many young intellectuals of his generation, Marx was both very impressed by Hegel's vision and convinced that it could be improved upon. Marx's effort was one of the most radical attempts to do so: it involved inverting Hegel, or standing him on his head, so that his thoroughgoing idealism was transformed into just as thoroughgoing a materialism. This strain of Marx's thought continues as a vital force in the social sciences today.

The Paradigm of Historical Materialism

Historical materialism is not a theory but a paradigm. In chapter 1, we noted that paradigms refer to very general sets of assumptions about how the world works, ones that we can use to create theories. The assumptions do not explain any concrete behavior themselves but, instead, advise us about how to do so, suggesting, for instance, where we are apt to find a good clue or independent variables and how to formulate effective explanatory arguments with them. Thus, paradigms give us guidance about how to solve problems, but they don't actually solve any problems by themselves.

Marx's paradigm of historical materialism, as I've indicated, was geared to guide our understanding of social structure and how it changes across time. By *social structure*, I mean recurrent patterns of interaction between and within categories of individuals. For instance, college classes have a social structure that consists of recurrent relations between professors and students and of relations among students. Among these relations are professors lecturing and students listening and taking notes; students raising questions with professors; professors answering students' questions; students making jokes among themselves about the professor; and so on. The pattern of these relations gives structure to classes, a structure that can change over time and from place to place. For instance, relations between professors and students are less distant and formal now than they were a hundred years ago. This increasing informality is an example of social change. Of course, this is change in a small social structure, or a *microstructure*. Marx was interested in the structure of an entire society, or its *macrostructure*, and why it changes. How should we begin to think about this?

The best summary Marx offered of historical materialism comes from one long paragraph of his 1859 essay "A Contribution to the Critique of Political Economy":

> In the social production of their life men enter into definite relations that are indispensable and independent of their will, relations of production which correspond to a definite stage of development of their material productive forces. The sum total of these relations of production constitutes the economic structure of society, the real foundation on which rises a legal and political superstructure and to which correspond definite forms of social consciousness. The mode of production of material life conditions the social, political, and intellectual life process in general. It is not the consciousness of men that determines their being, but, on the contrary, their social being that determines their consciousness. At a certain stage of their development, the material productive forces of society come into conflict with the existing relations of production or—what is but a legal expression for the same thing—with the property relations within which they have been at work hitherto. From forms of development of the productive forces these relations turn into their fetters. Then begins an epoch of social revolution. With the change of the economic foundations the entire immense superstructure is more or less rapidly transformed. (Tucker 1971:4)

Let us look very carefully at this paragraph, taking it phrase by phrase. It first suggests, "In the social production of their life, men enter into definite relations that are indispensable and independent of their will." The "definite relations" here are another way of saying "social structure," and the "social production of their life" refers to the coordinated activities through which people earn a living. In **agrarian societies**, for instance, particularly powerful people claim ownership of the land and charge others for the right to farm it, or perhaps they use slaves to farm it. Relations between landowners and the slaves or peasants who work the land are an important feature of the social structure of agrarian societies. Marx identified such groups as **social classes** that had different and antagonistic interests. Owners, for instance, could become richer if they charged more for the right to farm land. Similarly, peasants would be better off if they paid less to owners, and best off if they paid nothing at all, becoming owners themselves of the land they farmed. Thus, their interests were in conflict, and since owners had more military force on their side (a concentration of power!), their interests prevailed. The point here is that when Marx looked to describe social structure, the first thing that attracted his attention was the character of the economic system and the relative inequalities and conflicting interests between classes of people (such as landowners and peasants) that it entailed. Social structures, for Marx, were primarily the patterns of antagonistic relations among classes of people and, secondarily, the relations of cooperation within groups that are crucial to the production of goods: these are the "definite relations" indispensable to "the social production of . . . life."

Now, we get to a very important passage: "relations of production . . . correspond to a definite stage of the development of their material productive forces. The sum total of these relations of production constitutes the economic structure of society, the real foundation on which rises a legal and political superstructure and to which correspond definite forms of social consciousness." There are four key terms here:

1. material productive forces
2. relations of production
3. legal and political superstructure
4. social consciousness

If we really understand these terms and the relations among them, we will understand Marx's historical materialism. **Material productive forces** refers largely to technology: the tools, weapons, buildings, paths or roads, machinery, medical facilities, and so on, that we use to earn our living. Material productive forces should also include "human capital," or the knowledge and skills that people develop to use the technology they have available.

Relations of production refers to the relationships among people, by means of which they are organized in groups to earn a living. The most important general forms of these relations, for Marx, are power (in other words, who can command whom) and property ownership. The relations between a foreman and a work crew, between a contractor and a set of sub-contractors, between a professor and students, between the owner of a factory and the workers in it, all of these are relations of production. So are the cooperative relations among members of a work or a sports team. In primitive societies, the relation between men as hunters and women as gatherers is a relation of production. Primitive societies are unusual because they have few relationships of authority or ownership. Modern societies, in contrast, are filled with such relations. The main question, for Marx, was, who has the right or power to direct the work of whom? For instance, slave owners have the right and usually the power to direct the work of slaves, but an independent subsistence farmer's work isn't directed by anyone; nor is that of a hunter-gatherer. By and large, owning property, a factory, for instance, is what gives some people power over others, according to Marx. Together, the material productive forces and the relations of production seem to define the *mode of production*, although Marx sometimes uses this term to refer exclusively to the material productive forces. The mode of production is very different in hunting-and-gathering societies from what it is in agrarian or industrial societies, and we saw in the last chapter that Marx believed changes in the mode of production caused changes in the degree of alienation and exploitation.

The **legal and political superstructure** refers to the government, courts, police, and so on. For Marx, the legal and political superstructure enforces a given set of relations of production, making sure it stays in place despite complaints by disfavored social classes. For instance, when a family farm can't make mortgage payments, the police are there to support the "real" owner of the farm, the bank holding the mortgage, just as they will be if you don't make payments on your car.[1] If you want to change these relations, you have to work through the political superstructure to do so. This means having the laws changed so that they protect farmers or drivers against their creditors.

Social consciousness refers to the beliefs people hold that legitimate (which is to say, make appear reasonable) the existing relations of production or the existing legal and political superstructure.[2] Although we often don't talk much about these beliefs, they continue to be present, ready to step forward as justifications for existing relations of production. Sometimes we take social consciousness so much for granted that we can't even imagine things' being different. Most of us believe unreflectingly in private property, for instance. We claim ownership over things like our textbooks, our bicycles, or our cars. We don't realize that while almost all societies have some notion of private property, in many, it's very restricted. For instance, in most societies, prior to the invention of agriculture, no one "owned" land. Instead, it was held in common, communistically, rather like national parks are today. In order for land to be something you could own, people had to develop the idea of private property in land. This had to become part of the social consciousness. The people who develop ideas like this are sometimes called *ideologists*. They offer good arguments for specific relations of production. For instance, Adam Smith, in *The Wealth of Nations* (1776), developed good arguments for private property and the division of labor. He tried to make them seem like good things, and he was quite successful.[3] Thus, ideologists like Smith provide us with sets of arguments that work to legitimate particular relations of production.

The four concepts we've just introduced—material productive forces, relations of production, legal and political superstructure, and social consciousness—define what Marx believed to be the major analytical sectors of any society. In essence, in the passage, he's saying that you can always analyze a society into its technology, its authority and power relations, the legal and political institutions that support these relations, and the cultural ideas that legitimate (or challenge) its relations and institutions.

Now let's see what use he made of them. We proceed to another important passage: "The mode of production of material life conditions the social, political, and intellectual life process in general." Essentially, Marx is saying that the material productive forces (or mode of production) constitute the most influential of the analytical sectors. In other words, material productive forces are the place to look for independent variables explaining change in the other analytical sectors. The technology by which we earn a living has the greatest influence over power and property relations, over legal and political institutions, and over the ideological elements of culture. This is the core of Marx's historical materialism: technology, and changes to it, are the dominant forces in society and in social change.

We've already seen what this means in Marx's theory. The concentration of power is low in hunting-and-gathering societies, which have neither propertied and powerful people nor propertyless and powerless people. In fact, the hunting-and-gathering mode of production more or less guarantees that people live in rough equality because each individual has the ability to earn a living for him- or herself. By contrast, farmers can't escape domination as easily. They are tied to a specific plot of land. Even if additional land were freely available, it would take a lot of time to plant and harvest new crops, so farmers can't just pick up and leave when someone with greater power claims ownership of their land and coerces them into handing over a portion of their crops in return for the right to farm it. This circumstance is directly determined by their mode of production.

In general, materialists like Marx are interested in how new technologies change the playing field with regard to relations of production, increasing or decreasing concentrations of power. Let's take a very different example: while women have probably always been able to do hard physical labor almost as well as men, the mechanization of work over the last century has dramatically decreased the need for such labor and, thus, expanded the proportion of paid work in regard to which it is harder to discriminate against women. At the same time, advances in birth-control technology have given women much greater and less costly control over their reproductive lives. These advances have allowed women to enter the paid work force in unprecedented numbers since World War II (Oppenheimer 1982), changing their status dramatically. It is much higher in relation to men than it was just two generations ago, and this seems due, ultimately, to changes in technology. After all, feminist movements in previous eras had little success convincing people to change their social consciousness and allow women equality. Arguments such as the early feminists made don't change people's minds in the way that new material realities do.[4]

Marx next made just this point: "It is not the consciousness of men that determines their being, but, on the contrary, their social being that determines their consciousness." We cannot develop new social orders simply by dreaming them up and then persuading people to join us in constructing them.[5] The material grounds for new social relations must come into existence before the relations can be changed. Consider again the argument above about the success of contemporary feminism compared to the failure of its predecessors: the latter lacked the material circumstances to increase women's power vis-à-vis men.

Now comes a difficult passage: "At a certain stage in their development, the material productive forces of society come into conflict with the existing relations of production or—what is but a legal expression for the same thing—with the property relations within which they had been at work hitherto." We've already seen an example of this in Marx's causal narrative about the rise of manufacturing in conflict with the guilds and their feudal relations of production. Industrial manufacturing was in conflict with the legal and political superstructure of feudal society, which had written into law privileges for guilds that severely restricted the ability of manufacturers to market their products. In general, the business of guilds was to "restrain trade" (to manage and reduce competition) so that craftsmen could make a decent living. Competition (for instance, trying to sell goods for less than one of your fellow guild members did) was seen as bad practice in the social consciousness of the period, and the guilds used their political power (through the legal and political superstructure) to make it illegal as well.

This is what Marx meant when he said, "From forms of the development of the productive forces these relations turn into their fetters." The guild form of social relations (between master craftsmen and apprentices and between the guild and the surrounding community) had allowed a particular mode of production (the craft mode) to develop and flourish. But it stood in the way of a new mode of production (manufacturing) that merchant capitalists were anxious to introduce and that would eventually prove vastly more productive than the craft mode.

In Marx's vision, a new order develops inside the old order. As the new order grows, the relations of production, the legal and political superstructure, and the social consciousness of the old order conflict with it and "fetter" (restrict) it. People begin to take sides: you're either with the old order (the guilds) or with the new (the manufacturing capitalists or bourgeoisie). The new order comes to see that its growth and success must entail the destruction of the old order.

When this recognition occurs, Marx said, there "begins an epoch of social revolution." He had in mind as an example the French Revolution, which he saw as the political event by which the rising capitalists freed themselves of the fetters, the legal and political superstructure, of feudalism. The switch from craft production to manufacturing Marx saw as a change in the economic "base" of society. "With the change of the economic foundation, the entire immense superstructure is more or less rapidly transformed." The conflict between guilds and merchants drove the change to a fundamentally new order, that of capitalism. Soon, Marx felt, the conflict between capitalists and workers would drive the change to a still newer order, that of communism.

This is the paradigm of historical materialism that guides Marx's formulation of specific explanatory theories or causal narratives. The summary paragraph we have just unpacked presents the paradigm succinctly, but it might help to reduce it further to an illustration. At its core, we have an analysis of society into four sectors and a statement about the priority of causal influences among them. This aspect of the paradigm might be presented as in figure 3.1, in which the thickness of the arrows corresponds to the strength of the causal influence. On the left side, these influences flow upward among the analytic sectors, from the base of material productive forces in the direction of the less influential social consciousness. On the right side, causal

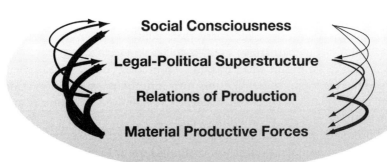

FIGURE 3.1
Causal Influences among Analytical Sectors in Historical Materialism

influences flow downward. The strongest influence is from the material productive forces upward, while the weakest is from social consciousness downward. The moral, or point, of this paradigm is most easily seen in examples
of social change, such as the rise in the status of women today. It suggests
that you can talk women's political and social equality all you want, trying to
bring about change by manipulating social consciousness, but you will have
little effect, at least until the material productive forces change to allow
women roughly equal positions within the relations of production. When
women work alongside men at equal pay, social consciousness of their equality follows naturally.

Of course, this states the matter too bluntly: it is always possible for
changes in social consciousness to affect the other analytical sectors of society, but this effect is less likely and apt to be weaker. It's almost always harder
to talk people into accepting changes than it is to induce change by altering
their material circumstances and trusting that their heads will gradually
follow.

Figure 3.1 summarizes Marx's presentation of historical materialism, but
only up to the difficult passage where he argues, "At a certain stage of their
development, the material productive forces of society come into conflict
with the existing relations of production. . . . From forms of development of
the productive forces these relations turn into their fetters. Then begins an
epoch of social revolution. With the change of the economic foundations the
entire immense superstructure is more or less rapidly transformed." This
aspect of historical materialism reflects Marx's assumption that modes of
production are discrete systems that develop according to a regular dialectical

dynamic (see appendix 2A). New modes are inaugurated by social revolutions, entailing changes in consciousness. In their early stages, they show only some of their true potential. With time, as they are fine-tuned, however, their productivity increases. They mature and flex their muscles, so to speak. Yet, the irony is that their maturation also entails increasing conflicts within them, as power shifts to previously subordinate social classes. And as these classes acquire power, they seek to overthrow the existing legal and political superstructure through revolution, inaugurating a new cycle.[6]

It is this portion of Marx's historical materialism that seems least viable today, in part because it was most influenced by dialectical thought and in part because it was based upon the questionable assumption, as I argued in chapter 2, that modes of production constituted discrete and highly integrated systems. Because they were discrete, changes between them had to be revolutionary: the old mode was so deeply reinforced by the legal and political superstructure and social consciousness that it could only be overturned through a radical upheaval. It is possible to dispense with this assumption and yet retain the view that changes in the mode of production can affect the concentration of power, shifting more into the hands of previously less powerful groups. For example, women as a group have gained significantly in power and status with the shift to a service-informational mode of production, without having to engage in revolutionary struggle.

The paradigm of historical materialism stood behind and guided Marx's theorizing. It represented his sense of how the world worked and, thus, allowed him to build his theories intelligently, rather than having to work blindly through the vast array of possible explanations for the social changes that interested him. In this way, paradigms allow us to economize on our theorizing efforts so that we don't have to start anew for each problem we want to explain.

The Legacy of Marx

The paradigm of historical materialism is an important part of Marx's legacy. It has been modified since his time so as to eliminate some of its weaker points, and it lives on in the program of analytical Marxism perhaps best exemplified in the work of E. O. Wright and his colleagues (1992, 1997), as well as that of Jeffrey Paige (1975). It has also given rise to two additional paradigms, each emphasizing a different aspect of historical materialism: the **conflict paradigm**, which draws as much from Max Weber as from Marx and stresses the latter's vision of social structure as importantly formed through antagonistic relations among groups, and **cultural materialism**, which focuses on the influence of people's material circumstances on their cultural beliefs and practices. We will look at each of these paradigms in turn. Being familiar with various paradigms is a great help when it comes to imagining what sorts of independent variables might plausibly explain events or conditions in the world around us. In a sense, they're like road maps that can direct us to the general vicinity of the answer we're looking for.

The Conflict Paradigm

The conflict paradigm, as indicated, borrows from Marx a conviction that enduring conflicts between groups are the skeleton of social organization. The paradigm recognizes that cooperative and relatively nonconflictual relationships constitute social structure as well, since the groups that are in conflict with one another are themselves composed of people who generally cooperate, be they families, the armies of warring countries, sports teams, or the like. But these cooperative relationships do not form the backbone of society as much as do the conflictual ones.

While Marx believed that conflicts between social classes defined social structure and were the major cause of historical change, the conflict paradigm broadens this perspective quite dramatically to look at conflicts across a wide variety of groups, formed on the basis of gender, status, religion, age, sexual orientation, race, and so on. The paradigm can be summarized in terms of some very general principles (based primarily on Collins 1975):

1. Humans, though highly social creatures, are motivated primarily by self-interest. We generally seek to maximize our material comfort, our sexual satisfaction, and our emotional fulfillment. We also seek to maximize the deference we are shown by others and to minimize the deference we have to show them. Given the option, we seek to avoid being coerced by others and would rather give orders than receive them.
2. In maximizing our satisfactions and avoiding coercion, we find it helpful to form alliances and pool resources with others, and we find it easiest to do so with people whose social characteristics or whose position in a society are similar to our own. In other words, we form socially homogeneous groups to pursue our interests. The social characteristics around which groups form include biological relatedness (family), age, gender, race or ethnicity, religion, or sexual orientation, while positions around which groups form include occupational specialty; status group; caste, estate, or social class; and so on.
3. Inequalities in the resources available to such groups allow favored

parties to take advantage of the less fortunate. Among such resources are physical violence, cunning, rhetorical skill in the presentation of one's case (persuasion), expertise in services broadly desired but little understood (religion and healing, for instance), ease of communication with one's allies, wealth, and political power.

4. Favored parties take advantage of the situation by constructing social arrangements by means of which more than their proportional share of wealth, deference, sex, or other desirable goods accrues to them. This flow of advantages is optimized at some point below a threshold, above which rebellion by those being taken advantage of is likely to occur.

5. Such unequal social arrangements are legitimated by an ideology that explains why a distribution of resources favoring the dominant group is "right" or "natural." Wherever possible, favored groups use their control of the political apparatus of society to write these social arrangements into law, and they monopolize the means of violence to insure obedience to the law.

6. As a result of an imperative, quite likely biological, to favor their own progeny, dominant groups create a system of institutions, such as inheritance laws, private schools, exclusive neighborhoods, clubs, and vacation retreats, to insure that prevailing inequalities are preserved from one generation to the next. Rules of inheritance are supplemented by norms and institutions insuring that group endogamy (marrying within one's group) is practiced where appropriate; in other words, we marry only our own "kind."

7. Subordinates in this system all want to think well of themselves, and, so, they often reject ideological legitimations of inequality that characterize them as undeserving or as "losers"—as too lazy or stupid to do better, for instance. Subordinates often turn the norms and values of the dominant group upside down so as to salvage self-esteem. (For instance, impoverished Christians argue, "The first shall be last and the last shall be first," meaning that in the afterlife, the system of inequalities in this world will be turned upside down so as to give poor Christians the advantages they now lack.)

8. Subordinated groups develop patterns of behavior that minimize the satisfactions and rewards of exploiting and exercising control over them. They occasionally take vengeance through direct harm to their superiors, but more frequently, they engage in passive resistance. The behavior of slaves was characteristic: they "shuffled" (moved slowly), acted dumb, broke or misplaced their tools, and so forth, so that man-

aging them became very trying and less profitable. Such behavior is a form of social control from below.

9. Any significant change in the distribution of resources that favors a subordinated group will lead to political conflict or violence aimed at redistributing advantages. In such conflicts, subordinate groups exploit the *counterideologies* they have employed to salvage their self-esteem, using them to delegitimate dominant ideologies.
10. When a previously disadvantaged group rises to power, it exploits its new position just as did the group or groups it has displaced.

In these ten principles, it is easy to see Marx's analytical sectors of society (material productive forces, relations of production, legal and political super-structure, and social consciousness) just beneath the surface. Yet, the locus of conflict has expanded far beyond the domain of social class so that history is no longer primarily the history of class struggles. In this regard, as in others, the conflict paradigm is more comprehensive than was historical materialism. Theories derived from it have been developed for the field of education (Collins 1979; MacLeod 1995), the legal system (Black 1976, 1993), and the analysis of the professions (Abbott 1988). And, these examples are only the barest sample. Among the paradigm's most important applications is the topic of gender relations, a topic Marx largely ignored, to which we now turn.

A Theory of Gender Relations

An interesting application of the paradigm is the theory of Marcia Guttentag and Paul Secord (1983).[7] The inspiration for their theory came while Guttentag was attending Wolfgang Amadeus Mozart's opera *The Magic Flute*, during which she was struck by how fervently the male characters were wooing the women. Comparing the characters' behavior with present-day standards of courtship made it clear that such fervor varied from one era to another: the sociological question was, why? What can it be that increases or decreases the vigor with which men court women? It seemed clear to Guttentag that men will invest more energy in courtship when and where women are prized, but what makes them more prized? Individually, of course, women might be prized for being accomplished, beautiful, or wealthy, but the question demands that we think of women collectively, as a group: where are women, in general, more prized and where less?

Guttentag came up with a surprisingly simple answer (which served as the stimulus for a more complex theory): all other things being equal, women are more prized where there are fewer of them in comparison to men. In fact, comparative rarity is a *resource* (see principle #3 above) that either gender can possess and that has a significant impact on the nature of gender relations. The scarcer gender will have more options in selecting a mate and more options to leave should that mate lose favor. Having relatively fewer options forces members of the opposite gender to compete for the opportunity to mate, and one manifestation of this is fervent wooing. Guttentag and Secord conceptualize the favored position of the scarcer gender in terms of **dyadic power**, which is the ability to get one's way in a two-person (dyadic) relationship. While many factors contribute to dyadic power, it is significantly increased by willingness to reject potential relationships or to leave a relationship should it prove unsatisfactory, and this willingness is in turn significantly increased by the ease with which new relationships, perhaps more satisfying ones, can be entered into, which, finally, is significantly increased by the relative scarcity of one's gender since this means more members of the opposite gender will be available. To turn this situation around, to lack dyadic power is to be dependent upon one's partner in a relationship and unable to contemplate leaving it easily. A woman lacking dyadic power, for instance,

> may have to put up with various behaviors on [a man's] part that she finds distressing or obnoxious. She may have to provide outcomes for him that are psychologically costly for her, while he can easily balk at providing outcomes for her if they are costly to him. . . . Thus, he has the power to control her behavior so as to maximize his own outcomes without at the same time having to make sacrifices that would keep her outcomes at a high level. (1983:162)

But this is only half the story. If the gender in oversupply (and, thus, lacking dyadic power) controls the political, legal, and cultural institutions of the society, it can use these institutions to blunt the dyadic power of the scarce gender. For instance, it could severely penalize those who try to leave relationships by forbidding divorce or stigmatizing individuals who resort to it, thus closing off or minimizing the options afforded by dyadic power. This ability to set the rules of the game through political and cultural control Guttentag and Secord refer to as **structural power**. Across history, men have always had more structural power than women (although how much more has varied), and they have used it to their advantage whether women held dyadic power (as they commonly do) or not. Where women are scarce, men use structural power to minimize the effects of women's dyadic power, generally producing a regime of gender relations that Guttentag and Secord characterize as "traditional." In such a traditional regime,

> For example, [men] would tend to devalue promiscuity for women so as to reduce the perceived alternatives for their female partners. Essentially, they

would favor monogamy. In some societies they might prize virginity in women up to the time of marriage. These moves are all designed to place constraints on women, constraints which raise the psychological costs of alternative relationships in order to prevent women from leaving existing relationships, and also to limit their power over men. (1983:24)

In extreme circumstances, men may create institutions like *purdah* that require adult women to hide their faces from, and sometimes to avoid the physical presence of, men outside their households. Such practices severely limit the ability of women to exploit their dyadic power by initiating contacts with available men.

By contrast, where men have dyadic power in addition to structural power, they will use these joint advantages to exploit women, who

would be more likely to be valued as mere sex objects. . . . The divorce rate would be high, but the remarriage rate would be high for men only. The number of single-parent families headed by women would increase markedly. . . . Women would not expect to have the same man remain with them throughout their childbearing years. Brief liaisons would be usual. Adultery would be commonplace. At the same time, men would have opportunities to move successively from woman to woman or to maintain multiple relationships with different women. Because of the shortage of men, these opportunities would be largely denied women. (1983:20)

Where men hold both dyadic and structural power, courtship is neither prolonged nor energetic since competition encourages women to bid down the price of access to them. Sexual norms become permissive and allow for mild promiscuity for both sexes outside of marriage, while virginity at marriage for women comes to be thought of as quaint. Serial monogamy becomes customary for men, who "trade in" wives for newer (and younger) ones, while divorced or abandoned women are left to raise children alone.

Guttentag and Secord thus theorize that the character of gender relations, whether "traditional" or "sexually permissive," is determined primarily by the interaction of two variables: dyadic and structural power as they fall into the hands of one or the other gender. Their theory is gender neutral[8] since it predicts that if women acquire structural power over men, they will behave just as men have in the past, creating "traditional," but upside-down, societies when men have dyadic power, and "sexually permissive" ones (where women exploit men), when women have both dyadic and structural power.[9] Guttentag and Secord use their theory to explain regimes of gender relations that existed in ancient Greece, in medieval Europe, and in frontier North America, as well as to address differences in gender relations between contemporary white and black populations in the United States.

While a full explanation of gender relations would require a more complex theory than Guttentag and Secord provide,[10] their work explains some of the variation that we see in how men treat women and vice versa. Further, it is rich in just the sort of implications that make it easy to test. Finally, as an illustration of the conflict paradigm, the theory has some interesting aspects. First of all, the groups formed by men, on the one hand, and women, on the other, have only the loosest of social structures, and in this regard, they are very different from tightly integrated groups, such as families. This structural looseness limits the degree to which men and women can organize for conflict with one another. Further, since individual men and women are bound together in the family as a procreative unit, they have significant common interests (for instance, in passing on whatever advantages they can to their children) that limit the overall degree of conflict that can develop between them as representatives of their groups. The structural weakness of genders as groups combines with the common interests of individual dyads to mute the degree of conflict we might expect to result from the often severe disadvantages that men have in the past imposed upon women.

The conflict paradigm suggests that changes in the distribution of resources that favor subordinate groups encourage political conflict aimed at redistributing advantages. We referred earlier in this chapter to the increased access women have had in this century to paid employment, a factor that has significantly increased their structural power in comparison with men. The result has been predictable in terms that flow from the paradigm: women have organized politically to strike down the legal disabilities (e.g., exclusion from voting) that men had previously imposed on them, while at the same time they have exploited ideologies they developed to salvage self-esteem (e.g., that women, though socially inferior to men, are their moral superiors) to occasionally advance such "gynocratic" claims as that the world would be better off if ruled exclusively by women.

We pointed out previously how ineffective feminist movements had been in the past, when unsupported by increasing structural power in the hands of women. This is just what Marx's historical materialism would have predicted, since Guttentag and Secord's variable of structural power is very similar to Marx's relations of production: as women acquire power in reference to the relations of production, they gain structural power. The same point flows from the second paradigm we want to look at here, the paradigm of cultural materialism.

The Paradigm of Cultural Materialism

Marx's historical materialism, supplemented by Darwin's theory of natural selection, gave birth to a second paradigm that continues to be influential in social scientific work today: cultural materialism. While we owe the promotion of this paradigm primarily to anthropologist Marvin Harris (1964, 1974, 1977, 1979, 1999), it has been exemplified in theories across the social sciences. Indeed, the explanation of cultures of honor offered by social psychologists Richard Nisbett and Dov Cohen in our first chapter was cultural materialist in inspiration.

In Harris's exposition (1999:141–52), cultural materialism begins by dividing societies into analytical sectors, just as Marx did, but collapses relations of production and the legal and political superstructure into one sector so that only three remain: infrastructure, structure, and superstructure. **Infrastructure** designates "modes of production and reproduction as constituted by a conjunction of demographic, economic, technological, and environmental variables" (1999:141). The **structure** joins together relations of production and the institutions that reinforce them in one analytical sector. Finally, the **superstructure** is the sector composed of the "symbols and ideas" that people use to make sense of the world and orient themselves to it.

Having made these analytical distinctions, cultural materialism asserts the "primacy of infrastructure," which

> holds that innovations that arise in the infrastructural sector are likely to be preserved if they enhance the efficiency of the productive and reproductive processes that sustain health and well-being and that satisfy basic human biopsychological needs and drives.
>   Innovations that are adaptive (i.e., that increase the efficiency of production and reproduction), are likely to be selected for, even if there is a marked incompatibility (contradiction) between them and preexisting aspects of the structural and symbolic-ideational [superstructural] sectors. . . . In contrast, innovations of a structural or symbolic-ideational nature are likely to be selected against if there is any deep incompatibility between them and the infrastructure—that is to say if they reduce the efficiency of the productive and reproductive processes that sustain health and well-being and that satisfy basic human biopsychological needs and drives. (1999:142–43)

Cultural materialism belongs to an even broader paradigm, called **functionalism**, which I will analyze in detail in chapter 7. Cultural materialism is functionalist because it suggests that beneficial innovations within the infrastructure (judged so because of their ability to enhance health and well-being) are apt to be preserved through selection of the groups or societies introducing them. The same is true for structural and superstructural innovations. Further, innovations to the infrastructure exert a strong influence on the structural and superstructural sectors, which are comparatively powerless to resist beneficial infrastructural innovations. In terms of a practical example, societies that develop or adopt modern medical technologies receive certain benefits thereby and are apt to thrive in comparison with societies that do not. Further, the organizations and ideologies within the adopting societies that oppose modern medicine are apt to decline and be displaced by those that accept it. Thus, folk remedies and exotic therapies, such as acupuncture, have proven relatively powerless in the face of "scientific" medicine.

Functional theories require careful attention to the social unit to which the benefits of innovations flow and upon which selection thus operates. Let us return to the example of cultures of honor from our first chapter to illustrate this point. Nisbett and Cohen suggest that since "herdsmen constantly face the possibility of loss of their entire wealth—through loss of their herds [to thievery] . . . a stance of aggressiveness and willingness to kill or commit mayhem is useful in announcing their determination to protect their animals at all costs" (1996:5). Here, the benefit of aggressiveness is felt by the basic herding unit, presumably the family, rather than by the wider society to which these families belong. Consider how a culture of honor might originally take hold: we can suppose that when herding was originally adopted as a society's basic mode of production, families varied considerably in the degree of aggressiveness they showed, perhaps on the basis of individual personality variations across the members of different families. Aggressiveness then spread (was selected for) among families because it contributed to the health and well-being of those who adopted it as a strategy for dealing with individuals who were not family members (and might be potential thieves). In other words, families with aggressive members did better than families without them. Even though aggressiveness is risky to the individual practicing it, families that benefitted from its protective aura were at an advantage in comparison with families that didn't.[11] Thus, the behavioral trait of aggressiveness was apt to spread because of its economic benefits to individual families, and, once spread, it could be gradually worked up into a cultural ideal (in the superstructure) through the ideology of personal and family honor. Consequently, aggressiveness might become common in a society without being beneficial to the society as a whole (or to individuals) since the unit being selected for was the family and not the society or individual.

In this example, we can again see how a specific theory flows from a paradigm. Nisbett and Cohen, in looking to explain the origins of cultures of honor, assume the primacy of infrastructure and the operation of selection by consequences, which is to say, the social preference for innovations that have positive consequences for the health and well-being of the social unit in question. The paradigm sets up an explanatory skeleton that we fill in with appropriate variables, such as aggressiveness and the benefit of this in terms of comparative resistance to thievery. The resulting explanation shows how a society that originally showed great variation in aggressiveness would necessarily evolve in the direction of a culture of honor in which aggressiveness was commonplace and deeply linked to social prestige. Further, were the infrastructure different, this evolution would not occur. This is the basic insight of cultural materialism, which we can see expressed in a further and final example.

Explaining Sacred Cows

Cultural materialism would not be a very helpful paradigm if we routinely found that social groups or entire societies adopted practices that clearly did not enhance their members' health and well-being.[12] The treatment of cows by the Hindu population of India is sometimes offered as an example of such a counterproductive practice. As part of the doctrine of *ahimsa*, which views all life as sacred, Hindus view cows as holy beasts, allowing them to roam unhindered, often garlanded with flowers, protected from slaughter and consumption, even in times of famine. Consequently, the entire "cow complex" in India has often been deemed economically irrational, with cows and their treatment being seen as a burden on this largely agrarian society, rather than as a contribution to human "health and well-being."

Intrigued by the phenomenon of sacred cows and the threat it posed to the paradigm of cultural materialism, Harris investigated it (1968, 1974:6–27). He concentrated first on calculating the often unremarked economic benefits that India derived from its large cattle population. For instance, dried cow manure is not only employed as fertilizer but is widely used as cooking fuel in circumstances where alternatives would be hard to come by. Harris showed how profoundly integrated into the Indian agrarian economy its cattle herds are, and his estimates suggest that having many cows around probably does contribute to, rather than detract from, human health and well-being. But this does little to explain why cows are viewed as sacred and why their slaughter is forbidden, even in times of human famine. Clearly, this would seem to be a case where people "shoot themselves in their feet" in order to indulge their religious sentiments. If beliefs and practices are selected for their consequences, isn't the sacredness of cows exactly the sort of belief we would expect to be selected against?

Yet, a singularly important function of cattle is to produce the oxen that Indian farmers use as draft animals for plowing. If, during a famine, a farmer slaughters his oxen and cows for the present benefit of their meat, he faces certain starvation the next year when he is unable to plow and plant his fields. Thus, as Harris writes,

The taboo on slaughter and beef eating may be . . . a product of natural selection. . . . During droughts and famines, farmers are severely tempted to kill or sell their livestock. Those who succumb to this temptation seal their doom, even if they survive the drought, for when the rains come, they will be unable to plow their fields. I want to be even more emphatic: Massive slaughter of cattle under the duress of famine constitutes a . . . threat to aggregate welfare. . . . It seems probable that the sense of unutterable profanity elicited by cow slaughter has its roots in the excruciating contradiction between immediate needs and long-run conditions of survival. Cow love with its sacred symbols and holy doctrines protects the farmer against calculations that are "rational" only in the short term. [Critics of the sacred cow phenomenon] don't realize that the farmer would rather eat his cow than starve, but that he will starve if he does eat it. (1974:15–16)

I have singled out here only one element in Harris's complex discussion of why it is beneficial to Indians to have sacred cows, but this element alone offers us a plausible explanation of the phenomenon: the comparative sacredness of cows (our dependent variable) is a function of how crucial oxen are to agricultural production in an agrarian economy subject to periodic drought and famine.

Harris does not discuss how cattle became sacred, but his reference to natural selection implies something like the following. In the early history of the development of India's agrarian infrastructure (perhaps several thousand years ago), cows were not held sacred. Then, for unexplained reasons, some religious visionary proposed the doctrine of *ahimsa* (the sacredness of all life) and chose cows as its foremost symbol. The belief spread among a small, local group of Indians influenced by this religious visionary and his or her charisma (see chapter 5). Then, a famine struck. This group recovered from the famine because it did not slaughter its cows, while neighboring groups did. This group then spread into the nearby lands previously occupied by "unbelievers," who slaughtered their cows and subsequently starved. Further, the group's success caused some of its new neighbors to become converts to the doctrine of *ahimsa*. Over the centuries, as famine after famine occurred in different regions of the Indian subcontinent, further growth in the group of believers and further cultural copying of their practices carried *ahimsa* far and wide, until the whole subcontinent subscribed to the sacredness of cows.

A moment's reflection will show that this process is identical to the one by which aggressiveness, and the culture of honor growing out of it, would have spread among cattle herders. Each case starts with variation in beliefs, attitudes, and behaviors: among cattle herders, a few people are aggressive while most are not, and among early Indian farming groups, one adopts *ahimsa* while the others do not. The two populations are then repeatedly stressed, the cattle herders by persistent thievery, and the farmers by famine. After each incident of stress, the beneficial trait (aggressiveness or *ahimsa*) spreads among the population, either by the physical reproduction of those who possess it or by cultural copying. Gradually, the successful trait comes to dominate the social system so that the original variety in beliefs and behaviors declines, having been selected out, and uniformity prevails. This is a consequence of the successful trait being functional for the group in question, and the overall explanation is a classic evolutionary one.

This explanation is materialist because it sees innovations (whatever the level at which they occur, be it infrastructure, structure, or superstructure) as being selected for or against primarily in terms of their ability to benefit the performance of the infrastructure and, hence, to improve health and well-being or to satisfy other fundamental needs. In this regard, we can see an affinity between conflict theory and cultural materialism since both make more or less the same assumptions about basic human motives.[13]

The explanations of sacred cows, of cultures of honor, and of differing gender regimes that I have reviewed in this chapter should make it clear how we draw upon paradigms for inspiration or guidance in constructing theories. Essentially, paradigms give us advice about where to look for variables that will solve the problem we set up by developing our initial empirical generalization and then looking for a matching empirical generalization to explain it.

Conclusion

I devoted the majority of chapter 2 to exploring the complex theory Marx developed to explain the origins and anticipated demise of capitalism as a mode of production. While the theory was clearly wrong in specifics, the paradigm from which it arose has given birth to three further paradigms that remain vital today: analytical Marxism (closest to Marx in inspiration), conflict theory, and cultural materialism, the latter two of which we've just discussed. Today, most sociologists view Marx as an important visionary. His ambition was to explain the workings of an entire social order, to see capitalism as a system with basic properties and processes, the essential relations among which could be described as a mechanism. Once this mechanism was fully analyzed, its present behavior could be explained and its future predicted.

In one sense, this desire to explain the workings of an entire social order continues to be the ambition of sociology. In the century since Marx's death, however, we have come to see social systems as considerably more complex than Marx's already complex theory envisioned. Thus, it is no longer clear to many of us that existing, large-scale social units, such as **nation-states** like the United States, can be understood as mechanisms, at least in practice if not in principle. At best, certain rules of thumb can be provided for aspects of such units or for their behavior,[14] rules that it is important to have but that fall a bit short of the encompassing vision Marx sought. In part, the restricted ambitions of contemporary sociology reflect an increased appreciation for the complexities of life, but they also reflect the impact of the next major theorist we will discuss, Max Weber. As indicated in chapter 1, Weber was so impressed with the influence of chance and contingency on human history that he believed the explanatory ambitions we find in Marx to be misguided. After all, if history is significantly influenced by chance events, the course it takes might be explained through a causal narrative, but not through the sort of theory Marx developed. Thus, the vision of Marx has had to be deferred in practice and, if Weber is right, might be mistaken in principle.

Notes

1. Conversely, when the Chrysler Corporation went bankrupt some time ago, it effectively lobbied the government to step in and bail it out at the taxpayers' risk. This reflected Chrysler's power.

2. Existing social consciousness can, of course, be challenged. Such challenges are one indication that power is becoming less concentrated.

3. By contrast, the early anarchist-socialist Pierre Joseph Proudhon (1809–1865), whose work influenced Marx, claimed that "property is theft"! Native Americans whose communally held lands were appropriated as private property by European settlers would probably agree with him. So might people who would like to enjoy the nation's beaches but find that so many of them have been bought up by private individuals. As I write, politicians are battling over whether to rescind laws that mandate taxing inheritances, and ideologists stand behind them, providing the arguments for and against this practice. The contemporary examples show that the issue of limits to ownership is still with us and that ideologists often strive as much to challenge the unself-consciously held beliefs in our social consciousness as to support them.

4. For a more extensive discussion of this example and the "materialist" point made through it, see Harris 1999:26–28.

5. It is relatively easy to do this in small groups that engage in "utopian" experiments but much harder to do so on the scale of whole societies.

6. Consider a simple example of what Marx had in mind: industrial capitalism drew scores of workers together in factories, facilitating communication among them and, thus, increasing the power of the working class to organize politically. Indeed, if industrial workers had grievances in common—gnawing poverty and long hours, for instance—their opportunity to "combine" and seek redress was enhanced by their

simple physical proximity. In a real sense, manufacturing as a mode of production was a precondition for **class consciousness** (awareness of common interests) on the part of workers and their organizing as a political force. (Recognizing this, British employers soon sought to forbid unions, as, for instance, by the Combination Acts of 1799 and 1800, repealed in 1824.) Yet, simple physical proximity remained a resource for workers that substantially altered their power vis-à-vis employers. Furthermore, as manufacturing became increasingly "capitalized," that is, as more owner money was sunk into machines and buildings, the real cost of strikes rose in proportion. Employers with little fixed capital (money invested in machines, buildings, and so on) could rely on savings to ride out strikes, but as the proportion of their capital that was "sunk" increased, the effect of "downtime" caused by strikes was more serious. It was more serious still if the sunk capital was borrowed since banks needed to be paid even when no money was coming in for the capitalist. Thus, ironically, investment in capital goods, although necessary to compete in the market, had the unforeseen consequence of shifting strategic political advantage at least somewhat in the direction of labor. This is the sort of irony to the development of a mode of production that Marx had in mind.

7. The actual intellectual historical framework out of which Guttentag and Secord's theory grew is in the exchange paradigm of George Homans, Peter Blau, and Gary Becker (see Guttentag and Secord 1983:157), a paradigm whose origins were in functionalism but which has increasingly incorporated conflict principles (see Turner 2003:299). The case we will consider is so infused with conflict as to make it an appropriate exemplar of the conflict paradigm.

8. A gender-neutral theory assumes that men and women are fundamentally alike and, thus, behave in the same ways when confronted with the same social circumstances. For example, as I have stated it above, the conflict paradigm is gender neutral. This assumption might be criticized in the case of gender relations by proponents of biosocial theories (e.g., Buss 1994), which argue that men and women have evolved somewhat different reproductive strategies as a result of the demands placed upon women by gestation and childbirth. Such biosocial theories would predict moderate differences in the way women (as opposed to men) would exploit possessing both dyadic and structural power.

9. In an upside-down traditional society, women would woo men and then restrict them to homemaking and child-rearing activities after marriage. In a sexually permissive society where women had structural power, they would exploit men in casual relationships or divorce husbands as they grayed in order to "trade up" to younger and more vigorous husbands.

10. For a discussion of the array of important variables involved, see Collins et al. (1993). For more extensive treatments, see Blumberg (1978) and Chafetz (1984).

11. The institution of the feud, wherein any (usually adult male) member of a family is "fair game" for members of another family claiming injury at the hands of a member of the first family, would distribute the individual risk in being aggressive more broadly.

12. As an example, consider the practice of therapeutic bleeding, which claimed George Washington among its many victims before it was retired in favor of more demonstrably beneficial treatments.

13. For a discussion of the ability of the cultural materialist paradigm to include elements of the conflict paradigm, see Harris (1999:143).

14. For instance, Randall Collins (1986) has pointed to certain properties of social units like empires that allowed him to predict (but not to time exactly) the collapse of the U.S.S.R. Similarly, Tilly (1992) is able to explain and predict certain basic properties of political systems. Both theorists, however, concentrate on very limited aspects of the social units they consider.

4

Max Weber and Capitalism

FOR MANY SOCIOLOGISTS, Max Weber (pronounced VEY-ber) (1864–1920) is the most interesting of the classical theorists. Born in Germany roughly half a century after Karl Marx, he was able to profit from the great flowering of comparative historical scholarship produced by intervening generations of scholars. Thus, while Marx was to some degree groping in the dark in trying to understand processes of social change across history, Weber was not. Further, Weber was a voracious reader with a great memory, qualities that allowed him to survey the development of entire civilizations, showing as much familiarity with their religions as with their economic foundations. At the same time, he was involved in empirical research on contemporary social problems in Germany and active in politics. Thus, he was by no means an ivory tower intellectual. A nervous breakdown, which occurred under very interesting circumstances and left him unable to work for several years, makes him psychologically intriguing as well. Indeed, it would be easy to spend a lifetime studying him and his work. Although the latter often seems dry (as an undergraduate, I always fell asleep trying to read him), one can only marvel at the depth and breadth of his scholarship and be captivated by the complexity of his views of society.

Weber's Program: Theoretical Modesty and Use of Analytic Typologies

Marx's theory of capitalism, as you've seen, is dauntingly complex, and, yet, one of our criticisms of it was that it may not have been complex enough. This is apt to be discouraging since it suggests that effective sociological theories must sometimes be conceptual mazes in which all but geniuses will become lost. Another conclusion we can draw, however, is that Marx was wrong to theorize about capitalism in the first place, and when we understand the point of view from which this criticism arises, we'll understand why Weber's theorizing takes a form quite different from Marx's.

Marx believed that capitalism's dynamics (its behavior as a system) could be understood in terms of a relatively small set of variables and properties, such as competition, technological innovation to reduce labor costs, falling rates of profit, concentration of industries, rising rates of unemployment, and the mobilizing effect of economic downturns. These properties and variables were parts of the capitalist mechanism, and once we understood its workings, we would be able to predict its future behavior. As a result of its very nature, Marx argued, capitalism would have to collapse and be replaced by a less alienating and exploitative mode of production, one he termed *communism*. Marx got some elements of the mechanism wrong, as we noted, but he also underestimated just how complex an institution a modern economy is; hence, our criticism that his theory was not complex enough. Yet, the problem may not be one we can fix by correcting his mistakes and adding a few more variables to make the theory more complex: today's economists, after all, with the advantage of much better data and much more sophisticated analytical techniques (and having had more than a century since Marx's death to put them to work) are not much better at predicting the behavior of capitalism than Marx was.

This should alert us to an important possibility: that the behavior of institutions like economies (or modes of production) may not be theorizable, at least, not according to the narrow definition of theory developed in our first chapter. A full discussion of this topic would take us far afield (see Jervis 1997; Hermann 1998), but at its core is a recognition that certain forms of complexity in systems can make predicting their behavior very difficult or impossible. We still have a hard time predicting the weather—say, the path of a hurricane several days into the future—although we know vastly more about the atmosphere as a system than we did in the past and have staggering amounts of data concerning it. Further, when we design enormously complex systems ourselves, such as nuclear power plants, we find it nearly impossible to foresee all the things that can go wrong with them, even when we apply our best efforts and know that errors on our part can literally be disastrous (Perrow 1984). Weber was aware of this particular aspect of complexity, and it drove him to the same conclusion he derived from the influence of chance and contingency in human affairs: certain phenomena may simply not be theorizable.[1] In practice, this made Weber believe that Marx's ambition to theorize about social change across history was misguided. Social change was not produced by such relatively simple mechanisms as Marx envisaged. Indeed, some important events causing social changes could not be explained at all but, instead, could only be descriptively narrated. Others might be explained by causal narratives, and still others by theories. In fact, understanding large-scale developments was likely to involve all three sorts of accounts, which gave theories proper a more modest role than Marx had expected for them.

It is important to emphasize that Weber did not believe causal theories were impossible in the social sciences; he merely concluded that they were ill suited to account for the large-scale social changes that were of greatest interest to nineteenth-century scholars and to which descriptive and causal narratives, he felt, were better geared. Weber's best-known work, *The Protestant Ethic and the Spirit of Capitalism* (1958a), illustrates this by combining a descriptive narrative with two causal theories to replace Marx's effort at a pure theory of capitalism.[2] The place of the descriptive narrative in Weber's account is so important that we can view him as suggesting that much social change is better understood historically than sociologically, which is not to say that we can't explain some of it but that we certainly can't explain all of it with theories.[3] For this reason, Weber could be said to have modest theoretical ambitions for sociology. But he compensates for this by having very broad analytical aims. Analysis, as I use the term here, refers to the process of decomposing the world into its component parts so that we can see what it consists of. Analysis explains the nature of things, and knowing their nature is just as crucial to theorizing as having causal accounts of their behavior. Analytical theories require an approach somewhat different from the one we developed in the first chapter (and illustrated in our discussion of Marx), however, and, thus, a treatment of Weber will allow us to expand our understanding of theorizing.

In this chapter, we first explore Weber's treatment of the origins of modern capitalism, his Protestant ethic thesis. My discussion emphasizes the ways in which this thesis is distinct from Marx's theory, as well as what Weber hoped to teach us about the scope of causal theorizing in sociology thereby. Chapter 5 will explore in some detail several of the theoretical analyses that Weber performed, using them to explore this distinctive approach to theorizing. I mentioned in the first chapter that theorizing involves more than causal models of the sort we have up to now been discussing, and we can use Weber's analyses to show this.

Weber's Protestant Ethic Account of Capitalism

As I stressed in the first chapter and illustrated through Friedrich Engels's observations of the difficult conditions of workers in Manchester, the impulse to theorize often arises in direct confrontation with puzzling conditions or incidents in the world around us. Weber's thesis didn't begin in direct observations, however, because a puzzle—the origins of capitalism—had already been developed for him by Marx. (Thus, sociologists just as often find their inspiration to theorize in the existing literature.) Weber found Marx's solution to the puzzle unsatisfactory in a way that pointed to two problems with the paradigm of historical materialism from which Marx's theory flowed: it was too materialist and too determinist. By too materialist, Weber meant that Marx's paradigm nearly precluded the possibility that important social changes resulted from changes in people's ideas (from social consciousness, or what cultural materialists call *superstructure*) rather than from changes in their material circumstances. By too determinist, Weber meant that Marx saw society as an easily predictable mechanism, whose workings had determinate (that is, precisely specifiable and certain) outcomes. In objecting to these two features of Marx's paradigm, however, Weber did not go to the other extreme, for instance, arguing that social changes are *always* caused by changes in ideas or that human social behavior has *never* had predictable, determinate outcomes: instead, he merely insisted that our paradigms should be more flexible, allowing ideas an important place when warranted and admitting how unpredictable complex systems often are. How better to make these points than to revisit Marx's central question of the origins of capitalism and argue that it needed to be addressed using a more flexible approach? Thus, Weber made his point by creating a rival account of the origins of capitalism and hoping it would prove superior to Marx's theory. How did he develop his account? He went directly to the stage of empirical generalization and started to work from there.

Catholic-Protestant Economic Differences: An Empirical Generalization

Weber begins *The Protestant Ethic and the Spirit of Capitalism* by noting an interesting empirical generalization, one already noted by others:

> A glance at the occupational statistics of any country of mixed religious composition brings to light with remarkable frequency a situation which has several times provoked discussion in the Catholic press . . . namely, the fact that business leaders and owners of capital, as well as the higher grades of skilled labour, and even more the higher technically and commercially trained personnel of modern enterprises, are overwhelmingly Protestant. (1958a:35)

In a series of footnotes to this passage and the paragraph it introduces, Weber provides some statistical data to support this generalization. In the terminology of our first chapter, he links the *dependent variable* of comparative economic success to the *clue variable* of Protestantism versus Catholicism. This provides us with a puzzle very similar to that of why the South should have high argument-related homicide rates. The question is, why should Protestants "do better" under capitalism than Catholics?[4] As we've seen, clue variables don't solve our puzzles; instead, they make them broader, but they often do so in a way that points us in fruitful explanatory directions. If there was something about Protestantism that encouraged capitalistic achievement, and if the Protestant Reformation preceded the origins of modern capitalism, then Protestantism could be responsible for capitalism's development. Any explanation of capitalism would thus have to look to the origins of Protestantism. Returning to our image of a whodunit, Weber wondered whether his empirical generalization perhaps identified Protestantism (or something associated with it) as the "perpetrator" of capitalism, a perpetrator that Marx had largely ignored. Further, if the origins of the Protestant Reformation were themselves inexplicable by the sort of theory Marx's historical materialism promoted, then this would make the case for a more flexible approach. So, the question became whether Weber could turn this hunch about the role of Protestantism into a convincing argument, and this meant searching for a *mechanism* that would explain why Protestantism produced capitalism.[5]

Conceptualizing Attitudinal Variation as the Cause of Variable Economic Success: Economic Traditionalism versus the "Spirit of Capitalism"

Weber's first step was to conceptualize the relevant difference between Protestants and Catholics that might be immediately responsible for their variable economic success under capitalism. In terms of the process of theorizing, his concern here was similar to Marx's when he wanted to conceptualize the condition of the Manchester workers. Marx sought concepts that would capture the relevant differences between the working conditions of the Manchester proletariat, on the one hand, and primitive hunters and gatherers, on the other, and he settled on alienation and exploitation. Alienation and exploitation are variables—something we can experience more or less of. Similarly, Weber needed to conceptualize the underlying factor that might account for the variable economic success of Protestants and Catholics and, thus, was looking for another variable. He found it in the realm of attitudes toward work. Protestants had more of a **spirit of capitalism**, he believed, than did Catholics. As with Marx's notion of alienation, "spirit of capitalism" designates a complex concept that's not easy to describe.

By the somewhat mystical-sounding phrase "spirit of capitalism," Weber meant that people vary in their orientation to work (and to economic life in general) in terms of how traditional versus how modern they are. Those who are most traditional have the least spirit of capitalism, while those who are more modern have more. Thus, the spirit of capitalism identifies one end of a spectrum of attitudes toward economic life, the other end of which is a traditional orientation. To understand the spirit of capitalism, it would be best to look first at **traditionalism**. Traditional attitudes were somewhat different for workers and craftsmen on the one hand and for merchants on the other. We will take these up in turn.

The traditionalism of workers is only roughly characterized in *The Protestant Ethic and the Spirit of Capitalism*. Weber noted three specific features:

- Traditional workers do not respond appropriately to productivity incentives. Their ambition is to earn enough money to get by on and no more. If wages are raised, they work less and enjoy the resulting leisure, instead of working longer to get ahead by accumulating savings (1958a:59).

- Traditional workers are resistant to innovation in labor practices, preferring old ways to newer, more productive, ones (1958a:62).
- Traditional workers discourage "rate busters," people willing to work harder to achieve higher pay, through informal social control (1958a:63).

Weber could be somewhat casual in his characterization of traditionalism because he knew readers would draw on their own impressions of cultural attitudes toward work prior to the flowering of capitalism. Europe in the period between, say, the twelfth and sixteenth centuries had been dominated politically and culturally by a combination of the nobility and the Roman Catholic clergy. Neither group, it was assumed, encouraged devotion to work.[6] Noble persons considered working for money to be socially debasing: they were noble in part because they had other people to work *for* them and, thus, did not consider money making, much less paid employment, a respectable endeavor. Nobles were superior people, a warrior and landowning caste; they did not labor but instead were owed the work of their inferiors as a basic right. The Church, for its part, considered work primarily a means of survival that enabled people to turn their attention to the important thing—their future status in the world beyond. These orientations to work among the social and spiritual elites meant that common people had little reason to see deep personal investment in their occupations as a means to fulfillment, prestige, and social (or godly) approval. To use an old phrase, they worked to live rather than living to work, and this attitude underlay the concrete qualities Weber attributed to the traditional worker that I've noted above.[7]

Merchants were characterized by a different but related set of traditional attitudes. Weber admitted that forms of capitalism existed prior to the Protestant Reformation, but he saw them as characterized by attitudes hostile to those of modern capitalism. On the one hand, if merchants were able to make a relatively comfortable living, they often sought to routinize their businesses, dealing always with the same suppliers and customers in the same way (1958a:66). The comfort of habit made them almost as resistant to innovation as the traditional worker. The remainder of merchants were overcome by what Weber called the "uncontrolled impulse to gain" (1958a:57) or "impulsive avarice" (1958a:172), hatching schemes to get rich quick or embarking on other high-risk–high-gain endeavors. Impulsive avarice was also expressed in the use of bribery or political favoritism to obtain monopolies from governments for trading in particular goods. Merchants seeking such monopolies were often more skilled in political manipulation than in business and, when successful, had little incentive to manage their monopolies skillfully. Weber also noted that many merchants adopted a "double ethic," according to which fellow countrymen were treated fairly, while foreigners were fair game to be cheated or otherwise ripped off.

We can see both the double ethic and an attitude of impulsive avarice nicely expressed in the business of piracy. Pirates (often with the encouragement of their governments) accepted very high risks in pursuit of equally high gains, preying upon foreign outsiders as a route to riches. They express perfectly what Weber meant by impulsive avarice, as did the conquistadors who sought gold in the Americas and thought little of stealing it from native outsiders. Both well represent what Weber styled "adventurer capitalism." This form of capitalism had an ancient pedigree and had never exerted much impetus to fundamental change in the societies it characterized.

When merchants acquired wealth, other traditional attitudes governed their use of it. They employed their profits to copy the lifestyles of princes, either living opulently in the cities or buying country estates to which they retired to pursue noble pastimes like hunting for sport (1958a:177). Thus, what the American sociologist Thorstein Veblen (1912) called **conspicuous consumption**, using one's wealth to impress others through wasteful leisure and purchase for display, was the norm among those who won in the high-risk game of commerce.

It might help to review the above in the format of our first chapter. Weber wondered not about an incident but about an empirical generalization: why do Protestants seem to succeed economically more than Catholics? Thus, he started with his dependent and clue variables already conceptualized for him. The theoretical question was why they should be associated. What was it about the two religions that produced this difference? Here, Weber conceptualized a possibility: perhaps Protestants developed specific economic attitudes that made them less traditional and, therefore, more apt to succeed. Figure 4.1 presents this relation among variables in the format of the first chapter. The question now became, was it something about Protestantism that caused members of that faith to adopt a new work orientation, or did it come from somewhere else? To pursue this, Weber first conceptualized what he called the "spirit of capitalism."

The Spirit of Capitalism

The attitudes of traditional workers and merchants, as well as of merchant adventurers, represent the traditional pole of variable attitudes toward work. Traditionalism did not threaten to transform societies in the way that modern capitalism did. This new form of capitalism was grounded in a quite different set of attitudes, so it had a different ethos, or spirit. This spirit is exemplified in economic endeavors that are

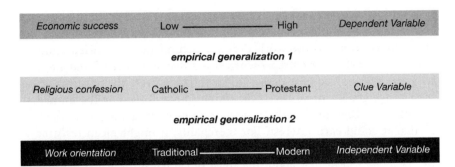

FIGURE 4.1
Weber's Basic Theory

rationalized on the basis of rigorous calculation, directed with foresight and caution toward the economic success which is sought in sharp contrast to the hand-to-mouth existence of the peasant, and to the privileged traditionalism of the guild craftsman and of the adventurers' capitalism, oriented to the exploitation of political opportunities and irrational speculation. (1958a:76)

No single passage in Weber's book is particularly good at explicating what it means to "rationalize on the basis of rigorous calculation," but we can best summarize and modernize his scattered comments by suggesting that it is like having a very well worked-out business plan whose goal is a regular increase in quarterly profits. By well worked out, I mean that the business plan analyzes a profit-increasing strategy into separate components and assesses each one in terms of its costs and benefits. By monitoring these components as we put our strategy into action, we hope to increase profits with as high a degree of certainty as possible. Risk, in other words, is something to be minimized by careful research, planning, and monitoring of progress. At the same time, predicting future profits requires good cost estimates, just as measuring present profits demands sound bookkeeping, both of which Weber felt reflected rationality based on rigorous monetary calculation. Finally, pursuing growth in profits demands a constant willingness to entertain and assess prospects for innovation. In a sense, the point to rationalizing on the basis of rigorous calculation is to be as methodical and risk minimizing in the pursuit of profit as openness to change and the desire to increase profits regularly will allow. Such an orientation constitutes the spirit of capitalism.

While this spirit seems most appropriate to business owners, Weber showed how figures like Benjamin Franklin applied it to workers as well. Every worker, Franklin argued, was able to save, and every penny saved could be put to work to increase one's future earnings. A worker alert to opportunity in this way would certainly respond to productivity incentives and welcome innovations to the work process. Behind this new orientation for workers, as well as for entrepreneurs, was a demand to check our impulses by subjecting our current desires to methodical oversight in terms of our long-range goals. For workers, this might mean foregoing the immediate pleasure of a beer after work in the interest of putting a penny in the bank so that it could earn interest. For merchants, it might mean resisting an impulse to "irrational speculation," say, the impulse to purchase stock on a tip. What was most new about the spirit of capitalism was that it subjected immediate desires to methodical evaluation in relation to long-range goals of growth and innovation. The rational character of the capitalist spirit demanded a devotion to disciplined economic endeavor that was missing in the various forms of traditionalism. This was the orientation that animated the distinctively modern form of capitalism, a form that was apt to have much more dynamic consequences for society.[8] (Here, we might reflect that whereas Marx saw greed as the motive for capitalist acquisition, Weber concluded that this motive needed to be carefully disciplined in order to get us beyond the stage of adventurer capitalism. Religion was the clue to this disciplining process.)

Explaining Variation in Capitalist Spirit: Background Information

Weber suggested it was the distinction between traditional and modern economic orientations that caused the difference in relative economic position between Catholics and Protestants in his own day. The question now became why members of the two religions should differ in their economic orientations. Could Protestantism somehow cause a modern orientation? If so, to explain the origins of modern capitalism would require us to move backward one causal step and explain the origins of Protestantism. But was this something that we could hope to do? In other words, was it something we could account for through either a causal narrative or a theory? Or was it, instead, a contingent event, which we could hope only to narrate descriptively?

To appreciate fully Weber's answers to these questions and the objections he saw them raising to Marx's historical materialism, we need a bit more background about the religious organization of European society prior to the Reformation as it appeared to Weber. Two features here are important: that a distinction was drawn between a class of religious specialists (the "clergy" of priests, monks, and nuns) and average believers (laypeople, or the "laity"), and that the orthodox doctrine of the Church was frequently challenged by ideas that were deemed heretical. Let us take these up in turn.

The Catholic Church, which had a monopoly on the provision of religious goods and services in European countries until the sixteenth century, had by the medieval period evolved into a "two-tier" system that opposed an exacting, strenuous religious life, usually monastically organized, with a less exacting lay existence in the world. The laity toiled to earn a living. They were expected to be good, to repent of their sins, and to go to church, partake of the so-called sacraments, and participate in religious festivals (which were quite common). The laity constituted one tier of the system.

Their religious needs, organized around the sacraments, were served by a priesthood of religious professionals. The priesthood formed part of the second tier, which was composed of people who gave their lives over to religion. This was seen as the superior option, and people who took it either became priests or separated themselves from the laity by joining monastic orders (or, for women, sisterhoods located in priories). While some monastic orders developed businesses by which their members earned a collective living (for instance, some Benedictines produced and sold a brandy, which today still goes by their name), many devoted themselves to lives of prayer and contemplation, supported economically by donations from the laity. Laity who died often bequeathed part of their estates to monastic orders, and some laity "tithed" (gave a tenth of their income) in part to support religious orders.

This two-tier system of religious specialists, on the one hand, supported by the laity, on the other, posed an important question to young men and women: in which tier did they belong? Although in practice the answer was often determined for them by their family circumstances, in principle, God was to indicate whether they were destined for the more strenuous life of priest, monk, or nun, or whether their place was with the laity. It was each person's obligation to "listen" spiritually for a "calling" from God in this regard. Those who were called upon to serve strenuously were said to have a "vocation," from the Latin *vocare* (to call).[9]

The second relevant feature of the existing religious organization of society was the presence of schism and heresy. Some religions, such as Christianity and Islam, develop an extensive list of doctrines (beliefs or propositions regarding religious matters), to which members are expected to adhere.[10] Such an orthodoxy, of course, can only arise through a process of disputing what members of a faith should believe, which means that disagreement is the original condition out of which an orthodoxy forms. But once doctrine is established, any person who wants to add to or to change it must seek the approval of the group. Approved new beliefs become part of a new orthodoxy, while disapproved beliefs may be judged heretical; that is, they may be banned as "improper" ideas. To persist in improper belief or practice is to be a heretic challenging the existing church (or a schismatic, who separates from it).

Heresy was a frequent companion to the Roman Catholic monopoly on religion, and the variety of doctrines that came under dispute was great. Doctrinal disputes led to careful consideration of the issues involved, often by gatherings of high Church officials, such as bishops, who then ruled either to adopt the new doctrine or declare the new idea a heresy. Once deemed heretics, proponents of the new doctrine had the option of recanting their beliefs or facing Church discipline, the worst sanction of which was capital punishment. Numerous heretics paid for their "persistence in error" with their lives.

For our purposes, it is important to realize that heresies and schisms arise out of reflection on ideas, as individuals try to make better sense out of the complex and often confusing amalgam of stories, parables, beliefs, and practices contained in a religious tradition. For instance, many religions face the problem of how to explain why a just, all-powerful, and loving God created an unjust world filled with evil (the problem of *theodicy*), and in early Christianity, this was occasionally solved by "dualist" or "Manichean" heresies that made evil completely independent of God. There are many further examples of such problems, each with its attendant orthodox and heretical solutions.

Note now that because heresies arise from reflection on religious ideas, they originate in the analytical sector of society that Marx termed the *social consciousness*. Indeed, rather than springing from changes in material circumstances, heresies seem to be a case where reflection on ideas—on religious "problems"—begets further ideas. Furthermore, heresies make their initial appeal to people *as ideas*, in terms of their ability to make sense of some of the difficulties inherent in religious belief. Consequently, in the case of heresies, social consciousness itself gives rise to changes in social consciousness. Thus, to the extent that any major social change is initiated either by heresy or by new doctrine, it issues from the top downward, in terms of figure 3.1, conflicting with Marx's paradigm of historical materialism by introducing an idealist explanation. As we will see momentarily, the way in which heretical ideas arise also affects the prospect that they can be explained by a causal model.

Protestantism and the Spirit of Capitalism: Calling, Predestination, and Worldly Asceticism

We are now prepared to explore the core of Weber's account of how attitudes toward work were transformed from traditional to modern, giving rise to

modern capitalism. The transformation, he argued, flowed from three innovative ideas, one of which we owe to Martin Luther and two, to John Calvin
and subsequent Calvinists.[11] Luther gave a new meaning to the idea of calling
or vocation, while Calvinism adopted the heterodox (not then accepted) doctrine of **predestination** and stressed the need to live an ascetic life (foregoing
pleasures or conspicuous consumption). These three ideas, Weber argued,
presented those who joined the movement to reform the Roman Catholic
Church with a set of mandates and problems to which they responded by
developing what he termed the **Protestant ethic**. This ethic in turn gave rise
to the spirit of capitalism, the new attitude toward economic life whose consequence was modern capitalism itself.

I will turn in a moment to explore each of the three innovative ideas and
the consequences Weber held they gave rise to, but we need to consider first
why he believed that their origin could not be explained sociologically, either
through a theory or a causal narrative. Weber was aware that we could explicate each new idea, in the process probing the possible motives that led
Luther or Calvin to entertain it, and then view these motives as the idea's
immediate cause. But we couldn't get back behind these motives to explain
their origin sociologically, in the way we did with the fictitious homicide I
explained though the culture of honor in the first chapter. (In that case, we
found that argument-related homicide varied regularly in relation to culture,
which in turn varied regularly in relation to the economic base of the society.) In other words, Weber had no theory of innovation in religious ideas
that would allow him to predict and explain the specific ideas Luther and
Calvin introduced. Nor could he place them in a causal narrative, viewing
them, say, as caused by the religious problems they purported to solve. After
all, orthodox ideas (as well as further heterodox ones) offered equally plausible solutions to the same problems. Consequently, just why these solutions
appealed to Luther and Calvin, when and where they did, was simply beyond
explanation, leaving us only the option of *descriptively narrating* their contingent occurrence. The sociological story thus begins with them: they cannot
themselves be explained causally.[12]

The above considerations underscore how important it is to distinguish
between phenomena that we can hope to explain sociologically and those we
cannot. They reinforce our ambition always to keep in mind the differences
among descriptive narratives, causal narratives, and causal theories, as well
as the phenomena to which we apply them. The distinctions are particularly
useful here because, as soon as Weber descriptively narrated the introduction
of Luther's and Calvin's innovative ideas, he proceeded to develop theories
to explain why they resulted in a new orientation to work and why this, in

turn, produced modern capitalism. Before we turn to these theories, however, we need to explore the three contingent ideas.

Luther's Idea of Calling

Weber argued that Luther significantly transformed the meaning of the religious idea of a **calling** or **vocation**. As we have seen, the Roman Catholic Church had evolved a two-tier system that distinguished clergy (religious specialists who committed themselves in principle to a demanding spiritual life) from laity (from whom somewhat less dedication was expected). Luther sought to erase this distinction, and his transformation of the idea of calling was key to doing so. *All* people, he suggested, were equally called to a demanding religious life. But rather than argue that everyone should become a monk, priest, or nun, Luther in effect proposed that these roles be abolished in favor of a universal priesthood that would express its exacting commitment to God not by withdrawing from the world (as did many monks and nuns) or becoming a provider of sacramental services to the community (as did a priest) but by commonplace work in the everyday world. Each activity in daily life, however humble it might be, could be transformed into a tribute to God if it were done in the right frame of mind. Weber argued that "one thing was unquestionably new" about Luther's concept of the calling, and that was its

> valuation of the fulfillment of duty in worldly affairs as the highest form which the moral activity of the individual could assume. This it was which inevitably gave every-day worldly activity a religious significance. . . . The only way of living acceptable to God was not to surpass worldly morality in monastic asceticism, but solely through fulfillment of the obligations imposed upon the individual by his position in the world. (1958a:80)

This meant that lay life was invested with a religious significance that the Roman Catholic Church had reserved for a clerical life. In a sense, then, Luther's idea of the calling meant the **monasticization** of the entire populace, as each individual was now called upon to express the same deep religious commitment through his or her *work* that the monks had been. Occupational dedication had become a spiritual value, so that one should now live to work rather than work to live.

As part of its monasticization of the populace, Protestantism de-emphasized the sacramental connection between Christians and their divinity (favored by Roman Catholicism) that necessitated a specialized priesthood. In place of the sacramental link, Protestant reformers recommended a more direct connection between Christians and their God, unmediated by a larger organization. In fact, it was partly to help establish this link that Luther set about translating the Bible from Latin (the priestly language) into German (the lay language of his country). At the same time, the monasticization of the populace made the monastic orders themselves redundant, so the reform movement could set about abolishing these institutions.

While all of this flowed out of Luther's modification of the idea of calling, Weber emphasized only the religious significance that it gave to people's worldly occupations.[13] For reasons we will shortly understand, he was able to pass over a practical difficulty that Luther's innovation entailed as I have described it above: the monasticization of the populace, in obligating all people to an exacting spiritual life, vastly expanded the total amount of religious dedication expected from people. But how was this great increase in dedication to be motivated? After all, people do not normally become energized just because we request them to: they need some incentive.[14] This incentive Weber found in a second innovative idea, predestination, for which Calvinism was responsible.

Calvin and Predestination

For Christians, an objective of every life is to wind up in heaven rather than hell. The different Christian churches and heretical movements, however, have sometimes developed quite contrasting views of how this is to be accomplished. In Weber's opinion, Calvinist churches adopted a view that, although it seemed to flow logically from God's omnipotence (all-powerfulness) and omniscience (all-knowingness), was particularly difficult to come to grips with. This view was that God had already destined each person, at the time of the creation, either to heaven or hell, and that there wasn't much we could now do about it one way or the other. As documentation of this view, Weber cited the Westminster Confession of 1647, promulgated by English Puritan followers of Calvin:

> Those of mankind that are predestined unto life [heaven], God before the foundation of the world was laid, according to His eternal and immutable purpose, and the secret counsel and good pleasure of His will, hath chosen in Christ unto everlasting glory, out of His mere free grace and love, without any foresight of faith or good works, or perseverance in either of them, or any other thing in the creature as conditions, or causes moving Him thereunto, and all to the praise of His glorious grace. (1958a:100)

As this passage suggests, neither one's good works nor one's faith could in any way draw out God's grace, although grace was the only passport to heaven. (After all, were faith or good works to have such power, we could control our own destinies, and God could not possibly be omnipotent.) It followed, then, that God's grace could only be distributed as God saw fit, "according to the unsearchable counsel of His own will," as the Westminster Confession put it.

The doctrine of predestination would be easy to accept if all but a handful of Christians had been "elected" for eternal salvation at the creation. But how could one know what proportion was elected? To do so, one would have to search the "secret counsel" of God's will, leaving it secret no more. That meant one couldn't know, though speculation naturally flourished, little of it optimistic. Richard Hamilton lists some British guesswork from the period:

> Lodowick Muggleton thought half might be saved, John Donne thought one in three, John Spittlehouse thought maybe a quarter. Arthur Dent's estimates ranged from one of a hundred to one of a thousand; Thomas Shepard also thought one of a thousand. John Bunyan, the most pessimistic of all, thought the chances of election were "perhaps one out of 1,000 men and one out of 10,000 women." (1996:73)

Even Muggleton's fifty-fifty odds raised the prospect that half of all lives lived in faith and filled with good works might "merit" hell—a disarming thought. Bunyan's estimate could only be profoundly dismaying to believers.

The doctrine of predestination, Weber believed, would likely arouse in such believers an intense interest in determining whether they were among the elect. Yet, there was no theologically legitimate way to know. As Weber wrote, Calvin "reject[ed] in principle the assumption that one can learn from the conduct of others whether they are chosen or damned," while one's own election depended upon receiving the grace God *might* meet out sparingly (1958a:110). Weber believed that predestination must produce in believers

> a feeling of unprecedented inner loneliness of the single individual. In what was for the man of the age of the Reformation the most important thing in his life, his eternal salvation, he was forced to follow his own path alone to meet a destiny which had been decreed for him from eternity. No one could help him. (1958a:110)

It was the difficulty of living in the face of this uncertain destiny that Weber believed had the most important consequences for Calvinist reformers, but before we turn to them, we need to register the third important idea introduced by the reformers, the demand for worldly **asceticism**.

Calvinism and Worldly Asceticism

By worldly asceticism, Weber meant a strong religious commitment to deny oneself common pleasures, or, as he put it "a fundamental antagonism to

sensuous culture of all kinds" (1958a:105). Ascetic attitudes are often carica-
tured in media representations of the American Puritan, clothed in severe
dress with a dour demeanor, and they are expressed today in the occasional
banning of alcohol, dancing, card games, and other popular entertainments
by the stricter Protestant sects and denominations. Prior to the Reformation,
asceticism had been a frequent practice of Catholic monastic orders, stimulated by a conviction that heavenly credit could be gained through earthly
privation, a conviction itself underlain by a sense that restricting one's comforts and foregoing personal enjoyment was a route to spiritual development.
In monasticizing the populace, Calvin and his followers recommended self-
denial to all believers.[15] In practice, this precluded a host of enjoyments common in the Roman Catholic world, from feasts to festivals, and discouraged
the conspicuous consumption commonly indulged in by nobles and successful adventurer capitalists. Asceticism would focus us on glorifying God,
whereas conspicuous consumption and worldly satisfactions were self-
glorifying.

In a sense, the call to asceticism merely reinforces the Protestant notion of
calling. It gives substance to the idea that all believers must commit to a
strenuous and exacting religious life. Comfort and pleasure imply relaxation
and, thus, a weakening of commitment. But this returns us to a question
raised above: if the Reformation called for a dramatic increase in aggregate
religious dedication, how was this to be motivated? Weber answered that the
conjunction of the three contingent ideas of calling, predestination, and
asceticism placed Calvinists in a spiritual or psychological quandary, the only
solution to which was to become highly motivated. Here, Weber proposed a
theory, albeit a psychological rather than a sociological one, to explain how
Protestants *must* respond to these three contingent religious innovations.

Signs of Election in Intense Occupational Activity

Agreeing to lead a strenuous spiritual life characterized by profound self-
denial with no guarantee of eternal reward would expose you, in vernacular
terms, to being had.[16] In other words, you might sacrifice much pleasure in
your life only to find that no eternal reward awaited you. Yet, if you believed
that the doctrine of predestination flowed logically from God's omnipotence
and omniscience, if you precluded any searching of God's "secret counsel"
to know whether you were among the elect, and if you admitted that God
would want a deep, ascetic commitment from all people, you'd see no logical
way around this potentially raw deal. You'd be stuck with it and simply have
to trust that it would pay off.

Weber assumed that commitment to this potential swindle was psychologically unsustainable among believers. Something had to give. In this sense, he saw the three contingent religious innovations of Protestantism as activating a psychological mechanism that would operate very much like Marx's capitalist mechanism: the religious deal would have to collapse, barring modifications to "sweeten" it, just as capitalism would have to collapse after progressing to unsustainable levels of alienation and exploitation. The difference was that the mechanism of Protestantism worked in people's minds, and by extension in the analytical sector Marx termed the *social consciousness*, while Marx's mechanism worked quite outside of minds as a mode of production.

But the deal did not collapse, Weber argued, since Calvinist believers found a way to sweeten it. The tension to which they were exposed could be reduced, he suggested, if they discovered a "sign of election," an assurance that their commitment and self-denial would be compensated in the afterlife. This led to an intense interest in such signs, that is, an interest in any indication that the believer was destined to be rewarded for his or her faith. Weber pointed to pastoral counsel that seemed to respond to this interest in signs:

> On the one hand it is held to be an absolute duty to consider oneself chosen, and to combat all doubts as temptations of the devil, since lack of self-confidence is the result of insufficient faith, hence of imperfect grace. . . . On the other hand, in order to attain self-confidence, intense worldly activity is recommended as the most suitable means. It and it alone disperses religious doubts and gives certainty of grace. (1958a:111–12)

Why did intense worldly activity act as a sign of election? While Weber's answer here is complicated, we can simplify it by saying that *worldly* activity was seen as helping God to build His (!) kingdom on earth, while *intense* activity, in which every moment was prayerfully planned and all impulses kept at bay, both averted the temptation to doubt and could presumably be sustained only by the elect. In practical terms, it simply did not make sense that God would build His kingdom on earth through believers' unremitting labor and not reward them. Put the other way around, God would not do His work through the damned. However little this assumption squared with doctrine (indeed, it resembled the Catholic notion of salvation by good works), it was psychologically impossible to reject. Thus, intense worldly activity "solved" the problem posed by the three contingent ideas introduced by the Reformation, and it was recommended as a way to reduce the unsustainable anxiety Weber assumed Calvinist doctrine would otherwise have caused.

Figure 4.2 summarizes Weber's psychological theory graphically. The figure allows us to see how Weber dealt with the problem of motivating the

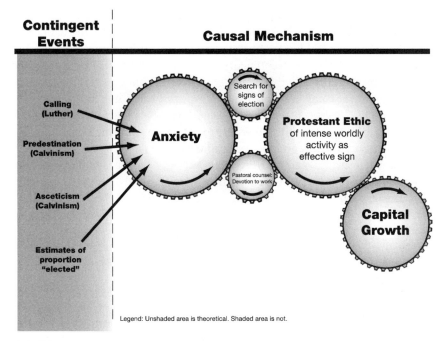

FIGURE 4.2
The Psychological Mechanism in Weber's Treatment of Capitalism

general increase in religious devotion needed to monasticize the world. The motive was anxiety reduction. Anxious to know their sacrifices were not in vain, members of Calvinist churches interpreted intense occupational dedication as a **sign of salvation**. Thus, the difficulty into which they were thrown by contingent and inexplicable religious innovations turned out to have a predictable consequence, explicable in terms of a psychological mechanism of anxiety reduction. Weber termed this consequence the *Protestant ethic*. The ethic combined an intense but methodical dedication to occupational life, seen as an expression of religious devotion, with an ascetic rejection of comfort and luxury. It involved just the sort of transformation in personal attitudes and identities that was needed to break through the economic traditionalism characteristic of European society and inaugurate modern capitalism.

From the Protestant Ethic to Capitalism and Its Spirit

We are now ready to conclude Weber's analysis of the origins of capitalism. He was well aware that capitalism was a complex institution, many of whose components could not be linked to Protestantism. For instance, capitalism benefited from forms of legal incorporation that would limit the liability of owners in the event of bankruptcy. Forms of limited liability were crucial to inducing investment in entrepreneurial ventures, but they had to be invented before they could provide this benefit. Similarly, technological developments in overland and canal transport, not to speak of oceanic shipping, vastly increased the markets entrepreneurs could hope to exploit, and so on. None of this, clearly, had much to do with Protestantism. But one significant feature did, Weber argued, and this was capital accumulation and reinvestment. It arose when profits came to believers intensely devoted to their occupations. Since they were prevented by their ascetic code from consuming conspicuously, profits accumulated and had to be reinvested. As Weber wrote,

> When the limitation of consumption is combined with the release of acquisitive activity, the inevitable practical result is obvious: accumulation of capital through ascetic compulsion to save. The restraints which were imposed upon the consumption of wealth naturally served to increase it by making possible the productive investment of capital. (1958a:172)

The diversion of profits from conspicuous consumption toward productive investment, Weber believed, significantly advanced the growth of capitalism, as did the transformation in attitudes toward work and business that Protestantism entailed. Enthusiasm for business and for success in it, he suggested, were further motivated by a sense that profits were a blessing from God and that the inspiration to new ventures—the essence of entrepreneurship—might itself be of divine origin. This new attitude would discourage the routinization of business by merchants seeking a comfortable life. On the other side of the equation, the new emphasis on method and calculation in business planning would discourage impulsive avarice. The novel attitude toward business that originated in the Reformation could then, he suggested, become culturally independent as the "spirit of capitalism":

> The religious valuation of restless, continuous, systematic work in a worldly calling, as the highest means of asceticism, and at the same time as the surest and most evident proof of rebirth and genuine faith, must have been the most powerful conceivable lever for the expansion of that attitude toward life which we have here called the spirit of capitalism. (1958a:172)

This transformation in attitudes toward work had initially needed religious inspiration to get off the ground, but, later, it could take on a secular existence free of religion. In fact, a commitment to "restless, continuous, systematic work" would, by its very success in the market place, now be forced on all who wished to remain in business, Weber argued, creating an "iron cage" from which few would escape and within which there would be little relaxation.

Back to Protestant-Catholic Differences? The Argument as a Whole

Weber argued, then, that Calvinist forms of Protestantism gave birth to the Protestant ethic, which, once established, could drop its original religious inspiration and become the secular spirit of capitalism. This spirit, considered as a cultural trait, then spread for the same reason that any advantageous physical trait might spread: it helped those who carried it to compete effectively against both routinized and adventurer capitalists of the traditional mold. As Weber wrote, "the capitalism of today, which has come to dominate economic life, educates and selects the economic subjects which it needs [i.e., entrepreneurs] through a process of economic survival of the fittest" (1958a:55). This is a functional explanation for why "restless, continuous, systematic work," born out of the contingent religious innovations of Luther and Calvin and the psychological machinery of anxiety reduction, became central to modern Western societies, in effect making them capitalist. It also constitutes a second explanation, one quite different from the mechanism of anxiety reduction that Weber used to motivate intense worldly activity. We will return to it in a moment.

The general spread of the spirit of capitalism, now independent of its Calvinist origins, poses a problem that Weber did not seem to recognize fully. He began his inquiry, as you'll recall, by noting the success of Protestants under capitalism compared to Catholics, and he might easily have succeeded in explaining this if the capitalist spirit had remained confined to its original Protestant seedbed. But in arguing that the spirit had become independent of religion and spread as a result of its functional superiority, Weber clouded the issue without recognizing it, for if the capitalist spirit, once having arisen in Calvinism, had spread independently of religious belief, why had it not spread thoroughly among Catholics in the intervening years, erasing the very differences Weber noted at the outset of his inquiry? We can imagine ways Weber might respond to this problem, for instance, by arguing that Protestants had longer and broader experience with the capitalist spirit than Catholics, but he simply did not address the issue.[17]

Thus, Weber's book, by failing to bring his account of capitalism's origin directly to bear on the supposed differences between Protestants and Catholics with which it began, does not close convincingly. Yet, *The Protestant Ethic and the Spirit of Capitalism* was a provisional and preliminary work. Weber was content in it to sketch an intriguing and plausible argument without tacking down all of its elements or conducting the rigorous research that would have been necessary to substantiate its claims. As his view of the matter matured, the argument of *The Protestant Ethic* became only one strand in a more complex picture of the origins of capitalism (see Collins 1986:19–44). Further, in that more complex picture, the doctrine of predestination no longer played a role. The Protestant Reformation itself remained important, but primarily because it destroyed the monasteries while motivating monastic devotion to work among believers. Calvinism and associated sects, writes Randall Collins in summarizing Weber's view, "were the most intense version of this motivation, not because of the idea of predestination . . . but because they required a specific religious calling for admission into their ranks, rather than automatic and compulsory membership in the politically more conservative churches" (1986:33). In a sense, then, it was more the voluntary nature of becoming Protestant, at the outset of the Reformation, that selected the most motivated believers and caused them to demand commitment from others, thus increasing devotion generally and transforming the culture of work.

We will not explore Weber's mature theory of capitalism further here, however; instead, we shall summarize the logical structure of the argument he made in *The Protestant Ethic*. As figure 4.3 shows, it falls into three sections, the first of which is a descriptive narrative. The second two are causal explanations of different types, a mechanism and a functional theory. On the left side of the figure are displayed four innovations in ideas (Marx's realm of social consciousness) that were produced by the Reformation. The occurrence of each of these ideas, not to speak of the grouping of the four together, is a contingent event. Each of them could just as easily not have become important to the Reformation or could have been substituted for by some other idea. Thus, there is no way to explain or theorize their occurrence: the best we can do is simply to narrate their appearance and incorporation into Reformation thought.

Once present, however, these ideas *necessarily* generate anxiety in believers, from whom extraordinary commitment is demanded with little assurance of reward. This necessity indicates that we are dealing with a mechanism, itself governed by a broader theory. Weber's psychological theory is that this level of anxiety is simply not endurable: believers would have to abandon or otherwise neutralize the effect of one or more of these ideas. Pastoral counsel and their own inclinations led them to conclude that there could be a sign of election in works (their deeds), with their own deep occupational commitment becoming an index of their salvation. This is the specific mechanism that accomplishes the anxiety reduction that Weber's theory argues is neces-

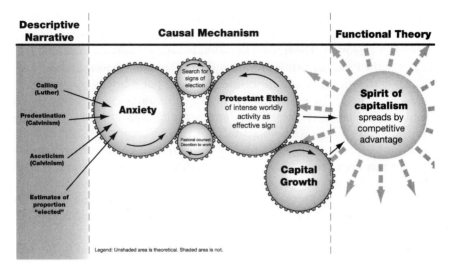

FIGURE 4.3
Weber's Full Treatment of the Origins of Capitalism and the Three Approaches It Involves

sary. The theory does not seem to admit exceptions: *all* people who adopt the four ideas will experience unendurable anxiety, although there might be several possible routes to escape from it. One route would be to abandon the beliefs altogether, and another would be to increase considerably the estimate of the proportion of believers elected for heaven: both count as alternative mechanisms, and Weber's theory does not explain why they weren't used (or used more often). It merely states that adherence to the Protestant ethic, in serving as a sign of election, was an effective means of reducing anxiety.

From this point, another argument takes over. The application of the ascetic mandate to the profits that come of intense worldly activity now gives rise to capital accumulation and reinvestment. This link, of course, isn't psychological. It's simply a practical likelihood. Intense application to business and a command to live frugally will frequently increase savings and allow for reinvestment. In a sense, we could say that the greater the Protestant ethic and the asceticism, the greater the capital accumulation. And capital accumulation was crucial to the development of capitalism.

Weber's account closes by explaining the transformation of the Protestant ethic into the spirit of capitalism through a second theory. This theory is used to explain the fact that the intense worldly activity characteristic of the Protestant ethic spreads beyond the bounds of Protestantism, no longer motivated by anxiety reduction. Weber does not fully develop this part of his account, but at its core is a model similar to the one Darwin developed for biological evolution. The intense devotion to rational business planning that is part of the Protestant ethic produces practical results superior to those produced by traditional economic attitudes: it is, to put it briefly, a better business orientation. The entrepreneurs and organizations exemplifying it will outperform old-style entrepreneurs and organizations, at least in the long run, and will thus spread both actively (by driving competitors out of business) and passively (in being copied by competitors). Because the remaining competitors need not be Calvinist, or even Protestant, the Protestant ethic is thus stripped of its specific religious aspects and made accessible to all as the spirit of capitalism. Further, once the superiority of this spirit is demonstrated, basically through its effect on the bottom line, it becomes unavoidable. People can't relax back into the older and more comfortable pace and style of economic life, back into traditionalism, even if they want to, because relaxation means failure in competitive markets—hence, the "iron cage" of intense and rationalized organizational activity of which Weber spoke.

   This theory is an early representative of what has come to be called *organizational ecology* (Hannan and Freeman 1989). Ecological theories attempt to explain the characteristics of populations of organizations, developing models to predict, for instance, the rate at which businesses will fail. Models of this sort belong to the broader category of functional theories that we will discuss in greater detail in chapter 7. An interesting feature of Weber's analysis is his argument that the spirit of capitalism could not have been inaugurated one business or one person at a time, presumably because it would have met with intense objection from traditionalists (1958a:55). Recall, for instance, that a characteristic of economic traditionalism among workers was disciplining "rate busters," people who worked harder than the norm. Weber implied that isolated embodiments of the spirit of capitalism would have met with a similar fate. It was thus crucial that it be introduced wholesale, as the outcome of a religious movement joined by many people for distinctly noneconomic reasons. This gave the spirit of capitalism the "critical mass" that it needed to prosper.

   Our description of Weber's account of the origins of capitalism is now complete. As you can see, it is divisible into three distinct components that work in sequence: a descriptive narrative (of theological innovations) and two causal explanations (of anxiety reduction and of the spread of the spirit of capitalism). Because it begins with a descriptive narrative of innovations in ideas, it illustrates nicely why Weber objected to Marx's historical materialist paradigm as too determinist and too materialist. If modern capitalism developed primarily as the unanticipated outcome of contingent religious doctrines, then there is simply no way to predict or explain its origins theoretically. Similarly, if it developed unexpectedly from an effort to reduce the anxiety these new religious ideas produced, then it grew from a change in social consciousness rather than from a change in material productive forces. At the same time, this does not mean that Weber is an enemy of theories since he uses them to explain how innovations in ideas translated into innovations in the economy. But he cautions us that we cannot explain everything theoretically: modern capitalism was a contingent development that did not have to happen when and where it did.

Evaluating the Protestant Ethic Thesis

Weber's account is obviously inventive and original, but this does not necessarily mean that it is right. We laid down in the first chapter a strategy for evaluating theories: test them first for robustness and then draw out and test their logical and substantive implications. We can't apply the criterion of robustness to the overall analysis here, however, because it isn't a theory and, thus, isn't broadly applicable. At the same time, I've already indicated that Weber's analysis apparently falters with regard to one of its logical implications: that the Protestant-Catholic difference noted in his original empirical generalization should have disappeared by the time he wrote. Further problems can be noted, most arising from the poor quality of evidence for several of Weber's most important characterizations. Very probing evaluations along these lines have been offered (Samuelsson 1961; Marshall 1982; Hamilton 1996), and they all conclude that Weber's argument is at best not proven and at worst quite unlikely to be correct. I will concentrate on Hamilton's discussion, which summarizes existing scholarship.

At the heart of Weber's argument is the psychological mechanism of anxiety reduction. His picture of the dilemma to which Calvinists were exposed by the doctrine of predestination is so compelling that the postulated anxiety seems inevitable. Yet, Weber produced scant evidence that it was actually felt by believers. Getting such evidence, of course, would not have been easy: the supposed anxiety occurred roughly two hundred fifty years before Weber wrote and existed as an internal psychological state. But traces of it should have been evident, one might argue, in believers' autobiographies or in their diaries, especially since these often focused upon spiritual concerns. In this regard, Hamilton (1996:71–73) cites the work of Kaspar von Greyerz, who reviewed sixty such diaries (of the roughly three hundred available from Britain in the proper period) and found little in them about the specific salvation anxiety Weber hypothesized, especially as stimulated by predestination. Further, on the basis of the diaries and autobiographies, the spiritual concerns of the literate segment of the population seem to have had little connection with the concerns of theologians. Thus, the documents that might offer the strongest evidence for Weber's argument lend it little support.

This may be because he emphasized a particularly harsh and unrepresentative interpretation of predestination. Weber focused on the Westminster Confession, as we have seen, but as Hamilton (1996:72) notes, the doctrine it contained was soon modified in ways that made its implications less severe. Further, the English theologian whose works Weber most frequently cited as an exponent of the Protestant ethic, Richard Baxter, was not a predestinarian and had rejected the doctrine of the Westminster Confession. This weakens our sense of a clear and necessary connection between Calvinist doctrine, salvation anxiety, and the Protestant ethic.

A second problem concerns the pastoral counsel Weber claimed identified hard work and worldly success as signs of election. Evidence of it, too, is hard to find, though there is the occasional suggestion that success indicates God's blessing (Hamilton 1996:74–75). Calvinists were often urged to diligence, but not as a proof of their election. Further, members of non-Calvinist groups were just as often encouraged to extend themselves. Thus, there is only the barest hint of Calvinists fastening upon "intense worldly activity" as a way of relieving anxieties caused by predestination.

Nevertheless, Protestantism or Calvinism might have induced a much higher level of commitment to work in believers, though it is hard to imagine just how evidence for this could be gathered so long after the fact. It remains the case, however, that Weber produced no such evidence; nor has any surfaced since. One would like autobiographies or diaries from the period to reflect this higher level of commitment, but they don't. Similarly lacking is much good evidence that Calvinist rates of saving and reinvestment substantially outstripped the rates of Anglicans or Catholics, though by implication they should have. Somewhat embarrassing in this regard, as Hamilton (1996:55) points out in another context, is Weber's reliance on Benjamin Franklin, whose writings are presented as prime examples of the Protestant ethic. Franklin himself, however, did not much observe this ethic: rather than reinvesting money his supposedly ascetic beliefs should have prevented him from spending, he used the modest wealth he gained through business early in life quite in the way of princes of old, eating well, enjoying himself at the theater, and pursuing his scientific hobbies. While his life in "retirement" was immensely active, it was lived in a way quite at odds with Weber's expectations.

Hamilton divides the argument of *The Protestant Ethic* into twelve distinct components and assesses for each the quality of evidence provided by Weber, as well as by subsequent research. He concludes that where Weber's argument is best supported, that is, in its discussion of the theological innovations, it usually needs some qualification. It is least supported in its positing of a psychological mechanism for relieving anxiety and in its functional argument for the development and spread of the spirit of capitalism. Hamilton devotes his most extensive discussion to the empirical generalization with which Weber began his inquiry: that Protestants fared better under capitalism than Catholics. He shows that the data upon which Weber most relied were gathered from only one German province, contain errors, and are subject to alternative interpretations that would make the association between religion and economic success spurious (that is, not causally connected to one another). Thus, the empirical generalization that Weber used to stimulate his account has only weak warrant.

Weber's fascinating account of the origin of modern capitalism, then, is far from being substantiated. As with Marx's theory of capitalism, we are apt to be disappointed by this, but as I noted above, *The Protestant Ethic* was not Weber's last word on the topic.[18] Furthermore, the question of the origins of capitalism remains unresolved today, so we cannot claim to have arrived at the "right" answer to a problem Weber got wrong.[19] Indeed, it is perhaps best to see his work as a significant step forward in recognizing just how complex and hard to answer are many of the questions that social scientists raise. And the effort Weber put forth remains interesting to us because of the contrast between its form and that of Marx's: the latter's determinism Weber counters with contingency; the latter's materialism he counters with idealism. That two such distinctive and different solutions to the same puzzle, the origins of capitalism, could be proposed tells us something about the diversity of perspectives in sociology. It also tells us something about how a research tradition develops. We rarely arrive at a solution to a problem (the guilty party, in terms of our whodunit metaphor) on the first try. Or on the second. Successive efforts refine our understanding of the problem by identifying some of its complexities, which become more apparent as easy solutions are dismissed. As we understand more about the problem and about the general form solutions to it have taken, our appreciation of it deepens and matures. This is how research traditions progress.

For many students, the origin of capitalism will appear to be of purely scholarly interest, and its fascination for Marx and Weber almost unintelligible. Yet, in a very real sense, no phenomenon more dramatically molds our lives today, or separates us more distinctly from ancestors perhaps twenty or so generations removed, than the eruption into the world of capitalism's dynamic force. Whether for good or for ill, it is massively important; thus, it seems only fitting that sociology should have cut its teeth trying to understand it and its origins and that it continues trying to this day.

Weber and Historical Idealism

We noted that Weber saw Marx's materialism as inflexible and tried to counter it with an idealist account of capitalism's origins. We need to pause briefly now to consider in greater detail what the term **idealism** means in sociology. In doing so, we are moving up from the level of theories to the level of paradigms, which, you will recall, consist of very general guidelines as to how theories should be formulated.

The term *idealism* is apt to be confusing because it has three distinct meanings in academic usage, two of which we need to exclude if we are to understand its sociological sense. First, both in academic writing and in common usage, "idealism" can refer to belief in and dedication to high-minded goals, such as ending poverty, promoting world peace, or abolishing racism, sexism, and so on. One contrast to idealism of this sort is *realism* (where we shun ideal ambitions in favor of more practical and easily achievable ones), while another contrast is *cynicism* (which assumes that such goals are not achievable because of fundamental flaws in human nature or society). However we stand on this, commitment to ideals is not what the term idealism refers to in sociology.

A second meaning that is definitely not part of common usage we owe to philosophy. There "idealism" can mean a conviction that the ideas or concepts we have of things are prior to, and more perfect than, the things themselves. For instance, the idea of a circle, one might argue, must exist prior to, and in greater perfection than, any circular object in the world around us. The idea of a circle must exist prior to such objects for us to recognize anything as circular in the first place; at the same time, it will be more perfect than them because it can be abstractly envisioned as lacking any of the imperfections that even the most finely crafted circular object will necessarily possess. The priority and perfection of ideas led philosophers like Plato to conclude that the world around us is only a derivative and imperfect copy of them, so that the realm of ideas is more fundamental than the realm of material things. It was Plato's preference for the former that made him an idealist. Again, this is not what the terms refer to in sociology.

In sociology, "idealism" refers to a hunch or conviction that social changes frequently occur as a consequence of changes in our ideas, and this hunch or conviction controls how we account for social institutions or social change. New ideas may cause social change intentionally or quite inadvertently, as we've seen in Weber's analysis of the supposed impact of Reformation theological innovations on capitalism. The sociological opposite of idealism is *materialism*, which refers to a hunch or conviction that social change normally results from changes in our material circumstances. (Sometimes **structuralism** is substituted for materialism here, referring to a conviction that changes in our ideas about social life frequently result from changes in the structural relations among individuals or groups. We will discuss structuralism in chapter 7.)

We have just explored a materialist and an idealist account of the origins of capitalism, so the contrast between the two stances should have a practical meaning for you, and it may help once again to refer to figure 3.1. But a further example should make the distinction very clear. Consider an interesting development in American social history. Joseph Smith, founder of the Church of Jesus Christ of Latter Day Saints (the Mormons), made it a part of early church doctrine that husbands could have multiple wives. While polygamy has been a relatively common form of family structure across history (and is permitted today by Muslims, among others), it was distinctly unconventional, and indeed illegal, among Western European societies and the colonists they exported. Whatever Smith's personal motives for instituting this unconventional family form, to promote it among his followers, he needed to give it a strong theological rationale, one that his followers would find both convincing and appealing. We might say that his success in doing so, along with his **charismatic authority** (see chapter 5), explains why, for a time, Mormons openly practiced polygamy, which was a feature of their social structure. Thus, Smith's innovative idea caused a social-structural modification from monogamy to polygamy, leading us to conclude that, here at least, changes in ideas cause changes in social organization. This seems a perfect example of idealism in action.

But consider the same example from a hypothetical materialist perspective. For instance, suppose that Marcia Guttentag and Paul Secord, whose theory of gender relations we have already discussed, were able to show that in societies where women outnumber men (a low sex ratio) and where men hold significantly greater structural power, polygamy is common. Suppose we further found that these conditions obtained in Smith's early circle of followers. Now we would have a plausible structural/materialist explanation of why Smith came up with his doctrinal innovation and why Mormon social structure changed as a result. (Again, this is a hypothetical explanation: I am asserting nothing about the causes of polygamy or about early Mormon sex ratios.)

This example illustrates the two points of view nicely, and it shows as well that debates between idealists and structuralists/materialists over the sources of social change can take on something of a "chicken and egg" quality. At question is where to locate the ultimate cause of some social change: in new ideas or new social or material circumstances. You should now be able to appreciate why this question is so important. As we saw with the new religious ideas of the Protestant Reformation, it is frequently very difficult to offer good sociological explanations for innovations in ideas. Unless the realm of ideas has a logic of its own for which we can provide a sociological underpinning,[20] we will be unable to explain and predict why and where a new idea will be launched. If so, however, we can only offer a descriptive or a causal narrative of a social change, and not a theory. And this was just the point Weber wanted to make in relation to Marx. Weber was a historical idealist not because he argued that social institutions and social change always resist theoretical explanation but because he believed they do so frequently enough, and in such important circumstances, that to embrace historical materialism would be a mistake.

Today, this issue is just as alive as it was a century ago. Over the past quarter century, sociologists have become increasingly idealist in their orientation, in part reacting to a heavily structuralist/materialist orientation (or paradigm) in the 1960s and 1970s. Contemporary idealism is expressed by its emphasis on agency, or the ability of social actors to create or transform their social environments, as well as by its emphasis on the *social construction* of everything from gender identity to social problems. The more we see social actors as free to create or mold their social environments, the less we can develop theories to explain the latter since they will originate in events we can only descriptively or causally narrate. Finally, idealism has been encouraged by a renewed emphasis on the importance of cultural differences in molding social organization (see Dobbin 1994 for a particularly interesting example). By contrast, structuralists and materialists emphasize how existing social structures and unplanned changes in them influence and constrain people's agency, allowing us to predict the social constructions they will create. Sociologists come to prefer one or the other orientation, idealist or structuralist/materialist, through extensive familiarity with the successes and failures of specific theories, as well as of descriptive and causal narratives, as they account for social phenomena. You see the problem illustrated nicely in the contrast between possible idealist and structuralist accounts of Mormon polygamy.

Weber and *Verstehen*

The foregoing examples also illustrate why Weber felt that an ability to understand other people's beliefs and motives sympathetically, a form of understanding captured in the German term **verstehen**, was an important part of the sociologist's equipment.[21] When we adopt idealism as a guide to formulating accounts of social phenomena, our starting point is always going to be in other people's minds. We have to understand their ideas or perspectives in order to see what motivates their actions. In other words, we have to be able to explicate their ideas or emotions in order to understand why they behave the way they do, and we do this best when we can somehow think and feel our way into their skins.

We saw how important this ability was when we developed our culture-of-honor explanation of argument-related homicide in the first chapter. Initially, it proved very hard to understand why someone at a party would get a gun and shoot another person, but as we came to understand better what a culture of honor means, thereby entering into it at least somewhat sympathetically, it became easier to see the human logic in such an act. Weber believed that this ability was crucial to good sociology, and a significant part of the discipline of cultural anthropology has also been devoted to sympathetically understanding foreign cultures. Weber's point here may seem so obvious that it's hard to imagine anyone disagreeing with him, but some social scientists have.[22] They worry about how we are to show that our imaginative construction of other people's motives matches what they're actually thinking and feeling. One problem, noted in chapter 1, is that people often do not know why they behave as they do (and only invent justifications for their behavior when called to account for it). If we impute motives to them in these circumstances, assuming that these must have operated beneath the person's consciousness, how can we establish that we have done so correctly?[23] And even when other people's motives are conscious, but we have no access to them, how are we to assure ourselves that the motives we suppose them to have had are the ones they actually did have?

We have seen how deep this problem is with Weber's reconstruction of the motives of Calvinist reformers. The salvation anxiety he presumed they must have felt and the means they adopted to escape it certainly make "perfect sense" as motives; thus, he seemed on the surface to have had a good "sympathetic understanding" of the reformers' difficult situation, but the fact remains that we have almost no evidence that they in fact felt the way that Weber supposed they did. Furthermore, it is reasonable to argue that we should find such evidence in their autobiographies, journals, and correspondence if they in fact experienced what he claimed. Put briefly, then, the problem with *verstehen* is that we tend to "read into" people's behavior motives that they did not experience. Thus, while Weber was right to emphasize the importance of sympathetic understanding in the social sciences, he probably did not stress enough the difficulty of ensuring that we understand correctly other people's internal states.

Weber's emphasis on sympathetic understanding has acted as a charter for **interpretive sociology**, a paradigm that connects social scientific understanding closely with humanistic disciplines that engage in textual interpretation.[24] Interpretive sociologists strive to understand the meanings that social events and institutions have for people and to explain the processes by which they create and react to these meanings. They differ over whether answers to these questions should aim for scientific validity or for a form of plausibility similar to that sought in the arts and humanities. Weber himself seems to have had clearly scientific ambitions for *verstehen* as a method, but the trouble he experienced with it in *The Protestant Ethic* perhaps suggests why some later scholars rejected this goal.

By examining Weber's early account of the origins of capitalism, we have been able to understand why he advocated idealism and sympathetic understanding. Both seemed called for by the nature of the phenomenon itself, at least in Weber's view of it. But, once again, Weber did not argue that sociology should be exclusively idealist or that it should only investigate how people understand their own behavior and the social world around them (as opposed to how both might appear to a more distant, and perhaps more "objective," investigator). Whether we develop idealist or materialist accounts or look at matters from the point of view of the actor or a more distant observer depends on the nature of the phenomenon we want to analyze. Thus, Weber stood for a flexible paradigm, embodying the wide array of approaches that the complexity of the social world, as he saw it, required.

Conclusion

In this chapter, we've reviewed Weber's account of the origins of modern capitalism. While this account can seem overwhelmingly complex, it can also be summarized and called to mind rather easily by reference to figure 4.3. Perhaps the most important lesson we gain from this account is that events of extreme importance and consequence need not be theorizable. They cannot be "explained," at least if we follow the meaning of the word as defined in this book, requiring that explanations provide causal accounts, whether through theories or causal narratives. At the same time, Weber's model of how salvation anxiety yields capital accumulation and his functional explanation of the spread of the spirit of capitalism both show us how psychological and sociological models can be linked to "chance" historical developments, such as the novel ideas Luther and Calvin introduced. Here, we see an interplay between historical and sociological modes of inquiry.

Now that we've come to understand Weber's general orientation, as well as the basis for his relatively modest ambitions for sociological theory, we're ready to look at one of his distinctive contributions to theory, the **analytic typology**. Investigating typologies will afford us the opportunity to discuss the explanatory practice of analysis in much greater depth than we have thus far.

Notes

1. Although Weber, of course, could not foresee the specific form modern complexity theory would take, his analysis of the complexity of both natural and social events in his early methodological essays (1975, 1977) seems to anticipate it. His views on the importance of chance are perhaps best developed in part 2 of a later methodological essay, "Critical Studies in the Logic of the Cultural Sciences" (1949:164–88).

2. Strictly speaking, as noted in the last chapter, Marx's explanation of the origins of capitalism (rather than of its behavior as a system) was a causal narrative rather than a causal theory. Whereas Marx would have seen this as a lapse from his ambition to produce causal theories, Weber would see it as the best we can hope to do. His *Protestant Ethic* book indirectly attacks Marx's ambition and substitutes a descriptive account for the first step in the origins of capitalism, while later steps involve causal theories.

3. Interestingly, the issue of the role of theory proper in explaining large-scale social change is still very much alive today, more than a century after Marx and Weber staked out their positions (see, for instance, Gould 2001). This indicates that the classical theorists put their fingers on some of the deepest problems in the social sciences, with which we all must still grapple.

4. It is important to note that this generalization, if true in Weber's time, no longer holds. As we will see, Samuelsson (1961:137–150) and Hamilton (1996:33–48) question whether it was true in Weber's time.

5. My discussion makes it appear as if Weber was concerned exclusively with refuting Marx's position. In reality, however, he was responding to a series of arguments that had developed in German historiography, in relation to which his criticism of Marx was a by-product rather than being central.

6. Randall Collins (1986:52–54), however, argues that monastic orders such as the Cistercians were in fact employing capitalist practices and "spirit" well before the Protestant Reformation.

7. You might compare the attitudes of Weber's economic traditionalists to those of some students with regard to their studies. Certainly most students "study to live," rather than the reverse, and this is responsible for the character of student culture on many campuses. As you read about Weber's theory, keep this analogy in mind and

ask yourself what would have to happen for students to change so that they "lived to study"!

8. I am putting aside the very interesting question of whether traditional and modern orientations identify poles between which people may vary continuously or whether they are tightly integrated "packages" of attitudes between which one would have to jump more or less at once across the chasm that separates them. (This is similar to the problem of whether the concept of modes of production defines discrete entities.) Put differently, it remains an open question whether economic orientation is better seen as a nominal or an ordinal variable. Reasons can be given for both views. You should be aware that the issue of variable attitudes toward economic life and their place in social change remains a very live topic in the social sciences. For an interesting anthropological investigation of the matter, see Foster (1967).

9. I give here the modern Roman Catholic understanding of the word *vocation*. Across time and religious confession, the meaning of calling (and the extent of the group conceived to be called) varies widely. At its narrowest, it refers to individuals such as prophets who are given specific missions directly by God. At its broadest, it refers to all people "called" to join in the worship of God, which is to say, to all members of Christian churches, whether they take on strenuous obligations or not. For our purposes, it is best to confine it to those adopting strenuous roles. For the early Protestant reformers, as we shall see, this meant every church member.

10. Other religions, such as Hinduism, are much more accepting of variation in members' beliefs. It is an interesting sociological question as to why religions vary in the degree to which doctrinal orthodoxy is seen as being crucial. For a broad analysis of heresy, see Collins (1986:213–46).

11. In a footnote, Weber (1958a:220n7) makes it clear that he is more concerned with ideas that developed within the various Calvinist denominations than with the specific ideas of Calvin. For a discussion, see Hamilton 1996:67.

12. My point here is not that sociological explanation of such ideas is impossible in principle but that we don't have even the faintest idea of how to go about it in this particular case. It would be like explaining why a novelist wrote the particular book she did (why, say, George Eliot wrote *Middlemarch*) in a period when other novelists wrote a variety of other books. This is not a task with which sociologists are apt to have much success. Some explanatory approaches to culture (see Douglas 1970 and our discussion of structuralism in chapter 7) suggest interesting ways to explain why certain concepts occur when and where they do, but they are unable to offer help with the three of concern to us here.

13. We can venture that the centrality Marx gave to work in people's lives, as reflected in the importance he placed on alienation from the process of labor, would have seemed to Weber culturally intelligible only in light of Luther's transformation of the idea of calling. Without this, in effect, the idea might never have occurred to Marx, who would instead have found other features of life more significant. A possible candidate might have been one's honor. For interesting discussions, see Miller (1993) and Patterson (1982).

14. I invite you again to consider the analogy to student life, where a few students live to study while a majority study to live. If all students were "called" to the scholarly life, this difference would disappear and universities would somewhat resemble

monasteries—as mine, the University of Chicago, did—devoted to the life of the mind.

15. Weber links denial to the goal of "self-control, which formed the end of the *exercitia* of St. Ignatius and of the rational monastic virtues elsewhere, [and] was always the most important practical idea of Puritanism" (1958a:119). We have encountered this theme before in Weber's discussion of the spirit of capitalism, which emphasized rational control over impulses.

16. This way of putting it is mine rather than Weber's, but I think he would concur. He was not religiously inclined and found predestination a "monstrous" and inhumane doctrine (1958a:104). The value structure of Puritanism, as exemplified in Paul Bunyan's *Pilgrim's Progress*, he viewed as perverse, especially as it favored religious self-interest over family ties and obligations. Interestingly, his mother, of whom he was very fond and respectful, was herself quite religious.

17. Had he taken this route, he would have had to face an additional implication of his argument: that inheritors of Calvinist forms of Protestantism should show greater capitalist success than inheritors of the nonpredestinarian forms, such as the Lutheran or Anglican-Episcopalian.

18. In addition to developing a somewhat different account of the rise of European capitalism in his later writings, Weber conducted comparative inquiries into Chinese and Indian cultural and social history in order to determine why these societies did not give rise to capitalism.

19. For a brief discussion, see Harris (1999:163–74). Focusing not on capitalism but on the rise of the West, the approach of Goldstone (2000) continues Weber's emphasis on the role of chance in history but locates the stimuli to Western development in a combination of entrepreneurship and engineering that originated in England as a result of a fortuitous conjunction of circumstances. Gorski (2003) offers an interesting reformulation of Weber's thesis that focuses on the contribution of Calvinist religious discipline to the formation of effective governments, which in turn provide the context for economic transformation.

20. As an example of such a logic, consider the argument made by historian Arthur Schlesinger (1986) that American political culture undergoes "pendulum shifts" from liberal to conservative (or vice versa) roughly once a generation. If we can find regular patterns in the development of ideas like this, their behavior becomes predictable, and we can use them in theories of social change. If the regular patterns are themselves caused by social factors, we can develop good sociological explanations for them.

21. When we use the term *sympathetically* here, it does not imply approval of the action in question but, instead, the ability to place oneself in another's shoes and imaginatively think and feel the way he or she does. Again, it's just the sort of talent a good detective must have in order to envision the motives various people might have had for committing a particular crime. Having this talent needn't imply agreement with or support of the motives but merely an understanding of them. *Empathy* is perhaps a better term here than *sympathy*.

22. The most thoroughgoing rejection of *verstehen* has been by behaviorist social scientists, who ignore people's internal states (e.g., their motives and sense of the meaning of their circumstances) on principle in favor of explaining behavior in terms

of measurable external factors. Less extreme positions simply point out, as above, that people often misunderstand the reasons for their behavior, as well as the character of their social surroundings, both of which may be better understood by observers less directly involved (and perhaps less biased) and who have professional training in social explanation.

23. For a thorough treatment of this problem through the lens of a classic study in cultural anthropology, see Schneider (1993:55–82).

24. See, among others, Nisbet (1976), Brown (1989), Geertz (1973), Lepenies (1988), and Taylor (1979[1971]).

5

Max Weber and Analytic Typologies

M AX WEBER DEVOTED THE beginning section of a major work, *Economy and Society* (1978), to outlining the sorts of phenomena sociology should explain and to establishing some of the categories into which these phenomena fall. In a sense, he wanted to sketch the various forms that human groups take and inventory the means by which the activities of people within them are coordinated. In addition, he hoped to account for some of the major transformations of these groups across time—a topic I'll return to in a moment. In the process, he developed **analytic typologies** that remain highly fruitful for us today. I noted in the first chapter that attention to analytic typologies expands our sense of what it means to theorize, directing our interest away from causal accounts (which explain why something happens) and toward analysis (which explains what something is composed of). While analytic typologies exemplify only one form of analysis (we could also analyze processes into their component activities or analyze the rules governing certain social practices, for instance), they raise interesting theoretical issues. I want to explore two typologies here, but before going directly to them, I need to better explain what an analytic typology is.

What Is an Analytic Typology?

Typologies are systems of classification; they sort instances of a phenomenon into different categories. You can think of them as creating a series of cells or pigeonholes among which instances of a phenomenon can be sorted so as to group similar ones together and to separate these from less similar ones. We have already introduced several informal typologies in earlier chapters, for instance, in distinguishing between argument-related and felony-related homicides or between materialist and idealist theories.

Sometimes our purpose in classifying things is purely **heuristic** (which means the classification merely helps us to think about the things classified), but, other times, we may believe that our system of classification captures real divisions in the world that exist independently of, and prior to, our invention of the typology. We can call the latter classifications **empirical** ones. An example of an empirical classification system would be the division of animals into species. An example of a heuristic classification would be the distinction between empirical and heuristic classifications itself, because we make this distinction just to help us think about typologies.

The analytic typologies we want to discuss here are empirical classifications, not heuristic ones. But empirical classifications themselves come in two types that I will call *open* and *closed* (to employ another heuristic distinction). An **open empirical typology** usually includes many types and may change across time, just as does the system of animal species. **Closed empirical typologies**—I'll switch to calling them analytic henceforward—have few types, which we normally assume to be permanent. Compare the distinction between species and between sexes among animals. Dividing animals into species gives us a very large set of types, numbering several thousands, while dividing them into sexes gives us only two. Why? Presumably because new species develop frequently, while new sexes have had a very hard time getting started. Thus, though evolution turned the ancestor of mammals into many successor species, all of these have had to follow the general rule for organisms that one sex is ok, two are better, but three would be a crowd.

Analytic typologies, as closed empirical classifications, are like the sex case rather than the species case. When we form an analytic typology, we don't want very large numbers of types to which we may have to add as we discover more (or as more evolve). Instead, we want a small number, and we'd prefer that they were permanent. The only way we can hold the number down is to assume that the categories into which we are dividing a phenomenon are relatively limited and closed rather than vast and open-ended: they're not something you expect to add to in the same way you expect to add new species to the category of mammals. I say relatively limited and closed because the property isn't simply a logical one, but rather an empirical one: it's logically possible to have more than two sexes, after all, and we can imagine other worlds on which multiple sexes might have developed, but the practical biological rationale for further sexes seems weak. Thus, in practice, all we get is two, and we don't expect more to arise, even though it's remotely possible that they will.

Let's consider another example. The Labor Department of the U.S. government has established occupational categories into which almost all the jobs that people have today can be sorted. There's, first, a very general set of job classifications, then intermediate-level sets of more specific categories, and, finally, a very detailed set of specific job types. The most general set consists of six categories: managerial and professional; technical, sales, and administrative support; service occupations; precision production, craft, and repair work; operators, fabricators, and laborers; and farming, forestry, and fishing. Beneath this is a set of twenty-three somewhat more specialized occupational categories. These categories, and the jobs they include, are added to and subtracted from as work types change with time: there were no computer programmers around, after all, when I was a child. The most detailed level of job types is meant to be purely descriptive and to cover the thousands of jobs that exist in the economy today.[1] The higher-level categories are meant to group job types that have significant resemblances. The whole system is a good example of an open empirical typology with several levels.

Now consider a very different sort of typology: the split of jobs into blue-collar (or manual) and white-collar (or cognitive/information processing). This is an analytical distinction drawn within a relatively limited and closed conceptual space, which is to say that it's hard to imagine there being a third component within it that the manual-cognitive distinction has missed (but see below). Both the open and the closed typologies use empirical distinctions: it's not that the manual-cognitive distinction doesn't refer to concrete jobs since the first three of the Labor Department's highest-level categories are primarily cognitive, and the last three primarily are manual, but this distinction intends to exhaust the conceptual space from which types of labor can be derived. By exhausting the conceptual space, once again, I mean that we don't anticipate a third type of work's being added to manual and cognitive types as the economy is further transformed technologically. In this sense, a good analytic typology should be good forever, while open empirical typologies are expected to change with the times.

An analytic typology thus sorts instances of a general phenomenon into an empirically (not logically) closed and small set of distinct categories. The set reveals important *nominal variation* in the phenomenon.[2] Because this concept is difficult to grasp, let me give one more example. If we look around the world, we will find many different religions: Shintoism, Buddhism, Christianity, Islam, Hinduism, Jainism, Sufism, Judaism, and so on (continuing into the several thousands through distinct religions practiced by smaller and smaller groups of people, many of them tribal). Listing these religions provides an open empirical typology of them, with all being identified as distinct from one another on the basis of their distinct beliefs and practices. Such a typology is not analytic. However, when we earlier distinguished between doctrinal religions (those that make adherence to a particular set of beliefs a criterion for membership) and nondoctrinal ones (those that don't), we were utilizing an analytic typology. The distinction we made is empirical, rather than heuristic, because doctrinal religions behave in distinct ways, often using quasi-judicial mechanisms to evaluate the orthodoxy of members' beliefs, for instance, that make them different from nondoctrinal ones.

I hope these examples make clear just what an analytic typology is and why we want to distinguish between analytic and open empirical typologies and then to distinguish both from heuristic typologies.[3] *An analytic typology establishes, on the basis of empirical differences, the small number of presumably permanent categories into which instances of a general phenomenon fall.* I want to turn now to some of the qualities that make for a good analytic typology.

As more examples accumulate, just what is theoretical about forming analytic typologies should be easier to see.

What Makes for a Good Typology?

A good analytic typology has three properties: its types are **exhaustive, mutually exclusive**, and explanatorily useful. I want to briefly discuss each of these qualities.[4]

Exhaustiveness

A typology is *exhaustive* when it specifies all of the relevant types encompassed by a concept and no others. Although it may seem easy to be exhaustive, it sometimes turns out to be difficult to know whether we've achieved our goal or not. Take the distinction between manual and cognitive labor above, and consider a possible third candidate for a basic form of labor: emotional work. Emotional work is done in a wide variety of occupations by practitioners ranging from ministers, to therapists, to stewards on airplanes (see Hochschild 1983). Now, it seems clear that emotional labor is distinct from manual labor since it doesn't involve acting on things physically. But is it simply one of the many forms of cognitive or information-processing/decision-making labor, or should it be made a category of its own? Until we decide this, we can't conclude that the manual-versus-cognitive distinction is exhaustive. (You might spend some time considering how you'd decide whether emotional work belongs in a category of its own, alongside manual and cognitive. This will give you a feel for the sort of theorizing that's involved in creating typologies.)

Mutual Exclusivity

A typology is *exhaustive* when it divides a concept into all its types (of one sort) and only these. A typology is *mutually exclusive* when each of the concrete cases it covers can be placed into one, and only one, of its types. Possessing this quality, a typology allows clear and clean sorting of concrete phenomena among its component categories. Thus, we won't find ourselves struggling to decide which category a given phenomenon belongs to. Rather like pigeonholes, our categories will have crisp edges (not fuzzy ones), and the objects we want to place in them will belong unambiguously in one or another. At least, this is the ideal.

Suppose we consider the manual-versus-cognitive distinction in this light.

Note that the question is not whether specific, real jobs can be unambiguously identified as exclusively one or the other—there aren't any jobs that are exclusively manual or mental—but whether the many different tasks a job entails can themselves be unambiguously designated either physical or mental, and whether we can evaluate the relative contribution of the two components so as to characterize the job as a whole. For instance, as I'm typing on my computer right now, most of you would conclude that the physical labor my fingers are doing is distinct from, and clearly subordinate to, the intellectual work involved in composing sentences that will communicate the idea of mutual exclusivity to you. Thus, it seems easy to classify the work I'm doing right now as primarily cognitive (even though it also involves physical labor), just as mowing my lawn is primarily physical labor. Indeed, most cases you spontaneously come up with will naturally sort themselves between mental and manual in this fashion.

But if you think about it for a while, you can spot some difficult cases, ones that don't easily sit in either category or that seem to sit equally well within both. One example might be musical performance—let's say the work of a jazz pianist (see Sudnow 1978). Is this physical or mental work? Can you say it is predominantly one or the other? So much physical skill (and practice to acquire and maintain it) is required of musicians that it might at first seem easy to classify the work as manual; but many performers are also expected to be creative, or at least to put their personal interpretive stamp on music that others have created, and this seems to be cognitive (or emotional?) work. So, how are we to pigeonhole the jazz pianist in terms of our manual-cognitive distinction? (For more detailed discussion of this point, see appendix 5A.)

There are ways of resolving this dilemma, but it's hard to conclude that any of them are completely satisfactory. And the issue isn't trivial because the problem that jazz musicians, and artists in general, pose for our distinction extends to many of the more skilled crafts, which often call for a good deal of intellectual or aesthetic input. These jobs show that our analytical categories do not have sharp edges; instead, there is a fuzzy area between them where jobs like jazz pianist or chef in a fancy restaurant seem to belong. Were there very many jobs of this sort, we might have to abandon our categories in favor of seeing the physical and intellectual aspects of jobs as continuously variable (see appendix 5A).

Our difficulties here at least help clarify why creating an analytic typology in sociology qualifies as theorizing: rather than explaining behavior directly, we are explaining the categories into which it falls. We first have to come up with a set of categories or types that accommodates our purposes. (This involves the same sort of conceptualization that we originally encountered in turning incidents into variables in the first chapter.) Then, we have to engage in a constant back and forth between the types we propose and the concrete, empirical cases we want covered by the typology. The only way we can tell that a proposed typology is good is to try it out on concrete case after concrete case, judging in each instance whether the criteria of exhaustiveness and mutual exclusivity have been met. Indeed, it's by comparing concrete instances in a rough way to begin with—that is, by looking for variation in them—that we get the initial ideas for creating our typology. The urge to typologize arises from recognizing that our cases vary in important ways, and this occurs to us as we scan an assortment of them, alert for possible variation, just as we did in our initial chapter. There, as I've indicated, our distinction between argument-related and felony-related killings presupposed an analytic typology of homicides. (You might ask yourself whether this typology is exhaustive and mutually exclusive.)

Usefulness

This leads us to the third property that makes for a good typology: explanatory usefulness. It is possible to create analytic typologies just for the fun of it, but sociologists expect them to pay off, and the payoff comes when we use our typologies as stepping stones to explanations. We can do so either by arguing that the different types we have identified behave differently and thus call for different sorts of explanations (as in the case of felony-related versus argument-related homicides) or that they are treated differently by people. For instance, there's not much point to distinguishing between mental and manual labor unless these categories are treated differently by people around us, with mental labor, for instance, somehow being seen as of higher status than manual work and, thus, worthy of higher compensation, all other things being equal. When such differences exist, we have something to theorize about: why, after all, should mental labor be considered superior in any way to manual? (Can you create a theory to explain this?)

This is only another way of saying that to be worthwhile sociologically, analytic typologies must carve up the world in ways that are explanatorily fruitful. The differences they recognize are associated with further differences that are socially consequential and, thus, sociologically significant. They make distinctions about which we can theorize or that we can use in our theories. (If doctrinal or nondoctrinal religions don't behave differently, for instance, there's no sociological value in establishing these categories.) Looking at this from the opposite angle, we'd worry that failing to make these distinctions would cause us to theorize clumsily, explaining less of the variation around us than we'd like to or, perhaps, overlooking important forms of variation altogether. (This is another way of indicating that analytic typologies are not just heuristic.) In the end, then, we can think of an analytic typology as a tool with which to theorize, a tool that works best when it's sharp, that is, when it's exhaustive and mutually exclusive.

Weber's Typologies

Weber began *Economy and Society* by distinguishing **social action** from other nonsocial forms of human behavior. Once he had done this, he proceeded to develop an analytic typology of social action, discussion of which I defer to later in this chapter. The rest of his immense book might be briefly described as aimed at developing open empirical typologies of the characteristic economic and political forms of association that pattern social action, as well as analytic typologies of the forms of power by which social action is hierarchically coordinated. Infused throughout is a concern to understand the historical forces that have caused changes in the economic and political forms of association across time. Here, I will concentrate on the analyses of authority and of action, taking up the former first because of the clarity with which it exemplifies the principles of typologizing. Somewhat later, we will see that the distinctions among forms of authority that Weber made are critical to characterizing and explaining historical change. As a way of approaching the typology of authority, let us first examine the more general category of power and become involved in typologizing ourselves.

Power

Power is one of the central means by which the activities of diverse people in a society are coordinated.[5] (You might stop here to consider how much of your daily activity, perhaps including your reading of this book, results from the power others have over you.) We can define *power* as the ability of one individual to get another to do what the first individual wants. Although the word "power" sometimes carries a negative connotation, we should remember that parents would not be able to socialize their children to be respectable adults without exerting power over them. Thus, it is impossible to conceive of societies in which power does not play an important, and usually positive, role (as it may in your reading this book).

Somewhat surprisingly, Weber did not construct an analytic typology of power itself.[6] He dealt only casually with its various types, without trying to exhaust the conceptual space they inhabited. I suggest you do this now as an exercise in analytical typologizing. Ask yourself what major means are available to any person to get another to do what the first person wants. Can you develop an exhaustive list of the categories into which they fall? How many types does it include? Can you think of cases that don't fit into any of your types or that seem to fit equally well into two or more?[7]

Your analysis will surely include both coercion and authority as types of power. Coercion gets people to do things by threatening to hurt them or, if threats fail, by actually causing them pain. Authority, on the other hand, gets people to do things because they view the commands issued by authorities as legitimate, as directives they should obey. Thus, it's hard to mistake instances of obedience resulting from coercion for instances of obedience to authority, and this makes these two categories mutually exclusive. We might view them as branches on a tree diagram, as in figure 5.1.

The tree diagram breaks down power into its constituent types, pictorially representing its analysis. As you complete the tree, you should concentrate on how you come up with additional types of power. Normally, doing so will require you to imagine numerous different cases, in each of which you get someone to do what you want and then figure out how to categorize (into types) the means you use in the different cases. One difficulty is assuring yourself that you've covered all the important differences.[8] Another is to categorize them at the same level of abstraction as the very general categories of coercion and authority. You don't want to develop a typology that mixes different levels of abstraction in its types, just as the Labor Department wouldn't want to set up categories of jobs reading "managerial and professional; technical, sales and administrative support; . . . short-order cook."

As you proceed with this exercise, you should consider how closely the process of constructing a typology resembles the process of theorizing we developed in the first chapter. It seems clear that we can use the same three general steps: setting up the problem, creating the typology, and evaluating the typology. But the nature of each step will be a bit different. We don't

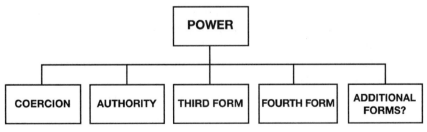

FIGURE 5.1
Outline of a Typology of Power

normally start to wonder about types of phenomena because of a particular incident that puzzles us, for instance. Instead, we start to wonder whether a concept, such as power, is unitary or is divisible into different types in a useful way. We decide this by exploring variation among phenomena that embody the concept. This is like turning an incident into a variable (see appendix 5A). Once we determine that important variations exist, we move to the stage of creating the typology. Our procedure here is quite different from that in the first chapter, however, since it involves establishing categories rather than seeking matching empirical generalizations. Finally, as we turn to evaluation, rather than drawing out testable implications of the typology, our procedure is to "throw" case after different case at it to see whether it works. (It does so when each case fits easily into one, and only one, category.) This is somewhat like testing for robustness. Since almost no typology will work perfectly, we have to decide if cases that don't quite fit damage our effort fatally or if we should put up with them because the typology nevertheless proves useful. We can provide a particularly nice example of evaluation as we examine Weber's typology of authority.

Authority

Authority is a distinct form of power. People who have authority get us to do what they want, and their power over us is characterized by its legitimacy, the sense we have that it is right for them to direct our activities. But why do we think it's right? Weber recognized that there are different sources for this general sense of rightness (in other words, that there is variation among them), which meant that authority itself could be analyzed into distinct types. In fact, it had to be thus analyzed to understand important variations in human behavior since "according to the type of legitimacy which is claimed, the type of obedience . . . and the mode of exercising authority, will all differ fundamentally" (Weber 1978:213). But before we look at his analysis, it would be useful to note that, for Weber, authority is a *relational phenomenon*: it always connects at least two people in a relation of domination and subordination. Furthermore, authority ceases to exist as soon as its legitimacy is questioned. Subordinates can always, in principle, ignore authority by refusing to grant it legitimacy, in which case the dominant figure in the relationship has to resort to other means, such as coercion, to see that his or her directives are obeyed.[9]

With this much behind us, let's see how Weber analyzed authority. He wrote,

> There are three pure types of legitimate domination [authority]. The validity of the claims to legitimacy can be based on:

1. Rational grounds—resting on a belief in the legality of enacted rules and the right of those elevated to authority under such rules to issue commands (legal authority).
2. Traditional grounds—resting on an established belief in the sanctity of immemorial traditions and on the legitimacy of those exercising authority under them (traditional authority); or finally,
3. Charismatic grounds—resting on devotion to the exceptional sanctity, heroism or exemplary character of the individual person, and of the normative patterns or order revealed or ordained by him (charismatic authority). (Weber 1978:215)

Weber's first type of authority obviously covers cases such as the lawful commands of government agents who have acquired their posts by proper means. This is the sort of authority that legislators and police officers possess. Why Weber styled this authority "rational" may not initially be apparent, however, and in tracing out his reasons, we can uncover an important flaw in his typology.[10]

To begin with, Weber considered the orders of government officials to be designed rationally to achieve specific goals, something we can see, say, in the orders of a police officer directing motorists so as to speed the flow of traffic. Thus, he viewed legal authority as significantly rational. Indeed, he saw the same rationality as infusing bureaucracies of all sorts, both public and private. As he wrote, "Experience tends to show that the purely bureaucratic type of administrative organization . . . is . . . capable of attaining the highest degree of efficiency and is in this sense formally the most rational known means of exercising authority over human beings" (Weber 1978:223). But he went on to identify the source of **bureaucracy**'s rationality as flowing out of something quite different from the "belief in the legality of enacted rules" that he used above as the "rational grounds" for legitimating legal authority. As Weber wrote, "Bureaucratic administration means fundamentally domination through knowledge. This is the feature which makes it specifically rational. This consists . . . in technical knowledge which, by itself, is sufficient to ensure it a position of extraordinary power" (Weber 1978:225).

Clearly, however, domination through superior knowledge has a legitimacy rather different from domination through "the legality of enacted rules." How can we show this? Consider: the motives that cause us to follow a doctor's orders (domination through knowledge) are different from those that cause us to obey laws that have been properly enacted. The latter we may obey even when we perhaps disagree with their aims or consequences, but we would never follow a doctor's orders if we believed they were mistaken. In the doctor's case, we submit to someone we presume knows better than we do (and wouldn't submit if we didn't presume this), while in the case of the law, we respect a process for being formally correct, even when it produces orders we believe substantively mistaken (consider, for instance, why military personnel fight even those wars they disagree with). Thus, the grounds of the two sorts of legitimacy must be different, and, as Weber has already indicated, this means we are dealing with different forms of authority.[11]

The development of Weber's argument here, which starts by explaining rational authority as "the legality of enacted rules" to which we submit and ends by finding it a form of "domination through knowledge," evidently involves a conflation (or mixing together) of two sorts of authority— *bureaucratic* on the one hand and *professional* on the other—that have distinctly different grounds. This means that instead of there being just three forms of authority (rational, traditional, and charismatic), there must be at least four (bureaucratic, professional, traditional, and charismatic). In other words, we have to split Weber's rational authority into bureaucratic on the one hand and professional on the other. I will proceed as if Weber accepted our evaluation and revision of his analysis.

We now have four forms of authority:

- *Bureaucratic*: the authority of office. We obey a person because he or she occupies an office legitimately granted the right to direct our behavior. For instance, we obey a police officer because the police are assigned by our political system the task of enforcing laws.
- *Professional*: the authority of expertise. We obey a person because he or she possesses knowledge or practical experience superior to ours. For instance, we obey a tow truck operator who tells us to take the car out of gear before towing it to the shop.
- *Traditional*: the authority of custom or precedent. We obey someone because he or she occupies a role customarily designated to have this authority or because that person has always had it. For instance, we often obey our parents out of custom.
- *Charismatic*: the authority of (what appear to be) mysterious powers. We obey someone because he or she has given prior evidence of being able to "walk on water" by means we do not understand.

Can you come up with further types? To prove the merits of the typology enumerated above, you need to take case after concrete case where people are willingly controlled by others and see whether each fits nicely into one of these four categories. If they all do, perhaps we have a good analytic typology here. If not, you can suggest an additional category and perhaps make a name for yourself as a sociologist. But to test the typology, you'll need to understand the forms of authority better, so we need to explore in greater detail the grounds or motives for submission to each of them.

The Grounds of Bureaucratic Authority

This authority attaches to offices and only through these offices to their occupants. We obey because the office has been granted authority according to a set of procedures (or other rationales) that are themselves legitimate. When this is the case, we may obey officeholders even when we believe their orders are substantively mistaken or misguided. This happens with some frequency in military organizations and on jobs.

Procedures like elections may be viewed as legitimate mechanisms for assigning specific people to offices, but so might be hereditary succession, as in monarchies. In addition to these sorts of legitimate procedures, there are rationales that give offices legitimacy. In organizations, for instance, someone often has to have the authority to make a decision that everyone else will follow, even if they believe it is the wrong one, if group paralysis is to be avoided. This problem occurs when a military unit must take one route or another when on patrol. Imagine that half the soldiers prefer one route and half the other, but the group must nevertheless stay together. In this circumstance, someone must be vested with the authority to make the decision. Hence, we have officers with the right to command.

Again, Weber points out that this kind of authority does not attach to specific people but to the positions or offices they hold. The specific person who makes the decision doesn't get to do so because he or she knows best (this would be an example of professional authority) but because he or she occupies the office that has been given the authority, in the overall design of the organization, to make the decision. We obey even when we believe the decision he or she makes is the wrong one, and we do so because the alternative threatens the breakdown of the organization of which we are a part.

The Grounds of Professional Authority

We often grant people the right to make decisions for us when they have expertise we lack, that is, when they have knowledge or capabilities superior to ours. We call such authority **professional** in the sense of "trained," "skilled," or "expert," words that are synonyms. We defer to professional authority because people who have it know what to do in situations where we do not. In principle, professional authority should always be justifiable in terms of the demonstrably superior outcomes that result from following its bearer's advice (or orders). If I have a problem with my computer software, for instance, I call my university's helpline. If the Help Desk people say, "Now click on Options, Attachments, then BinHex encoding," I do it. I believe following their orders will improve my interaction with my software much better than any efforts I might devise on my own. If my obedience didn't pay off in this way, I wouldn't call the helpline in the first place. Of course, I might occasionally get bad advice from the people there, but I take this in stride because their overall performance has been good.[12]

Obedience to professional authority makes sense because we assume that, had we the time and inclination, we could always acquire the requisite expertise and then direct our affairs ourselves. Were we to do so, we'd issue ourselves the same orders that professional authorities give us. In a sense, they simply help us out by acquiring knowledge that we don't have the time or inclination to acquire ourselves, although, in principle, we could always do so. Thus, we pay them to develop capabilities we lack so that they can act as agents for us.

The Grounds of Traditional Authority

Traditional authority, or the authority of precedent, is somewhat hard for us to understand today because we live in a society that doesn't much honor traditions. Nevertheless, precedent or tradition—which increase with the length of time some particular person (or category of persons) has directed our behavior (or that of people in our category)—can make this type of authority not just "right" but somehow almost sacred, as Weber has already noted. Just why this happens is something of a mystery that I invite you to ponder and perhaps theorize about. As you do so, be aware that if we equate tradition with the "tried and true," we've slipped over into the domain of professional authority: the "tried and true" is a form of knowledge that is privileged because it demonstrably works.

It isn't easy to find examples of traditional authority today, but consider societies in which parents choose mates for their children (the institution of arranged marriage). This is a good example of an exercise of authority that people come to honor. In fact, it can become so ingrained in a society that people who challenge it are seen as revolutionaries assaulting a society's foundations. In part because family units in previous centuries were much more important as economic institutions, children understood that their marriages were instruments for bettering the economic position of their families, but, by and large, they simply accepted the right of their parents to choose for them because this was the way things had always been done. This is thus an interesting case of traditional authority. Once again, you should be alert that if we view parents as *better able* to pick good mates for their children than are the children themselves, that is, if parents have expertise at choosing mates, we would consider this an example of professional authority. The sole motive for respecting traditional authority is the sense that the tradition of doing so is right (and occasionally sacred).

Traditional authority used to be much more widespread than it is today, being exerted by hereditary chiefs and rulers and by their designated representatives in small-scale societies and premodern states. Weber offered numerous historical examples of patrimonial or patriarchal offices or roles that relied primarily on traditional authority. In contrast to bureaucratic authority, obedience is owed to the person occupying such an office or role, and apart from being bound by tradition, this person may exercise his or her authority arbitrarily. As Peter Blau and Marshall Meyer write,

> There is no demand for consistent application and administration of rules. Clearly defined spheres of official authority; stable relationships of super- and subordination; appointment and promotion on the basis of merit, expertise, and fixed salaries—all of which are characteristic of bureaucratic administration—tend to be absent where traditional standards prevail. (1987:66)

As we shall see in a moment, the shrinkage of traditional authority is an aspect of the historical changes that Weber sought to describe and explain.

The Grounds of Charismatic Authority

We discussed charisma briefly in the last chapter in association with Joseph Smith's inauguration of Mormon polygamy. It is the hardest form of authority to comprehend. The word *charisma* is Greek and was used to refer to the "gifts," the miraculous powers, given to the Apostles by the Holy Spirit in the Christian New Testament. The Apostles (the first disciples of Christ) wondered how they were possibly to meet Christ's expectation that they convert the world to Christianity. After all, they were mostly just provincial fishermen with no background in evangelism or knowledge of foreign languages. But the Holy Spirit (a personified aspect of the Christian god) gave them the ability to "speak in tongues" (that is, to speak in a language that was universally intelligible),[13] to heal the sick, and the like. These miraculous powers, it was assumed, would allow them to demonstrate the value of Christianity as a religion since it gave them the power to perform miracles. Weber didn't believe in miracles, but he viewed charisma as "a certain quality of individual personality by virtue of which [the person] is considered extraordinary and treated as endowed with supernatural, superhuman, or at least specifically exceptional powers or qualities" (Weber 1978:241). Why are people treated this way? This is a complicated topic, around which a lot of argument swirls among sociologists. The shortest answer is that charisma accrues to people who succeed at doing notable things for reasons that others cannot quite fathom. The mysterious successes of would-be charismatics cause people to see them as infused with gifts for making decisions and taking action. So powerful is this impression that people often respond to charismatics by giving them great control over their lives. More than any other form of authority, charisma radiates influence into all aspects of our existence. Indeed, we may submit to complete personal transformation at the hands of charismatic figures, changing our lives to follow them: Christ, for instance, asked people to "leave all you have and follow me." We will return to this topic later.

You might ask how this form of authority differs from the professional form. The answer is that the knowledge on which professional authority rests can, in principle, be taught to anyone. The charismatic figure, on the other hand, has no communicable skill that legitimates the orders he or she gives. Instead, the gifts that ground the charismatic's orders are ineffable; we just can't explain how charismatic figures *appear* to do what they do.[14] And it's precisely because we can't account for the charismatic's qualities or capabilities that we believe it makes sense to follow his or her orders.

We now understand the grounds for each of our four forms of authority. Note: in arguing that they are mutually exclusive, we are not suggesting that specific people may not employ more than one of them. For instance, parents and military commanders might employ all of them in getting compliance from children or soldiers, respectively. But the motives for this compliance can always be apportioned unambiguously to one or another of authority's grounds. You will normally have no trouble concluding, for instance, that your professors are exercising professional rather than charismatic authority over you, though you'll sometimes find yourself submitting to them for bureaucratic and traditional reasons as well. Which form of authority is involved is something you can determine by asking yourself why you are obeying.

Further, unless you've come up with an additional form of authority, we're left to assume that our list of four is exhaustive, as well as mutually exclusive. I've always found this deeply mysterious. Why are there only four forms of authority (rather than, say, seven)? Might we some day evolve new forms of social organization that would produce a fifth type of authority? If not, have we perhaps discovered something about human nature in the fact that there are only four? That is, could it be that our brains are constructed in such a way that we only find four motives for submission to authority compelling? Will neurologists and sociologists someday team up to identify the brain structures that underlie each of the four forms and indicate why there are no others? If not, what could it possibly be that limits authority to only four types? These questions have gnawed at me for years.

One benefit of an exhaustive typology, nevertheless, is that it allows for a complete tree diagram such as that sketched in figure 5.2. As I indicated above, though analytic typologies can be created just for the fun of it, sociologists expect a payoff from them. Typologies of power and authority indicate to us the means by which people can be organized into groups so as to act in concert. Weber's point, however, was not simply to catalog or classify these means but to alert us to important variations among them. Being subject to charismatic authority is quite different from being subject to bureaucratic authority, for instance, and we cannot hope to explain the authority structures they produce, as well as the behavior that results from them, without understanding these differences.[15] We can also note that the evolution of human societies from hunting-and-gathering groups to postindustrial societies involves a dramatic change in the composition of authority in general, as bureaucratic and professional forms have grown in importance while traditional and charismatic forms have atrophied. This empirical generalization was very important to Weber's understanding of history. The next sections focus on charismatic and bureaucratic forms of authority as a way of illustrating the dramatic differences among the forms and exploring Weber's general understanding of history. Along the way, I'll introduce Weber's typology of action as a means of further clarifying his view of history.

It is interesting to note that the differences among the forms of authority influence the focus of sociological research interests. Both bureaucratic and professional authority, the "rational" forms, have motivational foundations that are so intuitively clear to us that they haven't attracted much attention.

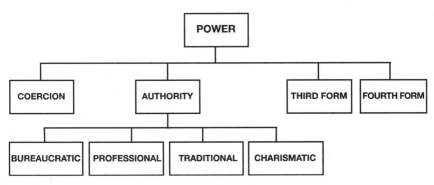

FIGURE 5.2
A Typology of Authority Added to the Typology of Power

Instead, sociologists have focused on studying the organizational milieus in which they exist—bureaucracies and the professions, respectively.[16] By way of contrast, the motivational foundations of charismatic and traditional authority remain much more obscure to us; thus, a good deal of our attention to them has focused on the nature of the authority relation itself and how it develops. Perhaps because it seems so exotic and so dramatic in its consequences, charisma has attracted more attention in this regard than traditional authority, so I will concentrate on it here.

Charismatic Authority and the Sociology of Charisma

As already indicated, authority is one of the prime means by which groups of people are held together and made to act in concert. By its nature, traditional authority causes groups to act in mostly predictable, orthodox ways since the dominant parties are bound to some degree by the very traditions on which their authority rests. Similarly, Weber argued, bureaucratic and professional authorities are constrained by the requirement that their commands be "rational," or at least be legitimated by "intellectually analyzable rules" (1978:244). Thus, the first three types of authority tend generally to be conservative.[17] They also exercise a comparatively narrow span of control over us: professors, for instance, can legitimately order students to do very few things. This is not the case with charisma: "Within the sphere of its claims, charismatic authority repudiates the past, and is in this sense a specifically revolutionary force" (Weber 1978:244). Often, the revolutionary vision of the charismatic leader is one basis for the claim he or she makes upon us: Martin Luther, Vladimir Lenin, and Adolf Hitler all followed Christ's pattern ("It is written, but *I* say unto you . . .") in rejecting the prevailing order and calling upon others to follow. Such calls, furthermore, may require us to refashion our lives completely, leaving our pasts behind to "come and follow" wherever and however the charismatic figure leads, even if it be to our doom, as with the Heaven's Gate cult or the People's Temple.[18] Thus, the scope of control that charismatic figures possess over their subordinates is normally much broader than that of other authorities.

These features of charismatic authority help us understand how gruesome incidents like Jonestown and Heaven's Gate can occur, while its revolutionary aspect helps us better see why Weber, unlike Karl Marx, dispensed with formulating theories to explain historical patterns of development. The new social worlds that charismatic leaders envision for us are unpredictable in their own right (as were the specific theological innovations Luther devised), and they are apt to have unforeseen consequences when adopted by followers. This means that history can occasionally take unanticipated paths—paths that it does not make sense to theorize about—as charismatically organized social movements redirect it.

This also means that charisma is both very interesting and very difficult to explain. In the years since Weber first discussed it, charisma has been written about frequently without this leading to any consensus among social scientists as to its nature or the processes by which it is acquired. In fact, there is deep division on both of these fronts, with some (e.g., Shils 1965) seeing it as a pervasive feature of modern institutional life and others (e.g., Friedrich 1961) viewing it as quite narrowly confined to explicitly religious contexts. Psychoanalysis (Camic 1980; Smith 1992), political science (Madsen and Snow 1991), psychology, and sociology have all been called upon to analyze it, without any field's making enough progress to claim success. Indeed, it has been suggested that falling under the sway of a charismatic authority is like falling in love (Lindholm 1990, Smith 1992), a process that social scientists don't understand very well.

We will not spend time exploring the general disarray with regard to charisma. Despite it, certain generalizations can be drawn from the literature:

1. Large numbers of people submit themselves to a charismatic authority only when other forms (bureaucratic, professional, or traditional) are perceived as ineffective in meeting widely felt needs.
2. Charismatic leaders "engage in exemplary acts that followers perceive as involving great personal risk, cost, and energy. . . . [These acts] must be novel, unconventional, and out of the ordinary" and used to underwrite a "vision that is highly discrepant from the status quo" (Conger and Kanungo 1987:642–43).
3. "The charismatic leader gains and maintains authority solely by proving his strength in life. . . . Above all . . . his divine mission must 'prove' itself in that those who faithfully surrender to him must fare well. If they do not fare well, he is obviously not the master sent by the gods" (Weber 1958b, 249).
4. "A charismatic leader must be a plausible vessel for divine grace: but the very content of 'plausibility' is itself culturally determined. It may be more than average endowment of energy, determination, fanaticism, and perhaps intelligence. Or it may be an altogether different set of attributes—epilepsy, strangeness, what we should regard as a mental disorder, or, particularly where children are regarded as prophets, even sheer innocence" (Wilson 1975:29).

In other words, the criteria for being deemed charismatic vary somewhat from one culture to another, although successful risk taking seems everywhere fundamental to the phenomenon, which persists only as long as successes continue and acquires broad sway only when other forms of authority are deemed wanting.[19]

Charismatic authority is relatively rare in national politics today, in part because it is potentially destructive to existing political organizations and in part because it finds scope only where other forms of authority are perceived as having failed. In other words, people only begin to look to risk takers for leadership when other forms of authority seem incapable of effectively organizing communal life. (This makes perfect sense in view of the fundamentally conservative nature of the other forms of authority: when the "old ways" of doing things seem ineffective, less predictable and perhaps revolutionary forms may become more appealing.) We can also turn this principle around in an interesting way: people may seek charismatic authority when other avenues to domination are closed to them. This may partly explain why young people often expose themselves to risk, say, in games of "chicken," in circumstances that adults find foolish and troubling. After all, young people have fewer avenues to domination available to them than do adults, yet have no less reason to find dominating others attractive. Thus, they may seek charismatic authority through taking risks, often at great hazard to life and limb.

At the same time, the significant differences of opinion among sociologists over the nature of the phenomenon and its sources suggest that we are still quite far from developing a theory to explain charisma. Indeed, it may be that we never will develop such a theory since the risk taking involved makes charismatic careers too chancy and contingent to be explained theoretically. If that is so, we'll at best be able to develop good causal narratives to explain the successes of individual charismatic leaders, something that would be worthwhile in its own right.

Bureaucratic Authority and the Sociology of Bureaucracies

With some understanding of charisma established, we must look to bureaucratic authority and bureaucracy to understand better Weber's view of historical change. If charismatic authority is mysterious, bureaucratic authority is just the opposite.[20] In fact, it is so reasonable that sociological attention has focused less on sources of the authority relation itself, as with charisma, than on the organizational context in which it occurs: bureaucracies. This form of organization, so pervasive today, was comparatively rare only several hundred years ago. Why?

Weber's answer to this question has two parts. The first involves an analysis of bureaucracies and the conditions that favored their formation. (This answer has since been supplemented in interesting ways, which we will attend to.) The second involves an overall view of history as influenced by **rationalization**, a phenomenon to which the spread of bureaucracies has contributed, as have such cultural developments as the scientific revolution. While Weber's view of rationalization is largely evolutionary, it retains a place for countervailing factors, often introduced by charismatic leaders, that complicate the picture and underline the differences between Marx and Weber. We will look first at Weber's analysis of bureaucracy and then at the process of rationalization. One component of the latter is an analytic typology of the forms of social action, which we will use as a second instance of typologizing. We will then return to Weber's view of history.

What Is a Bureaucracy?

Where I went to college, Weber's analysis of bureaucracy was required reading for all students, and I should confess that it put most of us to sleep, me included. In part, this was because Weber is dry to read, especially for people who don't have his grasp of the history of social institutions. But it was also because the phenomenon of bureaucracy seems on its surface uninteresting: unlike charisma, it's almost entirely without glamour. Eventually, however, I realized that the study of organizations, of which bureaucracies are today the most important form, is at the very center of sociology, and I came to regret that I'd never formally studied them. The literature on them is by now one of the most developed and most interesting in sociology, and as I'll try to show, even the sociological topics that are most engaging for students, such as popular culture, cannot be understood without some grasp of bureaucracy. Weber is still the place to start.

Since bureaucratic authority attaches first to positions (offices) and only through them to people, it can only exist in and through organizations. Weber defined a bureaucracy in terms of an **ideal type** that outlined its most characteristic features.[21] We can summarize these features as follows (from Weber 1978:220–21, 956–58):

1. The regular activities of a bureaucracy are divided into areas over which specific offices are given jurisdiction.
2. These offices are arranged in a hierarchy, with lower offices reporting to higher ones.
3. The orders and activities of offices are issued in, or committed to, writing and stored in files that may be subsequently consulted.

4. Officials do not own their positions (or the revenues that derive from them) but are salaried.
5. Performance in office "usually presupposes thorough training in a field of specialization" (Weber 1978:958), specialized knowledge of the organization itself, or both. Officeholders are selected and evaluated on the basis of training and performance and pursue advancement as a career.
6. The duties of office consume the full energies of the official (as opposed to being part-time or casual jobs). At the same time, officials are involved "only with respect to their official obligations" (Weber 1978:220) rather than their whole being (in, say, its religious or sexual aspects).
7. Recurrent operations are directed by rules of procedure so that they become routine.

While we might quibble with some elements of this definition,[22] it certainly includes various features of bureaucracies with which we are all familiar. Having characterized bureaucracies in this fashion, Weber turned quickly to what he called their **presuppositions**. I want to focus on one of these because of the importance of presuppositions (sometimes called **preconditions**) to theorizing in general, as well as to understanding Weber's analysis of bureaucracy.

Weber wrote that the spread of bureaucracy as a form of organization (and, thus, the spread of bureaucratic authority) presupposed a money economy (as opposed to an economy where people barter, are paid in goods, or both). As he made quite clear, this did not mean that no bureaucracies could be organized without money—he pointed to the government of ancient Egypt as an example—but instead that they are hard to form and comparatively unstable in its absence.[23] Why? Because it is exceedingly difficult to pay people regularly and consistently in kind (that is, in goods rather than in money). To avoid the difficulties of payment in kind, heads of bureaucracies may find it easier to allow officials to generate their own incomes by means of their offices. For instance, if a government needs judges (who must normally be paid), it might be easier to allow them to charge plaintiffs in kind per case than it would be to deliver goods to them regularly from a central storehouse. Yet, as soon as officials collect their pay themselves, those above them lose an important means to control or discipline them. Discussing government bureaucracies, Weber put the matter this way (and I quote him at length to give you a sense of how he reads in English translation):

> Without a money economy, the bureaucratic structure can hardly avoid undergoing substantial internal changes, or indeed transformation into another

structure. The allocation of fixed income in kind from the magazines of the lord or from his current intake—which has been the rule in Egypt and China for millennia and played an important part in the later Roman monarchy as well as elsewhere—easily means a first step toward appropriation of the sources of taxation by the official and their exploitation as private property. Income in kind has protected the official against the often sharp fluctuations in the purchasing power of money. But whenever the lord's power subsides, payments in kind, which are based on taxes in kind, tend to become irregular. In this case, the official will have direct recourse to the tributaries of his bailiwick, whether or not he is authorized. (Weber 1978:964)

The result of officials generating their own pay is that they become increasingly independent of those above them, and as their independence grows, the bureaucratic structure of authority weakens to the point where it can cease to exist. Yet, the specifics of this case are less important than the theoretical point behind addressing bureaucracy's presuppositions.

Note that Weber does not argue that a monetary economy causes bureaucracies to form. Bureaucracies are formed by specific individuals with specific purposes in mind—not by the pervasiveness of money. Yet, easy access to money profoundly facilitates their formation and maintenance, and Weber gives us a very specific and practical reason why this is so: it allows those in charge to retain their authority. Another way of putting this is to say that the empirical generalization "the more monetized an economy, the more bureaucracies" does not identify a causal connection between the two variables. Not only is money not a sufficient condition for bureaucracy (in which case it would be a cause), but it is not even a necessary condition.[24] This doesn't mean, however, it isn't important since it's only in relatively rare circumstances that we get bureaucracies in the absence of money.

A good deal of sociological explanation involves outlining presuppositions (or preconditions) in this way. We're interested not just in understanding the causal connections between independent and dependent variables, but in describing the circumstances that facilitate or impede the occurrence of our variables. If we think back to earlier discussions, we can note how presuppositions have already been at work in our analysis. For instance, in *Culture of Honor* (1996), Richard Nisbett and Dov Cohen argue that herding economies are apt to create the circumstances in which a readiness to resort to violence is functional and often gets dressed up culturally in codes of honor. In their case, herding stood to honor rather as money stands to bureaucracy for Weber. Neither of the former phenomena (herding or money) is necessary or sufficient to produce the latter (honor or bureaucracy), but each normally generates circumstances where the latter becomes much more likely. This sort of knowledge makes our theories or explanations much richer and more useful.

Because this point is so important, I want to make it again by means of an analogy. As I look out the window of my study right now, I can see cypress trees and cattails growing at the waterline of a small lake. Somewhat back from the waterline are oak trees. The positioning of the cypresses and cattails in relation to the oaks is not coincidental. Both of the former thrive in or near water, in circumstances where oaks would likely die. Let's call information of this sort *ecological*. Ecological knowledge concerns the conditions in which particular species thrive, do poorly, or fail to occur at all, as well as the relations among species. In terms of this analogy, when Weber discusses the presuppositions of bureaucracies, he is really establishing their social ecology—an understanding of the social and material circumstances in which they either thrive or fail to prosper. Once again, this is not knowledge of the causes of bureaucracy, just as the waterline is not a cause of the cypresses and cattails, but it makes the world much more predictable, which is an important goal of explanations.

As we will see in a moment, sociology has developed a much more abstract and detailed understanding of the social ecology of bureaucracy since Weber's time. But have we nothing to say about its causes? Not directly. Weber's analysis of bureaucracy is, appropriately, functional and evolutionary. As we've seen in discussing sacred cows, functional theories can explain why phenomena persist or spread, but they cannot deal with their initial causes. Weber argues that bureaucracies are a superior means of accomplishing certain collective activities:

> Experience tends universally to show that the purely bureaucratic type of administrative organization . . . is, from a purely technical point of view, capable of attaining the highest degree of efficiency and is in this sense formally the most rational known means of exercising authority over human beings. It is superior to any other form in precision, in stability, in the stringency of its discipline, and in its reliability. It thus makes possible a particularly high degree of calculability of results for the heads of the organization and for those acting in relation to it. (Weber 1978:223)

The efficiency and reliability of bureaucracies means that, where they come into existence, they will outperform and, thus, tend to displace other means of organizing collective activities.[25] They are, in this regard, similar to any other useful technological innovation or adaptively advantageous biological mutation. But, of course, their superiority does not help us understand how they came about, any more than the advantages of a particular mutation help us understand how and why it occurred. This doesn't amount to a fault in

Weber's analysis, however; instead, it suggests that the origins of particular bureaucracies are subjects for descriptive or causal narratives and not for theories proper.

As I've indicated, the study of bureaucracies is one of the richest and most developed areas in sociology today. In a sense, this topic has come to resemble the field of population biology, not least because bureaucracies are constantly being born, maturing, and, for the most part, dying off (as individual commercial companies come and go, say). And we've come to understand much better how they behave. Often, for instance, we find that the informal aspects of bureaucracies are more important to their efficient functioning than are the formal aspects that Weber stressed (see Blau and Meyer 1987). Out of this very rich literature, I have time here to emphasize only one advance in our understanding of the social ecology of bureaucracies.

The Social Ecology of Bureaucracies

Where do bureaucracies thrive? An interesting answer to this was provided by sociologist Arthur Stinchcombe (1959) in a seminal essay early in his career.[26] He began by noting that firms in the construction industry seemed to have fewer levels of hierarchy and fewer clerical staff devoted to keeping records—the second and third features of Weber's definition of bureaucracy—than did firms in other industries. Additionally, the lowest level of workers in the construction industry had a good deal more discretion in performing their jobs than did workers in mass production industries, such as automobile manufacturing. Stinchcombe focused on tract housing, where carpenters, for instance, have much more control over the sequencing of their labor in framing a house than do auto workers on an assembly line.

Another way to put this is to say that the hierarchy in construction firms is flatter than in mass production firms (which rise like a pyramid above the lowest level workers) and that the work of the lowest-level employees is more "professional" in that it requires high skill levels and allows considerable discretion. This pattern of a comparatively flat structure and a skilled workforce Stinchcombe designated *craft administration* of production in contrast to bureaucratic administration. Another way of characterizing this contrast is to say that the rules of procedure that regulate recurrent operations in bureaucracies (Weber's seventh defining quality) are only minimally developed in craft administration since so much is left to the discretion of the workers, who are normally organized in function-specific teams (plumbers, electricians, carpenters, and so on) led by subcontractors who report to a contractor. In contrast, the work routines of mass production workers are often planned beforehand in great detail by the central staffs.

Let us stop for a moment here to be clear about Stinchcombe's approach. As we would anticipate, he alerts us to an important aspect of variation among organizations involved in production. Some of these (the mass producers) are more bureaucratic than others (such as the construction firms), which is to say that some more closely approximate Weber's ideal type than others. The question is, why? Stinchcombe's answer is relatively simple: he writes, "The variability of the construction industry, its intimate dependence on variations in local markets, makes the development of bureaucracy uneconomical" (Grusky and Miller 1970:266). Thus, variability is the key ecological factor promoting variation in organizational character. Not only is construction work to some degree seasonal (because it is affected by the weather), but its volume can vary significantly from year to year. These effects are often magnified by the necessarily local nature of construction. The result is considerable variation in work flow, and this makes the growth of clerical positions in administration uneconomical: they represent large overhead costs when business is slow. Indeed, at the extreme, not only are clerical positions kept to the minimum in construction, but the whole organization that is assembled for a particular project may be disbanded as soon as it is finished, perhaps to be reformed (though often with different personnel) for the next project. This impermanence contrasts strongly with bureaucracies, which tend to be relatively stable across time.

If we want to generalize this argument, we can say that bureaucracies thrive where the demand for their products is relatively high and stable and where the products themselves can be made in routine ways that do not call for much worker skill or discretion. (Incidentally, this is also the classic recipe for worker alienation!) Mass production can take place only in these circumstances. On the other hand, where demand fluctuates significantly, where consumers seek individualized products (such as architect-designed houses), or where production cannot easily be standardized, bureaucracies cede place to professional or craft organizations (just as cypresses do to oak trees as we leave the lakeshore). Figure 5.3 depicts the relation among the variables graphically.

Once again, this argument, which explains variation between craft and bureaucratic organizational forms, will at first seem dry as dust. But it has very interesting applications. It explains, for instance, why it is so different to work at MacDonald's as compared to a gourmet restaurant (see Fine 1992). MacDonald's (and other fast food restaurants) succeed because many consumers are happy with highly standardized products and are willing to purchase a great deal of them. Gourmet restaurants succeed because other consumers demand varied and changing menus and often ask for adjustments to individual dishes to accommodate their tastes. MacDonald's

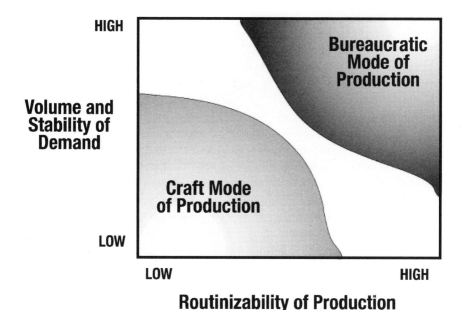

Routinizability of Production

FIGURE 5.3
The Social Ecology of Bureaucracy

employs an unskilled workforce in highly repetitive (and, therefore, potentially alienating) tasks, while gourmet restaurants employ highly skilled artisans (chefs with long professional training) and place a premium on their
creativity. Thus, these forms of organization look and behave very differently,
and they do so because they inhabit different regions of our social ecology.

The same argument can explain why movies, which used to be produced
in high volumes on the back lots of Hollywood studios, with actors, directors,
and production crews all on long-term contracts, are now mostly one-of-a-
kind products, often created by teams that are brought together for the single
effort and disbanded immediately afterward. In other words, the production
of movies has switched from a comparatively bureaucratic to a distinctly craft
mode of production. Why? Back when everyone went to the movies and
didn't care much what they saw (say, from 1920 to 1950), studios could be
more bureaucratized because demand for their products was high and uniform (see Crane 1992:51–55). The introduction of television changed the
demand for movies by reducing the size of the audience and increasing its
selectivity. With visual entertainment readily available in their homes,
would-be moviegoers had to be lured to the theater by better and more

expensive productions, which could not easily be made in rapid succession on sound stages or back lots. Further, consumer tastes, once they came into play, turned out to be relatively unpredictable. Some expensive movies won audiences while others didn't. This increased variability in demand was instrumental in moving the bureaucratic studios of old in the direction of today's craft production.

Thus, as I suggested earlier, understanding the social ecology of bureaucracy and other organizational forms, though it may seem the driest of subjects, can help us understand not just differences between how cars and houses are produced, but the nature of today's popular culture and how it gets produced, a topic much nearer to the concerns of the average student. In fact, sociologists have spent a good deal of time studying and explaining trends in popular music using theories that are adjuncts to Stinchcombe's (e.g., Peterson 1997). Once students encounter these fascinating studies, they develop a new appreciation for the social ecology of bureaucracy and understand the relevance of this apparently driest of subjects.

Rationalization and Historical Change

By this roundabout route, we've prepared ourselves to discuss Weber's second analytic typology and his overall view of social change across history. To proceed here, we need to understand better what Weber meant by rationality and rationalization. One of Stinchcombe's main points is that craft production is just as rational as bureaucratic production: in fact, it's a functionally superior organizational response to high variability in demand, a condition where bureaucracies function poorly. Thus, Stinchcombe's argument fleshes out the evolutionary and functionalist explanation Weber developed for the spread of bureaucracy by specifying important variables in its social ecology and showing how they affect organizational form.

People develop varied organizational forms to more efficiently exploit particular social ecological niches because they are motivated to economize, to get the most out of their effort. Doing so requires that they imagine an array of possibilities and then select the most efficient among them, perhaps through trial and error. In fact, each of us engages in this sort of behavior every day, for instance, when we plan the most economical route to several different places where we need to shop. Recall that in the first chapter, I noted that one way of explaining people's behavior is to look at their motives, and economizing of this sort turns out to be a motive that everybody immediately understands. When people are selecting the most efficient means to achieve some end, we don't ask, for instance, why they prefer more efficient to less efficient ones, and this is because their preferences seem so obvious to us all. Here we have one reason why efficient organizational forms like bureaucracies tend to spread: once people realize their usefulness, they get copied. Weber believed that to explain human behavior you really had to understand people's motives (as we've seen in discussing *verstehen*), and so he naturally wondered whether such motives could usefully be sorted into types. Let's see how he proceeded.

The Types of Social Action

Weber began his analysis by distinguishing social action from **individual action** and merely reactive behavior:

> We shall speak of "action" insofar as the acting individual attaches a subjective meaning to his behavior—be it overt or covert, omission or acquiescence. Action is "social" insofar as its subjective meaning takes account of the behavior of others and is thereby oriented in its course. (Weber 1978:4)

"Subjective meaning" means roughly the same thing as motive. Behavior that isn't consciously motivated at all, such as purely reflex behavior (e.g., jerking your hand back from a hot surface), doesn't qualify as action. Similarly, we need to distinguish social action from individual action (e.g., humming while you work alone). Thus, we get the analysis of behavior pictured in figure 5.4.

As soon as Weber made these distinctions, however, he spotted a problem with them in relation to our criteria for a good analytic typology. As he suggested,

> The line between meaningful action and merely reactive behavior . . . cannot be sharply drawn empirically. A very considerable part of all sociologically relevant behavior, especially purely traditional behavior, is marginal between the two. (Weber 1978:4–5)

FIGURE 5.4
A Typology of Forms of Behavior

In other words, there are occasions when people unthinkingly behave in customary ways (for instance, in automatically extending their hand to shake another's), and in these circumstances, it will not be clear whether the behavior is better seen as social action or as reactive behavior.[27] This means that we will occasionally have trouble sorting behavior among the categories of the typology.

Weber discussed this and other problems at length before turning to discuss social action, which is the appropriate subject matter of sociology. He pointed out,

> Not every type of contact of human beings has a social character; this is rather confined to cases where the actor's behavior is meaningfully oriented to that of others. For example, a mere collision of two cyclists may be compared to a natural event. On the other hand, their attempt to avoid hitting each other, or whatever insults, blows, or friendly discussion might follow the collision, would constitute "social action." (Weber 1978:23)

With this established, he proceeded to analyze social action, finding it divisible into four types (or categories of motivation) as represented in figure 5.5.

Affective action is simply another name for emotionally motivated behavior, as when we are driven by anger or pity to act in particular ways. (Like traditional action, this type is, on occasion, difficult to distinguish from reactive behavior.) **Traditional action** follows custom. As with driving on the right, which we discussed in the first chapter, people are often unable to give any reason for the details of such behavior (why the right rather than the left, for instance), though they know that what they are doing is socially expected of them. In this regard, traditional action is the social equivalent of a personal habit. **Instrumentally rational** (in German, *zweckrational*) **action** selects the most efficient among alternative means to the same end. It is motivated by a desire to economize, gain, or otherwise come out on top—and as we've just

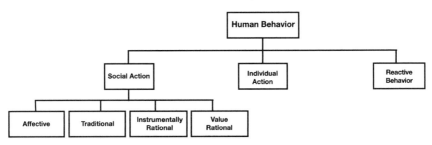

FIGURE 5.5
A Typology of Social Action Added to the Typology of Forms of Behavior

indicated, it's very easy to understand. **Value rational** (*wertrational*) **action,** in contrast, is perceived to be worthwhile in itself, either because it is morally or aesthetically preferable or because it is intrinsically rewarding. Strict pacifists, for instance, believe they must refuse combat duty regardless of the consequences to themselves or the society they live in. They have made nonviolence a superordinate goal. Somewhat similarly, one may play a game of racquetball because it is pleasurable in itself and be unconcerned with whether one gains anything as a result. Sometimes we find value rational action easy to understand (especially when it embodies our own preferences or prejudices), and sometimes we don't: I already indicated how hard it may be for us to understand why some people find pleasure in torturing animals, for instance.[28]

Let us continue with this theme. One way to familiarize yourself with Weber's typology is to see how people's motives vary in intelligibility across its categories. We've already seen that instrumentally rational action is immediately intelligible: in fact, it is so intelligible that we have trouble wondering about it. (For instance, we just don't ask people questions like, why are you buying that item on sale when you could pay full price for it?) This means there's not much call to explicate instrumentally rational action. Similarly, most affective behavior is immediately intelligible: we know why people become angry or offended when they are insulted (because this is just how we would react ourselves). When this isn't true, we worry that people are sick: inexplicably angry people may have brain tumors that cause their behavior, for instance, while people who are sexually excited by objects that leave us cold, such as shoes, are called *fetishists* and are considered to have a problem. Thus, unintelligible affective behavior could be a sign that something's wrong and in need of explanation (normally in nonsociological terms). By contrast, traditional behavior is never intelligible in its specifics because people never have reasons (motives) for traditional behavior. (We don't ask, why do you drive on the right rather than the left? because, apart from the instrumental aspect of avoiding collisions, nobody knows!) Thus, with traditional action, we can simply call off the search for motives since it won't lead us anywhere. It's enough to know that the action is conventional in the society in question.[29]

This leaves us with value rational action, and it's here that, much of the time, explication (and *verstehen*) really comes into play. To put this differently, we expect people to be able to defend the values that motivate their action, which is to say, to explicate its subjective meaning for us, and it is such arguments or explications that cause us to see their action as rational (*wertrational*), which here doesn't mean an efficient means to an end (*zweckrational*) but a well-reasoned end itself. Explication tells us why the actor believes a particular line of action is to be preferred morally or aesthetically (and independently of its instrumental value, should it have any). All of us are reasonably adept at making arguments and explications of this sort, but theologians and political or moral philosophers make a specialty of it, trying to develop particularly strong reasons for given lines of action, while a significant part of cultural anthropology is concerned with investigating the meaning of courses of action that initially seem peculiar to us because we aren't familiar with the ways of life in relation to which they make sense. A good deal of this goes on in sociology as well, as we've seen in dealing with a culture of honor.

Thus, just as the forms of authority each have a different ground or grounds, each form of social action has a different motivational basis and invites a different sort of investigation. This is useful to know.[30] But let's now see how the typology can help us understand Weber's view of rationalization. I've already remarked that traditional authority is no longer particularly important in modern societies, and a parallel argument would be that traditional action has slowly given way to *zweckrational* and *wertrational* action. (I think we can assume that the amount of affective social action remains relatively constant, although it is interesting to ponder whether the rise of ideologies of romantic love has perhaps marginally increased the portion in this category at the expense of *zweckrational* action, as when parents chose "profitable" mates for their children.)

Weber's own orientation to this development was exceedingly complex and interesting. One aspect of it involved a vision of the world as becoming gradually disenchanted, stripped of its old magical properties, with individuals increasingly being imprisoned in an "iron cage" of rationality. About this development Weber was ambivalent. A second aspect involved the limits of instrumentally rational action and its complex relation to value rational action, particularly when expressed in charismatic social movements. About these matters Weber was pessimistic. Let us take these aspects up in turn.

The explosion of technology associated with the scientific and industrial revolutions (and carried forward by the capitalist quest for new markets and manufacturing innovations) has made our lives vastly more predictable than in the past. Consider only a casual sample of ways this is true: modern sanitation and medicine now allow young people to plan for quite distant futures in relative security that they will live to enjoy them; market research reduces the risk to entrepreneurs of introducing new products; weather forecasting and monitoring allow us to predict hurricanes and floods; and the fascinating institution of insurance offers to compensate us (or our families) whenever we can't escape disasters. Our ability to avoid or diminish the downside of risk derives from our increased knowledge, and this separates us in a very fundamental way from earlier generations, who had to rely on religion or magic to deal with the downside of fate. Science and technology have success-fully displaced magic and religion in confronting risk because of their demonstrable technical superiority: to prefer modern medicine to older forms of healing is thus (usually) instrumentally rational action.

The spread of such action means that the world is no longer the enchanted place it once was: it has lost mysterious aspects that gave it certain charms.[31] Weber himself was immune to those charms, but that didn't prevent him from recognizing that an excess of instrumental rationality could blight our lives just as easily as an excess of superstition. We see this most dramatically in instruments like nuclear weapons (which may yet spell our doom if they fall into the wrong hands) and the "logic" of the arms race that caused them to become so widespread. And we see it less dramatically, but with greater poignancy, when older people are denied organ transplants (which are reserved for younger people, "rationally," because of the scarcity of organs) or when workers are forced to sacrifice their jobs so that manufacturing facil-ities can relocate, quite rationally, to areas where labor costs are cheaper.[32] Just as Marx saw industrial labor as often alienating, Weber saw the control over our lives exercised by "rational" institutions like labor markets to have similarly frustrating consequences; hence, Weber's image of an iron cage of rationality that imprisons us. This was accompanied, he believed, by a cul-tural flattening or loss of color:

> The fate of our times is characterized by rationalization and intellectualization and, above all, by the "disenchantment of the world." Precisely the ultimate and most sublime values have retreated from public life either into the tran-scendental realm of mystic life or into the brotherliness of direct and personal human relations. It is not accidental that our greatest art is intimate and not monumental. (Weber 1958b:155)

The comparatively low risk world that instrumental rationality had produced discouraged the very heroism that monumental art celebrated. Increasingly, great sacrifice was reserved for marginal people drawn to dubious prophets (like Jim Jones or David Koresh[33]) and not for our central social and cultural enterprises.[34] The storied battles of old seemed doomed to be supplanted by the hideous brutality of trench warfare, which made World War I such a human catastrophe.

Thus, while Weber profoundly respected the advance of science and the mastery over nature it afforded us and felt that disenchanting the world was a crowning human achievement, he also believed that it necessarily ate away at the "sublime values" expressed in the past. He was ambivalent about ratio-nalization, then, however inevitable it might be. At the same time, his analysis of the differences between instrumentally rational and value rational action caused him to see limits to the former, limits that might cause rationalization occasionally and unpredictably to be reversed. In particular, new forms of value rational action could be introduced by charismatic leaders (and the social movements they led) to challenge instrumentally rational action.

This prospect does not need to be underscored today, when extreme religious movements sanction terrorist attacks against the most effectively rationalized polities in the world. Indeed, the frequency with which powerful utopian visions (from Hitler's Third Reich to Pol Pot's Kampuchea) have over the last century been used to warrant genocide may be taken as an index of certain limits to rationalization.[35] As Weber suggested, the spheres of instrumentally rational and value rational action are entirely independent of one another since neither science nor economics has anything to say about the values that make life meaningful. As he wondered,

> Who . . . still believes that the findings of astronomy, biology, physics, or chemistry could teach us anything about the *meaning* of the world? If there is any such "meaning," along what road could one come across its tracks? If these natural sciences lead to anything in this way, they are apt to make the belief that there is such a thing as the "meaning" of the universe die out at its very roots. (Weber 1958b:142)

Neither science nor other forms of instrumentally rational action, he went on to say, can be used to answer the question "What shall we do and how shall we live?" (Weber 1958b, 143). These questions belong to the domain of value rational reasoning, over which theology and moral or political philosophy normally preside. Anyone who studies these disciplines will soon recognize that their arguments do not lead to generalized agreement among people but instead to diverse and contradictory views on how we should live. In Weber's opinion, these contrasting value positions are not reconcilable: any reasonable explication of why we should behave in one way can be countered by a reasonable explication of why we should behave in the opposite way. In concrete terms, "good" arguments can be made for torturing animals (by proponents of bullfighting, say) to counter the equally good arguments for banning the practice. More generally, as Weber argued, "the ultimately possible attitudes toward life are irreconcilable and hence their struggle can never be brought to a final conclusion" (1958b:152).

If we return now to our analysis of authority, we can recognize that one role of charismatic leaders is to introduce new attitudes toward life through their visions for change, providing novel answers to the question, how shall we live? These answers place their followers in conflict with the world around them, organizing them as a social movement for change. It is the leaders' success in surmounting risks, *by means that are inexplicable by science or instrumental rationality*, that underwrites their answers, which need not be beholden to rationalization and, indeed, can just as easily struggle against it, seeking to re-enchant the world, as we see being done by charismatic leaders of fundamentalist movements today. But this means that the process of rationalization is subject to reversal at the hands of particularly successful charismatic leaders and the social movements they organize. Furthermore, we already know from Weber's treatment of leaders like John Calvin and Martin Luther that the occurrence and the particular visions of charismatic leaders are unpredictable and not something we can develop theories about.

Weber's concept of rationalization deserves further scrutiny, but I'll relegate that to appendix 5B. On the basis of the foregoing discussion, we're fully prepared to appreciate Weber's view of history and understand why it departed so radically from Marx's. One side of Weber's view was evolutionary and saw history as characterized by the gradual spread of rationalization as the more efficient inventions of instrumental rationality came to supplant the less efficient. (These developments might be explained by a functional theory, whose general form we will discuss in chapter 7.) Occasionally, charismatic social movements such as the Protestant Reformation may unintentionally give rise to phenomena like capitalism that hasten this process of rationalization (as did the civil rights movement in our recent past).[36] But others, such as Pol Pot's, may seek to turn back time, rejecting industry and its instrumental advantages in favor of an agrarian utopia, while various fundamentalisms seek to make instrumental rationality distinctly subordinate to a religious view of the world. Thus, while instrumental rationalization has a certain appeal, particularly as it generally increases our comforts and protects us from risks, these advantages can unpredictably be countered by a compelling vision of a riskier or less rational social order. While we can sometimes explain these social movements in terms of appropriate preconditions (such as the failure of competing forms of authority), much about them can only be narrated descriptively. Consequently, the course of history must itself be largely unpredictable. No Marxian, classless utopia is its necessary conclusion: indeed, brutal "utopian" visions, such as the Nazi one, can just as easily be foisted on us by charismatic leaders. This left Weber pessimistic about the future.[37]

Stratification and Conflict

These reflections nevertheless reveal an aspect of social life with regard to which Weber and Marx largely agreed: that it was dominated by conflict. If

Marx believed that **social class** was everywhere the prime axis of this conflict (to be eliminated in the classless society of communism), Weber saw many axes to conflict and believed that, since the values that promoted it were often incommensurable (being *wertrational*), there was no prospect of eliminating it from social life. Weber's views in this regard have been among his most important contribution to sociology, and we can conclude our treatment of him by attending to them. While Marx concentrated on property ownership as the basis of inequality, Weber held a more complex view. Inequality existed along at least three separate dimensions: wealth, prestige, and power (embodied as social class, **status group**, and political party, meaning any group vying for power). Of these, his treatment of status groups has had the greatest influence.

Inequalities of wealth were primarily important for Weber as they affected our **life chances**, the prospects opened or closed to us by our particular economic location (prospects, for instance, for a long and healthy life or for particular jobs). For Weber, life chances weren't distributed in discrete clusters that would make the concept of social classes very useful. In other words, the people we might group together as "working class" could have quite varied life chances depending upon whether they had stable, well-paying employment versus casual, poor-paying employment. Thus, he didn't think class itself explained too much about what happened to us. Further, while it was possible that people in the same class would band together politically to acquire power, Weber didn't think this particularly likely since the differences between people in the same class, particularly status-group differences, were too great. Thus, for him social class was largely a name we attach for convenience to more or less similarly situated people, without this name referring to any real group that tends to act in concert. In other words, in Weber's view, classes rarely acted as groups, whereas Marx expected that they would actively struggle for control of the modern state.

With regard to inequalities of power, Weber was primarily interested in the effect of political parties, groups of people who have joined together to strive for political power. They could gain power through democratic elections, or they could gain it through force of arms: Weber's point was simply that political power is something different from the advantage we gain from either wealth or status. Parties could develop not just around classes or status groups but around ideological positions, such as classical liberalism, that would draw together people from quite different classes, status groups, religions, and so on. This just means that, for Weber, the basis of political organization looked much messier than it did for Marx. Indeed, just about everything looked messier for Weber since he saw social organization and historical change as more complex than did Marx.

Status, our third dimension of stratification, is the same thing as prestige: it's a question of the perceived worthiness of a person or group, often in moral terms:

> In contrast to the purely economically determined "class situation" we wish to designate as "status situation" every typical component of the life fate of men that is determined by a specific, positive or negative, social estimation of *honor*. ... In content, status honor is normally expressed by the fact that above all else a specific *style of life* can be expected from all those who wish to belong to the circle. (Weber 1958b:187, emphasis in original)

While a "style of life" is expressed throughout one's social actions, status is most importantly announced to others by what a person consumes. In fact, status groups are largely organized around common patterns of consumption. (We need to think of "consuming" here quite broadly: for Weber, the choice of a religion to participate in was as much a consumer choice as the type of car to buy. The point is to consume in ways that earn you social honor, which you normally do by choosing a good car over a jalopy and a high-status religion over a stigmatized one.[38]) Weber considered status groups to be as important to society as, or more important than, social classes. Members of status groups had real shared identities in ways that members of social classes often lacked. For instance, truck drivers and short-order cooks might both be members of the working class, yet not think of themselves as having a great deal in common. In contrast, members of a particular status group—consider punks (Fox 1987) or bobos (bourgeois bohemians, see Brooks 2000)—always have a good deal in common. Indeed, as soon as strangers from the same status group meet, they find they have a good deal to talk about since they can explore the details and particularities of their shared consumer preferences (DiMaggio 1987). Alternatively, people from different status groups can find interaction awkward since they may not share interests that will bear sustained conversation.

Weber believed that while wealth, status, and power tended frequently to be correlated, so that people with wealth, say, also had status and power, this need not be the case. The different dimensions of stratification can vary independently, as when wealthy criminals are denied either status or political power. Thus, one's ranking can either be consistent across the three dimensions or variable.[39] Since Weber's time, a major concern of sociology has been to investigate and theorize about the relations among these three dimensions, as well as the means by which rankings on them are passed down (or not) from one generation to the next.

At the same time, status itself has become a significant focus of inquiry, and I want to concentrate on just one aspect of it here as an illustration of

Weber's legacy to sociology.[40] He indicated that in some social systems, status groups are formally and legally recognized. For instance, this happens in caste systems, such as that of India (Milner 1994). There, different groups, usually based upon occupations, were historically ranked in terms of their moral worth, with Brahmins at the top and "untouchables" (such as street sweepers) at the bottom.[41]

An important property of status hierarchies is that people of high status avoid those of low status, contact with whom is seen as "contaminating," or "polluting." For instance, when anti-Semitism was rampant in America, very interesting studies (e.g., Baltzell 1964) demonstrated the lengths to which Gentiles would go to avoid contact with Jews. Wealthy Anglo-Protestants insured they would not be contaminated by Jews by excluding them from their social milieu. No Jew would be granted membership in an Anglo country club or business association, for example (not to mention college sororities and fraternities).

Thus, status hierarchies are maintained by the scorn of the higher for the lower groups, and these emotions may even acquire religious underpinning. As Weber wrote,

> Status distinctions are . . . guaranteed not merely by conventions and laws, but also by *rituals*. This occurs in such a way that every physical contact with a member of any caste that is considered "lower" by the members of the "higher" caste is considered as making for a ritualistic impurity and to be a stigma which must be expiated by a religious act. . . . In general, however, the status structure reaches such extreme consequences only where there are underlying differences which are held to be "ethnic." (Weber 1958b, 188–89)

Indeed, a good deal of the literature on race relations in the United States views ethnicity, following Weber, in status-group terms (see, e.g., Dollard 1949), with minority groups ranking lower in terms of status honor and institutions like segregation being implemented to prevent "pollution" through contact. Relations between the genders often possess similar status elements as well, interestingly complicated by the fact that men and women, as mating couples, cannot avoid certain forms of intimate contact.

Contemporary sociology has developed Weber's concern with avoidance as a property of status hierarchies through a generalized interest in status boundaries. Distinctions among status groups can only be created and maintained through the formation and policing of such boundaries, and sociologists are interested in when and how this occurs. My own work, for instance, concerns how boundaries have been drawn between scientific and occult modes of inquiry into nature, causing the latter to be stigmatized as low status (Schneider 1993). Others have looked into how boundaries have been drawn between different musical genres so that, for instance, consumption of heavy metal is stigmatized (Bryson 1996). The techniques and strategies (called **boundary work**) involved in creating or challenging boundaries have been investigated (Gieryn 1983; Lamont and Fournier 1992), as have the social movements that organize around the task. Indeed, we can view the civil rights and feminist movements as focused centrally on the destruction of boundaries that were created long ago by racist and sexist "boundary workers." Others (Douglas 1970; DiMaggio 1987) have developed very general structural theories of the circumstances that cause societies to admit more or fewer internal boundaries.

An adjacent focus of inquiry has been the relation between such boundaries and social classes (Bourdieu 1984; Willis 1983). This literature explores how the educational system, by systematically favoring some status cultures over others, causes parental class standing to be transmitted to children in a process of **social reproduction** (DiMaggio and Mohr 1985). This literature and a developing critique of it (Lamont and Lareau 1988; Lamont 1992; Peterson and Kern 1996; Erickson 1996; Bryson 1996) has stimulated a general inquiry into the relation between culture and stratification, a concern which, in a very real sense, we owe to Max Weber.

Thus, the analysis of social boundaries carries forward and significantly advances concerned with social structure and conflict within it that saw their origins in Marx and Weber. Anyone reviewing the literature I've just cited would have to be impressed not just with the continuity of contemporary concerns with those of the classical theorists but with how far sociology has come since their day. Marx forged sociology with a very blunt hammer, which Weber refined with sharper instruments. But neither of them had the resources for empirical research available to modern sociology that have allowed us to approach these topics with significantly greater sophistication. Although we have by no means arrived at a final understanding of social boundaries and stratification, we are distinctly nearer to this than we were a century ago.

Conclusion

The last two chapters have looked at numerous aspects of Weber's sociology. His treatment of the origins of capitalism, while not convincing, does show us why he had modest expectations for the ability of sociological theories to explain significant developments across history. Indeed, no theory explaining why capitalism arose when and where it did has met with broad consensus, which seems to confirm Weber's point of view. At the same time, the fact that he incorporated theories into his own treatment of capitalism indicates his respect for theorizing in general. Further, the core of this chapter has allowed us to look at his enduring contribution to theory: the analytic typology. This has permitted us finally to give due consideration to analysis as a form of theorizing, where previous chapters have stressed primarily explication and causal accounting. I've drawn a distinction between open empirical typologies, which catalog the often very large and changing number of types into which phenomena like jobs sort themselves, and analytic typologies, which classify the limited and presumably permanent number of types into which phenomena like authority can be sorted.

We've also used Weber to add the concept of preconditions to our understanding of theorizing. Preconditions are the circumstances that favor particular causal relations. They do not directly cause something to happen themselves but, instead, increase its likelihood by providing circumstances favorable to it. They act as facilitators, as we've seen in the case of monetization facilitating bureaucratization. Preconditions play an essential role in theorizing, being almost as crucial to it as maps are to travel. They tell us a good deal about the terrain in which social phenomena exist, and without this, we'd be left to stumble around partly blind. We've examined one instance of this terrain in explaining the social ecology of the bureaucratic and craft administration of production.

It remains regrettable that Weber has so little immediate appeal to students just beginning their sociological journeys. Having experienced this myself, I'm sympathetic. He is an acquired taste. In this regard, developing an appreciation of him can serve as a gauge of your growth as a sociologist. Émile Durkheim, to whom we now turn, is different in this regard: he's all there for you right from the beginning.

Appendix 5A: Mutual Exclusivity

Analytic typologies deal with nominal variables, and to work well, their types have to be discrete and relatively homogeneous. To take the example in the text, if the contribution of manual and cognitive labor to jobs varies continuously, we won't be able to meet these criteria. Here's a way of visually representing the problem. First imagine, as in figure 5A.1, that the manual and cognitive components of jobs vary continuously.

At the center point in figure 5A.1, jobs will be equally manual and cognitive; thus, if we cut the figure in half and call jobs on the left side manual and those on the right, cognitive, we will have created categories that are only arbitrarily discrete. (Obviously, a job that's 49 percent manual and 51 percent cognitive will have more in common with a job that's 51 percent manual and 49 percent cognitive than will either of these have with jobs near the poles of our newly created categories.) Put differently, we will not have formed homogenous categories; instead, they will include jobs more different from one another than they are from neighboring jobs in the opposite category. This would not be a good thing.

If figure 5A.1 accurately represents the distribution of manual and cognitive contributions to jobs, we'd probably be mistaken to employ a manual/cognitive typology. The latter works best when the categories of jobs look like they do in figure 5A.2. This figure indicates that manual jobs are qualitatively different from cognitive jobs in such a way that all of them have more in common with one another than they do with the cognitive jobs. Another way to put this is to say that we want the categories of our analytic typology to be homogeneous, with all the phenomena within them being the same with regard to an analytic property. Of course, neither of the two figures has to represent the real nature of jobs accurately; the point is that unless the phenomenon that interests us looks a good deal more like the second figure than the first, it's not going to be a good candidate for an analytic typology.

Appendix 5B: Measuring Rationalization

Weber's view of history as a process of rationalization has an immediate appeal since we are all accustomed to thinking of modern society as more rational than primitive societies and certainly have no reason to question that our technology represents an advance over theirs. In fact, the picture seems

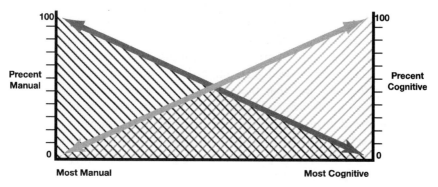

FIGURE 5A.1
Continuous Variation between Manual and Cognitive Contributions to Jobs

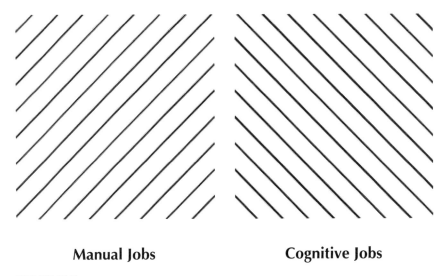

Manual Jobs   Cognitive Jobs

FIGURE 5A.2
A Representation of Manual and Cognitive Jobs as Discrete Categories

so reasonable that we may have trouble questioning it. But, as with many broad-brush pictures, it's always good to press it a little. (For some help in this regard, see Hollis and Lukes 1982.) Has Weber defined rationality and rationalization well enough that we can measure it and show that it in fact increases across time? Can we gauge its retreat (in relatively precise numerical terms) in the face of "irrational" social movements?

Often when we attempt to turn appealing concepts like rationalization into measurable variables, we find we have to be much clearer about them, giving them very precise definitions. (If you think back to chapter 2, for instance, you'll find that we weren't very precise about alienation.) Weber himself made no attempt to do this, and when we look at the examples he offered for guidance, we're apt to grow further confused. We've already seen, for instance, that Weber viewed value rationality as quite distinct from instrumental rationality and that these two can vary independently. Stephen Kalberg (1980) finds further distinctions: he suggests Weber had four distinct patterns of action in mind in the general concept of rationality. I want to review these here as a way of making this concept somewhat more concrete, although, in each case, I'll pass over the question of how it might be measured. You might try to answer this as an exercise.

Kalberg's *practical rationality* is perhaps the easiest to understand since it means the same thing as instrumentally rational action. When there are more efficient ways of doing things, we generally adopt them. This sort of rationality has always existed, but some cultures may encourage it more than others. Sometimes, practical rationality comes into conflict with traditional ways of doing things, and then we have to decide whether to sacrifice tradition to efficiency. Practical rationality is usually localized in that it provides solutions to specific practical problems, often by devising new rules of thumb for dealing with them, but this doesn't spread to other problems. In a sense, it is a form of tinkering driven by a concern for finding a better way of doing things.

Formal rationality refers to the development of standardized procedures, rules, or laws. For example, you'd probably worry if you thought your professors "played favorites" in a class, giving the highest grades to students they like. You'd be comforted if your professor adopted a standardized procedure for grading that guaranteed fairness all along the way. When professors do this, according to Weber, they're behaving in a formally rational way, and this is a large part of what bureaucracies are about.

Theoretical rationality refers to efforts to increase the internal consistency of a specific domain of thought or action, turning it from an amalgam of things into a system. Theoretical rationality turns a pile of baseball cards into a set catalogued by teams or organized by lifetime batting average. Or it tries to make a moral system consistent: must you oppose euthanasia ("mercy killing") if you're also an opponent of abortion? Today, the physical sciences are the premier enterprises of theoretical rationality as they try to organize and systematize our understanding of nature.

Finally, *substantive rationality* is used to organize our lives in reference to ultimate values. For instance, if we value eternal salvation—or personal pleasure or friendship—above all else, substantive rationality is used to organize our behavior into patterns consistent with our values. It is the domain of value rational action. It tells us how we should live, using reasoned arguments to relate each activity to our ultimate goals.

Each of these forms of rationality would have to be measured in a quite different way. Were we able to do this satisfactorily, would we find that they all "advance" or spread through an evolutionary process? When we ponder this, it seems apparent that a model like evolution applies best to the practical form of rationality. Innovations that work tend to spread (reproduce) and be maintained until something better comes along. Thus, it makes preliminary sense, while awaiting good measures, to assume that things like technologies evolve in a way roughly similar to organisms. But it's not clear that the other forms of rationality also evolve in this way. Consequently, just how we would measure rationalization as a global process seems unclear.

Notes

1. These job types should be distinguished from the assortment of tasks that real individuals might be hired to do as a "job" since actual jobs might combine the activities of numerous job types. In other words, the work that real individuals get paid for may come from several, perhaps unrelated, job types.

2. Methodologists differentiate between **nominal, ordinal,** and **interval variables.** Nominal variables divide a phenomenon into unranked types (e.g., female/male); ordinal variables rank a phenomenon in terms of more or less (e.g., high/middle/low income); and interval variables can be ranked in terms of precise quantitative differences (e.g., a salary of $25,000 versus $30,000). These distinctions (nominal, ordinal, and interval) represent an analytic typology of the phenomenon "variables."

3. In addition to analytical and descriptive typologies, sociologists also employ what I will call *dimensional typologies.* Dimensional typologies use two or more properties relevant to a phenomenon to separate instances of it into classes, usually organized in terms of cross-cutting tables. In chapter 7, for instance, I borrow from Harriet Zuckerman to divide scientific publications into those that get cited and those that don't (dimension 1), and those that are conformist and those that are deviant (dimension 2). These dimensions can be related to one another in a two-by-two table that discriminates among normal, moribund, quack/fraud, and revolutionary scientific work. A discussion of this form of typology is included in many methods texts (see Babbie 1999:166–67, for instance, and for a fuller discussion, see Sjoberg and Nett 1997:248–56). As far as I am aware, we have not developed a standard terminology for discriminating among types of typologies. Accessible short discussions can be found in social science encyclopedias (e.g., Bailey 2000; Tiryakian 1965).

4. For further discussion of these qualities, see Bailey (2000) and Tiryakian (1965).

5. Another important means is *markets*, which centralize and, thus, facilitate the voluntary exchange of goods and services between people who are in principle equally powerful (see Lindblom 1977). They play an important role in *Economy and Society* as well.

6. Indeed, his approach to the topic is uncharacteristically sloppy. He defined power as "the probability that one actor in a social relationship will be in a position to carry out his own will despite resistance" (Weber 1978:53). The reference to resistance can make his idea of power seem synonymous with **coercion** since coercion best overcomes resistance, while authority is completely powerless to do so, but Weber elsewhere made it clear that power is a much broader category, of which coercion and authority are types among others (such as a monopolistic market position). But he never systematized his view of power by trying to exhaust its types and show how they are different from one another. I remain wary of the inclusion of resistance in his definition of power.

7. When I have my students do this exercise in class, one of the most interesting cases that comes up is that of trickery. When one person tricks another into doing what the first person wants, is this a type of power in its own right, or does it belong

to another category? If so, to which category? Another interesting case involves the use of blackmail.

8. This is one reason why having a wide variety of experiences (or acquiring them vicariously by reading) is helpful to theorizing. Of course, it helps not just to have experiences but to accustom yourself to reflecting on them in somewhat abstract terms.

9. Thus, the 1960s dictum "Question authority!" is actually meaningless since authority ceases to exist as soon as it is questioned. The dictum would more appropriately be "Question authorities!" since *authorities*, people who hold an office or who are reputed to know a lot, should not upon those criteria alone necessarily be granted authority.

10. This problem with the typology was pointed out long ago by Talcott Parsons in his introduction to Weber's *Theory of Social and Economic Organization*. See Weber (1964:58–60).

11. This is just the sort of "testing with cases" that we need to employ to probe a typology for possible weaknesses. If we conclude that following a doctor's orders is motivated in a significantly different way from following properly enacted laws, then we have to rethink our typology. As we can see from this example, evaluating a typology involves throwing case after case at it to see whether it can handle them all.

12. Note that this is not always a matter of professional authority's being backed up by something like "science." Priests (or ministers) and shamans are professionals with regard to the spiritual world. They acquire their expertise by long study and training. Often we can't test their expertise, however, since the "proof" of it may not be available until after we die. Nevertheless, this is professional authority, even when we must "take it on faith" that the orders we are given will (eventually) work.

13. See Mark 16:17, I Corinthians 12:8–11, and I Corinthians 12:28–30 for the biblical basis for this "gift." The "speaking in tongues" that occurs in charismatic religious services today does not have the property of universal intelligibility.

14. I stress "appear" here because charismatic authority exists exclusively in the eyes of the beholder and not independently (or beforehand) in the person who is granted authority. This means, for example, that people can't somehow have charisma that others have not yet recognized. It also means that it doesn't matter whether the charismatic authority uses tricks to give the impression of having charisma, as long as we don't know she is using tricks. In the domain of charismatic authority, impressions (or appearances) are everything.

15. In a sense, this makes it clear why analytic typologies are an integral aspect of sociological theory: they outline dimensions of variation in the world around us and, thus, provide many of the concepts we will use in our explanations. Creating typologies, then, involves making conceptual distinctions that carve up the social world along the fault lines of its qualitative variation.

16. It is unfortunate that, for reasons of space, I'm unable to address the professions here, although they are the subject of important theorizing today. See, e.g., Freidson 1970, 1994; Abbott 1988; Brint 1994.

17. Of course, bureaucratic organizations like businesses can, collectively and across significant spans of time, be responsible for vast changes in our circumstances. But the innovations any single business introduces tend to be only marginally socially

transforming, especially because the businesses have to respect the relatively stable legal and political framework in which they exist.

18. Thirty-nine members of the Heaven's Gate cult, led by Marshall Applewhite, committed suicide on March 27, 1997, in expectation of being taken aboard a space-ship, and more than nine hundred members of the People's Temple cult, led by Jim Jones, were murdered or committed suicide on November 18, 1978, apparently in expectation of external intervention in their isolated community in Jonestown, Guy-ana. Information about these groups and others can be accessed through the Reli-gious Movements Homepage Project at the University of Virginia. See http://religiousmovements.lib.virginia.edu.

19. Note that if we attribute the charismatic's success at confronting risk to some learned skill or feature of character that enhances competence in dealing with jeop-ardy, our submission would be a case of professional, rather than charismatic, subor-dination. For instance, the grounds for obeying a warlord whose success in sacking enemy cities derives from craft knowledge of how to do so would be little different from the grounds for obeying a doctor skilled at surgery. For specifically charismatic subordination to occur, success must be marvelous and inexplicable, something that no one could teach or learn.

20. They contrast strongly in other ways as well. For instance, while bureaucratic authority is the form in which the nature or qualities of the person in authority are least relevant, charismatic subordination is dedication specifically to the person of the leader and is often characterized by extreme devotion in this regard.

21. Some ideal types, such as a perfect market or a perfect vacuum, do not exist in reality but serve as models that existing systems may more or less closely approxi-mate. Others, such as Weber's ideal type of bureaucracy, do in fact exist, even though some bureaucracies may not possess every feature of the definition. Ideal types have been much discussed by analysts of Weber's sociology. For a discussion of them in the context of typologies in general, see Bailey (2000).

22. It is unclear, for instance, whether either written files or specialized training are in any sense necessary to bureaucracy. Garston (1993:5), after entering some res-ervations about Weber's definition, offers his own: "A bureaucracy is an organiza-tional structure characterized by a hierarchy whose occupants are appointed, whose lines of authority and responsibility are set by known rules (including precedents), and in which justification for any decision requires reference to known policies whose legitimacy is determined by authorities outside the organizational structure itself."

23. Money is so common today that it may take some effort to realize that, although it is an ancient invention, its use was severely restricted until quite recently.

24. *Sufficient* conditions are those that are always accompanied by the phenome-non of interest to us. *Necessary* conditions are those whose absence will prevent the phenomenon from occurring but whose presence is not alone sufficient to produce it. It is often a necessary, but never a sufficient, condition of getting a degree in soci-ology that you pass a course in theory.

25. In this regard it is no accident that highly bureaucratic armies have displaced the sort of heroic military organizations that were common in tribal societies and depicted so effectively in Homer's *Iliad*.

26. I will cite the essay as included in Grusky and Miller's reader *The Sociology of Organizations* (1970). In line with my comments upon the sleep-inducing quality of Weber's analysis of bureaucracy, I can report that Stinchcombe's important essay usually ranks lowest in student appeal when I assign it in classes. There just seems to be something about bureaucracy that puts students to sleep.

27. At the same time that Weber wrote, Sigmund Freud created the discipline of psychoanalysis, in part by insisting that much behavior we think of as reactive or unintentional, such as slips of the tongue or dreams, is in fact socially meaningful in the richest sense and at some level "intended."

28. To some degree, the different types of action have come to be studied by different disciplines or subdisciplines in the social sciences and sociology: affective action by psychology and the sociology of emotions; traditional action primarily by anthropology; instrumentally rational action by economics, cognitive science in psychology, and the sociologies of science and organizations (as well as "rational actor theory"); and value rational action by anthropology and the sociologies of social movements, politics, and religion.

29. When you ask people to explicate traditional action, they ultimately have to throw up their hands and simply say, "I don't know. It's just our way of doing things, I guess."

30. I will leave it to you to consider whether the forms of social action meet our criteria for a good typology. Can you spot problems other than those Weber has already admitted?

31. In *Culture and Enchantment* (1993), I argue that this process of **disenchantment** has been in fact much shallower and less widespread than Weber himself anticipated. Large percentages of citizens of advanced industrial societies believe in UFOs, past lives, crystal power, and so on, and a smaller, but still significant, percentage believe themselves to have been abducted by aliens. Just as importantly, though disenchantment has been comparatively thorough in the narrow confines of the natural sciences (which are little understood outside universities), it has had almost no effect on the social sciences, which, for the most part, remain deeply magical in their accounts of human behavior.

32. Why the United States has chosen not to insure workers against this prospect is a failure of rationality you might want to ponder. The recent past has seen increasing protests against the supposed global economic rationalization promoted by institutions like the International Monetary Fund and the World Bank.

33. Jim Jones founded and was the charismatic leader of the Peoples Temple, more than nine hundred members of which were murdered or committed suicide in Jonestown, Guyana, in 1978. David Koresh was the charismatic leader of the Branch Davidian sect of Seventh-Day Adventists, more than eighty members of which died in a seige by the FBI on their Waco, Texas, compound on February 28, 1993, launched in an attempt to serve warrantts on Koresh. Information about these groups and others can be accessed through the Religious Movements Homepage Project at the University of Virginia. See http://religiousmovements.lib.virginia.edu.

34. The process of rationalization both highlights charisma (which is less common in a distinctly nonmagical environment) and makes it more difficult for it to occupy politically central positions, which tend to be shielded from it by rationalized governmental bureaucracies and political parties.

35. Of course, we need to recognize that genocide itself can be a highly rationalized enterprise, as were the Nazi gas chambers. At the same time, the supposed aesthetic or moral values supposedly embodied in the Aryan "master race" were purely *wertrational.*

36. The ability to select minorities and women for central economic and political roles expands the pool of talent available and, thus, should in principle better the performance of both business and government. Consequently, both civil rights and feminism can claim to be rationalizing social movements.

37. It is easy to view his brilliant essays on science and politics as vocations (Weber 1958b, 77–156) as suffused with a prophetic pessimism about the prospects of Weimar Germany, a pessimism that Hitler's rise to power, after Weber died, would show to have been warranted.

38. Weber would recognize that there's more to personal status than just consumption: it's related to the work you do and to particularly significant accomplishments as well. But status groups, that is, groups of people who share a common status, are almost exclusively defined in terms of common habits of consumption. This means that status honor is somewhat distinct in its origins from the culture of honor we discussed in our first chapter.

39. A classic argument by Lenski (1966) suggests that inconsistently ranked people are motivated to strive politically for changes, particularly changes that allow their lower rankings to rise to the level of their highest, while people consistently ranked should be more conservative (less open to political change).

40. Status was discussed independently by the American economist Thorstein Veblen (1912), whose work has also had an important influence on sociology.

41. Status groups need not always be ranked. For instance, in high school, "greaser" and "preppy" groups both see themselves as superior to the other. Similarly, some groups at the bottom of the status hierarchy—poor people without much education, for instance—may join religions that allow them to feel superior to those of the highest status in a society. Nevertheless, there is often an objective dimension to status that people can't avoid. Those who have only intermittent employment in bad jobs (and who need jobs because they lack independent means), for instance, will normally be shunned and discriminated against by members of mainstream society, who have the things such people would like, such as high pay and nice houses. Those less well off simply can't escape recognition that their status denies them access to these things.

6

Émile Durkheim on the Division of Labor and Suicide

A S WE TURN TO OUR THIRD THEORIST, it might be good to remark that if Karl Marx viewed society mostly as an *economic* system, and Max Weber viewed it as a *political* system, Émile Durkheim (1858–1917) saw it as a *moral* system. We have just seen that Weber saw the coordination of individuals in a society as normally accomplished by power, in one or another of its many forms, and he saw competition for power as being at the core of politics. We've also seen that Weber's interests included cataloging the varied institutional forms that the coordination of people took, such as bureaucracies, and explaining changes in them across history. Taking a somewhat different tack,

Durkheim focused on how people's activities were coordinated through subscription to common beliefs and values, from which were derived norms for behavior. One of his prime concerns was to explain variations in norms and in what caused people to subscribe to them across history.

In the process, he developed some of the most strikingly original applications of the functionalist paradigm in sociology. He employed this paradigm to construct theories about certain aspects of deviance, law, suicide, and social change. His first book argued that the division of labor, which we've already seen playing a prominent part in Marx's analysis of alienation, was itself a functional adaptation to increases long ago in human population density.[1] Essentially, he argued that the increased productivity resulting from divided labor allowed more people to live together with less conflict among them: this constituted the *function* of divided labor in human social organization. We have already reviewed similar arguments about the functions of two cultural phenomena: the culture of honor among the Scots-Irish and sacred cows among Hindus. Similarly, Weber explained the spread of bureaucratic institutions and of the spirit of capitalism functionally. I will reserve analysis of functionalism until the next chapter, however. Here, we will simply look closely at two of Durkheim's theories.

The Division of Labor

Durkheim's *The Division of Labor in Society* (1933) analyzed (among numerous other phenomena) an aspect of law that is very important to us today. You may be aware that European countries have abolished the death penalty, while the United States has not. Opposition to the U.S. death penalty is reasonably strong, however, both in Europe (where some countries will not extradite accused criminals to the United States because they might be subject to execution) and in the United States itself. Such opposition is sociologically fascinating since executions were common until fairly recently in the United States (to the point that lynchings, an illegal form of execution, were frequent) and in the somewhat less recent past in Europe. Indeed, we need only go back three centuries or so to find that, in Europe, executions were often prefaced by gruesome torture of the offender, a practice now widely deemed repugnant. Why has this change of attitudes with regard to the fitting punishment for offenses occurred? Why are we today concerned that executions, when we do conduct them, be as painless as possible? The qualms we express here would certainly mystify our ancestors, who often sought to extract maximum suffering from the condemned and saw the result as a form of entertainment.

Again, this is the sort of wonder out of which sociological theories grow. If you look at the paragraph above in light of the first chapter, you'll see that it contains two potentially interesting empirical generalizations. The first connects the presence or absence of execution with variation among nations, and the second connects the declining gruesomeness of punishment with the lapse of time over the past three centuries. Are the latter two variables clues that could lead to an explanation of why a phenomenon like torture, which was so common in the past, seems barbarous to us today? Could they help us explain why execution may be on the way out as a punishment even in the United States and why we increasingly substitute lethal injections for more painful means to bring about legally prescribed death?[2]

A version of these questions is at the core of *The Division of Labor in Society*, but Durkheim didn't use them to begin constructing his theory. In other words, he didn't begin with observations about variations in punishment that he conceptualized and then sought empirical generalizations for. Instead, he created the theory first and then applied it to a version of these questions. Thus, the path he took (at least as it is presented in the book itself) was the reverse of the one we took with our homicide case in the first chapter. Durkheim developed the theory and then used it to predict variation in the severity of punishment across different types of societies. To see why his investigation took this direction, we need to back up a bit and look at the larger concerns that animated his book.

The Forms of Solidarity

As we noted in introducing the classical sociologists, their primary ambition was to understand and explain the dramatic changes society was undergoing as a result of the industrial revolution and the political revolutions (French and American) of the eighteenth and nineteenth centuries. *The Division of Labor in Society* outlined Durkheim's vision of the fundamental nature of these changes. The preface to the second edition, published in 1902, makes the social concerns that drove him to write it very clear. The business world of his day, he explained, was sadly lacking in ethical behavior. Indeed, the very idea that the economic realm should be governed by ethics was only weakly developed, with the consequence that

> The most blameworthy acts are so often absolved by success that the boundary between what is permitted and what is prohibited, what is just and what is unjust, has nothing fixed about it, but seems susceptible to arbitrary change by individuals. . . . The result is that all this sphere of collective life is, in large part, freed from the moderating action of regulation. (Durkheim 1933:2)

His concerns remain relevant today: as I write, some corporate officers in the United States are under intense scrutiny for alleged fraud and for profiting personally at the expense of their shareholders and employees. Durkheim wished to diagnose the conditions giving rise to precisely such behavior, and doing so required, he felt, a very deep look at human social history. We will leave the diagnosis aside for the moment to join him in this investigation, which will quickly lead us back to the issue of the severity of punishment with which we began.

From the standpoint Durkheim developed, the revolutions of the eighteenth and nineteenth centuries were not complete novelties but, instead, represented a significant acceleration of a long-standing trend associated with occupational specialization, which he followed Adam Smith in referring to as the *division of labor*. Today, we have become so used to the enormous proliferation of different types of work that it takes some effort to recall that, when Durkheim was born in 1858, the overwhelming majority of people were farmers, doing more or less the same thing as everyone else in society did and as their forebears had done for many hundreds of years. Indeed, the farther we go back in history, the more this is true: among technologically primitive peoples, as we saw in addressing Marx's theory of alienation, there is very little occupational specialization.

To understand why Durkheim focused on the division of labor, we have to join him in asking a basic question: what is it that permits a society to cohere as a unit, to overcome people's individuality and conflicting, independent interests, and molds them into a group? One obvious answer to this is a common set of beliefs and values.[3] To the extent that we strongly value honesty, for instance, defrauding others will seem of little worth, however much it might be to our personal benefit. For Durkheim, beliefs and values that are shared constitute a **collective consciousness** (*conscience collective* in French) in which every individual in the group participates. Collective consciousness is perhaps a misleading term: Durkheim didn't mean that the group has a "group mind" but, rather, that all individuals in it must share some beliefs and values to constitute a group: all people in a group have at least some elements of belief in common that define them as members of the group, in spite of individual or family differences. In essence, the collective consciousness is formed out of these commonalities, and to the extent that these commonalities are distinctive, they draw a line between "us" and "them," that is, between members of our own group and members of other groups, helping to construct the boundaries discussed in chapter 5.

Now, when Durkheim looked at present-day societies, he wondered about what constituted their collective consciousness. People in modern societies are often so different from one another in beliefs and values that it's hard to see what they have in common. If someone asked each of us to define what it means to be American or Japanese or French, we'd have a hard time figuring out what characterizes us as members of the same society. (For instance, a significant portion of Americans believe in astrology and reject evolution, but most scientifically sophisticated people ridicule such beliefs. So, what holds these people together in the same society, apart from simple membership in the same political unit? The same could be asked even more strongly of differences between religious people and atheists.)

At the same time, when Durkheim looked back in human social history through the lens of contemporary primitive tribes, the answer to what constituted their collective consciousness seemed very clear to him: primitive people shared most of their beliefs and values. They lived together in relatively small groups, in which the same stories, religious practices, and ways of making a living were common to all individuals. So, when Durkheim asked why such people shared beliefs, the answer seemed simple: it was because their lives were so similar. In a primitive society, each person did more or less the same thing as every other person from dawn to dusk, with minor variations for men and women and for youths and adults. Similarity of lived experience, then, led to similarity of beliefs and values. One felt close to others in this circumstance, felt *solidarity* with them, because one shared so much of their experience of the world. In fact, one shared so much of this experience that it was rare for members of the group to disagree about basic beliefs and values in the way that religious people and atheists might—or so Durkheim believed.

He called this principle of social cohesion **mechanical solidarity**. *Mechanical* is perhaps an odd choice of a word here. Durkheim explained, "The term does not signify that it is produced by mechanical or artificial means. We call it that only by analogy to the cohesion which unites the elements of an inanimate body" (1933:130). He meant that the elements of an inanimate body, like a rock, can be fused together without being reciprocally dependent upon one another. Thus, we can throw a rock, or we can break it up and throw the pebbles that result, both in more or less the same way. This is not something we can do with a living body because reciprocal dependencies fuse its various parts in a different way, causing it to die if broken up. In societies, mechanical cohesion causes people to act in unison when together and similarly even when apart. The similarity results because their actions are motivated by the same beliefs and values, arising from the same lived experience. But they are able to survive when apart, as can the pebbles drawn from a rock, because they are not interdependent within society.

Durkheim then asked what happened to this principle of solidarity when people's lives became increasingly different because of the division of labor.

The division of labor posed a problem because it caused people to specialize, and as they did, they ceased to share experiences. Today, the experiences of a printing press operator are quite different from those of a construction worker, and neither has much in common with a professor. Thus, there's little basis for mechanical solidarity. How, then, do societies in which labor is finely divided avoid falling apart?

Durkheim reasoned that as mechanical solidarity declined, another form of solidarity arose to take its place. This he called **organic solidarity**. Just as the organs in a complex body specialize in function but are all dependent upon one another, so would people who had specialized continue to remain dependent upon one another through relations of economic reciprocity, even as they lost the commonality of life that buttressed the collective consciousness. As the collective consciousness weakened, people became increasingly bound to one another by their very specialization and, thus, interdependency. Professors, after all, cannot live without construction workers to build their houses and press operators to print the books they write and from which they teach. Thus, the division of labor simultaneously caused the decline of mechanical solidarity and the rise of organic solidarity, so that societies continued to cohere, even as they ceased to have as broad and strong a collective consciousness.

Figure 6.1 represents graphically the relation between mechanical and organic solidarity, as well as their relation to the collective consciousness. The figure indicates that as we move from mechanical to organic solidarity, we

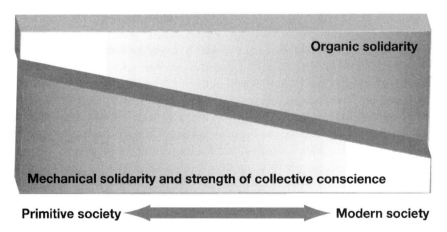

Organic solidarity

Mechanical solidarity and strength of collective conscience

Primitive society ◄━━━━━━━━━━━━► **Modern society**

FIGURE 6.1
The Contributions of Mechanical and Organic Solidarity as Components of Social Cohesion across Time

see a gradual weakening of the collective consciousness. As people shared fewer life experiences, their beliefs and values tended to diverge so that they had less and less in common, and the strength of the collective consciousness was proportional to the commonality of beliefs and values.

If we stop and look at figure 6.1 for a moment, we can see that it embodies an empirical generalization: variation in the composition of solidarity (that is, in the relative contributions of the mechanical and organic forms) is related to variation across time in the comparative modernity of societies. The latter thus offers a clue as to what causes change in our dependent variable. And it is obvious, given the title of Durkheim's book, that he saw the division of labor as the independent variable to which this clue variable pointed us.

Modes of Punishment Vary with Forms of Solidarity

We are now set to return to the point from which we started. Durkheim reasoned that the strength of collective consciousness in mechanically solidaristic societies would lead to severe punishments for those who broke the law. The anger that each individual felt when norms were violated would resonate with that of all other individuals, growing as it reverberated and, consequently, demanding more painful or even fatal expiation (atonement). In such circumstances, "A simple restitution of . . . order would not suffice for us; we must have a more violent satisfaction. The force against which the crime comes is too intense to react with very much moderation" (Durkheim 1933:99–100). This might explain how practices like torture could arise: only excruciating pain visited on offenders could quench an outrage increased by its mirroring within the group. If the collective consciousness weakened, however, so would the ability of the community to react as one to the assaults upon it which crime represented. As individuals ceased to share beliefs and values, the group would slowly be drained of the emotional energy that demanded maximally painful expiation of crimes. As this happened, physical punishments would be increasingly replaced by punishments seeking *restitution*, that is, a return to the state of affairs before the crime was committed. As Durkheim conceptualized this development, **repressive punishments** involving violence against the criminal gave way to **restitutive punishments** providing compensation for victims. For example, a repressive punishment for theft might involve chopping off the hand of the thief, while a restitutive punishment might merely involve return of the stolen items or compensation equivalent to them.

Translated into our framework, Durkheim argued that as the variable of collective consciousness declined (weakened), so did the severity of punishment.[4] Behind this stood a second theory: as the independent variable of the division of labor increased, the dependent variable of collective consciousness decreased. Graphically, the theory can be represented by figure 6.2, which shows the relations among our three variables: increases in the division of labor cause declines in the strength of the collective consciousness, which in turn cause declines in the severity of punishment.

It is not just that punishments decrease in severity as organic replaces mechanical solidarity, however: some categories of crime simply disappear. Consider an example: blasphemy and other "religious crimes" (crimes directed against collective symbols) were punishable in the United States some time ago, but they are no longer punishable today.[5] Durkheim's theory suggests that the existence and extent of religious crime was a reflection of the extent and strength of the collective consciousness. In fact, the stronger this was, the more would most crimes be seen as assaults upon the collectivity, assaults that take on the same religious character as blasphemy. As one commentator put it,

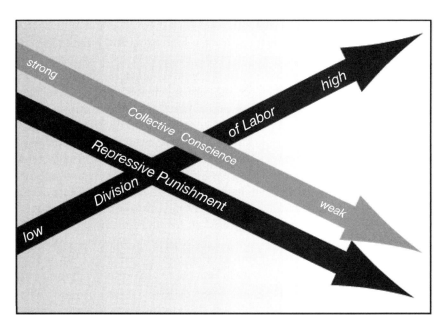

Primitive Society ◄─────────────► **Modern Society**

FIGURE 6.2
Division of Labor, Strength of Collective Consciousness, and Punishment Style

The progressive weakening of the *conscience collective* . . . helps account for the lessening of "religious crimes." . . . It is these crimes—offenses against public authority and its representatives, the mores, tradition and religion—which offend the collective conscience and call forth violent repression. Since social evolution diminishes the primacy of collective sentiments, crime comes to be defined in more individual terms, and punitiveness tends to be reduced. (Spitzer 1975:614–15)

Thus, the slow transition from mechanical to organic solidarity meant that the scope of crimes to which repressive sanctions were attached would shrink and that these sanctions would themselves lessen in severity. At the same time, a host of new crimes and entire areas of law (civil, administrative, and constitutional) evolved with the advancing division of labor, in part to regulate the increasingly important transactions associated with economic development. But all these new forms of law carried restitutive rather than repressive sanctions. Thus, restitutive sanctions came to replace repressive ones, and punishments like torture and execution came to be seen as "cruel and unusual" (to borrow the terminology of the Eighth Amendment to the U.S. Constitution).

Durkheim's vision of the transition from mechanical to organic solidarity was much broader than the above suggests. He believed, for instance, that the notion of *individual personality* only began to acquire meaning as people's experiences diverged with an increasing division of labor.[6] Further, the latter did not automatically produce an effective organic solidarity since only when the members of a group fully recognized their interdependence (and thus their importance to one another) did solidarity prevent them from taking advantage of their neighbors. Thus, the want of ethics in business of which he complained resulted from a failure to fully achieve organic solidarity and represented for him a **pathological** social condition arising from the very rapidity with which society was changing in his time. We will return to this theme of social pathology in chapter 7; our concern here is with the core theory that explains the forms and the severity of punishment in terms of the varying components of solidarity that hold a society together. How good is this theory? Will it stand up to careful scrutiny?

Evaluating Durkheim's Theory

In *The Division of Labor in Society*, Durkheim offered a good deal of *unsystematic* evidence to support his argument. A glance at history would indicate that many modern societies have substituted incarceration for the torture, mutilation, and execution that used to be common forms of punishment; have reduced the scope of collective crimes like blasphemy; and still reserve the severest punishment for crimes against representatives of collective authority, for instance, killing a police officer. But such observations by themselves don't prove Durkheim's theory, which requires that these developments be caused by changes in the bases of social solidarity. In fact, his observations were not systematic enough even to warrant the empirical generalization that punishments decrease in severity as the division of labor increases. Rather than look to the logical and substantive implications of the theory to devise new tests of it, then, suppose we simply look at the quality of evidence for the initial empirical generalization since, without its being true, Durkheim's theory will not have a leg to stand on.

Steven Spitzer (1975) decided to put the generalization to a more systematic test roughly eighty years after Durkheim proposed it. He gathered data on a sample of thirty societies at varying levels of "societal complexity," ranging from primitive hunting-and-gathering groups to industrial societies, assuming that complexity would correlate with the division of labor and, thus, with the transition from mechanical to organic solidarity. Spitzer also ranked societies according to the scope of crimes to which severe punishment was attached and the frequency with which it was meted out, winding up with the following scheme of four levels of severity:

> Punishments reported in Type I societies were the most severe and included aggravated capital punishment, mutilation, torture and severe corporal penalties for a wide range of offenses. Type II societies were characterized by less physical violence against offenders, and even though torture and mutilations were occasionally carried out, they did not represent routine features of official control. Societies classified as Type III might also rely on physical punishments for crime, but these sanctions were generally restricted to mild corporal punishment and capital punishment "pure and simple." Material penalties were found more frequently in societies of this type. Societies of the final type (IV) were distinguished by the dominance of material sanctions (e.g., fines, compensation in kind, confiscation or destruction of the offender's property) and/or confinement as modalities of punishment. In these societies the most "primitive" physical penalties are either unknown or extremely rare. (1975:620–21)

Thus, Type I societies utilize the most severe punishments and should, according to Durkheim's theory, be characterized by a strong collective consciousness and low division of labor, while Type IV societies should be characterized by a weak collective consciousness and extreme division of labor. What did Spitzer find?

In his sample of thirty societies, he found the distribution reported in table 6.1 relating relative complexity and punishment type (Spitzer 1975:623). This table shows that simpler societies generally use less severe forms of punish-

TABLE 6.1
Societal Complexity by Punishment Type

	Punishment Type				
	I	II	III	IV	Total
Simple	11.7%	23.5%	23.5%	41.2	
Societies	(2)	(4)	(4)	(7)	17
Complex	46.2%	7.7%	15.4%	30.8%	
Societies	(6)	(1)	(2)	(4)	13
Total	8	5	6	11	30*

*Data on societal complexity (Freeman and Winch 1957) were only available for thirty of the forty-eight societies studied.

Reprinted with permission from Steven Spitzer, "Punishment and Social Organization," *Law & Society Review*. © 1975 by Blackwell Publishing Ltd.

ment than do complex societies and that complex societies are either severe or lenient, without many falling in between. Thus, Durkheim's initial empirical generalization appears to have been wrong. If the collective consciousness is stronger in primitive than in modern societies, this clearly does not lead primitive people to seek violent expiation of crimes to satisfy their outrage. Instead, Spitzer argues, severe punishments are most common in highly stratified (and, thus, necessarily somewhat complex) societies that have not developed either advanced market economies or democratic political systems. He suggests that in such stratified societies severe punishment "is instrumental in consolidating a particular system of domination . . . [that] must resort to political and ideological controls to support the concentration of wealth" (1975:632). These are autocratic societies like the empires of Rome and China, as well as the European states prior to the industrial revolution. Such societies used grotesque punishments to frighten the lower orders by illustrating the power of their superiors. The spread of democracy and of control of the economy by markets lessened the need for such instrumental displays of power, with a consequent lessening of the severity of punishment; hence, the bimodal (twin-peaked) distribution of complex societies between severe and lenient modes of punishment, which reflects two very different stages in the development of complex societies—first autocratic and then democratic. Put in terms of our earlier discussion of Marx, Spitzer's data indicate that the severity of punishment varies with the *concentration of power* in a society. This reaches its height in agrarian societies ruled by a tiny minority of nobles.

Spitzer's sample of societies is small, and we would like to see his study repeated with a larger one, but it shows that Durkheim's empirical generalization probably can't pass an important initial test. This alerts us to how crucial it is to securely ground our empirical generalizations in evidence. In Durkheim's day, the wealth of anthropological research necessary to conduct a study like Spitzer's simply wasn't available; thus, he was forced to rely on more casual observations, from which it proved misleading to generalize. At the same time, we can probably conclude that Durkheim's theory placed too much emphasis on common experience as a source of outrage that was presumed to motivate severe punishment and not enough on the interests of powerful people and their willingness to use brutal means to advance those interests. In general, Spitzer argues, the degree and rigidity of stratification in a society, or the concentration of power, seems a better predictor of the severity of punishment than does the sharing of experiences among its members. At the same time, this doesn't mean that Durkheim's theory is completely mistaken since the strength of collective consciousness could, in principle, also contribute to the severity of punishment, though it does not seem to be as important as stratification.

Where does this leave Durkheim's theory? It seems clear that the independent variable of the strength of the collective consciousness cannot by itself explain the severity of punishments we mete out to criminals.[7] Thus, something must be wrong with the theory. Rather than criticizing him for this, however, we should appreciate the tradition of research he initiated. As noted before, it is rare in the sciences that questions are answered perfectly the first time they are asked. No lesson has stood out more strongly in the history of science than that research and theorizing are a cooperative enterprise, advancing as we improve both the quality of our evidence and the theories we use to explain it. We learn the same lesson from the study of suicide, to which Durkheim contributed dramatically. We will find that he set research on a path that today is uncovering some fascinating and completely unanticipated aspects of human behavior.

Durkheim on Suicide

Theories are efforts to relieve the itch that our wonder produces, and few social phenomena have caused people to wonder more than suicide. Why do people take their own lives? Such a drastic step often seems to defy explication, for though we can easily imagine people being depressed or embarrassed enough to "wish they were dead," most of us find it much more difficult to imagine actually taking the steps that end our lives. In a sense, we find the wishing easy to explicate, but not the doing. Thus, we have a certain macabre fascination with the details of people's suicidal motives and actions.

The fact that no other phenomenon draws us so compellingly into people's interior lives made suicide, for Durkheim, a prime strategic target for sociological theorizing. In the late nineteenth century, psychology had already separated itself from philosophy and established itself as an academic discipline, but sociology had not. Thus, Durkheim reasoned that if he could explain suicide—this presumably most psychological phenomenon—sociologically, he would make the strongest possible case for viewing sociology as a distinct science, without which we could not understand our behavior. Success here should earn sociology a place in university curricula, something Durkheim was determined to achieve.

Setting Up the Problem

His plan of attack involved some important initial skirmishes. Suicide had already been studied and theorized about somewhat, primarily by psychiatrists and political scientists.[8] Durkheim's first foray involved showing that existing theories could not explain important aspects of the behavior of suicide as a variable. Indeed, he made it clear in the course of this that sociology would not explain suicide (as an individual act) but, instead, would explain the behavior of suicide *rates* as they vary from one place and time to another. (This is something we are familiar with from considering variation in rates of argument-related homicide.) His second foray flowed out of this and involved showing that the behavior of such rates could not be explained by individual psychology. It was crucial in this regard that he distinguish between individual, psychological phenomena and social phenomena. The latter he considered **social facts** that existed independently of individuals in a realm of causes and effects quite separate from psychology. I want to focus on this second foray for a moment because it is crucial to Durkheim's exercise of sociological imagination, as well as to his campaign for the independence of sociology as an academic discipline.

He devised an ingenious way of blocking our natural inclination to explain suicide psychologically, which is to say, by explicating people's individual motives. He admitted that studies of the presumptive motives of suicides "show us the immediate antecedents of different suicides" (Durkheim 1951:148) but suggested that they could not handle variations in rates. He made this point by means of an interesting **thought experiment**,[9] in which I encourage you to join him. Suppose suicide rates were to double across a generation. If we believe that suicide can be explained by people's individual motives, this doubling would most easily be accounted for if people either developed some new motive for suicide or if one of the old motives was much more frequently activated. (Otherwise we would have to believe that the old motives had somehow become "doubly fatal," as Durkheim put it, which is implausible.) In other words, we would explain changes in rates by changes in the composition of motives, with some of them suddenly becoming much more prominent. For instance, if we suppose that people commit suicide more frequently when driven to despair by severe economic reverses, such as occurred during our Great Depression, then if suicide rates increased from twenty to forty per hundred thousand over a relatively short period of economically troubled years, we might speculate that this rise was due to increases in such despair. But these increases in despair would then shift the distribution of people's motives for committing suicide, becoming a greater proportion of them. By way of contrast, a doubling of the rate without any change in the composition of motives would be very puzzling: what could we infer, other than that these motives had somehow become doubly fatal? (Stop for a moment to consider: doesn't this argument stand to reason? In other words, doesn't it accord with your sense of how the world should work? This reinforces for us the importance of drawing out the implications of our suppositions about how the world works.)

Durkheim then used **empirical** findings about the presumptive motives of suicides (such as might be gathered from suicide notes) to show that while suicide rates had risen 40 percent in France over a generation from 1856 to 1878, the distribution of motives had remained the same. This was true in Saxony, as well, where suicide rates doubled over roughly the same span of time. Furthermore, suicides from very different occupational milieu, such as farmers versus professionals, showed very similar distributions of motives. Durkheim felt this left us no option but to conclude that "the motives thus attributed to suicides, whether rightly or wrongly, are not their true causes" (1951:149). Something was going on behind the scenes that caused rates to rise or fall while motives remained constant—something that people could not access through explication of motives, any more than Southern students could understand, without Richard Nisbett and Dov Cohen's help, why insults raised their cortisol and testosterone levels so much higher than those of Northern students. Thus, Durkheim inferred that the behavior of suicide rates would need a causal account that was independent of individual motives. And if he could explain the behavior of these rates, he would have made a strong case for sociology as a new discipline.

From Empirical Generalizations to a Theory

For many sociologists this interesting inference remains the bedrock upon which the discipline is founded. The arena "behind the scenes" that Durkheim postulated is the realm of *social facts* or *forces*, where currents flow that sweep our behavior along in ways we cannot understand by examining individuals or their motives. In a very real sense, these forces operate like the force of gravity, unseen and discernable only in their effects. Having envisioned such a realm of social facts, Durkheim was prepared to journey into it to construct his theory:

> Disregarding the individual as such, his motives and ideas, we shall seek directly the states of the various social environments . . . in terms of which the variations of suicide occur. Only then returning to the individual, shall we study how the general causes become individualized so as to produce the homicidal results involved. (1951:151)

But how were the "states of the various social environments" to be directly sought? Durkheim had two resources at his disposal. First, there were the theoretical intuitions about social facts that he had already developed in *The Division of Labor in Society* and which led him to view phenomena like social solidarity as important in regulating people's propensity to crime and their attitudes toward punishment. Perhaps similar phenomena controlled suicide as well, which was itself often viewed as a crime. Second, he had a set of apparently unrelated empirical generalizations about the behavior of suicide rates, some developed by previous researchers and some the result of his own research. Perhaps patterns could be found that linked them together, relating them to one another. If so, he could then move back and forth between the linked generalizations and his theoretical intuitions to see if he could specify the social forces, the independent variables, that were causing suicide rates to vary. Once he had conceptualized these independent variables, he could use them to make additional predictions about suicide rates that he could test by gathering further data.

The book *Suicide* does not allow us to look over Durkheim's shoulder as he employed this procedure. Instead, it gives us the result: packages of empirical generalizations that Durkheim had already linked to governing social forces. To give you a sense of the problem as he initially faced it, however, consider the following four generalizations, discussed by Durkheim in *Suicide*, that were known to students of suicide in his era:

1. Single people commit suicide more frequently than married people of the same age (176ff).
2. Military personnel commit suicide more frequently than civilians (228ff).
3. Periods of rapid economic growth or decline have higher suicide rates than periods of stability (241ff).
4. Slaves commit suicide more frequently than free people (276).

If unseen social currents or forces are causing suicide, these generalizations inform us that the currents are stronger for singles, for military personnel, for slaves, and for everyone during booms or busts, and they are weaker for the married, civilian, and free and for everyone during periods of stability. In each case, the question is, why? Our situation here reinforces the argument of the first chapter that we can only begin to explain phenomena by noticing how they vary. In what way do the first conditions (single, military, economically unstable, slave) differ from the second (married, civilian, stable, free) so as to cause higher rates of suicide among those marked by them? Each of the empirical generalizations serves as a clue pointing us toward a matching empirical generalization containing the independent variable that will explain variation in rates. Beyond our initial question of why, we need also to wonder whether the independent variable might be the same for all four of the generalizations above or whether each of them will need its own explanation. In other words, is there just one social force at work here, or two, three, or even four?

This is an intriguing problem to ponder, just the sort of thing that gets a theoretician's juices flowing. How might you solve it? You'd need first to conceptualize the dependent variable, suicide rates, as Durkheim did. In his view, the concept of suicide would include "all cases of death resulting directly or indirectly from a positive or negative act of the victim himself, which he knows will produce this result" (Durkheim 1951:44). This means that we would call the sacrifice of a soldier who throws himself on a grenade to save his comrades a suicide, similar in some ways to what happens in a suicide bombing. It would also mean that very risky behavior like games of competitive intoxication (in which people vie to see how much alcohol they can consume, sometimes to the point of acute poisoning and death) would qualify as suicidal just as much as Russian roulette.

We might now simply speculate about which qualities of single life, military life, and so on distinguish the two sides of our empirical generalizations in ways that would be relevant to suicide. But our speculation could use some guidance. Take the second generalization first. Military suicides generally occur under two sorts of circumstances that are quite different from one another. During warfare, some soldiers expose themselves to certain death in order to save their comrades (or to advance their cause, as in the case of suicide bombings). In a quite different circumstance, more familiar in previous centuries than in our own, a soldier who has behaved in ways that dishonored himself or his regiment would be expected to make restitution to his unit by killing himself. In both cases, Durkheim noted, the soldier is sacrificing himself for the group, and he styled these **altruistic suicides**. If we wanted to go outside the military, Durkheim pointed to additional cases where people choose death over dishonor, as well as to practices like the Hindu suttee, where widows commit suicide upon the death of their husbands, as examples of altruistic suicides that would cause rates to increase for particular groups. Thus, the concept of altruistic suicide allows us to bundle together certain empirical generalizations about suicide rates (e.g., higher for military and Hindu widows) and speculate that they might be due to the same social current.

Durkheim then speculated that the higher rate of suicide among single, as opposed to married, people might likewise be linked with other empirical generalizations, such as that suicides are relatively common among elderly widowed or divorced men, to constitute a second bundle of suicides characterized by relative social isolation. He styled these **egoistic suicides**, meaning not that such people were self-centered but that their isolation threw them back upon their own resources, resources that might prove insufficient.

Considering these two types of suicide more deeply, Durkheim found a way of connecting them. Altruistic suicides can only occur where individuals consider groups to which they belong to be more important than themselves. Drawing on his previous interest in social solidarity, he reasoned that groups will appear really important only when individuals are deeply enmeshed within them, tied to their fellows by relatively strong bonds. This is certainly true of soldiers, who have to depend on one another frequently for their very lives. Such individuals might be styled as very socially integrated. By contrast, the social isolates whose suicides he styled egoistic seem comparatively poorly integrated, having fewer strong bonds with others. One might say they suffered from a lack of **integration**. In contrast, altruistic suicides suffer from excessive integration. But this means that the same variable, **social integration**, explains our first two empirical generalizations: too much integration causes altruistic suicides, and too little causes egoistic suicide. Between these extremes, a moderate amount of integration protects people from suicide.

Figure 6.3 graphically represents Durkheim's first theory about the social currents causing suicide.[10] In it, we have been able to dispense with our clue variables to show the direct relation between the independent and dependent variables. It tells us that as we shift the amount of social integration in a society from either moderate to low or moderate to high, we raise the suicide rate. This is Durkheim's answer to the question of how suicide rates might double in a society while the distribution of motives remained the same. If a society became less integrated, for instance, this would impel more people to suicide without any change in their motives at all. In terms of our metaphor of social currents, a change in integration would simply sweep more people before it, not different ones. It's not their motives that somehow become

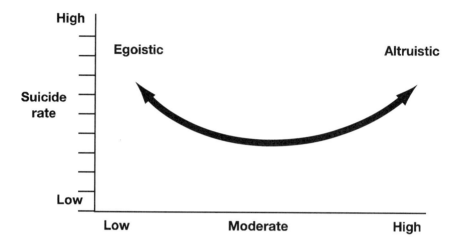

Social Integration

FIGURE 6.3
Social Integration and Suicide Rates

doubly fatal; rather, the social circumstances in which they find themselves become more deadly.

Durkheim now proceeded to deal with the remaining two empirical generalizations in the same fashion. His discussion of why suicide rates increase in periods of rapid economic growth and decline is particularly interesting. We have already mentioned the despair into which people might fall when they suddenly lose their fortunes in a market crash. But though such despair might account for rises in the rates during economic downturns, what could possibly account for rises during upswings? Why might people take their lives when they are doing better, so to speak? Durkheim developed an intriguing way to link the two. He noted that poverty alone could not account for suicide since suicide rates among the poor are not particularly high. But if poor people are accustomed to their poverty, better off individuals are not. Thus, when the well-off suddenly become poor,

> society cannot adjust them instantaneously to this new life and teach them to practice the increased self-repression [that poverty necessitates and] to which they are unaccustomed. So they are not adjusted to the condition forced on them, and its very prospect is intolerable. (1951:252)

The rapid change in their circumstances leaves them momentarily "at sea" as to social norms, without a sense of how to behave in or cope with their new circumstances. This sense of being at sea, Durkheim termed *anomie*, or normlessness. People whose old habits and norms for living are suddenly rendered ineffective are momentarily cast adrift and, during this period, might more easily question the **norm** that they should not take their own lives. Interestingly, Durkheim reasoned, the very same thing was true of people whose economic circumstances rapidly improve:

> Then . . . the conditions of life are changed, [and] the standard according to which needs were regulated can no longer remain the same. . . . The scale is upset; but a new scale cannot immediately be improvised. . . . The limits are unknown between the possible and the impossible, what is just and what is unjust, legitimate claims and hopes and those which are immoderate. (1951:252–53)

This is the circumstance of lottery winners and others who experience rapid rises in their fortunes. In our day, we see the deaths of rock stars like Jimmy Hendrix, Janis Joplin, and Curt Cobain as possible instances of **anomic suicide**. For them, previous limits have been removed by fame and fortune, and they easily find themselves going over the edge, engaging in risky or self-destructive behavior. (Anomie is also involved in risky activities like competitive intoxication that college students sometimes engage in upon being released from the normative control of the home environment into the freer atmosphere of college.)[11] Thus, Durkheim felt that the concept of anomic suicide could draw together various empirical cases, showing similarities between riches-to-rags, as well as rags-to-riches, circumstances.

As to the final generalization about slaves, Durkheim reasoned that if the circumstances of those who rapidly gained or lost wealth left them at sea, lacking norms to guide their behavior, the circumstances of slaves appeared to be just the opposite. Their activities are extensively controlled from without. Unlike a person who has suddenly acquired wealth (whose options multiply so rapidly that each day can be lived differently), slaves experience few options at all: new days offer them no novelties but only the same old limits. Durkheim styled theirs **fatalistic suicides**, indicating that their lives were outside their control.

Underlying anomie and fatalism, it seemed apparent, were vast differences in the degree to which people's lives were regulated from without. If we think of rock stars (or artists in general, according to the modern romantic image of them) as living unregulated lives, we can easily see that slaves represent the opposite: their lives are excessively regulated. Thus, Durkheim reasoned that **social regulation** operated just like social integration: a moderate amount prevented suicide, while too much or too little encouraged it. We graph this relation in figure 6.4.

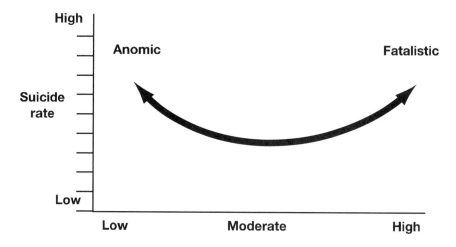

Social Regulation

FIGURE 6.4
Social Regulation and Suicide Rates

As you contemplate the relation between social regulation and suicide rates depicted by the graph, you can better appreciate the interesting train of reasoning that led Durkheim to it. Most people, in speculating about the suicides that sometimes accompany economic crashes, would stop looking for causes as soon as they considered the emotional distress of losing one's wealth. But Durkheim reasoned that, although such distress was a necessary precondition of suicide, individuals whose lives remain moderately regulated will less frequently carry out the act. Thus, the combination of distress with normative decompression (anomie) or compression (fatalism) is necessary for suicide rates to rise. This is what Durkheim meant in making the bold statement above that "the motives thus attributed to suicides, whether rightly or wrongly, are not their true causes." These lay in the social currents that caused the preconditions to have fatal results.

We can summarize Durkheim's theory by collapsing figures 6.3 and 6.4 into figure 6.5. This graph is an interesting sort of map. It depicts the relations of two independent variables, social integration and regulation, to the dependent variable of suicide rates. At the very center of the map, where integration and regulation are both moderate, suicide rates are the lowest. Each move away from the center, in any direction, increases the prospect that suicidal preconditions (normally the psychological aspects) will lead to suicidal

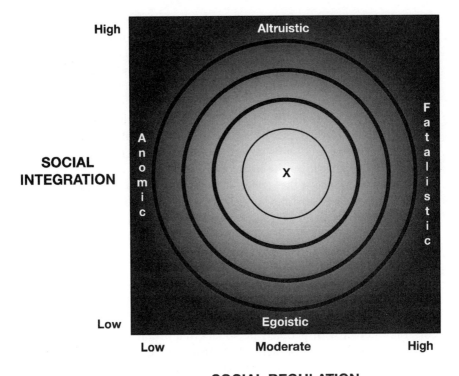

FIGURE 6.5
A Map of Suicide Rates and Types in Relation to Integration and Regulation

consequences. Conversely, the same suicidal preconditions will yield only low rates when they afflict people at the center of the figure.

The map outlines a territory in which both individuals and societies can be located and upon which they can move about. To take only one example, when individuals move to new communities, they are usually less integrated for a while than they were before. Thus, they move downward on the map from the center. As they acquire new friends and acquaintances, they move back upward. Similarly, some states in the United States, such as Nevada, Arizona, and Florida, have a high proportion of new residents, who will have had little chance to form ties to others. These states would be situated in the lower quadrant of the map in comparison to states, like Pennsylvania, that have few new residents. And at a higher level still, countries like the United States, where the average citizen moves from one community to another quite frequently, will be situated below countries whose citizens move about very little (all other things being equal). Similarly, but now considering the variable of regulation, the economic boom of the 1990s in the United States would have moved it to the left on the map, as the lives of individuals became less governed by norms. We would expect from this both higher rates of suicide and the increases in corporate crime that afflict us now and that worried Durkheim in *The Division of Labor in Society*. And we would expect them even more in countries like Russia after the breakup of the Soviet Union.

It is a useful exercise to plot both personal and national trajectories on this map. An individual who quits college to join the army, for instance, moves toward the upper right on the map. So, normally, does a country that goes to war. Mustering out of the service or winding down from war to peace, by contrast, moves us toward the lower left, as does a person who gets divorced or a country whose divorce rate increases. Somewhat fancifully, a person who leaves solitary confinement in prison to join a hippie commune moves from the lower right to the upper left; less fancifully, mass murderer Charles Manson followed just the opposite path.

The location of individuals and societies on the map corresponds to the strength of the social currents impelling them to suicide. The further we depart from the center of the map, the stronger these currents grow. The currents interact with people's personal circumstances or motivations to determine the likelihood of their self-destruction. Yet, although the currents act through individuals, their effects are invisible at the individual level and are only revealed through differences in rates across different categories of individuals. Thus, the map exposes the factors working behind the scenes to control our behavior, and it is easy to see why Durkheim would have chosen this topic to make his case for sociology. Sciences are most impressive when they reveal the hidden workings of nature, in this case workings that become visible only through sociological methods of inquiry. It seems only fitting, then, that Durkheim eventually won academic recognition for sociology in France.

Evaluating Durkheim's Theory of Suicide

To find Durkheim's theory intriguing and compelling doesn't necessarily mean to find it correct, as we have seen in preceding chapters. We need to see how it fares against our criterion of robustness, then to determine whether its implications are supported. Over the past century, a good deal of further work has been done on the subject of suicide, upon which we are able to draw.[12] Has Durkheim's theory survived? Our conclusion must be that it has only in part, or not without modification or significant reservations. Before

I address problems of robustness and unsupported implications, however, I want to discuss a problem with the measurement and **calibration** of Durkheim's variables. Having looked at all of these problems, I will bring up intriguing clues about mechanisms in the area where Durkheim's theory has experienced its most compelling success.

Measuring and Calibrating Integration and Regulation

In *Suicide*, Durkheim never measured his independent variables globally. Instead, he relied on very narrow **indicators** of them. Indicators are the measures that we use for more abstract, and often more general, variables. For instance, Durkheim assumed that, other things being equal, single people were less socially integrated than married people and that this could explain why the suicide rate for singles is higher than that for members of couples. Thus, he used marital status as an indicator for degree of integration. While this is perhaps reasonable, it would be preferable to measure the integration of individuals globally, say, by cataloging all of their social ties and getting a measure of the strength of each one. We could then sum these to arrive at an overall integration score for the individual.[13] Because this is enormously difficult and time-consuming to do for living individuals, and even harder for those who've taken their lives, it's perfectly understandable that Durkheim relied on indicators such as marital status rather than developing global measures. But without such measures, we can't actually be sure where to locate specific people or groups on figure 6.5. We can't actually establish their "absolute location" on the map. Unfortunately, it is the absolute location, according to the theory, that determines suicide rates.

Put another way, without a knowledge of absolute location, we can't calibrate our variables, assigning them standard units, then positioning our scale in relation to some phenomenon of concern. Let me explain why this is important. Using Durkheim's indicators, we can often infer people's relative locations vis-à-vis other people or groups (indicating that they are more integrated than others or less), but this doesn't help us understand where they belong absolutely. For example, all other things being equal, single people will normally be less integrated than married ones, but without more information, we don't know whether married or single people should have the higher rates of suicide. After all, we could just as easily argue that single people are moderately integrated while married people are excessively integrated as that single people are poorly integrated while married are moderately integrated (which was Durkheim's position). Without a calibrated scale on which to place them absolutely, we are really just assuming where they belong and basing our assumption on their suicide rate. In other words, we judge single people to be poorly integrated (rather than married people to be excessively integrated) just because they have the higher suicide rate.

This is fine as long as we are only trying out the theory in our minds, but it isn't alright if we want to evaluate it seriously. The problem is to avoid **tautology**, that is, assuming what we claim to be showing.[14] To escape the problem, we'd need both good global measures of our independent variables (integration and regulation) and calibration of their relation to suicide rates (our dependent variable). Just as we set the centigrade scale of temperature to zero at the point where water freezes, we'd set our integration measure at zero where suicide rates are lowest. Only in this way can we really establish whether, in moving from single to married status, we are generally moving closer to zero (Durkheim's assumption) or farther away. Once we did this for integration, we'd need to do it for regulation since the suicide rate is determined by an individual's or group's position on both variables. Only recently have efforts been made to address these problems, and only for the variable of integration (see below). Again, the reason is the immense expense involved in measuring these variables directly.

Even if we had the time and money, however, deciding how to measure the variables would present further problems. Barclay Johnson (1965) implied that Durkheim's definitions of integration and regulation are too vague to give us much guidance in developing global measures. In fact, Johnson decided that integration and regulation amounted for Durkheim to more or less the same thing. He pointed, for instance, to descriptions of integration that emphasized its regulative function, such as Durkheim's claim, "When society is strongly integrated, it holds individuals under its control" (1951:209, cited in Johnson 1965:883). This seems to indicate that the aspect of integration important in relation to suicide is actually its regulative function as it subjects us to control by others. But, if this is so, we now have just one independent variable, not two, since integration and regulation turn out, in practice, to be much the same.

Ways around this problem can be devised. For instance, we can stress the role of options in being regulated (having few options means much regulation; having many means little). After all, it seems clear that anomie consists of being cast adrift in a sea of choices, whereas fatalism consists of having too few to choose among: the sea has dried up. By contrast, integration might be measured by the reciprocity that ties with others normally entail (the more people to whom we would lend money, or who would lend money to us, the more integrated we are, for instance). This way, we can separate regulation and integration quite clearly in our minds and then decide upon ways to measure them. But because Durkheim's concepts are vaguely described, we can't be sure that these are the ways he would have selected himself, had he ever tried to measure the variables globally.[15]

Robustness and Dubious Ad Hoc Assumptions

Even as he was writing *Suicide*, Durkheim was grappling with evidence suggesting that his theory was not robust. To find ways around this evidence, he introduced, in an ad hoc fashion, some assumptions that have come with time to seem increasingly dubious. Let us look at some examples.

In Western societies generally, as in Durkheim's data for France, women commit suicide less frequently than men.[16] Further, marriage offers women less protection from suicide than it does men, and divorce affects them less. Why? Durkheim was unable to explain these empirical generalizations with his theory and resorted to ad hoc assumptions about innate gender differences, assumptions that are sexist by present standards, in order to do so. For instance, he assumed that men's natures made the regulative effect of marriage beneficial to them, while women's natures made it less so. Why?

> Woman's sexual needs have less of a mental character because, generally speaking, her mental life is less developed. These needs are more closely related to the needs of the organism, following rather than leading them, and consequently find in them an efficient restraint. Being a more instinctive creature than man, woman has only to follow her instincts to find calmness and peace. She thus does not require so strict a social regulation as marriage, and particularly a monogamic marriage. . . . By limiting the horizon, it closes all egress and forbids even legitimate hope [of divorce]. (1951:272)

This assumption allowed Durkheim to see marriage as integrating women but, at the same time, as overregulating them, leading to fatalistic suicides that lowered the benefit of marriage. In the nineteenth century, in his view, marriage produced effects similar to those of slavery for women, effects that the ability to divorce one's husband might temper. By contrast, men were both properly integrated and regulated by mandatory monogamy. It prevented them from constantly imagining relations with other women (thus experiencing sexual anomie) and, so, protected them from the effects of underregulation, which is to say, of too many sexual options.

While Durkheim may or may not have been right about the greater exposure of men to sexual anomie (see Buss 1994), he resorted to it as an ad hoc way of accommodating the awkward empirical generalization that men's suicide rates declined with marriage while women's did not.[17] This generalization seemed to indicate that his theory was not robust. Without his assumption about innate gender differences, after all, the theory predicted equal benefits to men and women from marriage in terms of social regulation; yet, this prediction was not borne out by the data. Durkheim resorted to a similar ad hoc adjustment when he found that men who married very young showed an increased tendency to suicide rather than the decrease his theory predicted (1951:158). The very young man's situation, he then claimed, was similar to that of a wife: he was excessively regulated by too early a marriage, having options closed off at a time when they should not be.

Theorists who encounter inconvenient data—inconvenient because they conflict with the logical or substantive implications of their theory—must walk a fine line between making legitimate adjustments that recognize the complexity of the world around us, on the one hand, and, on the other, going so far with adjustments that the theory is insulated against challenge through the available data. We need to scrutinize such adjustments on their merits.[18] The ones above have few.

Implications Unsupported by Data

Durkheim's theory yields several implications that have not found support. For instance, he argued that the rate of civilian suicides fell during wartime because society became more integrated, thereby reducing the number of egoistic suicides; at the same time, he explained the high rate of military suicides by the unusually high degree of integration shown by military units (1951:205–206). Their excessive integration makes soldiers prone to altruistic suicide. But if this is the case, it follows as a logical implication that the rate of military suicide should increase during wartime, when integration can be assumed to be even higher. Instead, it drops (Davies and Neal 2000:45–48), just as does the civilian suicide rate. Clearly, this presents a problem for the theory, a problem we call an **anomaly**. We have anomalous findings on our hands when the data we gather (for instance, about wartime military suicides) don't accord with what our theory has led us to expect.

Indeed, left unmodified, Durkheim's explanation of altruistic suicide would predict high rates among communal religious societies such as monastic orders. The degree of integration in monasteries or priories is probably comparable to that in the military, and, yet, suicide is comparatively rare—another anomalous finding (Davies and Neal 2000:48). Durkheim (1951:228) referred to waves of suicides that sometimes swept medieval monasteries, and we have seen numerous recent examples of mass suicides among communal religious sects, but these appear to be initiated by the occasional charismatic leader rather than to result regularly from high degrees of integration. Christie Davies and Mark Neal conclude that at the altruistic end of the integration spectrum, suicide rates "can be *either very high or very low* depending on circumstances that lie outside Durkheim's model" (2000:48, their emphasis), and they explain that this indeterminacy

> flows logically from the difference between the nature of egoistic-anomic and altruistic-fatalistic suicide. In an egoistic-anomic society individuals are weakly attached to groups but are feebly regulated. Therefore the nature of the group and the content of the regulations *does not matter*. All egoistic and anomic societies are the same, since all weak forces are *weak in the same way*. By contrast, if individuals are strongly integrated and strongly regulated, then their behavior, including the committing of or restraining oneself from suicide, must depend on the nature of the group and the content of the rules. (2000:48–49, their emphasis)

As we saw above, the rules of the military—which embody elements of a culture of honor, incidentally—used to make the suicide of dishonorable individuals customary, but the rules of monasteries did not. Thus, we would have expected high rates of military, but not of monastic, suicide, even though levels of integration and regulation may be similar. At the same time, charismatic figures can exploit the altruism of communal sectarian groups to precipitate mass suicide under unusual circumstances. Yet, the customs and rules, not to mention the charismatic figures, lie outside Durkheim's model. These cases suggest that high integration serves here more as a precondition than a direct cause for altruistic and, perhaps, some forms of fatalistic suicide.[19]

Another set of implications has to do with the age and gender distribution of suicides. As Chris Girard writes,

> Durkheim's argument that strong social ties protect against suicide suggests that suicide rates should decrease between adolescence and middle age and then increase in old age. However, in most economically developed countries, the suicide rate climbs steadily from adolescence to middle age. . . . Furthermore, the suicide rates for women in these countries often decline after ages 45 to 54 or 55 to 64. (1993:568)

While a full consideration of these anomalies would demand a chapter in itself, the pattern of declining suicide rates among women as they age is particularly problematic for Durkheim's theory "because it is in old age that a large percentage of women are widowed and living alone" (Girard 1993:568) and, thus, presumably experiencing declining social integration.[20]

Girard suggests that this anomaly and several others can be accounted for by a different approach to suicide, one that relates it to **identity spoilage**. To be happy with life, we need to be happy with who we have become, that is, with the identity we have developed and by which other people judge us.

In modern societies, an identity is something we must achieve, usually in competition with others.[21] If you'd like to become a doctor, for instance, you're going to have to prevail over a fair number of your comrades in the premed arena. Furthermore, once you achieve an identity, it can always be threatened, and if you can't ward off this threat, it can be spoiled. For instance, a doctor's identity can be spoiled by a particularly bad instance of malpractice. In fact, the malpracticing doctor could be stripped of her medical license and made to suffer humiliation among her peers. Girard believes that identity spoilage increases our exposure to suicide. Indeed, it was just because their identities were spoiled that military officers who behaved dishonorably were expected to commit suicide, contributing their altruistic suicides to the overall rate.

Girard next wonders whether there might not be differences between men and women as to the severity and the timing of threats to their identities and, thus, the likelihood of spoilage. He suggests men have traditionally faced greater competition in the achievement of desired identities than have women. While men's identities have focused on occupational success and physical vigor, women's have traditionally focused on familial roles and attractiveness. The former arenas are more competitive than the latter, Girard claims. This means that men are more exposed to identity spoilage, which may account for their much higher rates of suicide. But further, men face increasing challenges to identity as they age. They may be thrown out of work or face retirement without adequate financial security, and they will certainly lose their physical vigor. This explains why male suicide rates increase with age.

By contrast, challenges to women's identities peak in late middle age and then decline, according to Girard. The main obligation of a mother is to launch her children into life successfully. By the time she reaches late middle age, her children have either been successfully launched or gone astray. If they've gone astray, a mother's identity is somewhat spoiled in the view of the community. If not, she can relax and bask in her children's accomplishments. Further, by late middle age women may have passed the point where aging further threatens their attractiveness, which perhaps ceases to be as important to their identities. It follows, Girard argues, that men will commit suicide more than women and that their rate will continue to rise as they age, whereas women's rate will be comparatively low and drop in late middle age, which is just what the data show for developed economies.

Girard believes his theory of identity spoilage can explain many other suicide-rate patterns, especially in agrarian societies. There, suicides are often more common among young people than among the old and as common among women as men—just the opposite of the pattern in developed economies. Girard explains that major threats to identity (failure to acquire a farm or a trade for a man or failure to marry and bear children for a woman) occur comparatively early in life in agrarian societies (see also note 19).

Girard's theory might be deemed complementary to Durkheim's since we can argue that identity spoilage affects people more dramatically when they are socially integrated. People whose ties to others are few and weak, after all, are not apt to care as much if they are poorly thought of by others, and dishonored military officers might prefer to live out their lives if they could establish a new identity in a new community. It is their inability to escape existing social networks, a common feature of small towns and earlier centuries, that gives them no option (see Miller 1993), and this inability itself reflects a degree of social integration and regulation.

Yet, if the concept of identity spoilage can be seen as complementing Durkheim's theory, that it must be called upon at all indicates that anomalies remain which Durkheim's theory cannot handle by itself. The accumulation of these anomalies, as well as problems in measuring integration and regulation, have caused one of the foremost researchers in the area, K. D. Breault (1994), to conclude that anomic, altruistic, and fatalistic forms of suicide are less strongly supported than egoistic suicide. As to the latter, however, a particularly interesting line of research has developed lately that raises the prospect of spectacular success for the egoistic component of Durkheim's theory.

Social Integration and Mortality

Some of the strongest evidence that low levels of social integration cause suicide rates to rise comes from an interesting source. I've noted that social integration is rarely measured globally in studies of suicide but, instead, is inferred from indicators such as marital status. In recent years, however, studies of the determinants of health and sickness in populations have been conducted by sociologists of medicine in conjunction with epidemiologists, and these studies have measured social integration globally. They find that

> marital status, church attendance and membership, interactions with friends and relatives, membership in voluntary organizations and participation in social leisure activities—all Durkheimian social integration variables—are significant determinants of mortality after a battery of controls are employed, including physical and mental health. (Breault 1994:18)

Among the forms of mortality is suicide, but the results are much broader and more startling than this: *social integration protects not just against suicide, but against most causes of mortality!* To my mind, this is one of the most stunning findings the social sciences have ever produced. It means that we can significantly improve our prediction that a given person will die in a given year by knowing that individual's level of social integration. Consider figure 6.6 reproduced from James House, Karl Landis, and Debra Umberson (1988).

The figure shows the mortality rates for various populations, adjusted for age, at various degrees of social integration, from low to high. The individuals in these prospective studies have been checked for their medical histories and current health conditions so that all factors contributing to mortality can be held constant. Still, in every group studied thus far, the highest level of integration means a lower death rate. Consider the relative risk ratios for the populations: Evans County, Georgia: blacks, 1.09, whites, 1.83; Alameda County, California, 2.41; Eastern Finland, 2.63; Tecumseh, Michigan, 3.87; and Gothenburg, Sweden, 4.00. The risk ratio indicates how many times more likely, within a given year, you are to die if you experience low integration rather than high, and it varies from just slightly more likely (Evans County blacks) to four times more likely (Gothenburg Swedes)!

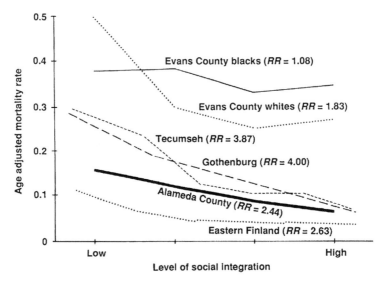

FIGURE 6.6
Level of Social Integration and Age-Adjusted Mortality for Males in Five Prospective Studies. RR is the Relative Risk Ratio of Mortality at the Lowest Versus the Highest Level of Social Integration.

To appreciate just how astonishing these findings are, recall that they apply to individuals of equivalent physical and mental health, at least to the extent this can be determined by medical exams and health histories. The studies show that poor social integration has about the same effect on longevity, all other things being equal, as does smoking. Suicide is thus only one of the factors that shortens the lives of people with few social ties. We have as yet no idea just why poor social integration produces shortened lives, but it is fair to assume that our immune systems are involved in some way. Tracking down the mechanism involved will be exceedingly difficult, but its discovery will, I believe, qualify as one of the most interesting and important scientific achievements likely in this century.

We can conclude that, while facing numerous anomalies in its altruistic, anomic, and fatalistic quadrants, Durkheim's egoistic explanation of suicide still appears to be on the mark. The fact that integration affects not just suicide, but most other forms of mortality as well, means that it has physiological effects that we may eventually understand as *mechanisms*. Just as Nisbett and Cohen are able to show how the culture of honor becomes, quite literally, incorporated in Southerners, we should eventually be able to show precisely how our relative social integration works upon our bodies, for good or ill. And we will have Durkheim to thank for the theory that led us to these mechanisms.

Conclusion

In this chapter, we've reviewed two of Durkheim's major works. *The Division of Labor* responded to a question many social theorists had been asking: what is it that holds modern societies together? The lack of ethics among businesspeople that worried Durkheim suggested that something was amiss in contemporary life, and in speculating about its causes, he developed a theory with very broad implications. Not only could it account for the behavior of people in business, but it seemed able to answer such questions as why gruesome punishments had slowly fallen out of fashion. Unfortunately, Durkheim's theory got off to a bad start because the empirical generalization on which he based it—that primitive societies are more repressive than complex societies—was wrong. But his underlying theoretical intuition that social solidarity was an important social fact, which is to say, an important independent variable, inspired his approach to suicide. The theory he developed to explain variation in suicide rates could lay claim to being the most influential single theory in the history of sociology. In part this is because it pointed convincingly to a realm of influences on our behavior that had not previously been recognized and that would require a new discipline, sociology, to investigate; in part, this is because it continues, a century after its publication, to inspire research that promises fundamental insights into the relation between individual well-being and social organization.

It may once again seem disappointing that only one aspect of the theory has found strong empirical support. Indeed, it may seem odd that we spend so much time analyzing a theory only to point to the many problems it encounters with regard to measurement, robustness, and unsupported implications. But these features make it a particularly good exercise through which to illustrate the skills we need to evaluate theories. In particular, we have seen how important it is to draw out the implications of a theory so as to be able to put it to tests. A good part of the "detective" aspect of theorizing relies upon exploring implications. Doing so is critical to building our case so that it can convince a skeptical jury.

In chapter 7, we turn to the general paradigm that guided Durkheim's theorizing. Functionalism would appear to be a relatively simple paradigm, but it is not. We will first see Durkheim put it to quite striking use in explaining the function of crime. We will then go on to explore the criteria for successfully using the paradigm, how demanding these are, and how infrequently they have been met in sociology. Here, we will find further illustration of the skills we need to evaluate theories.

Notes

1. Schmaus (1994:121–41) argues that it is a common misinterpretation of Durkheim to see the division of labor as caused by increasing population density. Instead, it is caused by increasing "moral density," which refers to people's perceptions of the number of social relationships they enter into. His point is important, but not crucial to our concerns here.

2. Our problem here reminds us that we often don't know why we behave the way we do. If we *explicated* our squeamishness over torture, we could certainly come up with good reasons or motives for it. Similarly, we can *justify* our opposition (or lack of it) to execution. But neither our reasons nor our justifications can explain why our motives are so different from those of our ancestors, who seem to have looked upon torture as a form of grisly entertainment. For a fascinating analysis of the latter topic, see Spierenburg (1984).

3. This is one of a number of answers that can be given. For some theorists (e.g., Hechter 1987), exchange between individuals, or *reciprocity*, is the fundamental glue of social organization. As we've seen, conflict theorists like Marx and Weber point to power (as coercion or authority) as the means by which groups are held together. For a discussion of prior answers most relevant to Durkheim's own analysis, see Lukes (1973:140–47).

4. Strictly speaking, Durkheim saw severity of punishment more as an index than an effect of changes in collective consciousness, but since I don't believe anyone would join him in doing so today, I feel free to make this minor modification for my purposes.

5. An example of a religious crime being contested in the U.S. today is flag burning (or other forms of disrespect for this symbol). The Supreme Court has declared flag burning "protected speech" that must be allowed under the First Amendment to the Constitution, although Congress, playing to popular sentiment, consistently tries to pass laws against it, laws that essentially make the flag sacred and burning it a religious crime. For Durkheim, the sacredness of collective symbols like the flag was the essence of religion. We will return to this topic in the chapter 7.

6. He fell victim in this view to one of the anthropological prejudices of his time, which saw both individualism and individuality as largely lacking in the simplest societies. A somewhat similar view, as Professor Thomas Burger pointed out to me, is put forward by G. H. Mead (see chapter 8) in arguing that the self becomes most fully developed by incorporating multiple generalized others, which is unlikely to occur in a primitive society.

7. I might again note that Durkheim actually uses severity of punishment as an *indicator*, or *index* (stand-in measure), of the strength of the collective consciousness, rather than viewing it as an dependent variable *explained by* the strength of the collective consciousness. If he maintained this position, however, Spitzer's data would force him to conclude that the collective consciousness is strongest in highly stratified societies with significant division of labor, causing him to abandon the notion that commonality of experience causes a strong collective consciousness. This would leave his theory in shambles, so it seems best to view severity of punishment as a possible effect of a strong collective consciousness rather than as a measure of it.

8. These occupational terms are anachronistic. Psychiatry itself was a barely established field that Durkheim referred to as the study of *mental alienation* and its practitioners as *alienists*. I use the term *political scientist* to encompass researchers called *moral statisticians* in Durkheim's day. Moral statisticians collected and analyzed information about social problems such as crime, prostitution, and suicide, using government and church records as data bases.

9. Thought experiments allow us to speculate about "what ifs" when we are unable to actually manipulate the variables involved experimentally. Drawing out implications, as you'll see in this example, is particularly important to developing thought experiments.

10. The figures I am using here to represent Durkheim's theory are similar to those used by Johnson (1965).

11. Underlying Durkheim's theorizing here is a conservative view of human nature. He believed that people were unable to regulate their desires and behavior by themselves but, instead, needed limits set for them by the surrounding society. Left to ourselves, we drink and eat too much, are overcome by lust, and aspire to preeminence among our peers. Only by having our desires moderated through the collective consciousness can we be kept from harming ourselves or others. This contrasts with the liberal view that most people are naturally self-regulating.

12. To deal with all the criticisms Durkheim's theory has faced would require a

small book in itself. Most prominent has been concern over whether official suicide statistics, upon which Durkheim relied almost exclusively, are trustworthy (Douglas 1967).

13. To do so, of course, we'd first have to define very clearly what we meant by *strength* of ties and decide how to measure it.

14. We are allowing our dependent variable (suicide rates) to serve as an index of our independent variable (integration), and when we do this, we can't be shown wrong by the data we gather: a false, but apparently strong, influence of the independent variable on the dependent is guaranteed by the fact that the latter is the measure of the former: thus, they must vary together.

15. The need for global measures and for calibration is underscored by a recent study (Breault and Kposowa 2000) showing that in the United States, singles in fact have lower rates of suicide than married people. This may be because the social integration of married people has changed across time in comparison to singles; because complex methodological problems have caused us (and Durkheim) to mistakenly conclude that married people have had lower suicide rates (see Breault 1994); or because Durkheim mislocated the difference between single and married states on an absolute map of integration and regulation. Without global and calibrated measures, we simply can't solve the problem that a study of this sort poses for evaluating Durkheim's theory.

16. At the same time, women attempt suicide as or more frequently than men. This raises a problem: which measure is the better test of Durkheim's theory, attempted or completed suicides? If women's attempts are less fatal than men's because they have less access to the most fatal means (guns), then we might prefer attempts. If we conclude women are less successful because they are using the attempts instrumentally and, thus, "don't really mean it," then we might prefer completed suicides. In contemplating this problem, be aware that in some cultures, women's rates of completed suicides are actually higher than men's, particularly among young women (see Girard 1993; Davies and Neal 2000).

17. As he put it, "we have now the cause of the antagonism of the sexes which prevents marriage from favoring them equally: their interests are contrary; one needs restraint and the other liberty" (1951:274). For a modern treatment of these issues, see the very interesting article by Kessler and McLeod (1984), as well as the chapter by Besnard (2000).

18. With regard to marriage, for instance, it would not be reasonable to argue that husbands in the nineteenth century faced the same degree of regulation as their wives. Marriage was simply much more restrictive for women than for men. Thus, the designation *married* on a death certificate meant something different for a male suicide than for a female suicide. Once again, this is a reason to seek global measures of our variable. In the case of young husbands, Durkheim is again inferring his independent variable from his dependent one: young married men are assumed to be excessively regulated solely because their suicide rates appeared to be high, not because their degree of regulation has been measured globally.

19. On fatalistic suicide, see Davies and Neal's very interesting discussion of the uncharacteristically high rates of suicide among young rural Chinese women (2000:40–45). They see this as fatalistic since, upon marriage, young women become

subject to the authority of their mothers-in-law, an authority so heavy that their condition resembles slavery.

20. I note that Breault and Kposowa (2000:166) suggest, "The older white female is more likely to become part of a social network compared to older white males who are widowed. . . . Thus the death of a spouse might increase the social integration of white women but decrease that of white men." In other words, widowed women may actually increase their integration compared to married age-mates, removing the anomaly. Once again, this points to the need for global measures of our independent variable.

21. By contrast, identities are more linked to ascriptive statuses (determined by race, gender, or lineage, for instance) in earlier societies. This makes it easier to fulfill the expectations of others, which Girard believes accounts for the generally lower rates of suicide in earlier societies.

7

Émile Durkheim and Functionalism

IN CHAPTER 6, we looked at two of Émile Durkheim's theories—those of variation in suicide rates and of variation in the severity of punishment—without indicating their relation to the functionalist paradigm from which they were derived. In this chapter, I want to use another of Durkheim's theories as a springboard to discussing the general nature of functionalism, viewed as a paradigm for creating theories. I'll discuss criteria that functional theories should ideally meet and develop a protocol by which their success in doing so can be evaluated. After developing the protocol, I'll apply it to several contemporary functionalist theories. My purpose in doing this is to outline critical strategies for evaluating functional theories. (This section of the chapter is unavoidably somewhat difficult, but its difficulty does indicate the rigor needed to successfully evaluate theories.) We'll conclude the chapter by examining the quite different explanatory strategy Durkheim used to account for the existence of religion as a belief system and social institution.

The Social Function of Crime

Functionalism is perhaps the most frequently utilized paradigm in the social sciences, but, as we will see, sometimes it is not well understood. To make sure that it is understood properly here, we will have to be very clear about its logical structure, and we can do this by slowly working outward from Durkheim's explanation of why crime is a **normal**, and indeed necessary, component of any healthy society. He made this counterintuitive proposal in the third chapter of a short book called *The Rules of Sociological Method* (published in 1895). When I say the argument is counterintuitive, I mean that it runs counter to our normal assumption that crime is everywhere a *social problem*, a pathology any society should be happy to rid itself of.

Actually, Durkheim (1938:67) admitted to having trouble breaking free of this assumption himself. He finally did so in the process of deciding whether it made sense to apply notions of health and sickness to societies as well as to individuals. Individuals clearly get sick (which they consider a bad thing), and sometimes even die from their illnesses (which they consider much worse). But claims that societies are "sick" seem disturbingly relative to the opinions of the observer,[1] and societies don't die in any way directly comparable to individuals. Could there be an objective way, then, to view some social phenomenon or condition as pathological? Was there any way to agree over what constituted a social problem?

Durkheim reviewed a number of ways that physical problems, such as illnesses, might be deemed pathological for individuals, but he judged none of them to be properly applicable to societies. He then attacked the problem from the opposite direction and argued that, at the very least, attributes that are universally possessed by societies should not be judged pathological and, therefore, not seen as social problems. Such attributes should be seen as normal to societies, which would preclude their being judged pathological. Durkheim (1938:58) noted that "it would be incomprehensible if the most widespread forms of organization would not at the same time be . . . the most advantageous." He was confident that readers would agree because they had come to share the Darwinian evolutionary view that disadvantageous traits could not spread through a population that already possessed more advantageous ones. If we view different societies (of the same type or stage of development) as constituting a population, the same principle should apply to them: if social traits are subject to a process of **selection** that eliminates the disadvantageous ones, those that remain and are widespread cannot be pathological.[2]

Durkheim immediately drove this point home using it to challenge the conventional wisdom on crime. Crime was a universal attribute of societies, he argued, and it had previously been universally deemed a social problem. But, if his principle of normalcy was right, the latter view had to be wrong. To show that it was wrong, he needed to indicate that crime *functioned* in a way that was evolutionarily beneficial to societies. In other words, crime had to be a functional attribute of societies that, once introduced, would spread through the population of societies by a process of selection.[3]

Defining the Problem

Let us stop for a moment to consider how Durkheim was setting up his problem. When we look at organisms and how they are designed, we sometimes find that they possess components whose purpose isn't immediately clear to us. This is true of our appendix, for instance, and I know I can't myself explain why my ears produce a waxy substance that I occasionally remove. If we look at societies on analogy to organisms, we can similarly wonder about the purpose of given institutions or practices. But only those that lack a manifest (obvious) purpose excite our wonder in this way. For instance, we have so little trouble understanding the purpose of an institution like medicine that the question of medicine's purpose doesn't elicit much interest. It's when we can't find any manifest purpose for a custom or institution that we grow intrigued. We then have to look for **latent functions** that the practice might be serving.[4]

Crime isn't a practice that initially invites this approach because we probably believe crimes have individual motivations but no wider social purpose at all. (If anything, crimes seem dysfunctional for society.) In other words, we seek the **manifest functions** of criminal activity at the individual level, in terms of payoffs to the criminals, without feeling any impulse to wonder about latent functions at the societal level. It was part of Durkheim's genius to use the concept of normalcy to force himself to wonder about the possible latent functions of crime. If they existed, we could perhaps demonstrate why crime would spread among societies by a process of selection and, thus, be present in them universally today.

Durkheim did not proceed immediately to this demonstration but first argued that, were crime a social problem (that is, were it pathological), there was simply no means by which it could, in practice, be eliminated from societies. In other words, he first suggested crime was an inevitable element of societies. Why? To see the force of his argument, it would help to consider a practical example. We are today much concerned with "child abuse" as a social problem.[5] Children can be abused in many ways, some very serious and others less so. Suppose we arrange these from the most to the least serious, as depicted in figure 7.1.[6]

With the exception of some societies in which child sacrifice is practiced, almost all societies forbid the most serious forms of abuse of children, those at the right of the list. Beyond this, however, we find a good deal of variation across history. Indeed, the writings of authors like Charles Dickens make it clear that children in previous centuries were routinely treated in ways we would today consider grossly abusive. Into the early twentieth century, the painful mutilation of girls by the practice of foot binding was the norm in China (Mackie 1996), while, in the United States, it was argued that failing to beat children was the real social problem since if you spared the rod, you spoiled the child. Our attitudes toward abuse changed in the mid- to late twentieth century, even though some groups still practice ritual mutilation of children (e.g., circumcision or ear piercing) without considering this abusive. At the limit of our current sensibility, some European societies today

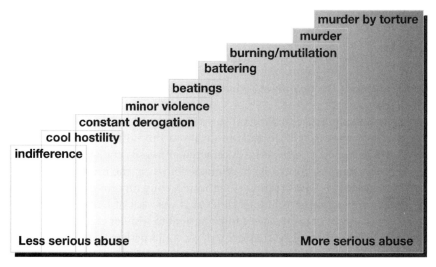

FIGURE 7.1
The Relative Gravity of Child Abuse

consider disciplinary spanking to be a punishable form of child abuse, while bumper stickers that ask us whether we have hugged our children today hope to control psychological abuse informally. In other words, over the course of the last century, we have lowered considerably the threshold over which acts must pass to be considered abusive toward children. In consequence, we are now horrified by behavior that would have been commonplace, and perhaps judged socially beneficial, at an earlier time in our own society.

Durkheim explored the social process by which changes of this sort occur.[7] We lower the threshold, he argued, by focusing the attention of the society on the most serious crimes, heightening our collective consciousness in relation to them so that we see them as even more serious. This can have the effect of suppressing them since individuals will be less likely to commit crimes that have generated increased concern and thus community surveillance. But the increased concern and surveillance automatically cause us to perceive less serious offenses as more serious, Durkheim argued, often criminalizing ones that were previously viewed as merely boorish or otherwise inappropriate. This raises the rate of offending anew, as the suppressed serious crimes are supplanted by less serious, newly criminalized ones—as with spanking in Scandinavian countries. These have now become more repugnant as a result of the very heightening of concern that suppressed their predecessors.[8] The lowering of the threshold is experienced as an improvement in moral character as we come to see our past practices as "barbaric."

It is worth quoting Durkheim's description of this process at length:

> Robbery and simple bad taste injure the same single altruistic sentiment, the respect for that which is another's. However, this same sentiment is less grievously offended by bad taste than by robbery. . . . That is why the person guilty of bad taste is merely blamed, whereas the thief is punished. But if this sentiment grows stronger, to the point of silencing in all consciousnesses the inclination which disposes man to steal, he will become more sensitive to offenses which, until then, touched him but lightly. He will react against them, then, with more energy; they will be the object of greater opprobrium, which will transform certain of them from the simple moral faults they were and give them the quality of crimes. (1938:68)

Although Durkheim's linking of lapses in taste to robbery may puzzle us, the social psychological mechanism he described is a very real one. For us to criminalize a practice like disciplinary spanking, we have first to view it as demonstrating poor taste in child-rearing practices, the sort of thing we might cluck our tongues at when our neighbors reveal that they employ it. Once the tongue clucking becomes widespread enough (say, as the result of efforts to heighten our collective consciousness about the fragility of children and the unstinting love and respect they need in order not to be profoundly damaged), we find it possible to visualize spanking as a crime. Of course, we never come to judge it as equal in barbarism to torture and mutilation or to child sacrifice—the heightening of collective consciousness does not eliminate all ability to discriminate in this regard, but it can pass over the threshold that separates bad taste from acts that elicit formal social control by the police, thus becoming crimes.[9]

While Durkheim did not give this process a name, I will call it **scrupulosity**. This term refers to a common experience in religious communities whereby minor faults in one's behavior or religious observance come to be seen as proportionally more important as one's most serious faults are eliminated. Scrupulosity is the social psychological process by which moral molehills gradually appear as mountains, and it is characteristic of individuals and communities that strive to heighten or intensify their collective consciousness so as to eliminate some perceived defect. (The movement to think and behave in "politically correct" ways today exemplifies such an effort to heighten our collective consciousness.) Durkheim was suggesting that scrupulosity is a social psychological *mechanism* that operates everywhere, with the consequence that crime is inevitable. It is inevitable because the same process that heightens our collective attention to address serious crimes and eliminate them at the same time lowers the threshold for what constitutes a crime.

This interesting argument was not a direct part of Durkheim's functional account of crime, however. He introduced it, I think, for two reasons. First, it weakens the grasp of received opinion on us since, if crime in general is inevitable, we will be less likely to view it as something we must necessarily try to get rid of. And, second, it prepares the way for a functional explanation by allowing us to view crime as a product not of individuals alone but of a distinctly social process that is built into the organization of our community life. And once we see crime as a social phenomenon, inevitably built into the constitution of society by the process of scrupulosity, it is certainly easier to wonder whether it might also be advantageous to societies. In other words, Durkheim has been taking elaborate care, in setting up his problem, first to draw us into his own sense of wonder. Once he has accomplished this, we are ready to tackle his main, functional argument. I will present it first as he does, then indicate one minor aspect in which it is wrong. Next, I'll restate the argument in the way I believe to be compelling.

Explaining Crime

Durkheim (1938:70) noted that for social change to occur, "the collective sentiments at the basis of morality must not be hostile to change, and consequently must have but moderate energy. If they were too strong, they would no longer be plastic." It follows that societies that heighten their collective consciousness so as to stamp out crime may become rigid in the process and, thus, hostile to innovation. Yet, some innovations will be beneficial, allowing societies to adapt better to their environments or respond to challenges they set. Rigid societies are unable to accept these innovations, which impedes their ability to compete with societies that do innovate or to respond successfully to changes in their physical environment. In other words, a society that is too scrupulous is also too inflexible to adapt and is apt to be selected against by pressures from the natural or social environment. From this it follows that crime "is useful, because these conditions of which it is a part are themselves indispensable to the normal evolution" of society (1938:70).

To drive his point home, Durkheim directed us to the case of Socrates, an innovative thinker who was no more interested than Durkheim in parroting the received wisdom. For failing to conform, however, he was judged a blasphemer by his fellow Athenians and executed. Excessive demands for conformity, the case of Socrates seems to suggest, cause societies to mistake innovative thought for blasphemy and to deny themselves its benefits. Inflexibility of this sort is simply fatal, evolutionarily speaking. Societies that practice it consign themselves to the dustbin of history. It follows that crime is itself evolutionarily beneficial.

This last conclusion seems wrong to me: it's not crime that is beneficial; it's the social flexibility, or tolerance, that accepts innovation but cannot exist without at the same time allowing for crime. This is what Durkheim means by referring to the "conditions of which [crime] is a part" in the quotation above. He never really meant that murder, robbery, arson, and other standard crimes were somehow in themselves useful to society; instead, he deemed useful the relaxed social control that, unfortunately, guaranteed that such crimes would be committed.[10] In other words, you can't have a society flexible enough to permit Socrates to live and to speak his mind without at the same time allowing people their murderous thoughts and actions. The one is the price of the other; yet, this needn't mean both are advantageous. Correctly stated, the presence of crime in a society is a possible index of the flexibility that allows for innovation, but it is not advantageous in itself.

Let's pause for a moment to consider the logical structure of Durkheim's argument. Almost without our being aware, it has taken on the traditional form of a theory, as figure 7.2 shows. There we see that the adaptive flexibility of a society decreases as its concern with stamping out crime increases. In fact, the rate at which crimes are committed can serve as an index of flexibility since the two variables behave in the same way.[11]

Societies that succeed in focusing a great amount of collective attention on

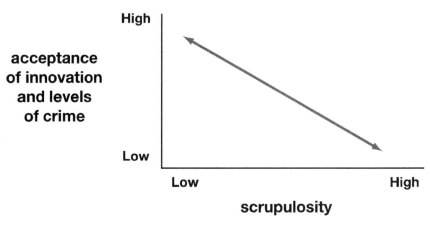

FIGURE 7.2
Crime Levels and Acceptance of Innovation Related to Scrupulosity

crime are apt to be **totalitarian**, demanding enormous and unstinting commitment from their members. This call for commitment makes these societies so hostile to individuality and individualism that they stifle any novel thinking. People become scared to think for themselves because of the likelihood that the result will be interpreted as blasphemy, as it was with Socrates. In totalitarian societies, individuals will consistently find their innovations mistaken for an attack on the society itself and, thus, become hesitant to voice them.

We see, then, that crime is not only inevitable but is an index of social health. By an index, I mean that it points to another condition, social flexibility, that is a desirable (functional) trait for societies to possess. In practice, we can't eliminate crime without also eliminating this flexibility. So, crime isn't directly functional but it is a necessary concomitant of a functional trait. Since we can't have flexibility without crime, we really shouldn't want to get rid of crime, odd as this conclusion seems.

An Illustrative Case: Fraud and Innovation in Science

It might help to make this argument concrete through a restricted, but I hope very convincing, example.[12] It comes from the field of science, where a premium is placed upon innovation. To set up the example, I need to make two sets of distinctions that we can apply to the research findings of scientists. The first is between findings that conform to the conventional wisdom in their substance and methods, on the one hand, and findings that are deviant, challenging the conventional wisdom in either substance or method, on the other. The second distinction is between findings that history judges to have been productive contributions—I'll call these "good science"—versus those upon which scientists are judged to have wasted their time, which I'll call "bad science." These two sets of distinctions allow us to form what's called a two-by-two table, such as figure 7.3. Take a moment to consider what types of work might fit into the boxes it offers us.

Let's explore the upper right box first: it contains bad conformist science. What does such science look like? Every year, scientific journals publish enormous numbers of articles and reports of research findings, the majority of which are never referred to again (that is, they are never cited by other scientists in their own work, which is the best way we have of measuring the influence that research has had). Thus, much research simply disappears after publication, without any discernible impact on the scientific community. While it enters the archives, it does so without any consequence and, thus, could be deemed wasted effort. To judge it "bad" might seem a bit harsh— Harriet Zuckerman (1977:88) terms it merely "pedestrian"—but it is, technically speaking, worthless, which isn't much better than "bad." In principle, the money spent producing it would have been better spent elsewhere.

By contrast, "good" science influences the work of other scientists, as is shown by their citing it in future publications. Good conformist science gets noticed by others and has an effect on their research but is not seen as being strikingly innovative. Thomas Kuhn (1962), a philosopher of science, referred to such work as **normal science**: it solves problems without changing people's orientation toward solving problems. It leaves people's habits of

	Good science	Bad science
Conformist science		
Deviant science		

FIGURE 7.3
An Empty Two-by-Two Table Relating the Relative Quality and Normalcy of Scientific Work to One Another

thought and laboratory practice in place, merely adding further pieces to the jigsaw puzzles upon which scientists are working. On the other hand, what Kuhn calls **revolutionary science** changes the nature of the puzzle itself: it challenges our habits of thought or our sense of what counts as good evidence for our ideas.

That Kuhn's revolutionary science belongs in our good deviant box will be clear from one case. In 1912, a meteorologist named Alfred Wegener presented evidence to the German Geological Society that the continents had originally been connected to one another but had, over a very long span of time, drifted apart.[13] Wegener was not the first to notice the correspondences between the shapes of South America and Africa—they had been remarked on by Francis Bacon in 1620—but he was the first to produce good geological and paleontological evidence that there had originally been one supercontinent that split into mobile fragments. This notion contradicted the prevailing understanding of how the earth and its continents were formed, however. Although Wegener wasn't laughed off the podium when he presented it, his theory was met with a mixture of interest and incredulity. One scholar characterized Wegener's theory as "delirious ravings"; a gentler view saw it as a "fairy tale" (Schwarzbach 1986:109,112). While it gained some support, this collapsed under aggressive attack from other scientists in the late 1920s, so when Wegener died in 1930, his position was considered distinctly deviant within geology. New support for continental drift was found in the 1960s, however, and it is now firmly established as geological orthodoxy. Thus, we've come to look back on Wegener as a bold thinker, a revolutionary who was able to see beyond the conventional wisdom of his time. This is just the sort of nonconformity we need: it is deviant but good science, and we can point to the work of Nicolaus Copernicus and Galileo Galilei for additional instances.

We've now found examples to fill three of our boxes: what remains is deviant bad science. This is represented by quack ideas and fraudulent findings. Quack ideas abound in every era: some arise within the scientific community itself and then have to be exiled, while others arise on its margins and have to be kept out. Homeopathic medicine is an example of the former, and "creation science" of the latter. The work that scientists do to police their enterprise and to exile or keep out quack interlopers has been styled **boundary work** (Gieryn 1999). Without boundary work, science would be an incoherent enterprise, with too much time and energy devoted to researching topics that would eventually prove fruitless.

To avoid both fruitlessness and positive harm, science must also guard itself against fraud. The frequency with which fraudulent findings are concocted by scientists is hard to gauge, but cases like that of immunological researcher William Summerlin[14] indicate that it does happen (see Hixson 1976 and, for additional cases, Miller and Hersen 1992). Both fraud and quackery threaten to undermine science and, thus, qualify as both deviant and bad for the enterprise.

We've now filled in our two-by-two table so that it looks like figure 7.4. We can use this table to make Durkheim's point.[15] Transferring his argument to the field of science, it says that if we somehow got all scientists to be very concerned with policing boundaries to eliminate fraud and quackery, they would, having become too scrupulous, automatically mistake revolutionary ideas for scientifically blasphemous ones (i.e., for quackery). And fear of being judged blasphemous would make scientists unwilling to publish revolutionary ideas. In other words, a campaign vigorous enough to stamp out quackery and fraud would cause figures like Wegener to clam up and keep their novel ideas to themselves since these ideas would initially appear as quackery—or as delirious ravings—to the community. Thus, successfully stamping out fraud and quackery means at the same time stamping out revolutionary ideas, which would routinely be mistaken for "bad" ones. But without revolutionary ideas, science will slowly become stagnant. So, we can't get rid of the lower right-hand box without also getting rid of the lower left.

Conversely, permitting the relatively relaxed atmosphere that encourages revolutionary ideas automatically also permits a degree of fraud and quackery. Indeed, it will often take some time to sort the revolutionaries from the quacks, as the career of Wegener's idea suggests.[16] This means that the presence of fraud and quackery among scientists is an index of the very community flexibility toward new ideas that will allow for revolutions to occur.

	Good science	Bad science
Conformist science	normal science	unnoticed work
Deviant science	revolutionary science	quackery & fraud

FIGURE 7.4
A Completed Two-by-Two Table Exemplifying the Relation between the Quality and Normalcy of Scientific Work

Thus, odd and counterintuitive as it may seem, the presence of quackery and fraud is a good thing for the scientific community. This is not because they make positive contributions themselves but because they are present whenever there is healthy flexibility in the system.

I hope that using the field of science to illustrate Durkheim's point makes it thoroughly convincing. It should also be clear that sociologists must often get beyond the conventional wisdom to investigate how the social order works. This is often true when we seek the latent functions of social phenomena, and it is testament to Durkheim's genius that he was able to think so clearly and forcefully in the counterintuitive mode. Of course, we have yet to evaluate his explanation of crime, but we can do this best in the course of our analysis of functionalism as a paradigm.

Functionalism as a Paradigm

Having looked at a classic example of functional analysis, we can now turn to the paradigm itself to examine its logical structure. I've already indicated that it is not well understood, but perhaps I should say it is not well followed, because its standards (which are severe) are infrequently met in practice. Indeed, few instances of its use in the social sciences have been entirely convincing, either because they have been poorly thought through or because the data needed to support them cannot be gathered. The best instances of it sway us because, even without good data, they appear to be on the right explanatory track. Yet, while we can hope to improve them, perfection will rarely be reached because social scientists are limited in their ability to design the sorts of laboratory or field experiments that have made functionalism so successful a paradigm in the biological sciences.

As I've already suggested, functionalism is the approach we "naturally" take whenever we're puzzled about why an organism possesses a trait that lacks an obvious purpose (or, in Durkheim's case, when we're puzzled about a feature of society that seems harmful but is universally present). A quick way to get an answer is to remove the structure and see what happens to the organism. For instance, we attempt to discover the functions of particular genes by removing them from the DNA of germ cells and seeing what happens as the organism develops. In applying functionalism in the social sciences, we make a provisional assumption that it makes sense to view social groups on analogy to organisms or machines in order to raise questions about what their "parts" are doing, that is, what they're there for. Again, we won't normally have questions if the functions are manifest because these are known to us to begin with. It's the latent functions we're after, and the easiest way to discover them is to remove the part and see how the group reacts. The problem is that we often don't have any easy—or even hard—way to do this. Recognizing that we don't, we're apt simply to speculate about possible functions that we'll never actually be able to demonstrate. This is standard operating procedure in the social sciences, and, unfortunately, it sets a very low standard of practice.

I want to outline a higher standard here. I'll do this as a series of steps that constitute what we can call a *protocol* for functional analysis. If we can successfully complete all of the steps, we will have made as strong a case for our analysis as possible. If we can't, which is most of the time, we should be clear about why we haven't been able to and about how much damage this does to our case.

My protocol for functional analysis consists of ten steps. I'll present them individually with some commentary on most of them.

1. *First, we must identify clearly the attribute or process whose function we want to understand. This means we should define it clearly enough that independent observers would agree that it is present or absent in a given circumstance and to what degree.*[17]

I note that Durkheim confused us about the identity of his attribute because, while he indicated it was crime, he seems really to have meant social flexibility, for which the presence of crime was merely an index.

2. *Next, we must specify the social unit for which the attribute provides a function. This might be an individual, a family, an organization, or a political unit (town, state, nation, and so on). The specified unit will be analogous to the organism in biology. The attribute is seen as being a part of this unit, and we are curious about whether and how it is functionally necessary or beneficial.*

If the unit is "society," as in Durkheim's case, we should make every effort to specify what this very vague term designates since this is crucial to taking the next step.

3. *We must specify the population to which the unit belongs. This population should consist of similar units among which our unit resides: individuals must belong to some specified population of individuals (e.g., a college, town, company, state), organizations to a specified population of organizations (e.g., industry, national association), and so on.*

As we'll see, the population is the testing ground upon which we can demonstrate the benefits of the attribute in question since beneficial attributes should spread through the population. Durkheim is unclear here, though we can surmise that his population consists of a group of societies, today probably corresponding to nations.

By completing the first three steps, we've prepared ourselves to offer a functional explanation of the attribute. We've done the easy part. What follows is a lot harder.

> 4. *Next, we must suggest a benefit the attribute provides to the unit. This is the same thing as indicating its role or function within the unit.*

How do we settle upon a benefit? We can perform an experiment in our minds (a thought experiment) by eliminating the attribute (e.g., social flexibility) and asking ourselves what might happen to the unit (e.g., the society), or we can compare the unit with others that lack the attribute (comparing, for instance, the relatively flexible United States to the relatively inflexible Afghanistan under the Taliban regime) to see how they are different. Units lacking the attribute must be placed at a disadvantage thereby, since otherwise there would be no point in having it in the first place. The process here is just like the search for matching empirical generalizations we outlined in our first chapter.

> 5. *If possible, we should specify the precise mechanisms by which the attribute provides its benefit to the unit. This makes clear how the attribute plays the role we have just allotted it. Are the benefits manifest or latent? Reversing this, we should also specify the mechanisms by which the attribute is maintained by the unit. How is it kept viable?*

Durkheim indicates that social flexibility allows for innovations to be accepted. Social flexibility means that innovators will not have to risk punishment (or death) for advancing ideas that may initially seem strange. Thus, we have at least a modest sense of the mechanisms by which flexibility produces an advantageous result and can give examples. It keeps people from clamming up. We should also try to specify the mechanisms, such as rules guaranteeing academic freedom, that maintain the beneficial social condition.

> 6. *We must next estimate the magnitude of the benefit to the unit. How much better does the unit perform for having the attribute rather than lacking*

it? If there is a mixed picture of advantages and disadvantages, we need to total them up and estimate the scale of the net benefit.

Most functional analyses get through steps 1 to 4 without much difficulty, although they are often very casual about steps 2 and 3. Where they begin to disappoint us is with steps 5 and 6. (Sometimes this is unavoidable since mechanisms can often be very hard to investigate.[18]) Durkheim's analysis of crime, for instance, gives us some sense of the mechanism by which flexibility could produce benefits, but he leaves the magnitude of its effect largely or entirely vague. He says that the mechanism encourages innovation but gives us no sense at all of the magnitude of the benefit this provides. In fact, he really does no more than appeal to the story of Socrates in order to convince us that social flexibility is a benefit.

Steps 4 to 6 constitute the core of a functional analysis of the attribute. The steps that follow allow us to explain the attribute's spread from its place of origin to other units in the population we specified in step 3. In the social sciences, these steps are usually left implicit. This is unfortunate because it's here that the real explanatory power of a functional explanation is revealed. Further, contemplation of these steps can often identify disabling flaws in functional explanations, an example of which we will meet later.

7. *If possible, we should estimate the selection pressure on the population to which the unit belongs.*

Selection pressure is a fancy term, but it really just refers to the sorts of factors affecting the population that would increase or decrease the speed with which new, beneficial attributes spread across it. Selection pressure can vary, among other ways, according to the degree of competition among units in the population or how exposed they are to predation by units in other populations; how scarce the resources are that these units need to maintain themselves; and how easy it is for new units to enter the population. Aggressive, exposed, and resource-poor units that are challenged by new entrants into the population are subject to high selection pressures. They must really struggle to survive, and this means that the return to them on any beneficial innovation will come rapidly, with the consequence that it should spread quickly to other units in the population. The opposite circumstances yield a low selection pressure, making it questionable that innovations will spread at all. Where there is no selection pressure at all, functional analysis is meaningless.[19]

8. *We should identify the mechanism or process by which the attribute spreads from the initial to subsequent adopters. Some can spread by mod-*

eling as less successful units in the population copy the innovations of more successful units. Others will spread by conquest, migration, or still other processes.

For example, it is possible that the military occupation of Afghanistan by the United States will lead to greater social flexibility there. Thus, the mechanism in this instance is military conquest.

9. *Next, we use the estimates of benefit (step 6) and of selection pressure (step 7), along with knowledge of the mechanism(s) in step 8, to estimate the speed with which the attribute will spread through the population.*

This step causes us to wonder: if the benefits of flexibility are great, it must be that selection pressure is low because many societies seem to resist moving toward flexibility.

10. *Finally, we derive implications from steps 4 to 6 and steps 7 to 9 that allow for varied tests of the theory.*

While this ten-step protocol ignores some nuances that would be included in a "professional" version, it's perfectly adequate for our purposes.[20] It should be used to evaluate any functional explanation you encounter. I will use it in a moment to point out some problems with contemporary functional analyses, but I want now to use it in a loose way both to compliment and to criticize Durkheim's theory.

It is an interesting property of Durkheim's analysis of the function of crime (or of social flexibility) that, once we properly understand it, it seems obviously correct. Even though it barely gets past the fourth of our ten steps, it so appeals to our rough sense of how the world works that we are likely to be thoroughly convinced by it. We then relax, unconcerned about completing the steps in the protocol, even as a purely critical or evaluative exercise. While I think this reaction is a testament to the value of Durkheim's counterintuitive insight into society, it cuts off the possibility of further insights and prevents us from entering certain reservations about Durkheim's theory.

Consider a possible reservation: one reason Durkheim's theory seems obviously right to us today is that we are aware of the prominent failures of rigid totalitarian regimes in the twentieth century. The eclipse of fascist and communist totalitarian governments has contributed to our background sense of how the world works. It seems reasonable to attribute the demise of these regimes in part to their inflexibility, which we see exemplified today in a state like North Korea, a state certainly beset with problems. So reasonable is this that we're tempted to see flexibility as being self-evidently functional so that people should prefer it just as they would prefer the telephone to the telegraph.

But there are two problems with this view. First, it simply assumes that the failures of totalitarian governments in the twentieth century were functionally ordained, whereas they may have been the result of contingent events of the "for want of a shoe" variety that we analyzed in the first chapter. Nazi Germany and its allies might have won World War II, after all, in which case rigidity might appear the more functional social attribute. We cannot really know whether totalitarianism's inflexibility, on the one hand, or contingent events, on the other, account for the downfalls until we have a sufficiently large sample of cases by means of which to evaluate the two possibilities responsibly.

The second problem is that totalitarian governments, such as the Taliban in Afghanistan or the somewhat less stringent House of Saud in Saudi Arabia, seem still to arise anew, despite the supposed costs of their inflexibility. At the very least, this means that these costs are certainly not manifest to everyone. At the most, it causes us to wonder whether social flexibility really does spread very far through the population of states on its merits. Varieties of fundamentalism, from Christian to Stalinist to Islamist, clearly have their attractions (at least for government leaders) and may call out in citizens a willingness to sacrifice that allows fundamentalist states to engage in wars of conquest as well as urgent proselytizing and conversion across borders. At the present moment, it is not clear whether the more or less flexible states will prevail or whether a certain mixture of flexibility and totalitarianism is perhaps a permanent feature of the global organization of states.

I bring these matters forward to indicate that we in fact know very little about how to measure the benefits of flexibility to states (taking these as our units) or about the selection pressures to which these states are subject—with the consequence that we can't really say whether flexibility should drive totalitarianism out of the population of states, either by success in war or by being copied. And this means that, although Durkheim's functional explanation of flexibility may seem obviously true when we initially understand it, it still needs to be demonstrated empirically for very important populations like modern states.[21]

I hope this illustrates why it is important to have a very clear idea of the standards we'd like functionalist arguments to meet. Functionalism fell quickly and deeply into disrepute in the 1960s, in part because it had been employed so sloppily before then. It has slowly been revived, largely as a result of uses that, like Durkheim's, have been convincing without necessarily living up to the standards we've just laid out. We've already encountered two of these: Richard Nisbett and Dov Cohen's functional explanation of the spread of a reputation for violence among male members of families in herding economies, and Marvin Harris's explanation of the spread of cow worship among populations on the Indian subcontinent. You should take the opportunity now to go back and review these arguments, evaluating them in terms of the standards of our protocol. (You'll find they leave a good deal to be desired.) Another example that you may not have immediately recognized as functional was Arthur Stinchcombe's explanation (see chapter 5) of the circumstances in which bureaucratic (as opposed to craft) administration of production thrives. His explanation is particularly interesting because it illustrates how we can use an understanding of factors like the volume and stability of demand for a product to predict how broadly a trait like bureaucratization will spread through the population of productive organizations. Where demand is not stable or high enough, bureaucratic administration becomes dysfunctional and is replaced with craft administration.

These three arguments are each very interesting, if still quite provisional. Their shortcomings indicate how hard it is to do functional analysis well, while their obvious appeal suggests how hard it would be to get along without functional analysis at all.[22]

Functional Explanations of Stratification and Poverty

I want now to look at two further applications of functionalism. The first is Kingsley Davis and Wilbert Moore's explanation of stratification, which is perhaps the best-known use of the functional paradigm in twentieth-century sociology. The second is Herbert Gans's use of the paradigm to explain the persistence of poverty, a case that illustrates some important pitfalls to be avoided in applying the paradigm. The two cases together will allow us both to understand functionalism better and to understand its relation to the conflict paradigm (discussed in chapter 3).

Davis and Moore on Stratification

Davis and Moore outlined their functional theory of stratification in a short article published in 1945 in the *American Sociological Review*. They focused on explaining why the various positions in society, for which we can let "occupations" stand in, receive greater or lesser rewards. (Doctors, after all, earn more than trash collectors, and the differences in rewards they receive are one basis for a prestige hierarchy that ranks doctors above trash collectors.) Their answer flows from a series of propositions: that positions vary in their importance to the societies in which they exist; that they also vary in the talents and training required to perform well within them; and that individuals in a society differ in their abilities and their diligence. Given these variations, it is beneficial to a society to recruit the more able and diligent individuals into the more important positions. To do so, it is necessary to offer differential incentives, with recruits to important positions receiving more of valued goods and social prestige than recruits to less important positions. The result of this is stratification, "an unconsciously evolved device by which societies insure that the most important positions are conscientiously filled by the most qualified persons" (1945:243).

Note that this argument says nothing about the degree of difference in incentives that is required to recruit talented and diligent people to the important positions. As far as Davis and Moore's argument is concerned, this difference could be quite small, provided it worked. Further, if the incentives are monetary and the differences allow some individuals to accumulate wealth over the course of a career in an important position, nothing in the Davis-Moore theory suggests that this wealth should be allowed to pass to their children through inheritance. Thus, the theory explains only a certain, probably quite small portion of the stratification existing in actual societies, but it insists that this portion is functionally necessary.[23] Unstratified societies with highly differentiated roles would be at a disadvantage in competing against similar, but stratified, societies because the unstratified societies would fail to allocate motivated and talented individuals to the crucial roles.

If you reflect on the above, it will soon be apparent that Davis and Moore's theory is as underdeveloped with regard to our protocol as is Durkheim's, although, in some ways, it is more straightforward. Just as Durkheim argued that the universal nature of crime pointed to its functional potential, so did Davis and Moore with stratification. Also like Durkheim, however, they made no effort to assess the net benefit it offers society or the selection pressures to which such societies are exposed. Nor did they produce a very firm sense of how one crucial variable, the functional importance of positions, could be accurately gauged.[24] Despite these and other problems, however, their theory remains just as convincing as Durkheim's: we are apt to admit that it is "right" even though it meets few of our criteria.[25] In part, this is because the ubiquity of stratification stands as an obstacle to testing the theory, just as the ubiquity of crime stands in the way of testing Durkheim's theory.

In the first chapter, however, we saw how important it is to derive implications from a theory so as to provide tests of it. Are there ways of doing this with the Davis-Moore theory? Noting how few empirical studies the theory had generated, Stinchcombe (1963) suggested several possible tests. In the first of these, he pointed out that, while it is very difficult to measure the functional importance of the different positions in a society, we can roughly assess changes in the functional importance of the same position over time. For instance, Stinchcombe pointed out that having good people in command positions in the army is not crucial to a country when it is at peace but becomes absolutely vital when it is at war. Davis and Moore's theory implies, then, that the differential reward for army command positions should increase in time of war and decrease thereafter. This seems to follow from the theory as an implication, and it is an empirical generalization that we should be able to test easily.

On another front, Stinchcombe pointed out that organizations vary in the degree to which adding a single highly talented or motivated individual can make a difference to the performance of the whole organization. For instance, to use one of his examples, finding a star willing to act in a hum-drum movie will increase one's profits far more, proportionally, than will finding an extraordinary housepainter to join a crew of housepainters on a given job. It follows that there should be greater differences in rewards in the former type of organization than in the latter. Again, this is something we can test empirically, and, as with our discussion of Nisbett and Cohen's the-ory, each test that the theory passes increases our confidence that it is right, which means it is the best we can do for the time being. At any rate, with some ingenuity in drawing out its implications, the Davis and Moore theory can easily be put to tests.

There is also an implication that can be drawn negatively and that makes clear the theory's relation to the conflict paradigm. Davis and Moore speci-fied only that a vaguely defined threshold level of inequality was necessary to attract talented, motivated, and trained people to important positions. But most societies probably have far more inequality than this minimum. Realiz-ing this, we can reverse Stinchcombe's approach to argue that, when a posi-tion is filled by equally talented and motivated people who are nevertheless differently rewarded, the difference cannot be functionally explained by Davis and Moore's argument. An example will make this complicated point clear. At the turn of the twenty-first century in the United States, chief execu-tive officers of major corporations received compensation at least two hun-dred times that of the average production worker, while in Japan CEOs received about ten times the compensation of average workers.[26] If we assume that, in the long run, U.S. and Japanese corporations are equally well (or poorly) run, then it seems clear that none of this large difference in com-pensation can be explained functionally. Instead, it must result from the greater power of U.S. executives to receive, in their compensation packages, more than they are due. To explain exactly how they manage this, we would have to call on the conflict paradigm, not on functionalism.

The comparison between levels of compensation for Japanese and U.S. executives does not establish that the Japanese level is functionally necessary. In fact, we could only determine what is functionally necessary by driving down compensation to executives until they decided to leave and take other positions, no longer finding the rewards of their old positions great enough to draw out their talents and energies. Despite our not being able to determine this threshold, however, the case clearly shows that only conflict explanations can account for compensation higher than the Japanese receive since this must be above the functionally necessary threshold.

We can see from this that functional and conflict explanations are often complementary. Particularly when we are trying to explain phenomena like stratification, they may both be necessary. Figure 7.5 attempts to make this clear using real-world examples. In this figure, we arbitrarily set the threshold for the functionally necessary minimum differential at seven, although we really have no idea where it lies between one and ten. Above seven, we enter an area that could be explained either by functional or conflict theories, between which we could decide only by experiments driving down executive compensation. Above ten, however, we're confident that we've entered exclusively conflict territory, for which the Japanese case sets a lower limit. Thus, it seems evident that to explain all of the variation in rewards attached to positions, we need both paradigms.

Herbert Gans on Poverty

Thirty years after Davis and Moore published their theory, Gans (1972) tackled the problem of stratification once again by looking at the possible ways that poverty serves society. Like crime and stratification, poverty seems to exist everywhere, which can make us wonder whether it perhaps serves some latent purpose or purposes of which we are not aware. Gans was able to list fifteen of these latent purposes, which he thought might explain why poverty did not disappear, even though American society supposedly "waged war" on it in the 1960s.

Here, I want to use Gans's argument to illuminate problems that occasionally crop up in functional analysis and that we can avoid by carefully following our protocol. An initial problem is that Gans never defines poverty or the group ("the poor") it characterizes. Thus, we don't know how large a group this is or who, precisely, is in it. As Gans turns to the unit or units for which poverty is beneficial, furthermore, he switches back and forth between the society as a whole, on the one hand, and various groups within society, such

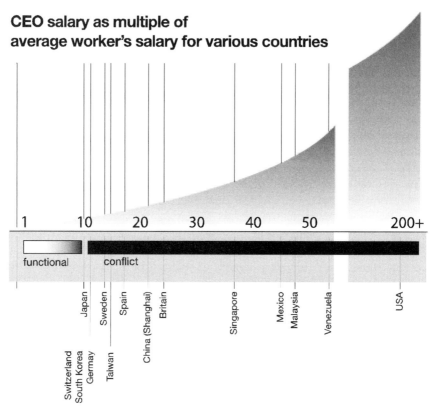

CEO salary as multiple of average worker's salary for various countries

FIGURE 7.5
The Contribution of Functional and Conflict Paradigms to Explaining Stratification
Data source: "Spreading the Yankee Way of Pay," *Business Week*, April 18, 2001

as the rich or the helping professions, on the other.[27] The latter step violates the second principle of our protocol. That principle indicates that the trait or attribute we intend to analyze must be a part of the unit receiving the benefit. But the poor aren't a part of the rich or of the helping professions; they're a part of the society to which the rich and the helping professions belong alongside the poor. Put more bluntly, poverty is not a trait that characterizes the rich or social workers and, so, can't be functional for them.

The example of Gans's third function for poverty will make this problem clear. He writes,

poverty creates jobs for a number of occupations and professions which serve the poor, or shield the rest of the population from them. As noted already, penology would be minuscule without the poor, as would the police, since the poor provide the majority of their "clients." (1972:279)

Indeed, a very similar explanation is often given by students when I ask them to anticipate Durkheim's explanation of why crime is functional: they echo Gans by saying that crime persists because it provides jobs for the police. But a little reflection will indicate that this cannot be the case. Were crime to decline, maintaining police forces at current levels would only be functional *for a society* (as opposed to the police themselves) if there were no better use for the money that pays for the now-superfluous police. But since the money saved could be diverted to employ engineers, teachers, nurses, military personnel, or other producers of more valuable goods and services, this is clearly not the case. Thus, giving up the policing we no longer need should make our society *better* able to compete on the world scene. Indeed, societies whose lower crime rates allow them to divert resources out of policing should be at a clear advantage, all else being equal, in comparison with societies needing large police forces. So, while it is certainly true that crime employs police, we simply can't say that crime persists to employ police.[28] The same will be true for any occupation, such as social worker, whose services are disproportionally utilized by the poor.

This problem will occur whenever we assert that a trait belonging to one group proves functional for another group of the same sort, rather than for the unit to which both belong. Compare the police example with a properly functional explanation that Gans offers. In this case, the unit of analysis is the society:

> In addition, as Barry Schwartz pointed out . . . the low income of the poor enables the rich to divert a higher proportion of their income to savings and investment, and thus to fuel economic growth. This, in turn, can produce higher incomes for everybody, including the poor, although it does not necessarily improve the position of the poor in the economic hierarchy, since the benefits of economic growth are also distributed unequally. (1972:279)

Here, we have a suggestion that while the rich indeed become richer for the sacrifice of the poor, so do the poor themselves. According to an interesting argument made by political philosopher John Rawls (1971), the poor should willingly forego income now if this is the only or fastest way to get more income later. Further, if we assume that "higher incomes for everybody" are a benefit to the society in competition with other societies, depriving the poor of higher incomes now may possibly show functional benefits for the society as a whole later. This is a legitimate functional explanation in principle, and, indeed, it is often utilized in practice by politicians seeking to reduce the tax burden on the rich.

But what happens if only the rich, and not society as a whole, benefit from the fruits of the income that the poor forego? Now we are squarely back in conflict territory. As we saw in chapter 3, the fourth principle of the conflict paradigm is that "favored parties [in this case, the rich] take advantage of the situation by constructing social arrangements by means of which more than their proportional share of wealth, deference, sex, or other desirable goods accrues to them." Indeed, when Gans identifies functions that the poor provide for the rich, as opposed to society as a whole, he often merely renames conflict explanations as functional ones. And this happens because he doesn't follow the second principle of our protocol.

Since the general point here is very important, let me make it in another way. Suppose the poor provide the majority of boxers, and the well-to-do, the majority of ticket-paying fans for boxing matches. Let's also suppose that the poor who enter boxing see it as one of the few avenues available for them to make "big money" and that they wouldn't box if there were other, less painful and dangerous means open to them. Now we can casually say that one role of the poor is to box before the well-to-do and even style this as one of their "functions." But having a function in this way is not being functional in the framework of a functional explanation. The latter requires, as part of steps 4 to 6, that we specify the benefit gained by a unit to which both the rich and poor belong so that this unit gains a competitive advantage within the population of units specified in step 2. It would be extremely difficult to do this in the case of boxing as a professional sport, with society as the unit receiving the benefit, regardless of how thrilled the well-to-do are by boxing matches. Would a society without boxing matches be at a competitive disadvantage against other societies? Put differently, we cannot explain why the poor box (rather than the rich) in terms of the benefit in this to society at large. Instead, we do so by exploring variations in the opportunities the rich and poor have that cause the latter to box and the former to pay them to do so. But this involves a conflict explanation, not a functional one. Again, we should not mistake the casual meaning of the terms *function* or *role* for the more rigorous one we need in functional analysis.

A final problem arises from ignoring the seventh item on our protocol: selection pressure. In identifying another function of poverty, Gans writes,

> The poor buy goods which others do not want and thus prolong their economic usefulness, such as day-old bread, fruits and vegetables which would otherwise have to be thrown out, second-hand clothes, and deteriorating automobiles and buildings. (1972:279)

Here, the unit receiving the benefit is appropriate (society), and the benefit seems at first glance obvious. Shouldn't societies that avoid waste have some advantage, all else being equal, over societies that don't? Yet, this will be true, in practical terms, only where extreme general poverty (across societies) places a competitive premium on such conservation. As societies grow richer, the selection pressures to which they are exposed on this score drop correspondingly. In fact, very rich societies like ours may need to waste in order to keep their economies healthy. Thus, we scrap automobiles that Cubans would care for lovingly and maintain across the years. Likewise, the consumption of day-old bread may be functional for very poor societies but is not of measurable advantage to those where the average citizen is significantly overweight. Thus, a formally correct functional argument here is made worthless by the absence of any realistic selection pressure.

Concluding Remarks on Functionalism

From the examples we have chosen, it should be clear that the functional and conflict paradigms can complement one another in explaining social phenomena. We needn't ally ourselves with one or the other paradigm exclusively; instead, we should learn to employ each when and where appropriate. In some cases, such as stratification, it's clear that they are both needed to explain the phenomenon, at least in societies with a complex division of labor.

At the same time, the functional paradigm clearly has had a mixed track record. Its best examples are convincing even when, for practical reasons or out of laziness, they don't meet all (or, normally, even half) of the demands of our protocol. Further, counterintuitive examples of functional theories, such as Durkheim's of crime or Harris's of sacred cattle, often give us just that experience of adopting a novel explanatory viewpoint that makes becoming a social scientist so exciting. This is to the great credit of the paradigm. At the same time, careless or poorly conceived examples show us how hard it is to use the paradigm well, and it has rarely lived up to the promise that Durkheim and other early social scientists saw in it. Its future depends in part on whether its track record can be improved, and this may well happen if part of sociology becomes more allied with biology through human **sociobiology**, where standards for its use are sometimes higher.[29]

Structuralism: Durkheim on the Origins of Religion

We will conclude our discussion of Durkheim by reviewing his theory of religion. This was provided in his deepest and most interesting book, *The Ele-*

mentary *Forms of the Religious Life* (published in 1915). His approach to the topic was complex and involved several different forms of explanation (including a functional component), but at its core was a form that I will call *structural*. Rather than spending time exploring the full complexities of *The Elementary Forms*, I will highlight its structural core and several modifications to it offered by later scholars, then close with some reflections on structuralism. This is the backbone of contemporary sociology—so much so that it has not really been articulated as a separate paradigm.

The Problem of Religion

The domain of religion presents a fascinating field for inquiry by social scientists. Like magic, religion is populated with entities (e.g., gods, miracles, and sacred objects) whose existence or spiritual qualities are not detectable by the accepted methods and instruments of science. This means that scientists cannot accept explanations of religious phenomena from within religion. Although believers may have a very strong sense of the reality of religious entities and be convinced of their effects within their lives, the evidence believers can offer for this doesn't meet scientific standards. This leaves scientists no option but to seek other, nonspiritual explanations for religious phenomena. They are forced, regardless of their personal beliefs, to adopt what sociologist Peter Berger (1967:179–88) calls "methodological atheism" as a principle of inquiry. Thus, while social scientists may themselves be believers (as was Berger), for the purpose of developing theories to explain religious phenomena, they must put belief aside and construct naturalistic explanations.

When they do, the problem posed by religion becomes apparent. If spiritual phenomena do not register for science, why do societies universally posit their existence? Indeed, though all societies probably contain nonbelievers, almost all place religious phenomena at or near their center of their attention. But why? We have no problem discerning why gathering and processing food is important to societies since they quite quickly die out if they stop believing in or practicing this. But we can't say the same for religion, which makes it a particularly perplexing social phenomenon. Why is something that is so poorly motivated (from the standpoint of methodological atheism) both so central and so ubiquitous?

Durkheim dismissed some of the easier answers to this question that had been provided by scholars in the nineteenth century. These answers assumed that religion resulted from flawed thinking on the part of primitive people (from whom, just because they were so "primitive," no better could be expected). For instance, scholars had accounted for belief in souls and spirits by assuming that people in simple societies were perplexed by the phenomenon of dreams and invented the concept of a *double*, able to leave the body and travel long distances at high speeds, to account for dream experiences they remembered upon waking. As an immaterial (or only weakly material) entity, the double might live on after the physical death of the individual and become a *spirit* with aspects of sacredness, serving as the basis for full-fledged divinities with highly sacred properties.

Durkheim complained that this **animist**[30] explanation assumed primitive people were stupid. Individuals considering immaterial doubles as a way to account for dream experiences would obviously confer with friends they had met in the dream state and learn that the doubles of these friends did not share their experiences. Since this would cause us to abandon the idea of a double, Durkheim reasoned it would do the same for people in simple societies. Expanding on this point, Durkheim wrote,

> It is inadmissible that systems of ideas like religions, which have held so considerable a place in history, and to which, in all times, men have come to receive the energy which they must have to live, should be made up of a tissue of illusions. (1915:69)

It was certainly hard to see how you could use the animist explanation to account for the cultural endurance of religion across time (although some scholars at the time assumed that religion was on its last legs, being only an illusion that was finally to succumb to human enlightenment). Yet, Durkheim doubted that religion was merely an immature phase in human intellectual development, as it had been characterized by Auguste Comte, the founder of sociology. If religion was to be explained by social science, Durkheim asked, "What sort of a science is it whose principle discovery is that the subject of which it treats does not exist?" (1915:70). Thus, the question became, what is the real and continuing foundation in human experience upon which religion grows?

To investigate this, Durkheim first needed to define *religion*. He dismissed arguments that the core of religion was a belief in the supernatural (since many people did not distinguish the natural from the supernatural) or in divinities (since some religions, forms of Buddhism, for instance, lacked them). Instead, he argued,

> All known religious beliefs, whether simple or complex, present one common characteristic: they presuppose a classification of all things, real and ideal, of which men think, into two classes or opposed groups, generally designated by two distinct terms which are translated well enough by the words *profane* and *sacred*. (1915:37)

The distinction between the **sacred** and the **profane** was unique, Durkheim believed, because it was seen as being absolute. Unlike *good* and *bad*, which might shade into one another at their borders, the sacred had to be kept perfectly insulated from the profane in ways that allowed the two to be defined by one another: "The sacred thing is *par excellence* that which the profane should not touch, and cannot touch with impunity" (1915:40).

Having decided that the sacred/profane distinction characterized all religions, Durkheim made it the centerpiece of his definition of religion:

> A *religion is a unified system of beliefs and practices relative to sacred things, that is to say, things set apart and forbidden—beliefs and practices which unite into a single moral community called a Church, all those who adhere to them.* (1915:47)

Thus, to explain religion, we need to find some real and continuing human experience that gives rise to the distinction between sacred and profane. Durkheim reasoned that the best way to find such an experience would be to look at the simplest societies then known, examine what they held sacred, and then speculate about the experiences that might underlie this belief and the practices associated with it. He assumed that examples of existing simple societies would be the best models for early human societies, potentially giving us access to the origins of the sacred/profane distinction and, thus, of religion itself.

Explaining Religion

For his example of an existing simple society, Durkheim chose Australian aborigines. Their form of religion is called **totemism** and consists of beliefs and practices related to symbols associated with each clan within a larger association of clans. The clans drew their names from the totems, and the totems themselves were drawn from actual objects existing in the environment, ranging from inanimate objects like clouds, to insects, to more imposing birds or marsupials. That many of the totems were very ordinary creatures or objects meant that there was nothing about the objects themselves that could explain their being seen as sacred. And, yet, they were treated with great reverence.

Durkheim reviewed a good deal of anthropological literature on totemism to argue that totems were treated reverently because they were perceived to possess spiritual power of a sort that was common to them all. It was this power that made the totems sacred and explained why being an ordinary object was no hindrance to totemic status. Different simple societies gave this power different names (e.g., *mana, orenda, wakan*) and totems were "the material form under which the imagination represents this immaterial substance, this energy diffused through all sorts of heterogeneous things, which alone is the real object" of religious observance (1915:189).

> This is the original matter out of which have been constructed those beings of every sort which the religions of all times have consecrated and adored. The spirits, demons, genii, and gods of every sort are only the concrete forms taken by this energy . . . in individuating itself, in fixing itself upon a certain determined object or point in space, or in centering around an ideal and legendary being, though one conceived as real by the popular imagination. (1915:199)

Thus, the sociological problem now became to explain the origins of this spiritual energy. Why was it everywhere appreciated, given that it had no properties that would reveal it to scientific scrutiny?

Durkheim reasoned that since this spiritual force was able to impose itself upon us, was due respect, and was immaterial, whatever real and continuing experience caused people to conceive of it should have the same properties. A likely candidate was society itself, in its guise as the moral authority that obligates us to conform, regardless of our personal interests. Early in life, we experience this authority as commands from particular individuals (usually our parents), but as we become fully socialized, the source of obligation dematerializes into the collective unit to which we show allegiance. This unit continues to exert pressure upon us and, thus, control over us, and such immaterial pressure serves as the real experience that people in simple societies construe as mana and embody in symbols like their clan totems:

> Since it is in spiritual ways that social pressure exercises itself, it could not fail to give men the idea that outside themselves there exist one or several powers, both moral and, at the same time, efficacious, upon which they depend. They must think of these powers, at least in part, as outside themselves, for they [the powers] address them [men] in a tone of command and sometimes even order them to do violence to their most natural inclination. It is undoubtedly true that if they were able to see that these influences which they feel emanate from society, then the mythological system of interpretations would never be born. But social action follows ways that are too circuitous and obscure, and employs psychical mechanisms that are too complex to allow the ordinary observer to see whence it comes. (1915:209)

This solution to the problem may initially seem a bit disappointing since the degree of reverence we show to divinities and the aura of sacredness they possess seem an order of magnitude greater than the everyday pressure to conform we feel flowing from the society around us. So, what about society could give rise to impressions of sacredness?

But here Durkheim stepped in with an additional real experience, which he termed **collective effervescence**. This is the experience of being transported beyond yourself through group-based emotional intoxication. It can occur in protest marches, when thousands gather to express themselves, or in lynch mobs bent on summary justice. Durkheim spoke of

> periods in history when, under the influence of some great collective shock, social interactions become much more frequent and active. Men look for each other and assemble together more than ever. That general effervescence results which is characteristic of revolutionary or creative epochs. . . . Men see more and differently now than in normal times. Changes are not merely of shades and degrees: men become different. The passions moving them are of such an intensity that they cannot be satisfied except by violent and unrestrained actions, actions of superhuman heroism or of bloody barbarism. (1915:210–11)

The difference between everyday life (which is humdrum) and periods of collective effervescence (when we are transported out of ourselves) mirrors the distinction between the profane and the sacred. But this only reinforces Durkheim's claim that the "real" entity underlying religion is society itself. In worshiping gods, people are really paying respect to the social units whose pressures they always experience and which occasionally become vehicles that transport them to a realm beyond the everyday.

Thus, Durkheim found in two real and continuing human experiences, namely, collective moral authority and collective effervescence, the powers and feelings that people interpreted (or misinterpreted) as sacred spiritual energy. Since this energy could make people do quite extraordinary things, it was natural that its source would be transmuted from the correct one, society, and allocated to something more interesting: the totem itself and the spiritual energy it embodied. As societies became more complex with the division of labor, an entire institutional sector, religion, came to be devoted to spiritual forces and to managing our behavior with regard to them. Thus, Durkheim believed he had solved the profound puzzle religion presents to methodological atheists.

Evaluating Durkheim's Explanation

In *The Elementary Forms of the Religious Life,* Durkheim did not draw out and test any implications of his theory. One barrier to doing so was that it didn't take the form we've recommended. Religion was viewed as a universal with its source in universal experiences, like the collective moral authority of the group. But, if this were the case, religion should be a universal constant. Although Durkheim was well aware it wasn't, he didn't stress its variable nature in ways that could be linked directly to the real foundations he out-lined for religion.[31] This left his argument somewhat unconvincing, and for a long time, it remained "merely theoretical."

In a book titled *The Birth of the Gods* (1960), however, Guy Swanson took up the challenge of deriving testable implications from Durkheim's theory. Durkheim (1915:226, 294) had argued that "the god is only the figurative expression of the society" and suggested that different forms of divinity, from local clan totems to "great gods" symbolizing tribal unity, expressed different levels of complexity in social organization. Swanson developed this insight in an interesting way. He first differentiated raw spiritual energy (mana) from spirits. Mana, much like electricity, has no purposes of its own but, instead, has to be put to work by people or spirits. Spirits, like people, are distin-guished by having their own purposes and agency (the ability to act accord-ing to their intentions). Swanson thus felt that mana and spirits might express different aspects of society, and I will here concentrate on his expla-nation of spirits since it is more straightforward.

Because spirits have intentions and agency, Swanson reasoned that they must express real experiences that we have with groups, groups that have intentions and agency themselves. In his terms, such groups have **sover-eignty**:

> A group has sovereignty to the extent that it has original and independent juris-diction over some sphere of life—that its power to make decisions in this sphere is not delegated from outside but originates within it, and that its exercise of this power cannot legitimately be abrogated by another group. (Swanson 1960, 20)

Although we usually apply the term *sovereignty* only to states, social units like families possess it as well since they are usually seen as having jurisdiction over a wide spectrum of issues having to do with child rearing and the forma-tion of marriages. In complex societies, the same is true of political units, such as townships, counties, and states. (In contrast, organizations like schools or military units lack sovereignty since their authority is delegated by political units superior to them.)

Swanson was now ready to form a theory making explicit the connection Durkheim saw between different levels of social organization and different forms of divinity. Spirits can belong to worlds teeming with other spirits, none of whom has much authority over the others, or they can all be coordi-nated by a "high god" who is seen as the originator of the universe and the ultimate power within it. In some forms of monotheism, in fact, there may be only one god, conceived of as extremely powerful and remote (though most high gods have choirs of lesser spirits, such as angels, to serve them).

Other religions may have innumerable minor spirits without anyone to rule over them. Thus, religions vary in the relative elevation of their gods and the degree to which ultimate authority is vested in only one, which is only to say that the spiritual world varies in concentration of power, just as does ours.

Swanson speculated that the more people experienced their social and political life as organized though multiple levels of sovereign groups (as in city, county, state, and nation in the United States), the more they would deem a high god, one responsible for the origin and coordination of the universe, fitting. By contrast, if people experienced few levels of sovereign groups (say just family and tribe), this would predispose them to find multiple lower-powered spirits fitting. In other words, the spiritual world would be modeled on the political order in terms of its relative coordination by a distant and august entity. To test this theory (as well as numerous others that we won't review), Swanson gathered data from a representative sample of fifty human societies available through an anthropological data bank called the Human Relations Area Files. What did he find? Table 7.1 presents the striking results. Swanson found it difficult to judge whether high gods were present in eleven of his sample societies, but the overall trend would not have been changed by such data one way or the other. The trend is strong, despite three cases (two with few groups but high gods and one with more groups but no high god) that go against the grain.

The data suggest that the preferred forms of gods are strongly determined by the character of a society's political organization. If so, this seems a good indication that Swanson (and, behind him, Durkheim) was on the right track: if we can show that observed variation in religious belief is socially determined, it seems reasonable to argue that the phenomenon of religion itself has its origin in discernable social forces in the general domain that Durkheim identified (more on this in a moment).

Thus, Swanson slightly modified Durkheim's theory and then developed

TABLE 7.1
Number of Sovereign Groups and Presence of High Gods

Presence of High God	Number of Sovereign Groups		
	One	Three	Four or more
Present	2	7	10
Absent	17	2	1
Total	19	9	11
Percent present	11	78	91

Reprinted with permission from page 65 of *The Birth of the Gods: The Origin of Primitive Beliefs* by Guy Swanson. Ann Arbor: University of Michigan Press. Copyright © 1960 University of Michigan Press.

numerous implications that allowed him to test the modified theory. Not all of these tests produced the sort of clear-cut results we see in table 7.1, but they do give us some confidence that we can use sociology to explain some of the variation across time and space in religious beliefs and practices.

Durkheim's theory of the social bases of religious experience continues to animate sociological theorizing. For instance, it inspires a broad-ranging subparadigm, articulated by Randall Collins (2004), for analyzing social interaction and social structure as "interaction ritual chains." Earlier, it provided a significant stimulus to the insights of Erving Goffman, whose dramaturgical approach to interaction we will encounter in chapter 8. Indeed, few works have had as much continuing impact on contemporary sociological theory. One may even see it in the outlines of an additional paradigm designated "structuralism."

On Structuralism

The approach that Swanson took in explaining variation in religious beliefs is best termed *structuralism*. Structuralism accounts for variation in some aspect of social life (e.g., belief in high gods, our dependent variable) by linking it to variation in social structure (e.g., the number of sovereign groups, our independent variable). Of course, *social structure* is one of those vague terms than can encompass a great deal, but essentially it refers to the character of relations among individuals and groups within a society, evidenced in recurrent patterns of interaction. In its simplest form, social structure can be thought of as having vertical and horizontal dimensions (Black 1976). The vertical dimension situates individuals and groups in terms of their relative power and prestige and identifies who has precedence and who gets to direct whom within the society. This is the dimension Swanson draws on in analyzing sovereign groups extending upward from the family. The horizontal dimension situates equally powerful people and groups in terms of their connections with one another. These can be direct or indirect, and direct connections can vary greatly in terms of their relative intimacy. Thus, the horizontal dimension measures how "distant" people are from one another, with some individuals being strangers to one another and others being deeply intimate. Further, we can map the network of relations among individuals and groups to show that some are "better connected" (or more central) than others (who are thus more peripheral) within the society.

An extended discussion of social structure is beyond our concern here, which is simply to illustrate how it is used in formulating theories. Once again, the basic principle is to look for variation. Social structures vary from one group, society, or social stage of development to another, and individuals or groups vary in terms of their position within a structure. We can use such differences as our independent variables. According to Donald Black (1976), for instance, when we compare societies in which most individuals know (or know of) one another with those where two average individuals will be strangers, we find that the former society will have much less law than the latter. Societies where individuals mostly know one another handle disputes informally, while societies where most individuals are strangers need a legal system to manage disputes. Thus, the lower the horizontal distance among average individuals in a society, the less law. Turning to variation in vertical position within a society, we can say that individuals who are higher up will be better able to mobilize the law against individuals who are lower down. Thus, law is utilized more in a downward (from top to bottom) direction than in an upward direction in societies.

We can, then, argue that the use of law varies both in terms of the overall structure of society and in terms of the relative positions of disputants within it. Functional and conflict theories can also be developed to account for some of this variation, but the scope of structuralism extends into regions that neither functional nor conflict theories can easily enter. For instance, anthropologist Mary Douglas (1970) argued that a preference for ritual forms of expression (for instance, for having an old-fashioned wedding ceremony as opposed to writing your own or skipping one altogether) characterizes societies with relatively permanent and well-defined groups whose roles are defined in terms of one another. It's societies with more fluid and ill-defined group structures that find rituals hollow and, so, either avoid them or emphasize being creative rather than following hallowed traditions. Douglas thus uses the overall character of social structure (her independent variable) to explain people's relative acceptance of ritual (her dependent variable).

Neither the conflict nor the functional paradigm suggests explanations for this sort of cultural variation. Of course, such variation might be the result of purely conventional choices (in the terms of our first chapter), but structuralism works by explaining phenomena we might otherwise assume conventional. As we establish such explanations, we begin to define a dividing line between sociocultural phenomena that are freely chosen (and, thus, not susceptible to theoretical explanation) and those that are *conditioned by the character of the social relations in which people are bound up*. When this conditioning occurs, certain ways of doing things just "feel right" to people for reasons they are unable to understand or explain. Indeed, this is another reason why explication (or Weber's *verstehen*) can only get us so far in sociology: people often do not know why they prefer the things they do. As Durkheim suggested, only sociology can investigate the structural influences, the social facts or forces, that people themselves are unable to see.

It would be easy to go on at length about structuralism here, but perhaps the most effective way to exit our discussion is to reflect that Durkheim's explanation of suicide perfectly exemplifies this strategy of explanation. In chapter 6, we saw that Durkheim didn't believe that suicide rates could be explained by people's individual motives in committing suicide. As he developed his theory, he came to conclude that features of their social structures, such as relative social integration, were primarily responsible for the variation in rates we find from one society or time to another. This is a purely structural argument: neither the functional nor the conflict paradigm leads to it.[32] Thus, while we have presented Durkheim largely as a functionalist, two of his major theories, those of religion and of suicide, are primarily structuralist in flavor. Structuralism, it has been claimed (Black 2000), offers the clearest way to establish sociology as a discipline distinct from psychology and the other social sciences. Accomplishing this was one of Durkheim's fondest wishes, and through his theorizing we still find guidance to this goal.

Conclusion

I have used this chapter to explore functionalism as a paradigm and to offer a very brief introduction to an additional paradigm, structuralism. Over the last century, functionalism has probably been the paradigm most utilized by sociologists, and, yet, I've argued that it has often been employed in a slapdash manner and, on occasion, incorrectly. Some slapdash uses leave us convinced that they must be on the right track, even though much more evidence would need to be gathered in order for them to become convincing. The incorrect uses leave us wondering how functionalism came to be so misunderstood in sociology.[33]

Durkheim's explanation of crime, like the explanations of cultures of honor or of sacred cows in earlier chapters, shows us the power of the functionalist perspective to point out the latent functions of institutions or practices. Explanations of phenomena through their latent functions have been one of the primary strategies through which sociology has warranted its ambition to be a separate social science. When we perceive latent functions, we look into the domain of what Durkheim called *social facts*, where forces operate to control or mold people's behavior outside their awareness. Structuralism has also explored this domain, seeking to explain variations in behavior through variations in the structural circumstances in which it occurs, variations of which actors are unaware. Durkheim's profound work on religion pointed us in this direction.

The approaches of Karl Marx, Max Weber, and Émile Durkheim are alike in that they sought to address large-scale social change, as well as in their assumption that the theories or causal narratives that explained these changes would employ factors of which most people were unaware.[34] Thus, each gives us a sense that sociology is a necessary and revolutionary discipline, needed because a new realm of mechanisms has been discovered. These mechanisms work behind the scenes, so to speak, to determine the outcomes we experience in our lives. For me, the allure of sociology has always been in this peek it gives us behind the scenes, into areas of which pre- or nonsociological folk are unaware.

Chapter 8 will look at a very different paradigm in sociology, one that started out by rejecting the entire general strategy we've been exploring thus far through the work of Marx, Weber, and Durkheim. All of these sociologists were interested in developing theories and in using them to explain large-scale social changes. Their work exemplifies the conflict, functionalist, and structuralist paradigms. Our next paradigm, *symbolic interaction*, began very differently, without any interest in large-scale social change or any ambition to produce theories. One strand of it has retained this stance, while another, as we shall see, has become increasingly theoretical.

Notes

1. For instance, people who are not religious sometimes view religion as a social problem in that religious controversies so often turn violent. On the other hand, theists see atheism as a pathology that is dangerous to societies. Here, as in so many other cases, what is seen as a social problem seems to be determined by our own particular point of view and not, as with diseases, by the nature of things independent of our opinions. (Of course, there are religious perspectives from which disease itself may be viewed as beneficial and not something we should combat.)

2. This view assumes that traits are completely independent of one another. Yet, if pathological properties arise necessarily from otherwise advantageous traits, Durkheim's argument would be in some trouble. This is in fact the case with crime and necessitates a modification to Durkheim's argument that I make below.

3. By a process of *selection*, I mean that societies possessing crime would be favored in competition with those that didn't and, thus, would be picked out (or selected) to spread across time and space. There are many processes by which such spreading occurs: migration, military conflict, increased birth rates, borrowing the favored traits of competitor societies, and so on.

4. The contemporary theorist Robert Merton (1949) initially developed the distinction between manifest and latent functions.

5. For a fascinating history of this concern, see Pfohl (1977), and for later indications of it, see Best (1990).

6. My array assumes that psychological abuse is less serious than physical abuse. This is probably true at the extremes but quite arguable in between. Children (or the

adults they eventually become) might prefer occasional beatings, for instance, to being constantly badmouthed by their parents.

7. His interest has expanded into a significant focus of contemporary sociology, which is on the social construction of social problems. See, e.g., Becker (1973), Schneider (1985), Best (1990), and Hacking (1999). We now have a much more nuanced understanding of this process than Durkheim did but the general outlines of his approach remain in place.

8. Kai Erikson, in *Wayward Puritans* (1966), has developed this point to argue that rates of offending should be relatively constant in societies, with scrupulosity creating waves of newly criminalized behavior whenever it suppresses the rates at which the old crimes were committed.

9. From the perspective of children's rights, we would say that the exception to the crime of assault that allows parents to attack their children (under the guise of discipline) is finally being withdrawn so that the law is becoming consistent and non-discriminatory.

10. Durkheim did point out that the often intense reaction to crimes that arises in communities serves to better define, and strengthen commitment to, social norms. For this to be functional, however, we would have to assume that commitment to norms naturally weakens in the absence of such responses to crimes and does so to a point that would threaten a society's survival. This is a questionable assumption. Even were it the case, could the problem only be solved by new crimes? Or could reflection on the old ones serve this function? Do we really need a new Hitler every few generations to strengthen our conviction that genocide is evil?

11. This is an oversimplification. For ease of exposition, I have ignored the downside to very low levels of scrupulosity, which is a "decadence" in which most crime is defined away as a matter of personal choice. Decadent societies have so little "collective consciousness" that they may have trouble agreeing on any collective projects. They are the opposite of too rigid, being instead too flaccid to resist attack or combat environmental challenges.

12. In this example, I am applying to Durkheim's original argument a set of distinctions made by Harriet Zuckerman in her essay "Deviant Behavior and Social Control in Science" (1977).

13. For a review of Wegener's contribution, see Schwarzbach (1986).

14. Summerlin, a researcher at the Sloan Kettering Institute for Cancer Research in the 1970s, appears to have faked results indicating successful suppression of immunological rejection of skin grafts between different strains of mice, as well as of human corneal implants into rabbits. See Hixson (1976) and, for additional cases, Miller and Hersen (1992).

15. We can also use it to reflect on the difference between a two-by-two table and an analytic typology. Compare the types of work distinguished in this table with the types of authority distinguished by our analytic typology in chapter 5. Are they different? If so, why?

16. For an extended analysis of this problem, see Schneider (1993:124–42, 194–204). It can also be very difficult to determine whether fraud has occurred (see, e.g., Jensen 1992).

17. Note that the issue of how the attribute arose in the first place is completely

separate from a functional analysis. We must not imply that the function it serves is the cause of its origin since this is **teleological** reasoning, which impermissibly makes later consequences the cause of earlier events. What we can sometimes offer is a causal or descriptive narrative of its origin, recognizing that this is quite independent of the functional account.

18. For instance, it is socially beneficial to humans to be taller rather than shorter, and we can even calculate these benefits with some precision, say in terms of the higher compensation earned by tall people (2.2% more for each additional inch) or their more frequent occupancy of leadership roles. How and why do taller people, other things being equal, wind up ahead? Researchers are only beginning to track down the mechanisms that produce this effect (see Persico, Postlewaite, and Silverman [2004]). One of the ways that normal science progresses is by patiently tracking down mechanisms. You might reflect that only a hundred years ago, we were ignorant about the functions of many bodily organs, but our achievements in physiology and microbiology over the last century with regard to this have been truly astonishing. The social sciences are only beginning to concern themselves with such patient analysis of mechanisms.

19. It would be good to recall here that we can't give a good reason for why people drive on the right versus the left. Contingent social practices (mere conventions) like this cannot be explained functionally. They have no demonstrable benefit for societies and are not "selected for" under pressure.

20. A professional version would introduce the concepts of path dependence (Dobbin 1994) and of inferior conventions (Mackie 1996) and alert us to modeling processes that are nonrational (DiMaggio and Powell 1983; DiMaggio 1997). It would also indicate that positive functions for one level of units (say, families) can have negative impacts on higher or lower levels (societies or individuals). It is certainly not clear that the benefits of a culture of honor to families in herding economies are equally beneficial to the societies in which they live.

21. I suspect it would be easier to demonstrate in the field of science by pointing to the demise of certain schools like that of Lysenko in genetics, but it's hard in science to specify the unit to which the benefit accrues.

22. One of the most thoroughly researched and critically analyzed functional explanations is Rappaport's (1968) treatment of the role of ritual in the relation between humans and their environment in the New Guinea highlands.

23. In this regard, it is simply a modified version of "meritocracy," because it shows how important positions get allotted to meritorious individuals by necessarily bearing higher rewards.

24. We may initially assume that doctors are more important than sanitation workers, for instance, until a sanitation strike threatens to spread disease far more rapidly than doctors can cure it, demonstrating that the sanitation workers actually occupy the societally more crucial position. Davis and Moore recognized this problem and indicated some ways it might be handled, noting as well that positions varied in the amount and sophistication of training they required: for some, nearly any individual will do; for others, only the most highly trained. Such factors can explain why sanitation workers are less well rewarded than doctors, even though they are arguably more functionally important to society.

25. For a brief overview of criticisms of the theory, see Abrahamson (1978:62–74), who concludes that "in the more than thirty years since its presentation, the functional theory is yet to produce anything resembling definite evidence in support of it" (74). At the same time, Abrahamson (1979) has provided one of the most interesting and rigorous applications of the theory in analyzing whether the differential rewards allocated to the different positions on professional baseball teams can be explained functionally. Despite his success with baseball, he indicates how difficult it is to apply such an analysis to societies as wholes rather than to an organizational arena like baseball that is unusually rich in relevant statistics.

26. These figures, as well those used in figure 7.5, are drawn from "Spreading the Yankee Way of Pay" (*Business Week*, April 18, 2001), which uses data developed by the consulting firm of Towers Perrin. Average employees are assumed to work in industrial firms with about $500 million in annual sales. It is interesting to note that in 1997, one U.S. chief executive, Michael Eisner of Disney, was estimated to have received more in compensation than the *Top 500* British CEOs. Over several recent years, *Business Week* estimates of the U.S. CEO/average worker ratio ranged from 200-to-1 to 561-to-1 using different bases or time periods.

27. Gans suggests that Merton (1949) authorizes this in his discussion of the functions of political machines and in his discussion of the postulates of functionalism, but I believe Gans misinterprets the passages he cites.

28. An additional problem, arising from the fifth provision of our protocol, is that it is difficult to identify mechanisms by which police (or the wider society) maintain the crime that employs police (or the poverty that provides social workers with their clients) *and to which maintaining police (or social workers) is necessary.*

29. For a novel example of a human sociobiological functional theory, see Schneider and Hendrix (2000). For serious criticisms of human sociobiology and complaints of low standards even there, see Kitcher (1967).

30. In Latin, *anima* means "soul." The "doubles" people were thought to have concocted to explain their dream experiences were progressively empowered and made more sacred through the degrees of soul, spirit, and god; hence, the designation of the explanation as *animist*. In critiquing animist explanations, Durkheim dealt primarily with the writings of Edward Tylor and Herbert Spencer. For an overview, see Evans-Pritchard (1965).

31. This is a problem with many explanations of religion. If we see religion as a solution to our inability to face our own mortality or as the sole way to "objectively" ground contestable values (so as to make them less questionable), we are settling upon universal problems of human existence that cannot easily be made to vary. This leaves us unable to explain why some people believe and others don't, or why some divinities regulate human morality and others don't.

32. Of course, one can integrate this explanation with a functional one by pointing out that a beneficial degree of social flexibility will necessarily allow for some deviance, of which suicide is a form. But, once again, this is not to say that suicide is itself functional: it's merely a consequence of a structural condition that is functional.

33. For an additional example that seems to misunderstand functionalism, see Etzioni 2000.

34. While Weber did not assume this in principle, instead giving importance to *verstehen*, he almost always did so in practice.

8

G. H. Mead and Symbolic Interaction

THIS CHAPTER REVIEWS A PARADIGM that has come to be called **symbolic interaction**, which developed out of the social psychology of George Herbert Mead. Mead himself, as we will see, produced little sociological theory, yet he remains significant because his work (along with that of Georg Simmel) successfully brought sociological attention to direct human interaction—the arena of what we call **microsociology**. Some who've followed Mead into this arena have themselves shown little interest in theory, and for reasons similar to those we've already encountered with Weber. Social interaction, they believe, is too fluid to be causally modeled and can at best be explained through causal narratives. This strand of symbolic interaction thus remains primarily descriptive rather than theoretical.

Another strand of symbolic interaction, however, has striven to develop theories of interaction, some primarily analytical in orientation and others employing causal models. After reviewing the work of Mead, we will turn to exemplars of this strand, looking first at the fascinating work of Erving Goffman, who brings the concerns of Durkheim to focus on explaining interaction, and then briefly addressing a **subparadigm** within symbolic interaction styled **affect control theory**. A reasonably thorough treatment of Goffman or of affect control could each easily occupy a full chapter, so our treatment will have to be quite sketchy; yet it should illustrate the interesting ways in which interaction has come to be explained theoretically.

Mead and Social Behaviorism

Mead was primarily a philosopher and belonged to a school known as **pragmatism** (of which his friend and colleague John Dewey was perhaps the foremost exponent). Pragmatism focused on the way people use knowledge to adapt to the world around them, and Mead concerned himself with the social component of this world. His philosophical concerns directed him to the development of the *self*, which he saw as formed in interaction with other human beings by particular processes he sought to analyze. Thus, he focused on small scale social units where individuals were usually in face-to-face contact, so that his orientation was to **microsociology** in contrast to the **macrosociological** interests of Marx, Weber, and Durkheim. Furthermore, because he sought to outline the most general processes by which the self was formed and then acted back on the world, he was interested in phenomena that didn't vary from one time or place to another. Thus, he sought to establish universals of human social activity rather than to explore change and variation across societies, another characteristic that separates him from our first three theorists.

The nature of Mead's microsociological approach made him look closely at people's use of gestures and language to communicate their intentions to others, as well as their need to interpret the behavior of others so as to respond to it appropriately. We will look briefly at the ideas Mead developed to analyze the self and its development in the process of socialization. They have become common currency (that is, are widely employed) across the social sciences, forming the basis for several quite different subparadigms, some theoretical in orientation and some not.

Behaviorism

When I was a young child, I used to bring my grandmother books to read to me. She would let me lie down on the sofa beside her and put my head in her lap as she read. I found this delicious, and believe it's one reason I still enjoy reading books so much. It also expresses a basic principle of **behaviorism**: that we behave in ways that bring us pleasure (or rewards) or that help us avert pain (punishment). Behaviors that produce rewards are reinforced and tend to be produced again, while those that do not tend to be discarded as ineffective.[1]

Thus, how we come to behave is conditioned by the pattern of reinforcements provided by the environment around us. As individuals enter a specific environment, they may initially use trial and error to cope with it. Certain of their trials are apt to be rewarded, while others are not. The former are then repeated in the expectation of further rewards. The process amounts to learning. Why one person likes books so much and another likes cooking can be explained by causal narratives depicting the pattern of rewards and punishments to which they have been exposed.[2]

Using the lens of pragmatism to view this process caused Mead to focus upon the formation of the self. How do infants, as they grow into children, acquire a sense of self? What factors are crucial in its formation? How does the child, as it comes to possess a self, deal effectively with its environment? How do individuals transform environments through their own actions? It is surprising to realize that in even asking these questions in this form, Mead expressed his independence from early twentieth-century ways of thinking. Most thoughtful people of his era would have explained variation in personality or character across individuals very simply: it was variation in heredity that caused variation in character. You inherited your character from your forebears just as a race horse inherited its speed. So much was this the conventional wisdom that many people would have seen Mead's questions as uninteresting to ask. People already *knew* that heredity was crucial to the formation of the self and could explain variations across individuals, so why even ask the questions in so general a way? Behaviorism, however, took a very different view of the matter, explaining variation in character through variation in the environment. But to establish a basis for behaviorism, Mead felt he had to get back behind variation to ask more basic and universal questions about the formation of the self *in general*. His answers can prepare us to form theories but are not theoretical themselves, and thus can't be presented in the format of chapter 1.

To answer his very general questions about the *self*, Mead believed, he had to introduce the notions of *mind* as the instrument by which individuals come to perceive their environment and plot courses of action within it, and *society* as the structure of groups which serve as the social environment in which the self is formed and through which individuals work collectively to cope with the physical environment and transform it. Thus, one of Mead's most important books was titled *Mind, Self and Society* (1934).[3]

Infants begin to develop minds as they perceive regularities in their environment and in their interaction with it. They advance significantly when they discover *symbols* as a means of representing elements of this environment and *gestures* as a means of communicating symbolically with the people in it. Mead drew upon Darwin (1872) in viewing gestures as the primary means of communication among higher animals. A dog uses a growl, for instance, to warn other dogs to stay away while it is eating. The growl conveys, we presume, the dog's willingness to fight for its food should other dogs try to take it away. Gestures such as this are built into many animals by evolution, and can be viewed as largely "hardwired" or genetically determined through the animal's biological constitution. Humans vastly expand their repertoire of gestures by establishing *conventional* linkages between gestures and meanings.[4] (The words on this page are one of the most successful examples of this.) Furthermore, humans consciously intend their gestures in a way that Mead assumed animals did not. Animal gestures are primarily reactive and automatic, and so do not involve conscious deliberation. Occasionally, human gestures are "thoughtless" in this way, but more often they are deliberate, intended to evoke in another person the conscious meaning they have for the gesturer. As Mead wrote:

> When . . . [a] gesture means this idea behind it and it arouses that idea in the other individual, then we have a significant symbol. In the case of the dog-fight we have a gesture which calls out appropriate response; in the present case we have a symbol which answers to a meaning in the experience of the first individual and which also calls out that meaning in the second individual. Where the gesture reaches that situation it has become what we call "language." It is now a significant symbol and it signifies a certain meaning. (1934:45–46)

In order for effective communication to occur, people who employ gestures must assure themselves that their intended meaning is actually being conveyed to others, and to do this, they have to figuratively step into the shoes of the persons to whom they direct their gestures so as to correctly infer how they are being received. This Mead referred to as "taking the role of the other," and it was the imaginative act upon which the successful alignment of individuals with one another in their conversations or other group activities could occur. As Mead wrote,

> the individual's consciousness of the content and flow of meaning . . . depends on his thus taking the attitude of the other toward his own gestures. In this way

every gesture comes within a given social group or community to stand for a particular act or response . . . its meaning as a significant symbol. (1934:47)

By successfully taking the role of the other, we can anticipate how people will respond to our gestures; and because gestures come to have conventional meanings, shared throughout the community, it is often easy to correctly anticipate others' responses. Weber made much the same point in distinguishing **social action** from **individual action** or **reactive behavior**. Because social action was "meaningfully oriented to . . . others" (1978:23), it needed to employ gestures that successfully conveyed one's intentions.

The Formation of the Self

Mead argued that we acquire a *self* as we come to anticipate how others will respond to our gestures. Essentially, we develop the ability to see ourselves as others see us, making our *selves* an object of our own contemplation and evaluation. This is not something that very young children can do. Thus, he suggested, "the problem . . . presents itself as to how, in detail, a self arises" (1934:144).

Mead did not formally study children to answer this question, but instead drew upon our common stock of knowledge to plausibly sketch out steps in the process. Much of his analysis focused on the play and games children spontaneously indulge in:

> A child plays at being a mother, at being a teacher, at being a policeman; that is, it is taking different rôles, as we would say. . . . He plays that he is, for instance, offering himself something, and he buys it; he gives a letter to himself and takes it away; he addresses himself as a parent, as a teacher; he arrests himself as a policeman. . . . Such is the simplest form of being another to one's self. (1934:150–51)

In such forms of play (the "playing-at-being" or "pretend" forms), we see children trying on roles, imagining themselves into the shoes of other people. In solitary play of this sort, children appear minimally able to view themselves from the outside, which in turn implies that they have developed some sense of self. At the same time, collective role playing, as in the games "House" or "Cops and Robbers" increases their skill at stepping outside of themselves and into roles that are governed by rules. These rules structure their interaction with other participants in the play.

The **play stage** in the development of the self eventually gives way to the **game stage**. As Mead wrote:

If we contrast play with the situation in an organized game, we note the essential difference that the child who plays in a game must be ready to take the attitude of everyone else involved in that game, and that these different rôles must have a definite relationship to one another. . . . If he gets in a ball nine [baseball game] he must have the responses of each position involved in his own position. He must know what everyone else is going to do in order to carry out his own play. He has to take all of these rôles. . . . The game represents the passage in the life of the child from taking the rôle of others in play to the organized part that is essential to self-consciousness in the full sense of the term. (1934:151–52)

In the game stage, children come to see themselves in relation to multiple others, and to respond along with them in a coordinated fashion. Out of this experience of having to take the roles of multiple others, Mead indicated, children gradually form an image of the "**generalized other**" and thus enter the final phase in the development of the self.

Mead was not entirely clear about how a sense of the generalized other is arrived at from the experience of the roles and attitudes of multiple concrete others with whom children interact in games. He argued that in games,

[the child] is controlled by his being everyone else on that team, at least in so far as those attitudes affect his own particular response. We get then an "other" which is an organization of the attitudes of those involved in the same process.

The organized community or social group which gives to the individual his unity of self may be called "the generalized other." The attitude of the generalized other is the attitude of the whole community. (1934:154)

Although the process by which the child abstracts from given concrete individuals to generalized group attitudes is left unclear, the result is that people can anticipate not only how specific individuals would respond to what they intend to do, but how *any* individual (to the extent she is a representative member of the group) might respond. Further, by encountering members of still *other* groups, for instance through travel or through reading the books they write or other records they leave behind, people can form images of numerous generalized others, ones whose attitudes might differ significantly from those of the local groups in which they live.[5] At this point, the self is most fully and completely formed:

This getting of the broad activities of any given social whole or organized society as such within the experiential field . . . is . . . the essential basis and prerequisite of the fullest development of that individual's self. (1934:155)

Individuals with such selves can be accounted *socially competent.* They can correctly anticipate how others will respond and thus plan strategically, whether alone or in groups, courses of action that are effective.[6] As they mature, they develop a repertoire of selves appropriate to the different roles they play, each perhaps geared to membership in a different group and thus to a different generalized other. In sketching out this process, Mead laid the foundation for a behavioral social psychology that was very different from the **hereditarian** assumptions of his age. He then developed this social psychology by analyzing the self into distinct *phases*.

The Phases of the Self

Mead dissected the self into two phases: an "I" and a "me" (for convenience, I will simply italicize these henceforward rather than putting them in quotes as did Mead). The *I* is the self-in-action, when it is least self-conscious. To return to Mead's favorite example of ball games, a fielder is in the *I* phase when concentrating on catching a fly ball, moving gracefully to position himself for an easy catch. The effort of concentration places the fielder deeply *in* the action, to a degree that the presence of others may be momentarily forgotten—so much forgotten that collisions between outfielders are sometimes quite serious. The *I* is so engrossed in what it is doing that it cannot be self-conscious. By contrast, the *me* is self-conscious. It is the self as it reflects on the just completed performance of the *I* that it can scrutinize in memory. The *I* becomes an object to the self in this way, as its performance can be reviewed and evaluated. Furthermore, since it will be evaluated according to the attitudes of a generalized other, Mead (1934:175) argued that "the 'me' is the organized set of attitudes of others which one himself assumes. The attitudes of the others constitute the organized 'me,' and then one reacts toward that as an 'I.'"

While Mead vacillated between viewing the *me* as simply the record of the actions of the *I* as they are stored in one's memory on the one hand,[7] and as the imagined attitudes of others toward our performances as *I*s on the other, his central thrust seems clear. We continually switch into and out of "self-consciousness," and this marks the transition between the *I* and the *me*. The *I* acts and the *me* reflects on these actions as they would appear from the viewpoint of others. In other words, the *me* is the self in the phase of being conscious of how its behavior appears to others. As Mead wrote:

> . . . it is due to the individual's ability to take the attitudes of . . . others in so far as they can be organized that he gets self-consciousness. The taking of all of those organized sets of attitudes gives him his "me": that is the self he is aware of. (1934:175)

In changing the direction of their attention, people switch back and forth between *I* and *me* as if between the two sides of a coin: one or the other side must be facing up (or in our attention), but *only* one side faces up at a time.

I realize that Mead's discussion of the self can easily seem tedious. Why go into such analytical detail about the self, especially when the concepts involved seem relatively simple? But the appearance today of tedious simplicity in Mead's analysis in part reflects his success in getting us to think of selves as *socially* formed, complex entities. Mead spent so much time driving this home because he wrote against a backdrop of deeply ingrained hereditarian assumptions. His ideas would have seemed much fresher and more necessary had you been sitting in his class on social psychology at the time of the First World War. But, further, though Mead's initial discussion is somewhat tedious, he is laying the foundation for more interesting observations that we can try to test on ourselves.

Because the *me* evaluates the performance of the *I*, and does so on the basis of an "organized set of attitudes" taken over from others, Mead (1934:210) saw it as the phase in which social control occurs. The *me* informs us of errors in our performance (as *I* s seen from the imagined standpoint of others) and urges us to try again in hopes of improvement. As we "try again," we return to the *I* phase. But our efforts as *I* s, Mead argued, are inherently unpredictable (though sometimes within very narrow limits). Just what the *I* will do is something we can never be certain of beforehand: "Perhaps he will make a brilliant play or an error," wrote Mead (1934:175), reverting again to baseball imagery. We come to know what the *I* does only *as it does it*, being as much spectators to ourselves in this regard as are those around us. (Here, I hope you will agree, Mead's argument becomes much more interesting!) Whenever we have not had time to carefully plot courses of action (and sometimes even then), what we do is apt to at least modestly surprise even us. For instance, in everyday speaking we launch upon sentences, seeking to express our intentions, without knowing what precise course they will take, and we really learn of this only alongside those who are listening to us. Because of this, as Mead wrote,

> The "I" gives the sense of freedom, of initiative. . . . We are aware of ourselves, and of what the situation is, but exactly how we will act never gets into experience until after the action takes place. (1934:177–78)

Thus, the *me* and the *I* together account for conformity and for innovation in our social life: if the self "did not have these two phases there would not be conscious responsibility, and there would be nothing novel in experience" (1934:178). As Mead went on to note:

> The "me" is a conventional, habitual individual. It is always there. It has to have those habits, those responses which everybody has; otherwise the individual could not be a member of the community. But an individual is constantly reacting to such an organized community in the way of expressing himself. . . . The attitudes involved are gathered from the group, but the individual in whom they are organized has the opportunity of *giving them an expression which perhaps has never taken place before.* (1934:197–98, emphasis mine)

This ability of the *I* to introduce novelty meant that society was constantly, if usually in tiny increments, changing. The novel actions of the *I* can cause changes in the attitudes of others, which means that the *me*'s of all those involved undergo change, at least in very minor ways. This means that the generalized other is always changing, and that society is always in modest flux. Really significant change, on such an account, occurs when particularly forceful and original *I*'s appear, causing correspondingly great transformations of the *me*'s with whom they interact: "Great figures in history bring about very fundamental changes," said Mead (1934:202) in subscribing to the so-called **great man** (!) "theory" of social change.[8]

Mead's discussion of the *I* and *me* constituted his *analysis* of the self. We see him dividing it into phases that allow for both stability (the *me*) and change (the *I*), for conformity and innovation. Like any analysis, this one indicates what some broader concept (the *self*) is composed of. Yet, the mere provision of these phases, though it explains the composition of the self, does not allow us to explain or predict any concrete behavior. It provides an analytical rather than a causal model.

Mead's conceptualization of the *I* and the *me* has additional properties that can inform our understanding of theory, and we should take a moment to reflect on these now. In the first place, and reiterating what I said in introducing Mead, the concepts are presented as universals: what they refer to is said to be present in all competent adults in all societies and all historical periods.[9] Second, the particular analysis they provide cannot be evaluated with empirical data. You can evaluate them introspectively, looking into your own experience to see whether, for instance, you learn of what you do or say only as others around you do, indicating that your *I* is indeed unpredictable. But you can't *demonstrate* the *I* and *me* to anyone who doubts them. Suppose you explicated them to a friend, for instance, and that your friend responded, "You know, those are interesting concepts, but while I clearly have a self, *my* self doesn't *have* phases of *I* and *me*, at least as far as I can tell." This would stump you. It's not clear how you could convince your friend she was wrong, because the concepts are not empirical. They don't refer to anything we can point to or measure with instruments in such a way as to convince skeptics of their reality.[10] Nor, at least in present form, do they allow us to make the sort of predictions about variation in behavior that would cause a skeptic to say, "Well, though I can't find a basis for the *I* and the *me* when I look inside *myself*, you use them so successfully to explain and predict people's behavior that I'll just have to conclude there's something wrong with my **introspection** rather than with the concepts."

Note that this is not true of Mead's notion of *stages* in the acquisition of the self. We would presumably be able to point out to a skeptic that children have to develop competence in trying on the roles of others (the play stage), and that they do this well before they become competent at keeping multiple roles in mind (the game stage).[11] The fact that these two skills are acquired at different ages and always in the same sequence would be enough to convince us of their existence. Although we might wonder whether play and game represent entirely discrete stages, or perhaps suggest these are not the best or only ones, we would be convinced by experience (the data) that *some* form of development had occurred, and that this development was relevant to the formation of a self.[12]

Finally, I should note that Mead provides us with no mechanisms for explaining where and when we shift back and forth between the self's phases, or how we progress from play stage to game stage and then to an appreciation of the generalized other. The former is something we might eventually understand through brain sciences and the latter through developmental social psychology, but Mead did no more than outline themes for future research.

It is likely that Mead spent so much time discussing the *I* and *me*, despite their nonempirical status and his inability to address mechanisms, not only because he was more a philosopher than a social scientist (though these roles had not quite separated when he began his career), but because he wanted to combat longstanding conceptions of the self as entirely individualistic, self-interested, and determined by one's nature. His focus on the *me* allowed him to argue that our selves developed *relationally* in interaction with others (whose views were incorporated into the *me*) rather than *individually* in opposition to others. It followed that selves were not determined by one's given nature, but by one's social environment. This idea provided an underpinning for a major political achievement of early twentieth-century social science, which was to displace *racist* (and other genetic or hereditarian) explanations of cultural and behavioral variation with *culturally relativist* ones.[13] As I suggested above, **racism** saw variation among humans as flowing from fixed, inherited, racial differences—our racial *natures*—that expressed themselves as we matured, while **cultural relativism** saw variation as flowing from cultural conventions that were implanted in us through socialization. An implication of this latter view was that selves could be changed as one changed the social relations through which they were constituted. Using Mead's terminology, if we change the generalized other, we change the selves that incorporate it through socialization. This was the *nurture* side of the **nature versus nurture debate.**

This debate lives on, informed now by somewhat better (but by no means conclusive) science. A form of it arises when we consider whether peoples' selves become fixed rather early in their lives, or are always subject to relatively easy remolding. We argue, for instance, over whether and how criminals can be "reformed," whether schools can positively remold children's self-images and what effect this might have, whether individuals are responsible for their actions (or whether the "generalized other" perhaps bears the burden for their misdeeds), and so on. Here, social science meets up with social policy in a way that Mead would have found stimulating. Indeed, it is in part because of his work that we debate these issues in this form today.

We have now looked at Mead's ideas about **mind** and **self**, but have not discussed the third term in the title of his book, *society.* Unfortunately, Mead had little to say about society that has proven of enduring interest, beyond its role in the formation of selves. We could spend some time demonstrating this, but it seems best to move on immediately to outline some of the significant contributions to sociological *theory* that have grown out of Mead's **social behaviorism** as it was slowly transformed into symbolic interactionism and other forms of microsociological analysis. There is little theory in Mead himself, but he (along with George Cooley and Georg Simmel) refocused the interest of sociology upon the microsociological domain of interaction. As we will see in a moment, Mead's concern with the self was continued in the work of Erving Goffman. Much of Goffman's theorizing is analytical, and exploring it will allow us to expand our understanding of analysis beyond the appreciation we developed in reviewing Weber's analytic typologies. But Goffman, influenced deeply by Durkheim in this regard, also generated causal models of interaction that continue to be of great importance to sociology.

Erving Goffman and Symbolic Interaction

As I suggested above, one school of interactionist sociology has been hostile to theorizing. Herbert Blumer (1969), leader of the so-called Chicago school, emphasized the capacity of the *I* to respond in novel ways to its social environment, leaving the latter always somewhat in a state of flux. The unpredictability of the *I* made the direction or outcome of social interaction uncertain, which meant we could offer only descriptive (or occasionally causal) narratives of it, and not causal models. Taking Weber's position to an extreme, Blumer dismissed Durkheim's view that unseen social forces controlled people's behavior in predictable ways. Instead, behavior was molded by the meanings people attached to it (and to the social setting in which it occurred), and since these meanings were not fixed, behavior was largely the result of unpredictable and changing conventions. It was "socially constructed" through informal negotiations among individuals in interaction. Together, individuals arrived at a "definition of the situation" that colored how everyone thought and felt about the goings-on. But what was negotiated in this way could always be renegotiated: definitions of the situation were always subject to change. Whether and when they changed, on this view, was no more foreseeable than were the theological redefinitions by which Luther and Calvin redirected European faith in the Reformation. Because of this, sociology was primarily a descriptive enterprise, punctuated with causal narratives.[14]

Goffman understood this point of view, but maintained a greater confidence in the prospects of theorizing in the tradition of Durkheim. He is often recognized as the most subtle and informative analyst of social interaction in the tradition Mead initiated. His approach, sometimes styled **dramaturgical analysis**, viewed social life as collective performances that people put on, much like actors do on the stage. In taking this approach, he drove the metaphor of a social *role* much further than Mead had taken it, and explored in greater detail the consequences for our *selves* of success or failure in our roles. Fully describing Goffman's approach would require a very long chapter in itself, but I will briefly review here three features of his work: his inquiry into the rules by which interaction is structured; his treatment of the interactive strategies by which institutions attempt to remold individuals; and his efforts to model variation in interactive styles.

Explaining the Rules of Interaction

In the first chapter, I suggested that if we were to explain a game like football to a foreigner, we would do so in part by describing its rules and showing how they govern particular plays. Mead's treatment of play and games suggested attention to rules of interaction, and yet he made little effort to analyze these rules himself. Much of Goffman's intrigue for us, by contrast, lies in his ability to tease out rules that govern our behavior, often beneath our awareness. As Philip Manning has written in a book about Goffman:

> Curiously, we are quite unable to explain how or even why we do most of the things we do with supreme practical ease in our daily lives. Whether walking

down a street or answering a phone call, the way we perform these activities is both more intricately patterned and more important than most of us could possibly believe. In our daily lives we often act on autopilot: we comply with a set of implicit instructions that govern our behavior. (1992:4)

Nowhere is this "autopilot" clearer than in speaking, where grammatical rules govern the construction of our sentences in ways of which we are normally unaware. Grammarians must infer these rules from instances of speaking, and Goffman did much the same for interaction. I will explore here only a few examples and then discuss their relevance to theory.

Social interaction varies across what we might think of as social space. Drawing on his theatrical metaphor, Goffman (1959:106–40) analyzed this space into distinct areas or arenas. Stage actors prepare for their performances in dressing rooms and warm-up areas that are **backstage**, out of the view of audiences. In moving onto the stage itself, and especially **frontstage**,[15] actors abruptly enter the roles they have prepared for and practiced backstage. The transition is marked by changes in demeanor, posture, voice, and so on. By these means, actors become different persons for the audience, as opposed to who they are for themselves and for their fellow actors backstage. But the same is true of life in general, Goffman argued. All of us prepare for public performances "backstage," using the privacy of bedrooms and bathrooms to groom ourselves and otherwise strive for the effect we want to achieve when in public. Transitions between the two arenas are often marked by distinctive gestures. Before leaving the backstage, we check one last time in the mirror for our appearance, correct our posture, and perhaps take a deep breath; while upon return we may exhale explosively, kick off our shoes, and flop down on a couch. When surrounded backstage by intimates, our speech and dress are casual and we may feel free to perform grooming exercises that are taboo in public, while in the furthest recesses of our backstage, we carry out acts of extreme intimacy or of fundamentally private grooming. Re-entry frontstage causes all these informalities and tabooed behaviors to be left behind. Our behavior now has to conform to explicit standards of correctness—*formalities*—that can be arduous to learn and exacting to perform. As Goffman wrote:

Throughout Western society there tends to be one informal or backstage language of behavior, and another language of behavior when a performance is being presented. The backstage language consists of reciprocal first-naming, co-operative decision-making, profanity, open sexual remarks, elaborate griping, smoking, rough informal dress, "sloppy" sitting and standing posture, use of dialect or sub-standard speech, mumbling and shouting, playful aggressivity and "kidding," inconsiderateness for the other in minor but potentially symbolic acts, minor physical self-involvements such as humming, whistling, chewing, nibbling, belching, and flatulence. The frontstage behavior language can be taken as the absence (and in some sense the opposite) of this. (1959:128)

Goffman thus dissected social space, analyzing it into distinct arenas where quite different rules govern our behavior. He did so by employing a metaphor—life as theater—that made sense of observed variation in behavior (here between comparatively public and private domains). What is appropriate to one arena is not to the other.[16]

As I have presented it thus far, Goffman's treatment of behavioral variation in social space is almost exclusively descriptive. In the terms of our first chapter, his analysis results in an empirical generalization: the relative formality of our behavior is associated with our relative familiarity with those around us. We are most familiar with ourselves and least with strangers, while family, friends and acquaintances fall in between. Thus, we may pick our noses with relish in private, do so furtively among close friends, but not at all in public. This empirical generalization, however, does little to improve upon our everyday understanding of how the social world works. The more interesting question is *why* some forms of behavior are designated casual and others formal: why is slouching seen as casual and sitting up straight as formal, and not vice versa? Why are these variations in the meaning of our postures embodied in the particular ways they are?

Asking this somewhat odd question reminds us that we are often so accustomed to "the rules" that we don't think to question how they arise. Doing so requires that we defamiliarize them (viewing them as a stranger might) so that it occurs to us to wonder why they take the form they do and how they arise. Before we can know how to approach these questions, we have to speculate about whether the rules are pure conventions (which thus could easily be changed or, indeed, reversed), or whether that they are somehow necessary. If they are conventions, we would account for them through causal narratives explaining how they came to be, or provide histories of them through descriptive narratives. But if they are somehow *necessary*, we will have to look deeper for some causal model to explain them. The narratives would give us a "shallow" answer to how they arise, and a mechanism or causal model a "deeper" answer.

Let me put this in a slightly different way. If tomorrow we were able to redefine the situation and erase distinctions between front and backstage altogether, or perhaps to reverse the behaviors, moving today's informalities into public view and reserving current formalities for private use, Goffman would have known that he was describing mere conventions. The rules would be purely "social constructions" subject to change by collective agreement, just like driving on the right versus the left. If we found them to be so, there would be nothing to theorize about. The best we could do would be to assemble descriptive or causal narratives to show how these particular conventions came to be adopted.[17]

But Goffman was convinced they were *not* mere conventions, and he had an underlying view of the self that explained why.[18] The self that we all hope to present in everyday life is an *idealized* one that we carefully construct backstage, often with the help of other performers, with the aim of gaining an advantage in interactions that occur frontstage. Goffman noted that, though there are some occasions upon which the idealized self we enact in public is geared to underrepresent our real estimations of our worth, we normally claim slightly more than our due.[19] But doing this always puts us "on edge" during a performance, worried that we may be seen through, so that our public pretensions preclude the sort of ease and inattention that we are allowed backstage. For instance, mumbling and substandard grammar simply can't validate the self we normally lay claim to in public.[20] This means, however, that the behavioral distinctions that mark front- and backstage differences *can't* all be conventional. Many of them are determined by the universal aspirations of selves and the requirements audiences place upon us for validation.

We are apt to gain more, after all, if our frontstage performances are flawless and seamless, because these qualities make the person we *claim to be* consistent with the impressions we give of who we *are*. A successful match between the claimed and the performed self stimulates our audience to validate our claim. In asking for a first date with someone to whom we are attracted, for instance, it is generally better to appear calm and confident, rather than rattled or hesitant. Similarly, a public speech is flawed by the profuse sweating or shaking hands that reveal how nervous we feel at the prospect of making fools of ourselves. Further, our claim on the audience in both circumstances would be put in question by poor grooming, flatulence, weak handshakes—the whole litany of miscues that our parents instructed us against. These flaws undermine our ability to enact an idealized self before our audience, and indeed may catastrophically underrepresent our true worth.

This need for audience validation was at the core of Goffman's view of human beings. As he wrote in a later essay:

> The individual may desire, earn, and deserve deference, but by and large he is not allowed to give it to himself, being forced to seek it from others. In seeking it from others, he finds he has added reason for seeking them out, and in turn society is given added assurance that its members will enter into interaction and relationships with one another. (1967:58)

In addition to presenting ourselves to others in ways that strategically maximize the benefits that flow from interaction, then, we are also linked to our audience in reciprocal exchanges of deference.[21] We have to *give* in order to *receive*, and many of the formalities of interaction consist of rituals that ensure this exchange.

These observations, to sum up, suggest a mechanism that restricts our ability to freely (that is, conventionally) assign particular behaviors to any arena we wish. As a consequence, we are *everywhere* apt to find the same core differences between back- and frontstage behavior, whatever the time or society. To explain why, Goffman offers a mechanism that relates the aims people pursue in interaction and the characteristics of successful performances.[22] Together, these effectively structure interaction, eliminating many options and thus ensuring that the differences between front- and backstage behavior are *not* simply the result of conventions. Thus, Goffman's approach does more than simply *describe* the rules that govern interaction: it *explains* certain of them by means of a mechanism, showing why they take a specific form that is *not* conventional. Let us reinforce this point through an additional example.

We often feel mildly uncomfortable riding with strangers in elevators, and not just because they are strangers. The problem arises from a social dilemma: both casual acknowledgment and studious nonacknowledgment are permitted among strangers forced momentarily into close physical proximity, as in elevators or public lavatories, and we are never clear which rule should be followed. Just as claustrophobic physical circumstances can produce unease, so does the lack of a single rule governing proper elevator behavior, and the uncertainly involved ensures mild social discomfort. We deal with this either by silently staring above us at the floor indicator (or below us at our feet) or by seeking plausible ways to innocuously address our momentary companions–"Cold today, isn't it?" A similar problem occurs when an elevator empties piecemeal as it rises. As spaces in it open, Goffman suggests, we must decide whether to reposition ourselves vis-à-vis the remaining occupants:

> Thus, as the car empties, passengers acquire a measure of uneasiness, caught between two opposing inclinations—to obtain maximum distance from others and to inhibit avoidance behavior that might give offense. (1971:32)

Here, Goffman explains our unease with a theory: social discomfort arises from circumstances where competing rules govern our behavior, and the more rules come into conflict (or the weightier the rules), the more discomfort we will feel. Explanations of this sort are especially illuminating when we have not been conscious of the rules in the first place—as I was not conscious of what lay behind the repositioning problem in elevators.

In analyzing such situations, Goffman viewed himself as exploring social order. Social order is a web woven of rituals of interaction, each with its own rules. Selves traverse this web, seeking a share of respect and normally cooperating with others to provide them *their* share. Awkward situations are sites in the web, such as elevators, where conflicting rules leave us unsure of how to act. Or they are occasions where individuals slip up in their ritual performance of roles. Awkward people (those who are maladroit at the rituals of interaction) suffer embarrassment for their failures and cause discomfort to those around them, spoiling the cooperative effort. Consistently or profoundly maladroit people may even be viewed as mentally ill, and suffer severe withdrawals of social respect . . . to the point that they may be forcibly removed from society.

Social Processes in Total Institutions

People, like the mentally ill, who are severely deficient in interactive competence are often dealt with by institutions that attempt to reform or resocialize them. Among the institutions that attempt resocialization are what Goffman called **total institutions:**

> The total institution is a social hybrid, part residential community, part formal organization; therein lies its special sociological interest. There are other reasons for being interested in these establishments too. In our society, they are for forcing houses for changing persons; each is a natural experiment on what can be done to the self. (1962:12)

Examples are prisons, mental hospitals, monasteries, and boot camps. These institutions all work to remold selves, and they do so through a regular series of processes. Almost all begin with a ritual profanation of the individual's existing self:

> The recruit comes into the establishment with a conception of himself made possible by certain stable social arrangements in his home world. Upon entrance, he is immediately stripped of the support provided by these arrangements. . . . He begins a series of abasements, degradations, humiliations, and profanations of self. His self is systematically, if often unintentionally, mortified. He begins some radical shifts in his **moral career,** a career composed of the progressive changes that occur in the beliefs that he has concerning himself and significant others. (1962:14, emphasis in original)

In its early pages, Goffman's book *Asylums* provides us with a catalog of techniques of mortification. For instance, Goffman describes a particular style of assault on the self, designated "looping," in which the responses to humiliation that people use outside total institutions to protect their self-respect are systematically broken down:

> Deference patterns in total institutions provide one illustration of the looping effect. In civil society, when an individual must accept circumstances and commands that affront his conception of self, he is allowed a margin of face-saving reactive expression—sullenness, failure to offer usual signs of deference, *sotto voce* profaning asides, or fugitive expressions of contempt, irony, and derision . . . . [But] in total institutions, the staff may directly penalize inmates for such activity, citing sullenness or insolence explicitly as grounds for further punishment. (1962:36)

In his discussion of total institutions, Goffman analyzes the initial techniques of abasement by which old selves are undermined, the "reorganizing" efforts by which the inmate's self is remolded, the characteristic responses of inmates to these efforts, the cultures that develop among inmates, and the adjustments inmates undergo upon exit from the institution. Thoroughly exploring these stages or features of total institutions would occupy us far too long, but we need only point out here that, while Goffman's analysis occasionally seems merely a catalog of techniques, its aim is to provide general outlines of a universal process by which societies attempt to remold adult selves. While their efforts often fail with specific individuals, the techniques of existing total institutions show considerable similarity across time and cultures. They are, as Goffman suggested above, the result of "natural experiments" in human reformation, and the particularly ineffective ones tend to die out quickly, leaving little record, while those that succeed, even modestly, apparently utilize quite uniform strategies for remodeling people. Thus, we learn something generalizable from Goffman's analysis of processes in total institutions. It is theoretical to the extent that it identifies widespread *mechanisms*, such as rituals of mortification, that regularly produce similar results, such as the erosion of confidence in the self with which we entered a total institution.[23] We could use the functional paradigm to explain the spread and maintenance of such mechanisms.

Goffman's analysis of total institutions and their mechanisms for remolding the self, as well as his analysis of interaction rituals, carry us far, both descriptively and theoretically, beyond the limited discussion of social interaction Mead provided. At the descriptive level, as the quotation from Manning has already stressed, Goffman alerted us to behavioral rules to which we have always conformed without perhaps being aware of it.[24] His observational ability in this regard was so acute that we are apt to despair of being able to emulate him. But beyond alerting us to rules and processes, which is primarily a descriptive enterprise, Goffman offered us the deeper theoretical understanding, usually by specifying causal mechanisms. The analyses we have just looked at share Mead's interest in outlining universal aspects of interaction, sometimes concentrated in organizations like total institutions. I want to conclude our look at Goffman by outlining some of his efforts to explain variation in interaction using causal models of a structural sort.

Structural Models

While there is considerable insight to be gained from Goffman's descriptions of rules of interaction, their greatest value from the viewpoint of sociological theory is that they open vast arenas to causal modeling. For instance, his division of social space into front and back stages that vary in formality alerts us to the prospect that this spectrum *itself* varies from one society to another. Some societies or eras place great weight on a rigid segregation of front and back stages, populating the former with elaborate formalities, while other societies and eras are much more relaxed and informal generally. This returns us to a theme we introduced in discussing structuralism in the last chapter. There I referred briefly to anthropologist Mary Douglas's (1970, see also Elias 1978) interest in explaining why some societies value formalities (such as traditional wedding ceremonies), and see them as deeply meaningful, while other societies find them hollow. The former generally create much greater distance between front and back stages and respond with more severe sanctions to displays of informal behavior in public circumstances. Structurally, Douglas argued, such societies are characterized by significant stratification, with firm and relatively permanent boundaries between status groups. Societies that less firmly segregate front and back stages tend to have low degrees of stratification and/or fluid boundaries among status groups. Thus, we can develop the outlines of a causal model that explains and predicts the degree of separation between front and back stage in terms of differences in social structure.

Goffman provides similar models himself, though they sometimes go unremarked in the flow of his description and analysis. In a celebrated essay on "The Nature of Deference and Demeanor" (1967:47–95), for instance, he discussed the ceremonial rituals by which people convey respect for one another. Some such rituals are symmetric, with equal degrees of formality required of both sides. He noted that:

> in some societies, Tibetan for example, salutations between high-placed individuals can become prolonged displays of ritual conduct, exceeding in duration

and expansiveness the kind of obeisance a subject may owe his ruler in less ritualized societies. (1967:59)

While Goffman mentioned this only as a possibility, we may infer from his discussion that, across societies and in general, the higher the status of any two social equals, the more elaborate will be the ceremonial greeting rituals between them.[25]

Let me introduce a related causal model using the format of chapter 1. Early in his career, Goffman did research on interaction among members of communities in the Shetland Islands, which are in the North Sea to the northeast of Scotland. He observed that when Islanders ate around a table, they often sat very close to one another. This contrasted with seating practices he had already observed in Britain, where people sat farther apart. Thus, he was able to formulate the empirical generalization we find in figure 8.1. But what could have caused this variation? Goffman realized that the mere difference in location between Britain and the Shetland Islands was in fact incidental. It wasn't a matter of variation in local conventions, because he had been observing *middle class* customs in Britain, while the people in the Shetland Islands were primarily *working class*. Thus, he could propose a second empirical generalization, and then dispense with his clue variable to form the theory presented in figure 8.2.

Eliminating the clue variable, we get figure 8.3.

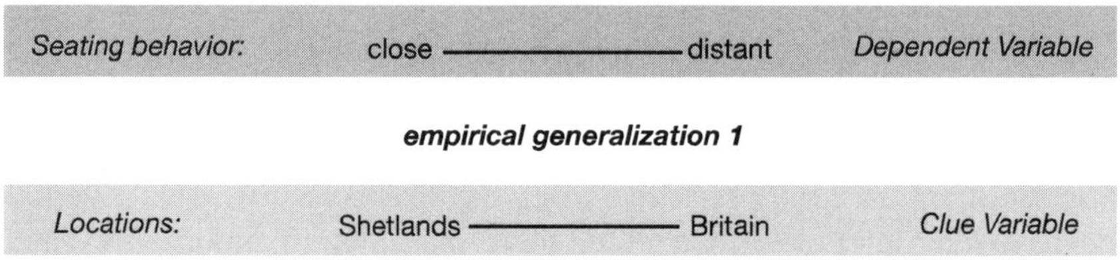

Seating behavior:	close ——————— distant	*Dependent Variable*

empirical generalization 1

Locations:	Shetlands ——————— Britain	*Clue Variable*

FIGURE 8.1
An Empirical Generalization about Seating Behavior

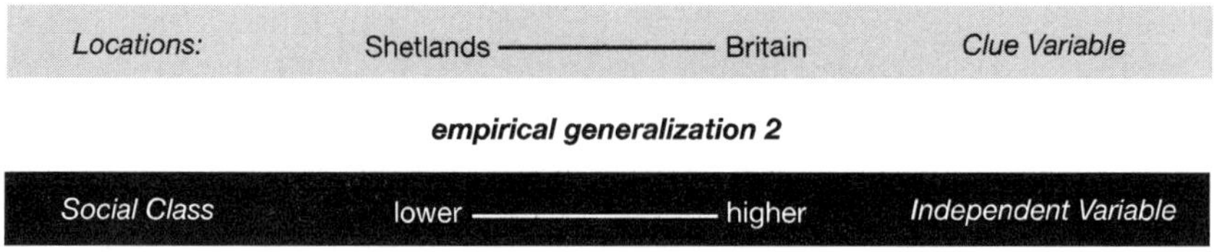

Locations:	Shetlands ——————— Britain	*Clue Variable*

empirical generalization 2

Social Class	lower ——————— higher	*Independent Variable*

FIGURE 8.2
Adding an Independent Variable to Explain Seating Behavior

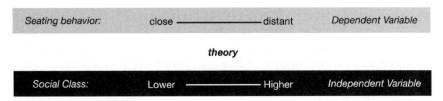

FIGURE 8.3
A Theory of Seating Behavior

To provide a mechanism for this causal relation, Goffman introduced the principle of an **"ideal sphere"** (or personal space) that surrounds people and that cannot be infringed upon without their permission. Drawing on German sociologist Georg Simmel's discussion of the matter, Goffman wrote that:

> Here . . . is one of the important differences between social classes in our society: not only are some of the tokens different through which consideration for the privacy of others is expressed, but also, apparently, *the higher the class the more extensive and elaborate are the taboos against contact.* (1967:63, emphasis mine)

While he proposes this causal model only for "our society," it is likely to apply everywhere: in all societies, higher status people have larger ideal spheres—personal spaces that have to be honored not just by greater physical separation but by more elaborate rituals of greeting or parting. Goffman used similar principles to explain and predict the nature of ceremonial relations between people of unequal status. Here, asymmetrical rules require subordinates to behave more formally than their superiors, with the degree of difference corresponding to the status differential involved. This explains, incidentally, why students usually address their professors formally (Doctor or Professor Last Name), but are first-named in return.

Thus, we can find many causal models embedded within Goffman's analysis of interaction.[26] Where did the inspiration to produce them come from? In introducing the above essay, he wrote that its purpose was

> to explore some of the senses in which the person in our urban secular world is allotted a kind of sacredness that is displayed and confirmed by symbolic acts . . . .[In doing so] I will try to show that a version of Durkheim's social psychology can be effective in modern dress. (1967:47)

Goffman here is connecting the interactionist paradigm to the orientation Durkheim developed in *Elementary Forms of the Religious Life* (see also Collins 1988b, Schneider 1996), and I have already noted the rich connections that can be made between symbolic interaction as a focus of sociological concern and the structuralist paradigm. The study of symbolic interaction, in part because it is primarily descriptive in its orientation, exposes broad fields of behavioral variation that can be conceptualized as variables and, hopefully, explained through structural means.

Let me conclude this discussion of Goffman by reiterating some important points. Throughout this chapter, I've stressed the distinction between behavior that is and isn't *conventional*. When behavior is purely conventional, we'd be wasting our time seeking a theory to explain it. Conventions, as we've seen, are arbitrary, and the best we can do to explain them is to offer a causal narrative of their origins.[27]

Now if the rules that govern how higher and lower status people address one another were also arbitrary, it would be incidental whether students addressed professors formally and professors addressed students informally or vice versa. After all, the same status distinction could be maintained by the reversed pattern of address—with professors being called by their first names and students being addressed as Mr. or Ms. Last Name. In other words, the *difference* in status can be "marked" or noticed equally well by either pattern of address. But it is universally true that only one of these options is chosen: higher status people are everywhere addressed more formally by lower status persons rather than vice versa.[28] Thus, this is *not* a convention, but instead a regular social pattern that can be causally modeled—that is, explained through a theory such as Goffman provides.

Establishing these patterns (which are really just empirical generalizations) takes us only half the way to a satisfying causal model, however, because we remain unclear about the *mechanism* that links status differences so firmly to only one of the two possible ways they can be marked. I have outlined such a mechanism elsewhere (Schneider 1996) by developing Goffman's notion of ideal spheres, but rather than review the somewhat complex argument involved, let's consider a simpler example. A tendency to associate good things with the direction "up" ("things are looking up!" or "up in heaven" for instance) and bad things with "down" ("what a downer!") also seems nearly universal. Sociologist Barry Schwartz (1981) has explained this symbolism by means of the universal experience of children looking physically upward to their parents, in whom they see a source of sustenance and physical comfort. Babies nurse looking upward, after all, and such an experience may build into us a sense that it is more appropriate to associate "up" with good than it is to associate it with "down." Thus, while the concept "down" would serve just as well as "up" to mark good things, it is empirically very rare that it does so, and it is rare not just in our usage, but everywhere.[29]

Schwartz found in the childhood association of up with sustenance and care a mechanism that can produce this nonarbitrary structural relation.

Goffman's sociology provides us with causal models of this sort. They show us why specific patterns of behavior are *not* conventional, but instead are determined by certain regular features of social life. Thus, Goffman's writings often give us two distinct levels of illumination: they first alert us to the rules that govern our behavior, often without our being aware, and then they indicate how these rules are mandated by aspects of the social order. And where he offers us no causal models, we are invited to provide them. Before attempting to do so, we need to ask ourselves whether the rules are simply conventions, and thus not worth theorizing about in the first place. If they are not conventions, we can with some ingenuity propose causal models that explain them. This prospect makes structuralist symbolic interactionism one of the most intriguing areas of sociological theory today.

Goffman's theorizing arises out of supremely close and acute observation of everyday human interaction. In fact his acuity is sometimes unnerving, since he is able to notice patterns or rules to our behavior when we are unable to do so ourselves. In this regard, he often appears vaguely alien, like a Martian visitor to whom *our* habitual practices, which have become invisible to us just because they are so commonplace, stand out strikingly. As sociologist Bennett Berger has written,

> Goffman was so sensitive to the most routine sorts of social interaction that he frequently startled his friends and acquaintances by his detached insights into the structure of their interaction, even as it was being enacted with him simultaneously both participant and commentator. (1986:ix)

His acuity has set a hard standard to live up to. In part because his insights are so hard to duplicate, Goffman can't be said to have established a subparadigm within symbolic interaction that continues to be consistently employed—though certain of his ideas animate research in areas such as social movements. The next approach we will consider, by way of concluding this book, is quite different in this regard. It is the basis for a collective endeavor around which a research community has coalesced, and which gathers data not in the somewhat haphazard manner of Goffman, but much more systematically. Although it styles itself a *theory*, in the terms we are using here, it is really a subparadigm in the wider paradigm of symbolic interaction. It, along with similar subparadigms like *expectations states* theory (see Collins 1988a, 239–42; Wagner and Berger 2002), develops broad and systematically related sets of ideas that indicate how theories explaining particular sorts of behavior can be formed and tested. It is a bit unfortunate that we can't spend more time with it and expectations states theory: they have been more consistently, coherently, and thoroughly developed than most other paradigms in sociology, and because of this give us a very clear picture of the sort of conceptual equipment that is useful in constructing theories.

The Affect Control Subparadigm

To introduce affect control as an orientation, let's return to the hypothetical incident that started us theorizing in the first chapter. There someone was shot. One male student killed another who had made advances to the first student's girlfriend. This caused us to *wonder*. Our wondering prompted us to seek an explanation of the shooter's behavior, and as sociologists we developed a theory to provide one, a theory involving an interesting and lengthy intellectual journey into the functional origins of cultures of honor. But the paradigm of affect control identifies a different source of wonder in this event. It wonders why we wondered about this shooting to begin with. Here, *our reaction* to the event becomes what we want to explain, and not the event itself.

Now it might seem that this is a bad question. After all, the answer to why we wonder seems obvious: one student murdering another is so striking an event that we just *naturally* wonder why it happened. What's there to wonder about, we might ask, in our wondering? But affect control sees in this the key to an important reconceptualization of human interaction, and one that corrects a significant defect in Mead's approach to it. How so? To being with, as I presented our wondering in the first chapter, it was *intellectually* motivated: the shooting presented us with a puzzle that we set out to solve, and the means we used to do so were all clearly *cognitive* (as opposed to emotional) in character. But it is rare, suggest proponents of affect control, that wonder is intellectually motivated. Normally, it is sparked by emotional or *affective* responses to incidents. Indeed, it is when something seems affectively *wrong* in an incident that we are jarred off autopilot and forced to take stock. An adequate explanation of this process, suggests affect control, will require us to remold our approach to symbolic interaction substantially.

In our murder, two of the things that seem wrong are that a *college student* is doing the killing and that it happens at a *party*. These features motivate our reaction, since we would not be as surprised if a shooting occurred on the streets between gang members in a dispute over turf. In order to set up a consistent comparative framework for analyzing such reactions, affect control theorists (Smith-Lovin 1988; MacKinnon 1994:19) suggest we consider events as consisting of actors (A) behaving (B) toward objects (O) in situations or contexts (S). While witnessing any murder would obviously be disturbing, what especially knocks us off auto-pilot in our case is the sense that *students* (A) shouldn't be doing *this* (B) to other *students* (O) at *parties* (S). In other words, the **ABOS configuration** of the event seems shocking to us, and our initial reaction to it occurs through *impressions* or *feelings* of *wrongness*, nicely captured in the notion of a *shock*, and not initially through thoughts or through thinking about the event at all. To put this somewhat differently, according to affect control we are almost always stimulated to think by impressions that are initially *felt* rather than thought about by means of concepts. We respond to emotional as opposed to intellectual stimuli, and this means that understanding our feelings will be the key to explaining our reactions.

As we learned in the first chapter, the second step in forming a theory is to turn incidents into variables. In this case, the incident is an instance of wondering, and affect control suggests that we conceptualize it as belonging to a very general category of responses to ABOS configurations called **deflections**. Deflections are instances of being knocked off autopilot by impressions of wrongness that are elicited by specific events. What is most interesting about the affect control paradigm is that it offers us a method for analyzing and comparing impressions of wrongness across all events that can elicit them, as well as for analyzing and comparing the features of events that cause these impressions. In other words, it explains deflections (or their absence when we continue on autopilot). The deflections or their absence thus become the dependent variables that affect control explains.

We might note that in taking this approach, affect control continues the ambition of symbolic interaction to understand universal features of interaction. The analytical and explanatory strategies of this paradigm can in principle be applied to any incidents, anywhere, across history and cultures. In practice, however, the paradigm requires us to collect very specific sorts of data about people's impressions of the individual components of any ABOS configuration and about people's reactions to the way these components come together in an event. Explaining why requires us to back up a bit.

In the 1950s, psychologist Charles Osgood and colleagues (1957) developed a very general method for analyzing the "meaning" of objects or events. This was called the **semantic differential test**, and it involved asking people to rate concepts that categorize persons, events, or objects—such as *mother*, or *breastfeeding*, or *crib*—along twenty abstract dimensions, each defined by polar terms such as good and bad, or quick and slow, with steps in between so that there was a neutral middle. While this can initially seem a bit nonsensical, as more and more information was gathered about people's ratings of concepts, two things became clear. First, ratings were relatively consistent from person to person within the same culture or subculture. This meant that researchers could claim to understand, albeit in a rather peculiar way, the attitudes that for Mead constituted the *generalized other*. In a sense, our ability to "take the role of the other" means understanding how this other would rate objects, persons, and events on a semantic differential test! More generally, socialization might be understood as the process by which people come to understand and accept the ratings prevalent in the communities in which they live.

Second, researchers used statistical methods to show that the twenty abstract dimensions of the semantic differential test could be grouped into three more general categories. These were **evaluation** (which captured a set of "good/bad" dimensions), **potency** (which captured "strong/weak" dimensions), and **activity** (which captured "active/passive" dimensions). Thus, any concept could be given an average "EPA" (Evaluation/Potency/Activity) profile in terms of the numerical scores it received across raters on the dimensions involved in each category, and you could use statistical methods to gauge how strong or weak agreement was over these average **EPA profiles** within a population. It is this EPA profile that generates the particular *feeling*, or affective tonality, that accompanies concepts for us and for the people around us. From this perspective, Mead's generalized other is the set of EPA profiles that show strong agreement within our community, and we come to adopt them, incorporating them into our *me*'s, as we work our way through play and game stages of socialization. These function to coordinate our EPA profiles with those of others around us.

The first advantage of this somewhat quirky view of things is that quite precise *quantitative* values can be used to replace the notoriously vague notion of what something *means* to people. For the purposes of the affect control paradigm, something *means* its EPA profile. A concept like *mother*, for instance, is only partly understood through its verbal (or dictionary) meaning. It carries as well an affective tone that the dictionary meaning can't easily convey. We can get at this affective tone through EPA profiles. The second advantage is that the meanings of concepts, reduced to their quantitative EPA profiles, can be compared across subcultures, cultures, and historical periods—as long as we can administer semantic differential tests (this is the practical difficulty I mentioned above).

I expect that the application of this method to our incident will already be apparent to you. Each component element of the incident—student (A) shooting (B) student (O) at party (S)—has an EPA profile stored away within our generalized other. The affect control paradigm refers to these individual profiles as the **fundamental affective meaning** for each concept. We experience deflection because the *transient affective meaning* that *this particular* *incident* generates (its ABOS profile) is inconsistent with the fundamental meanings of its components. Thus, a deflection occurs, and we get kicked off autopilot. This happens whenever transient meanings conflict with fundamental ones. In concrete terms, students and parties are too good and not potent enough to allow for an act like murder (which is bad and very potent), and thus we are shocked. By way of contrast, a culture of honor presumably consists of component fundamental EPAs that would cause considerably less deflection when brought together in this event. In a culture of honor the event would be an anticipated consequence of violations of sexual property, and male students would have higher "potency" scores to begin with. Parties would end in assaults or duels with enough frequency to change the fundamental affective EPA of parties in general. Thus, we would not expect a similar incident to cause the same degree of deflection in a culture of honor.

It will be apparent now that we have successfully turned our wonder into a variable, as well as devised an independent variable to explain it. Our dependent variable is measured by the degree of our deflection, and our independent variable is measured by the degree of contrast between the transient affective meanings elicited by the event and our fundamental affective meanings for its components. The greater the contrast, the greater the deflection—and our wonder. By an extension of this argument, we understand why we are quite a bit more apt to be deflected by our shooting than would be a participant in the culture of honor, where there is less contrast between fundamental affective meanings and the transient impressions the event creates. Hence *we* wonder and *they* do not.

Of course, there is a sense in which the affect control paradigm merely applies new terms and methods to factors and processes that we can understand in everyday terms. But its methods also allow it to develop mechanisms and use them to make rather precise predictions that are quite impossible otherwise. Consider, for example,

> an individual who acquires a transient self-impression that is much more negative than the individual's identity—say, as a result of being derogated in public. Affect control theory predicts that the stigmatized individual will engage a valued other in an especially positive action in an effort to pull the transient impression of self up to a more positive value. . . . On the other hand, individuals with negative self-sentiments—especially those who are too submissive and passive to depend on active behavioral strategies—need assurance from others that their low opinion of themselves is justified. They seek others who criticize them, even when the derogations are emotionally painful, because being criticized is an experience that confirms negative self-sentiments. (Heise 2002:25–26)

Had we more leisure, we could explore further examples like the above. Through them, affect control presents us with an unusual and very general perspective on the relation between society and self—one that, in combination with its mechanisms and quantitative predictions, takes us far beyond Mead. As most simply expressed by David Heise, the chief architect of affect control, this perspective suggests that:

1. Individuals create events to confirm the sentiments [the EPA profiles] that they have about themselves and others in the current situation.
2. If events don't work to maintain sentiments [i.e., if deflections occur], then individuals reidentify themselves and others.
3. In the process of building events to confirm sentiments, individuals perform the social roles that operate society—the principle of affective rationality. (2002:17)

In other words, we construct our social interactions (events) so as to minimize the prospect of deflection. If we can't avoid deflections, we change our EPA profiles so that deflections will be less likely in the future. And, driven by these factors, we find ourselves constituting societies.

Earlier in this chapter, I wrote that for Goffman, the social order was woven of rituals of interaction, and that "selves traverse this web, seeking a share of respect and normally cooperating with others to provide them with *their* share. Awkward situations are sites in the web, such as elevators, where conflicting rules leave us unsure of how to act" (p. 287, above). The general vision of affect control is allied to this but somewhat different. Selves cooperate to construct events that enact fundamental affective meanings (that is, that do not cause deflections), and when they are unsuccessful, have to remodel either their fundamental meanings or their *selves*. This process is one of continual feedback between selves and society (in Mead's terms, between the *me* and the *generalized other*), a cybernetic (feedback) process that has its intellectual roots in pragmatism and Mead (MacKinnon 1994:3). This process can be firmly connected to macrosociological forces. As we have seen by using affect control to explain the hypothetical deflection we experienced in the first chapter, as well as the lesser deflection that would be experienced in cultures of honor, affect control allows us to easily connect variation in interaction to macrosociological variations between, as Marx might say, different modes of production. Some of these modes of production breed cultures of honor, ours today does not.

Conclusion

In the end what may be most impressive for our purposes in this book is the thoroughness and care with which the affect control paradigm has been worked out. What had begun long ago, in Mead's work, as very general reflections of the relation between self and society, acquires in affect control theory a degree of explicitness and, consequently, measurability that allows theories to be formulated and tested. Thus, subparadigms like affect control and expectation states stand at the opposite pole from nontheoretical strands that also remain current in symbolic interaction. Further, because they do not call for the faintly Martian ability to become strangers to our own practices that Goffman possessed and that caused his work to be inimitable, they allow for research communities to form within the domain of microsociology, slowly pushing forward a collective investigation that promises a more and more thorough theoretical understanding of the interaction order. This is what science is about, and it is a fitting place to close down our discussion of sociological theory.

Notes

1. We can see from this that behaviorism represents an application to psychology of ideas similar to those Darwin applied to biology to explain evolution. If an organism acquires a new capacity through mutation or genetic recombination, this capacity will persist if it produces a selective advantage, allowing for more offspring to be produced. Behaviorism views specific behaviors similarly: if they provide advantages to the individual, they are maintained. Both evolutionary theory and behaviorism are forms of functional theorizing, and Mead himself was much influenced by Darwin's *The Expression of the Emotions in Man and Animals* (1872).

2. As suggested in footnote 1, the model here is very similar to a functional or evolutionary one. If people make blind attempts to cope with their environment, merely trying out approaches without much forethought to see whether they will work, we will only be able to offer descriptive narratives of their behavior rather than explain it. But the process by which some trials come to be rewarded and others not is something we can explain in terms of the environmental reward pattern (which is called a *reinforcement schedule* in laboratory experiment with animals). Looking at this from the other side, if we can control the environment so that it rewards just those behaviors we value, individuals should come to behave in just the ways we would like them to. This raises the prospect of utopian "social engineering," with environments being designed to reward only those patterns of behavior of which we approve. See the utopian proposals of behavioral psychologist B. F. Skinner in *Walden Two* (1948) and *Beyond Freedom and Dignity* (1972).

3. Mead did not publish this book. It was assembled from lecture notes his students took and published after his death.

4. Albert Bergesen (2004) has used the linguistic theory formulated by Noam Chomsky, as well as findings from cognitive psychology, to question certain aspects of Mead's discussion of gestures and how they are acquired. His article reflects another aspect of the nature–versus–nurture debate.

5. As Mead wrote, "The only way in which we can react against the disapproval

of the entire community is by setting up a higher sort of community" that includes "the voices of the past" as we encounter them in folktales or books (1934:167–68).

6. By contrast, children in the play stage are not yet competent. As Mead wrote, "you cannot count on the child; you cannot assume that all the things he does are going to determine what he will do at any moment. The child has no definite character, no definite personality" (1934:159). This definite character comes only with conceptions of the generalized other achieved through games. It is the organized attitudes of the generalized other that give structure and consistency to the self: "What goes to make up the organized self is the organization of attitudes which are common to the group. A person is a personality because he belongs to a community" (1934:162).

7. He once referred to the *I* as a historical figure: "If you ask, then, where directly in your own experience the "I" comes in, the answer is that it comes in as an historical figure" (1934:174).

8. I put *theory* in quotation marks here because, as you should now anticipate, the great man approach to change is not a theory in the sense that we are using the term here. Instead, it reflects Weber's conviction that innovations are often contingent phenomena that can only be narrated and not explained.

9. For an interesting, if somewhat oblique, challenge to this, see Julian Jaynes, *The Origins of Consciousness in the Breakdown of the Bicameral Mind* (1977). Jaynes argues that self-consciousness was absent from humans as recently as Homeric times. This is one way of turning the *I* and *me* into variables. Had Mead done so, he might also have argued that sociopaths, for instance, have acquired defective *me*'s and are, thus, socially uncontrollable.

10. Of course, we might be able to use scanning devices to show that different areas of the brain are activated during different phases of the self, thus indicating a neurophysiological basis for these distinctions. If so, we could show them to be empirical phenomena.

11. A good deal of experimental work was done by the Swiss psychologist Jean Piaget (see, e.g., 1970) on stages in children's intellectual development. While Piaget's experimental studies do not deal explicitly with Mead's concepts, they provide evidence within roughly the same ballpark.

12. You might reflect on whether analyzing the development of the self into stages results in an *analytic* or an *open empirical* typology, to use distinctions developed in chapter 5. Classic behaviorist psychology would point out that the self itself is not something we can demonstrate.

13. For an excellent history of this development in the field of anthropology, see Harris (1968).

14. A treatment of the interactionist tradition that emphasizes its descriptive side is available in Charon (1995), while an extensive review of both the nontheoretical and theoretical sides of the tradition can be found in Turner (1998:343–465). Nontheoretical interactionists normally confine themselves to providing descriptive or causal narratives. Consider this illustration of causal analysis from Charon:

> Any given act along the stream of interaction is caused by the individual's *decisions* at that point. A given decision in turn is caused by the individual's *definition of the situation* at that point. . . . The definition of the situation the individual arrives at in turn is influenced

by two things: *interaction with self* (thinking) and *interaction with others*. I took a job at Moorhead State University long ago. I took it because of several decisions I made at the time: to leave my previous job and community, to move from Minneapolis, and to stop looking for other jobs. These decisions were made on the basis of the goals I defined for myself at the time: to become a college professor, to finish my doctorate, and to settle in a community close to my family. (1995:129, emphases in original)

This causal narrative continues for some time, listing additional factors relevant to the decision. Sometimes with symbolic interactionists it remains unclear, as it does above, what is specifically sociological about the causal narrative provided.

15. Goffman usually refers to "front regions" rather than "frontstage" but almost always uses "backstage" rather than "back regions." I have decided to consistently use *front-* and *backstage*.

16. Such segregation allows behavior to convey explicit meanings that people can employ strategically. For instance, to behave *informally* in public usually conveys disrespect for those with whom we are involved. Because this meaning is explicit, it will be seen as intended and will be remarked by those around us. By contrast, behaving *formally* in formal situations implicitly conveys a respect that normally goes unremarked just because it is expected.

17. Behind this topic, very deep questions lurk about what it means to be human and about the nature of the social sciences. See the discussion by Peter Winch (1958) and the controversy that has arisen out of it. Briefly put, if rules are purely conventional, highly sophisticated machines might eventually prove indistinguishable from humans. On the other hand, if conventions are regulated by a deeper, intuitive understanding of collective "meaning," machines might always prove subhuman. This issue animates the movie *Blade Runner*, which is something of a cult classic.

18. This theory explains some core differences between front- and backstage behavior, but would need to be supplemented by others to explain why further behaviors wind up on one or the other side of the distinction. Still other behavior might prove to be merely conventional.

19. Goffman (1959:35) borrowed this claim from Charles Cooley, a colleague of G. H. Mead. As examples of underrepresentations in interaction, Goffman cited women who conceal their intelligence from men in order not to show them up and Southern blacks who conceal their self-respect from whites in order not to appear "uppity."

20. The notorious grammatical and lexical slips made by President George W. Bush in formal situations, which caused many people to view him incorrectly as somewhat dim, illustrate this point nicely.

21. Compare this point of view to the first postulate of conflict theory discussed in chapter 3.

22. Some of these latter are based in uniform physiological responses to embarrassment, which Goffman discusses in an interesting essay (1967:97–112).

23. Here, we might note the similarity to Weber's explication of the psychological mechanism by which anxiety over salvation supposedly produced uniform patterns of behavior among early Calvinists.

24. For instance, I had never noticed that people taking a stool at a bar or lunch counter immediately between two strangers who were already seated there may be

briefly examined sidewise by these strangers while being obligated to look straight ahead (or at the bartender/counterperson) and not to reciprocate the scrutiny. How people learn such rules is something of a mystery. It may be that they are derived from deeper principles, in which case their explanation would involve theory.

25. For an analysis of the mechanisms underlying this causal relationship, see Schneider 1996.

26. Donald Black's (1976:1993) structural sociology makes extensive reference to these causal models and represents a good place to learn about the connections between social structure and regular features of interaction as they mutually constitute "social order."

27. Because the concept of conventions is so important, let me underscore it with a further example from language, where the particular sounds that we use to express concepts are arbitrarily assigned and vary from language to language. For instance, English speakers designate a particular political office as *queen* while Spanish speakers designate the same office as *reina*. The difference exists because Germanic and Romance language families (to which English and Spanish belong, respectively) have only distant connections with one another and developed differently across time. These developments were governed by chance and contingency and are not something sociologists would seek to theorize about.

28. An interesting exception to this occurs with celebrities, a social category that cries out for deeper sociological understanding. Strangers tend to assume a familiarity with celebrities, to the point of sometimes feeling free to touch them (thus, violating a taboo against familiarity with nonintimates) that is neither warranted by normal rules of interaction nor explained by our sociological understanding of status differences.

29. The phrase "down to earth" would be one of the rare instances where "down" is associated with good rather than bad.

Postscript

I N THE PREFACE TO THIS BOOK, I noted the pedagogical challenge in teaching theorizing as a skill. Because there is almost no tradition of doing this, I've had to borrow from existing work on theory construction and then strike out on my own, hoping to make progress. Whether I've succeeded is for you to judge, and I certainly hope that your reactions (to which I look forward) will improve subsequent editions of this book, so that they make more progress than this one.

At the very least, you should now better appreciate my claim that the broader world is hostile to theorizing. That world expresses distaste for the complexity involved. Outside academic contexts, the difficult intellectual work required for theorizing proves irksome to most and can seem eccentric in a cultural time and place where simplistic thinking and rapid gratification are the norm.

To satisfy our wonder as only theories can, however, we must set ourselves apart from this broader world and assume the burden of actually *thinking*. Thinking takes different forms in different disciplines, but in the sciences it normally begins with the exploration of patterned variation, which you will now recognize means that it begins in a curiosity about empirical generalizations. These generalizations indicate that variation in one property or activity is linked to variation in another. When we begin to see patterns of this sort, we can enter into the detective work of tracking down their general causes and evaluating the candidates we come up with.

This is the elementary form that theorizing takes in sociology, and so I've focused my treatment on it, which is to say on causal models. Becoming acquainted with causal models seems to me the soundest path of entry into theorizing, as well as the strongest base from which to move outward into other forms. As to these other forms, I've spent some time discussing typologies as a way of illustrating the analytic mode of theorizing. But analysis can involve more than typologies and often explores the internal workings of social processes, treating them more or less as mechanisms. Process-analytic theorizing sets forth the common and necessary relations among parts or phases in a process, giving us another vantage on "how things work." But fully exploring this and other modes of theorizing would make for a much longer and more involved book.

Because my treatment of theory has been elementary, it's best to think of this book as a primer. I don't mean by this that the theories I've discussed are simple (far from it!), but that the series of steps to which I've reduced theorizing, so as to demystify it and allow you to approach it as a graspable skill, are comparatively simple and straightforward. To see what lies beyond the routine I've outlined, the best place to go is perhaps Jonathan Turner's *The Structure of Sociological Theory* (2003), which offers a broader view of theorizing as well as a relatively comprehensive treatment of contemporary theoretical paradigms. Familiarity with these diverse paradigms will drive home my point that theorizing in sociology is nearly incoherent as a practice; but, with your feet firmly on the ground in causal models, and having a clear sense of how such models are formed, this diversity should prove less disorienting. At any rate, this core to sociological theorizing is always available as a safe haven to which to return.

Students who proceed further into the thickets of theory will eventually encounter antitheoretical sociological paradigms such as postmodernism, critical theory, and critical feminism. For these paradigms, the habits of mind involved in theorizing are seen as themselves bound up with oppressive power structures, serving more or less as their handmaidens. Unlike the broader world for which theorizing is too difficult and irksome, these paradigms view it as naive and/or dangerous. They propose more sophisticated and politically purer forms of understanding with which to replace it. That these paradigms also claim the title of *sociological theory,* of course, only contributes to the difficulty novices face in determining what sociologists consider theorizing to be.

The modes of theorizing that people find congenial, then, clearly vary. Further, there is no solution to the incoherence of theorizing within sociology. (Interestingly, we can actually explain why incoherence prevails by means of a sociological theory that I won't go into here [see Fuchs and Turner 1986, Fuchs 1992]). In part because sociologists have so many modes of theorizing to choose among, their preferences tell something about their character as thinkers. My own character will be conveyed indirectly by the choices I've made in writing this book. For me, the central attraction of conceiving of sociological theory on the standard model of the sciences has been well captured in a lecture Max Weber gave in 1918 that was later published under the title "Science as a Vocation" (1958b:129–56). In speaking of science as a *vocation*, as you will now be aware, Weber implied that people were "called" to it as their central mission in life. As a vocation, its allure lay, Weber believed, in its ability to pay back our commitment with a unique sense of accomplishment. By doing science, after all, we participate in an enterprise that is more demonstrably *progressive* than any other available to us:

> Science has a fate that profoundly distinguishes it from artistic work. Scientific work is chained to the course of progress; whereas in the realm of art there is no progress in the same sense. . . . A work of art which is genuine "fulfillment" is never surpassed; it will never be antiquated. . . . [But] In science, each of us knows that what he has accomplished will be antiquated in ten, twenty, fifty years. That is the fate to which science is subjected; it is the very *meaning* of scientific work . . . It asks to be "surpassed" and outdated. (1958b:137–38)

Science, he indicated, never arrives at "the truth," but only at provisional ways of explaining things—ways that we hope will eventually be surpassed. What is so satisfying about this? It is the recognition that subsequent investigators cannot advance beyond us without using our own work as a stepping stone for theirs. Thus, though our contributions are ephemeral (i.e., temporary) in one sense, they drive knowledge forward *permanently*—at least as long as the enterprise of science itself survives. Devotees of science link themselves to predecessor and successor generations of scientists who share the same devotion, and whose reward is the further refinement and deepening of knowledge.

Advances in science, Weber believed, call for passionate commitment. The long training we need to reach the forefront of a field and the attendant narrowing of our vision as we concentrate upon a particular topic exert strains. Doing science can be boring at times and the specialization required is increasingly constricting. A greater strain, however, arises from the threat that a casual attitude entails:

> Whoever lacks the capacity to put on blinders, so to speak, and to come up to the idea that the fate of his soul depends upon whether or not he makes the correct conjecture at this passage of this manuscript may as well stay away from science. . . . Without this strange intoxication, ridiculed by every outsider; without this passion . . . you have *no* calling for science and should do something else. (1958b:135, emphasis in original)

Finely trained athletes and musicians experience a similar demand for rigor, and live in a world similarly foreign to the often relaxed attitudes of everyday existence.

Most students, of course, are not "called" to science. A conviction that the fate of their soul depends upon a correct conjecture is not their preferred route to intoxication. Still, it's only with a certain degree of rigor that we can satisfyingly scratch the itch that our wondering produces. Here, I've tried to suggest a set of routine steps by which to scratch, but *taking* the steps is not itself routine, since each of them demands both creativity and care.

They require this because the world doesn't lend itself to easy explanation. In taking the time to evaluate some of the classical theories, we've seen that ingenious theories proposed by very bright people can often be shown to have holes you could drive a truck through. Recognizing this can be disconcerting. But it's also an indication that, with our own creativity and care, we can clearly do better. And that's what attracts us to science.

In the interlude between the first and second chapters, I indicated that though the concerns of the classical theorists can initially seem foreign, they are easily linked to concerns of our own. Will the Internet and other means of nearly instantaneous communication allow a truly global society to develop? If so, will the national and local cultures in which we live today be fundamentally transformed in the process? If there is to be a global world, can it sustain the level of inequality that exists today? If not, does this mean bringing the rest of the world to the level of consumption enjoyed in advanced industrial societies? If so, how will we deal with the insult to the environment that may be involved? If not, how can wealthy nations scale back *their* consumption?

It is not clear that we can develop social scientific knowledge rapidly enough to answer these questions—and answers are necessary if we are not to be overwhelmed by the events themselves. Unfortunately, it is not even clear that we can sustain the social flexibility necessary preserve an atmosphere in which revolutionary insights into these problems won't be judged blasphemous. But *if* we can sustain this flexibility, I think we can safely predict that, before the turn of the next century, we will understand why—to take just one example—a relatively dense network of social bonds lowers our risk of dying, and we will have plumbed quite thoroughly the mechanisms by which this occurs. In all likelihood, I won't be around to relish this achievement, but successor generations of sociologists will. They will see it as discernable progress, and part of their enjoyment will come from looking back down a long path that connects their knowledge with Durkheim and the classics. To have become sociologists, of course, they'll have to have learned more than just Durkheim's theories. They'll have to have incorporated his habits of mind, his capacity to theorize. The payoff in doing so is profound. As I indicated in the preface, it's what has made our world so different from those of the past.

This is why I suggested that the acquisition of no other skill more fittingly embodies the values of a liberal education. If we are to intelligently confront (and perhaps gain control over) a world that is rapidly changing, theorizing is the *only* means at our disposal. Thus, nothing could be more valuable to learn, nor satisfying to teach.

Glossary

ABOS configuration. A way to represent an event according to the affect control paradigm. The configuration consists of EPA profiles for the actor (A), the behavior of that actor (B), the object acted upon (O), and the setting (S). When any of the four values for the given event differ from the fundamental affective meanings we generally assign the A, B, O, or S, we experience deflection.

activity. The A component in an EPA profile. It registers the activity/passivity dimension of a concept as measured by the semantic differential test. It is one of the three dimensions, along with evaluation and potency, by which results of the semantic differential test can be summarized. We can establish an EPA profile for any concept, such as "mother" or "jumping," by using the semantic differential test. When many test takers rate a concept similarly, this defines its emotional meaning within a culture or subculture. This is a way of representing what Mead called the "generalized other."

adventurer capitalism. The frequent practice among merchants or military adventurers prior to modern capitalism of accepting very high risks in anticipation of equally high gains. Pirating exemplifies this practice.

affect control theory. A subparadigm within symbolic interactionism that views interaction as guided by an effort to maintain the sentiments (the fundamental affective meanings) we attach to concepts of ourselves and others as we act in different situations. When these sentiments are challenged by a particular event (an ABOS configuration), we experience deflections, which in turn cause us to reevaluate our fundamental affective meanings in predictable ways. The affect control subparadigm allows for theories to be constructed within symbolic interaction, which is often a purely descriptive paradigm.

affective action. Weber's category of meaningful behavior of an emotional sort. Becoming angry at an affront would be an example of affective action.

altruistic suicide. The style of suicide that occurs when people are so closely tied to others (are so highly integrated) that they can more easily sacrifice their lives for those others.

agency. The ability of social actors to control or modify social circumstances or social structures. When people are free to choose among various options in this regard, the results of their agency are contingent phenomena that cannot be understood theoretically. Thus, explanations of such phenomena resort to causal narratives.

agrarian society. A society where farming is the primary activity. Here, the mode of production is dominated by agriculture and handicrafts, and the political system is usually controlled by a class of aristocratic warriors who claim ownership of the land and employ slaves or charge common people rent to work on it.

alienation. A complex variable that captures both how varied the capacities called for in most jobs are and how much of our potential as a species is expressed through our collective efforts at production. The first component (Marx's alienation from the process of labor) might be measured in part by job satisfaction, while the second (Marx's alienation from the species-being) can be crudely estimated by a measure like productivity per capita.

analysis. A mode of explanation that divides a concept (or conceptualization of a process) into its component parts and indicates the relations among them. Analysis is used to explain what entities or processes comprise.

analytic typology. A classification that establishes, on the basis of empirical differences, the small number of presumably permanent categories into which instances of a general phenomenon fall. The categories of good typologies are exhaustive (i.e., closed) and mutually exclusive, as well as sociologically useful.

animism. In Durkheim's *Elementary Forms*, a religion that arises from an assumption by primitive people that a soul (Latin *anima*) must be postulated to account for the experiences they have in their dreams, where their consciousness seems independent of their body and able to travel at will. Once this nonmaterial entity is accepted, it can slowly develop into the notion of a divinity. (Animism also refers to religions organized around dealing with the spirits inhabiting objects.)

anomaly. An empirical finding that conflicts with the logical or substantive implications of a theory. We can adjust our theory to explain away an anomaly (as Durkheim did with the anomaly that women's suicide rates did not decline with marriage), but when too many occur, we normally have to abandon our theory.

anomic suicide. The style of suicide that occurs when people are poorly regulated and left with too many choices to make. With a general weakening of social norms (anomie means normlessness), a sense of limits weakens as does the norm against suicide itself.

aristocracy. The social class that owns the land in many agrarian societies and passes it on to descendants by inheritance. Aristocrats normally acquire land through military conquest or through gifts from other aristocrats for providing military support.

asceticism. A regimen of norms requiring avoidance of worldly pleasure, conspicuous consumption, and, as Weber said, sensuous enjoyments of all sorts.

authority. Noncoercive power in which one's control over others is viewed by them as legitimate.

backstage. For Goffman, the sector of social space in which we can behave in relaxed ways and conduct intimate relations. We also use the backstage area to groom and otherwise prepare ourselves for frontstage appearances in which we try to make a good impression upon audiences.

behaviorism. A paradigm in psychology that views behavior as conditioned by our environment, which reinforces some of our actions and discourages others by meting out pleasure or pain. Actions that bring pleasure we are apt to repeat, and those that bring pain we are apt to abandon.

boundary work. The social and political efforts people make to establish some groups as prestigious and others as not, and then to erect social walls between them. For instance, evolutionary biologists perform boundary work to keep themselves separate from, and superior to, "creation scientists," who argue against evolution in favor of divine intervention in the origins of species. Evolutionists would experience mixing with "creation scientists" as polluting.

bourgeoisie. The social class that owns the means of production and exchange in a capitalist economy. (The adjectival form is *bourgeois*, as in "bourgeois culture." The term originally meant simply "city dweller.")

bureaucracy/bureaucratic administration of production. The organizational form characterized by hierarchical authority (a table of organization), salaried office-holders, standard operating procedures, written communications, and a generally low degree of discretion among production workers (as opposed to the greater discretion of managers). Bureaucracies tend to develop where production can be routinized and demand for a product is high in volume and consistent across time.

calibration. The act of fixing gradations, in standard units, for a variable and positioning the result in relation to phenomena of interest. We calibrate the centigrade scale of temperature so that the phenomenon of water freezing becomes its zero point, and a hundred standard units separate this point from that at which water boils. Durkheim failed to calibrate the variables of social integration and regulation, leaving us unsure about the implications of some of his propositions about suicide rates.

calling. An indication from God that we are to lead an exacting, rather than a more relaxed, spiritual life. Among Catholics, a calling or vocation indicates that one is to become a priest, monk, or nun, in other words, a member of the clergy. For Luther, all people were called to a spiritually strenuous life, which meant that the idea of a separate clergy could be done away with.

causal account (or causal model). An abstract representation of causal links among variables in a process. Models are improved by specifying the mechanisms involved and detailing how the variables are linked in the manner outlined.

causal narrative. An explanation of why something occurs, using a sequence of events, each of which causes its successor. Because causal narratives often involve "chance" events' linking different causal orders, the explanations they provide are not generalizable and should not be styled theories.

causal order. A group of causes that belong to the same domain (e.g., physical, chemical, biological, psychological). Causal narratives often link together different causal orders, and we interpret such links as "chance" events.

charismatic authority. The authority of (what appear to be) mysterious powers. We obey someone because he or she has given prior evidence of being able to "walk on water" (or do other extraordinary things) by means we do not understand. Both Christ and Hitler exercised charismatic authority.

class consciousness. Marx's term for the awareness a class has of itself as a political agent pursuing its interests in opposition to other classes.

class struggle. Conflict between groups that occupy different positions, with competing interests, within a mode of production. Class struggles inaugurate new modes or relations of production. Within a given mode of production, class struggle decreases with the concentration of power and increases as it wanes. Marx saw class struggle as the primary engine of historical change as victors would introduce new technologies or forms of political organization.

classical sociology. Works that we look back upon today as forming the foundation of the new discipline of sociology, generally from the period before 1920.

classless society. A circumstance in which everyone's relation to the means of production is the same. Classlessness characterizes hunting-and-gathering societies, and Marx believed it could be achieved once again through communism, where ownership of the means of production would be socialized (made collective).

closed typology. A typology whose categories fully and permanently exhaust the concept analyzed. Such typologies normally have relatively few categories. The term is synonymous with analytic typology.

clue variable. A variable that is linked to our dependent variable through a matching empirical generalization and that points us in the direction of likely independent variables that will match both clue and dependent variables.

coercion. The exercise of power by inducing pain or threatening to do so.

collective consciousness. The beliefs and values to which most members of a group subscribe and which define them as a group. For Durkheim, collective consciousness (or conscience) could vary in strength. Collective consciousness is the basis of mechanical solidarity and arises out of common life experiences.

collective effervescence. The emotional arousal, often to the point of ecstatic transport, that can occur when people, in one another's presence, focus their attention on unusual objectives. Such objectives might range from lynchings, to protests, to carnival celebrations like Mardi Gras.

communism. For Marx, an economic system in which the means of production are collectively owned by all members of a society and in which work is allocated in ways that allow individuals to explore and achieve their creative potentials.

concentration of power. The relative inequality in people's control over others. If each of us controls only him or herself, power is equally distributed, and concentration is at its lowest; if one of us gets to direct many others, however, power is considerably more concentrated. When power is concentrated, those lacking it may be forced to work in alienating conditions.

concept. An abstract term that groups together specific concrete phenomena in the world around us on the basis of their similarity. Concepts can often be ranked by degrees of abstraction: *woman*, for example, is less abstract than *female*.

conflict paradigm. A set of principles that view conflictual relations among a wide range of groups, differentiated in terms of their access to resources, as the key to social structure and changes in it. Social change occurs as the distribution of resources shifts, with resource-rich groups using their advantages to exploit groups that have fewer resources.

conspicuous consumption. A pattern of spending on luxuries so as to impress others with one's wealth that characterized the nobility, as well as adventurer capitalists, and that was discouraged by Calvin's call to asceticism. The term we owe to Thorstein Veblen.

contingent. Incidental, uncaused, or caused by chance (that is, by factors of no interest to us as sociologists). Contingent phenomena might just as easily not have occurred or have occurred differently. Social conventions, like driving on the right, are often contingent phenomena. They cannot be explained theoretically.

craft administration of production. An organizational form characterized by a low degree of hierarchy and high degrees of discretion exercised by production workers. Craft organization tends to develop where production cannot be routinized and when demand is low and irregular.

crisis of overproduction. A glut of goods in a market economy, caused by increasing mechanization that lowers production costs. Crises cause massive unemployment. Marx believed that when such unemployment became deep enough, workers would rise up in revolution to take control of the economy themselves.

cultural materialism. A subparadigm of functionalism that views cultural innovations as spreading throughout populations, primarily as a result of the material benefits they bring to people. Cultural materialism divides societies into infrastructure, structure, and superstructure and sees structural and superstructural changes as likely to take root when they benefit people through the infrastructure. Harris argued this was true of cow worship in India.

cultural relativism. The general position that cultures are coherent entities whose shared patterns of behavior are intelligible and meaningful to members and which argues that cultures cannot be ranked in terms of their comparative overall excellence.

dependent variable. The variable whose behavior we want to explain.

deflection. For affect control theory, the emotional recognition that something is wrong. It arises when the ABOS values for a particular event are out of synch with the fundamental affective meanings we have assigned the actors, behavior, objects, and situation that are involved in the event. When deflections are significant and cannot be explained away, they cause us to change our fundamental affective meanings.

descriptive hypothesis. A proposition about a state of affairs (e.g., there are more people in casinos than in church on Sundays) that is subject to empirical evaluation, that is, to evaluation through data meeting generally approved standards, such as those of courtrooms.

descriptive narrative. A chronicle of the incidents that lead up to, but cannot be seen as causing, some phenomenon of interest to us.

deterministic theory. A theory that produces precise predictions about the future state of a system, ideally based upon a thorough understanding of the mechanisms that produce this future state.

dialectic. An analytic framework (like a paradigm) that views social systems as dynamic entities that undergo change through regular stages of internal conflict defined in terms of thesis, antithesis, and synthesis.

disenchantment. Weber's descriptive term for the process of historical change by which our world becomes more rationalized and less infused with, or governed by, magical or spiritual forces. How far disenchantment has occurred is subject to dispute.

division of labor. The process by which the separate tasks involved in producing an item are allocated to specific individuals, who then specialize in them, as opposed to being performed by a single worker who is broadly competent. According to Adam Smith, dividing labor should lead to increased productivity as each worker becomes more competent at his or her own task. Marx believed that division of labor led to increasing alienation for many workers.

dramaturgical analysis. The name for a subparadigm in symbolic interaction, created by Goffman, that uses the metaphor of theater and theatrical performance to guide the analysis of interaction.

dyadic power. The ability to have one's way in a two-person relationship. Dyadic power is significantly a function of one's willingness to leave a relationship, which is usually conditional upon the ability to form alternative dyads.

dynamic system. A system of social organization that changes as a result of factors that are built into it.

ecology. See social ecology.

egoistic suicide. The style of suicide that occurs when people are so weakly tied to others (so weakly integrated) that their death seems largely their own concern, without a broader impact.

empirical. Observable; able to be demonstrated by experience across individuals, according to the standards of courtrooms or the accepted methods of science.

empirical generalization. A descriptive hypothesis stating a relation between two or more variables that is generalized from numerous individual cases in which this relation can be shown present empirically: for instance, argument-related homicide rates (variable 1) are higher in the rural South (variable 2) than elsewhere.

empirical typology. A typology whose categories exist, independently of our inquiry, in the world itself. Empirical typologies may be open or closed.

EPA profile. A summary score for a concept created through the semantic differential test. It includes values for evaluation (E: good/bad), potency (P: strong/weak), and activity (A: active/passive). The EPA profile results from averaging the rankings that many people in a culture or subculture give to the concept. When their scores are largely similar, EPA profiles give us a way of quantitatively describing what Mead called "the generalized other." Individuals' EPA profiles for a concept describe its fundamental affective meaning for them.

evaluation. The E component of an EPA profile. It registers the good/bad dimension of a concept as measured by the semantic differential test and is one of the three dimensions, along with activity and potency, by which results of the semantic differential test can be summarized. We can establish an EPA profile for any concept, such as "mother" or "jumping," by using the semantic differential test. When many test takers rate a concept similarly, this defines its emotional meaning within a culture or subculture. This is a way of representing what Mead called the "generalized other."

exhaustive. A typology is exhaustive when it specifies *all* of the types (categories) constituting a more general concept and *no others*. All concrete instances of the general phenomenon should fit into one or another of these categories.

explication. A mode of explanation that provides a meaning for a gesture or occurrence when this was previously obscure. Explications normally involve assertions about the intentions or motives of agents.

exploitation. The variable capturing the degree to which superordinates (e.g., employers) derive benefits from depriving subordinates (e.g., workers) of compensation for their accomplishments. Exploitation assumes that the subordinates aren't freely giving up this compensation but, instead, have no ready alternative. Exploitation is reduced to the degree that superordinates contribute to the accomplishments of subordinates.

fatalistic suicide. The style of suicide that occurs when people are excessively regulated and left with very few choices to make. Durkheim used the example of the suicides of slaves.

frontstage. For Goffman, the sector of social space where we try to control strategically the impressions we give others so as elicit optimal responses from them. We prepare for frontstage performances by using the backstage area to groom ourselves and rehearse lines of action that we hope will elicit favorable responses.

functionalism. A paradigm that explains the persistence or spread of an activity (or institution) in terms of its benefits for the social unit or units that adopt it.

fundamental affective meaning. In affect control theory, the emotional tonality a concept has for us, as measured in terms of its EPA profile. When the EPA scores for the actor, behavior, object, and situation involved in a particular event don't correspond with our fundamental affective meanings, we experience deflections.

game stage. The second of three stages through which Mead viewed children as passing on their way to social competence. In the game stage, children acquire the capacity to adjust their behavior to *multiple* roles being played by others, as might occur in an organized sports game. This prepares children to develop a conception of the generalized other, which summarizes the general attitudes of others about appropriate behavior.

generalized other. The set of organized values and norms that characterize a particular group. When individuals develop a sense of the generalized other and can use it to plan and adjust their behavior strategically, they are fully socially competent. For Mead, achieving a concept of the generalized other signaled the third and final stage in the development of social competence.

great man approach to change. The position that significant social change occurs through the actions of particularly significant individuals, perhaps as charismatic leaders. Mead subscribed to this position. It is a nontheoretical one, inimical to sociological theories of social change.

guild. In agrarian societies, a local union of craftsmen working in the same trade (e.g., metal smiths or barrel makers) that sets prices for their product and controls the recruitment and education of apprentices.

hereditarian. An adjective describing the belief that important variations in behavior across individuals can be explained by inherited biological differences. Late-nineteenth- and early-twentieth-century popular social science was primarily hereditarian and often racist. Mead's social behaviorism was antihereditarian.

heuristic typology. A typology that makes distinctions to aid our thinking but that we don't claim exist, independently of our thinking, in the world itself.

historical materialism. A paradigm that points us to changes in technology as the prime cause of social change and that sees class conflict as its mediating instrument. Marx's historical materialism viewed changes in material productive forces as the general source of change in the relations of production, the legal and political superstructure, and social consciousness.

hunting-and-gathering society. Societies where people hunt for game and forage for other food sources. Specialization in the production of goods and services is very low, as is the degree of social stratification. Social classes are normally absent. This mode of production has predominated across human history.

I. The phase of the self, according to Mead, that is unselfconscious because it is deeply engrossed in action. The *I* is the unpredictable and innovative aspect of the self, in contrast to the *me*, which evaluates the performance of the *I* in light of the responses of others to it.

ideal sphere. Goffman's term for the physical space surrounding an individual into which others are not supposed to intrude without permission. The size of the ideal sphere varies with the status of the individual.

ideal type. A model in which the most characteristic features of a particular social institution or process are described and related to one another and their characteristic operations are analyzed. An ideal type is drawn from, but need not in its specific form actually exist in, empirical reality. A "perfect vacuum" serves as an ideal type in physics, as does a free, open, and competitive market in economics.

idealism. The position that the origins of social change lie in changes in people's ideas. Idealism is the opposite of materialism and was forwarded by Weber in contrast to Marx.

identity spoilage. The damage to the image others hold of us that occurs when we fail to meet their expectations.

ideologists. People who create and spread the ideas or arguments that give legitimacy (or take it away) from given social institutions. For Marx, ideologists help create our social consciousness.

implication. A proposition that can be derived from a theory, assuming it is true. Empirical tests of implications allow us to evaluate a theory.

independent variable. The variable that we use to explain variation in our dependent variable. It is assumed to be a cause.

indicator. A measure, sometimes partial, of a more global concept. Durkheim used marital status as an indicator of relative social integration, although it measured only one aspect of this global concept.

individual action. Weber's term for behavior that is meaningful to us but that does not engage, and is not meant for, others. Whistling to oneself might be an example.

infrastructure. The cultural materialist term for the analytical sector Marx called the mode of production, with an added concern for the relation of the mode of production to the physical environment. Changes in infrastructure condition changes in the structure and superstructure.

instrumentally rational action. Weber's category of meaningful behavior in which we select the most efficient means to a given end. In German, this is called *zweckrational* action.

integration. See social integration.

interpretive sociology. A paradigm devoted to the explication of social situations in terms of people's understandings of them. Interpretive sociology sometimes draws on methods used in humanistic disciplines, viewing social behavior as similar to a text that calls for interpretation.

interval variable. A measure of variation using specific units (intervals). With interval measurement, the difference between any two cases can be indicated precisely. Salaries, with differences measured in dollar units, would be an example. Interval variables make differences much more precise than ordinal variables.

introspection. A method of inquiry by which we evaluate propositions about our internal lives by "testing" them through careful attention to the workings of our own consciousnesses, emotions, and so forth. Introspection may be used to evaluate Mead's propositions about phases of the self, but the results are normally not considered empirical. Thus, when my introspection disagrees with yours, we have no way to settle our differences.

latent function. A role or purpose of a practice or institution of which members of the society are unaware but which can be demonstrated through an effective functional analysis.

legal and political superstructure. For Marx, the analytical sector of society that includes the organizations (and relations among them) that regulate and enforce the relations of production.

life chances. For Weber, the prospects and possibilities opened to us through the social position or positions we occupy. Being male or wealthy has traditionally improved one's life chances (say, to graduate from college), as has membership in dominant religious or racial groups. Weber saw variation in life chances as a major effect of social class.

linear. A relationship between two variables in which a change in one is always related to a fixed amount of change in the other. When the relationship is graphed, it proves to be a straight line.

logical implication. Proposition deduced from a theory, usually by generating if-then arguments (or syllogisms). Example: if a culture of honor arises in herding economies, and if herding in the U.S. South is largely confined to Piedmont regions, then we would predict argument-related homicides to be higher there than in the non-Piedmont (lowland) regions.

macrosociology. The study of large-scale social units and the long-term social processes occurring within them. Occasionally, the term *mesosociology* is used to refer to the study of particular social organizations or groups, like a university or a soccer league, that are intermediate in size between micro- and macrosociological levels.

manifest function. An instrumentally rational role or purpose attributed to a practice or institution, of which individuals in a society are aware. One manifest function of military organizations, for instance, is to defend the populace.

material productive forces. For Marx, the analytical sector of society that includes the technology by which it earns its living, as well as the human capital (or knowledge) necessary to run and reproduce the technology.

me. The phase of the self, according to Mead, that reflects on and evaluates the performance of the *I* in light of the responses of others. The *me* is the phase through which social control is exercised and the means by which we can, by employing the generalized other, plan our future behavior strategically.

means of production. See material productive forces.

mechanical solidarity. For Durkheim, the cohesive force in society that results from a strong collective consciousness. Mechanical solidarity arises from similarity of life circumstances.

mechanism. Our abstract representation of the specific, detailed means by which a change in our independent variable causes a change in our dependent variable.

mechanization. Replacing human workers with machines to produce goods. This lowers unit costs and potentially allows innovators to increase their market share or profits. For Marx, mechanization eventually reduces surplus value and causes a decline in the rate of profit. Declining profits cause industrial concentration as more successful businesses buy up less successful ones in an effort to increase access to surplus value, which can only be done by employing more workers.

microsociology. The study of direct human interaction, usually in small, face-to-face circumstances. Occasionally, the term *mesosociology* is used to refer to the study of particular social organizations or groups, like a university or a soccer league, that are intermediate in size between micro- and macrosociological levels.

mind. Mead's term for the faculty that allows us to plan strategically our interactions with others and to respond to their behavior toward us. We do so by using gestures and significant symbols to communicate, as well as by imagining (through taking the role of the other) how our communications will be received by our audience.

mode of production. For Marx, the system of economic and social relations growing out of a dominant technology for producing goods. Hunting and gathering, agriculture and crafts, and industrialism are modes of production. Modes are conceived of as dynamic entities, increasing their productivity until contradictions that grow within them fetter them and encourage the development of new modes of production. Marx thought of modes of production as discrete entities, between which changes were revolutionary, but this is questionable.

monasticization. The process of infusing monastic standards of devotion and asceticism into an entire society. Luther's idea that all people were called to a strenuous religious life, when combined with Calvin's call for worldly asceticism, meant that all people were to labor for the glory of God as only monks and other clergy had under the Catholic regime.

moral career. Goffman's term for the trajectory of changes in our selves that occur when we enter a transforming environment, such as a total institution. These internal changes reflect changes in our social status and, consequently, in the behavior of others toward us.

mutually exclusive. The quality possessed by a typology when each instance of a general phenomenon can be placed in one, and only one, of its analytic categories. Mutually exclusive typologies have sharp edges separating their pigeon holes.

nation-state. A sovereign political unit generally governing people who are culturally similar.

nature versus nurture debate. Arguments between, for instance, hereditarians and behaviorists over the comparative importance of our biological makeups versus our environments in molding our behavior.

necessary condition. A variable that must be present for another variable to occur but which is not sufficient to produce the second variable on its own.

nominal variable. A nominal variable identifies the unranked types into which instances of some phenomenon fall. Religious affiliation and gender are both nominal variables, as would be citizenship.

norm. A shared cultural prescription encouraging or discouraging a particular form of behavior.

normal. Durkheim's characterization of those attributes of societies (or forms of organization) that, because they are widely distributed and have not been eliminated over time by competitive pressures, cannot be judged pathological.

normal science. Scientific research that conforms to standard methodologies and conventional theorizing in solving problems.

open typology. An empirical typology, such as of job classifications or animal species, to which we expect to add new categories when new instances of the general phenomenon arise. Consequently, the categories involved are often very numerous. Analytic typologies are closed rather than open.

ordinal variable. A variable involving a dimension of ranking (e.g., lower, middle, and upper class), permitting distinctions of more or less but not permitting precise measurement of differences between instances.

organic solidarity. For Durkheim, the cohesive force that arises out of social and economic interdependence that is brought about by the division of labor.

paradigm. A general model, or set of guidelines, for creating theories. Paradigms do not explain events or states of affairs themselves, as do theories, but instead give us guidance as to how promising theories can be formed. They are orientations to constructing theories and may compete with or complement one another.

pathological. Durkheim's characterization of social conditions that arise from maladjustment among societal components as elements of a functioning whole. Pathological conditions (such as extremely high rates of suicide) result in net pain to the society that could be eliminated by better adjustment among components.

play stage. The first stage in the development of the self, according to Mead, in which children become competent at playing as if they were others. Mead assumed that such play allows children to acquire an initial sense of self, which is to say, a sense of who they are in relation to others.

potency. The P component of an EPA profile. It registers the strong/weak dimension of a concept as measured by the semantic differential test and is one of the three dimensions, along with evaluation and activity, by which results of the semantic differential test can be summarized. We can establish an EPA profile for any concept, such as "mother" or "jumping," by using the semantic differential test. When many test takers rate a concept similarly, this defines its emotional meaning within a culture or subculture. This is a way of representing what Mead called the "generalized other."

power. The ability of one individual (or group) to get another to do what the first individual (or group) wants.

pragmatism. A philosophical school that seeks to understand how people cope successfully with their environments. Pragmatists believe that the "truth" of an idea is best judged by its success or failure in helping us deal with the world around us. Mead's social behaviorism was pragmatist in its orientation.

precondition. A variable whose presence does not directly cause, but is nevertheless necessary for (or significantly beneficial to), the existence of some other variable. Facilitators are weak forms of preconditions. Weber viewed a monetized economy, for instance, as a facilitator of, or precondition for, bureaucracy.

predestination. The doctrine that one's spiritual destiny is fixed in God's mind from time immemorial and is beyond one's personal ability to affect.

presupposition. See precondition.

productivity. A variable measuring the quantity of goods and services produced by a worker in a given time. This variable can be used as a rough indicator for Marx's concept of alienation from the species-being. When productivity is low (for instance when workers are only able to produce enough goods and services to maintain their immediate families), alienation from the species-being is high, and vice versa.

profane. The quality that allows an entity to be treated without the special respect due sacred entities. Durkheim saw the sacred/profane distinction as the defining property of religion.

professional authority. The authority of expertise. We obey a person because he or she possesses knowledge or practical experience superior to ours. For instance, we obey a tow truck operator who tells us to take the car out of gear before towing it to the shop.

proletariat. The class of people who sell their labor power in a capitalist society, working on machinery owned by the bourgeoisie. (The adjectival form is *proletarian*, as in "proletarian rebellion.")

proposition. A statement relating concepts to one another; used in an explanation.

Protestant ethic. Weber's term for the economically modern attitude toward work and commerce that was supposedly inaugurated by the Protestant reformers. This attitude favors calculable increases in productivity or profit through hard work and maximum openness to innovation when risk has been minimized.

racism. A belief that significant variation in behavior across individuals can be explained in terms of variation in their racial ancestry.

rationalization. For Weber, the historical process by which we develop calculable control over events and to which science and bureaucracy contribute most heavily.

reactive behavior. Weber's term for largely reflex behavior that happens beneath consciousness and is not meaningful.

relations of production. For Marx, the analytical sector of society composed of the organized social relationships by which the production of goods and services is coordinated. The factors most important to defining relations of production are relative control of one's labor power and the tools by which work is accomplished. Failure to control these leaves us under the direction of others. Slaves own neither their labor power nor the tools they use. Artisans usually own both. Workers own their labor power but not the tools they use, which are owned by capitalists. For Marx, relations of production determined one's social class and the relations among classes.

repressive punishment. Punishment of people for crimes through the infliction of pain. Durkheim hypothesized that resort to repressive punishment would correlate with the strength of the collective consciousness, but it appears he was wrong.

restitutive punishment. Punishment that attempts to return the circumstances of the victim to the status quo ante (the state they were in before the crime was committed), usually by means of financial compensation.

revolutionary science. Science that departs either from standard methods or from conventional ways of theorizing about problems and does so in ways that cause permanent change in our approach to solving scientific problems.

robustness. The quality a theory shows when its propositions are supported empirically in many different settings. Robustness is similar to replicability, or the capacity of an experiment to yield the same results over repeated trials.

sacred. The quality that requires an entity to be dealt with circumspectly, observing special procedures setting it apart from the everyday world.

scrupulosity. The psychological mechanism whereby minor faults come to be perceived as major failures and that occurs when we are able to eliminate our major faults. Societies that raise collective awareness about crimes to the point that they are eliminated often come to see their less serious issues as more serious, lowering the threshold for criminalizing them.

selection. The process by which advantageous or disadvantageous traits either spread through a population or are eliminated from it.

selection by consequences. In cultural materialism, the social preference for innovations that have positive consequences for the health and well-being of members of the social unit that adopts them.

selection pressure. A way of characterizing how rapidly the overall environment in which units exist selects for or against novel traits. Selection pressure is a function of such qualities as scarcity of resources, competition among units for access to resources, rates of predation, ease of entry into or exit from the environment, and so forth. Selection pressure must exist for functional explanations to work.

self. Mead's term for the agent that acts in and adjusts to the social environment by using symbols and reflecting on the responses of others.

semantic differential test. A test developed by Osgood in which people rate concepts in terms of multiple abstract dimensions (such as hot versus cold or hard versus soft) as a means of quantifying their meaning.

sign of salvation (or election). An indicator that one is among the elect who will eventually join God in heaven. Weber believed Calvinists sought signs of election to reduce religious anxiety arising from the potential of being swindled through predestination. They came to see intense commitment to their worldly enterprises as a sign of election on the assumption that God would build a kingdom on earth through intensely dedicated individuals like them.

social action. Weber's term for behavior that is meaningfully oriented to the actions of others. Social action, he believed, is different from both individual action (meaningful, but oriented to self) and reactive behavior (like reflex activity).

social behaviorism. Mead's term for his paradigm, which later came to be called *symbolic interactionism*.

social boundaries. See boundary work.

social class. A grouping of people who occupy a common general position within a mode of production, usually in terms of ownership. Slave owners, as a social class, own both the labor power of slaves and the tools by which the slaves do their work. Capitalists own the tools but purchase the labor power to work with them.

social consciousness. For Marx, the analytical sector of society that includes the ideas or arguments that support or legitimate particular sets of social institutions.

social ecology. An approach to understanding the social and material conditions underlying important dimensions of societal and cultural variation, usually in terms of sets of preconditions.

social facts. Durkheim's term for the features of social structure that influence our behavior, normally without people's being aware of this influence. For Durkheim, the purpose of the new discipline of sociology was to discover social facts, measure their influence, and create theories to explain them.

social integration. The variable measuring the density (average number) and depth (reciprocity) of ties between individuals in a group. For Durkheim, low integration meant excessive egoism, while high integration meant excessive altruism, both of which increased suicide rates.

social regulation. The variable measuring the control of the group over individuals, potentially measured by the relative availability of choices. For Durkheim, low regulation meant excessive anomie, while high regulation meant excessive fatalism, both of which increased suicide rates.

social reproduction. The process by which parental social-class position is passed on to children. While this used to be a function of inheritance of land or money, in the view of Bourdieu, it is increasingly accomplished by an educational system that rewards students who possess more "cultural capital" or approved knowledge and tastes. They initially acquire this cultural capital from interaction with their parents.

social structure. Recurrent patterns of interaction between and within categories of individuals. Characterizing these patterns defines particular social structures. For instance, structural relations between professors and their students are embodied in their recurrent patterns of interaction.

sociobiology. A field in science that investigates the biological foundations of social behavior across species from insects to humans.

sociological imagination. Mills's term for the style of thinking or habit of mind that allows us to connect individual problems (such as spousal abuse) to variation in group processes or structures (such as dyadic or structural power). In making this connection, we are alerted to possible ways of eliminating the problems.

sovereignty. Independent jurisdiction over (that is, ability to make rules for) a group of people. Swanson uses the number of hierarchically organized sovereign groups in a society to predict the presence or absence of high gods in a religion.

species-being. Marx's term for the creative potentials humans possess as a species.

spirit of capitalism. The economically modern orientation to work and to enterprise that seeks a regular increase in wealth through acceptance of innovation and rigorous planning and cost accounting.

spurious relationship. A "false" link between an independent variable and our dependent variable that occurs because both are linked to a third variable that explains their apparent relationship and indicates that it *can't be* causal. Annual summer rises in gasoline prices don't *cause* corn to grow. Both are effects of higher summer temperatures, although for very different reasons (or causal mechanisms).

status boundaries. The socially recognized borders between status groups. When these borders separate groups differing significantly in rank, they will be energetically "policed" and border crossers will be shunned. The effort to create boundaries has been called "boundary work."

status groups. Categories of people who consume similar goods and identify themselves thereby. Status groups are normally ranked in terms of prestige or worthiness according to general perceptions of the merit or value of the goods they consume.

structural power. The ability to set the rules of the gender game through control of the political and economic institutions of a society.

structuralism. A paradigm that accounts for variation in some aspect of social life (e.g., belief in high gods) by linking it to variation in social structure (e.g., number of sovereign groups).

structure. The cultural materialist term for the analytical sector that combines relations of production and the legal and political superstructure.

subparadigm. A specific paradigm belonging to a more general one. The affect control and dramaturgical subparadigms both belong to symbolic interactionism.

substantive implication. A prediction made by a theory when its propositions are connected to knowledge drawn from another field.

sufficient condition. A variable whose presence guarantees the presence of a second variable, normally because it acts as a cause.

superstructure. The cultural materialist term for the analytical sector that Marx called social consciousness.

surplus value. For Marx, the difference between what workers are paid and the market value of the goods and services they produce. The ratio of surplus value to market value measures exploitation.

syllogism. A pattern of three propositions in which a specific consequence is derived logically from two more general, preceding propositions (e.g., if Socrates is a human, and if humans are mortal, then Socrates is mortal).

symbolic interactionism. A microsociological paradigm that focuses on the coordination of people's activities through communication about, and adjustment in relation to, one another's intentions.

sympathetic understanding. See *verstehen*.

tautology. A flaw in an argument that arises when our conclusion is assumed in our premises so that we assume what we claim to show. In sociology this happens when we allow measures of our dependent variable (conclusion) to serve as indicators of our independent variable (premise). We gain no insight from the fact that these vary together since they could not do otherwise.

teleological. A form of explanation in which some desirable goal (Gr. *telos*) is claimed to cause progress toward itself, as when we say that birds grew wings in order to fly.

theory. An integrated set of concepts, formed into propositions, that explain particular conditions or events in the world around us.

thought experiment. An experiment that we run through in our minds rather than in the laboratory or the field. We speculate about "what ifs" to test the possible consequences of our ideas when we are unable to manipulate the variables involved experimentally.

total institution. Goffman's term for organizations, like monasteries, military boot camps, or prisons, that attempt to transform individuals through modification of their selves.

totalitarian. An adjective describing political regimes that attempt to control the whole (totality) of citizens' lives, rather than confining themselves to restricted areas like the provision of military defense, regulation of currency, and maintenance of infrastructure. Totalitarian regimes seek a heightening of collective consciousness in an effort to instill and enforce a broad range of "politically correct" behaviors.

totemism. A form of religion in which clan-level societies identify individual clans by symbolic items (totems) that are perceived as sacred and become the focus of ritual observances. The symbolic items are generally drawn from the natural environment.

traditional action. Weber's category of meaningful behavior that is conventional and customary.

traditional authority. The authority of custom or precedent. We obey someone because he or she occupies a role customarily designated to have authority or because that person has always had authority. For instance, we often obey our parents out of custom.

traditionalism. An attitude among workers, encouraging resistance to innovation, the disciplining of rate busters, and insensitivity to productivity incentives; among merchants, an attitude favoring routinization of business relations or, at the opposite extreme, adventurer capitalism.

value rational action. Action that is valued for its own sake, either because it is intrinsically pleasurable (like games) or morally preferable (like being kind). In German, this is called *wertrational* activity.

variable. A category of empirical condition that shows differences within it. The differences may be qualitative (nominal variation, for example, between female and male or between forms of authority) or quantitative (ordinal variation between more or less of something, or interval variation, where precise degrees of difference can be measured according to a scale).

verstehen. The form of understanding that results from occupying another's shoes to fathom his or her motives. Weber believed *verstehen* was critical to understanding human behavior.

vocation. See calling.

wertrational **activity.** See value rational action.

zweckrational **activity.** See instrumentally rational action.

Bibliography

Abbott, Andrew. 1988. *The system of professions: An essay on the division of expert labor.* Chicago: University of Chicago Press.

Abraham, M. Francis. 1982. *Modern sociological theory: An introduction.* Delhi: Oxford University Press.

Abrahamson, Mark. 1978. *Functionalism.* Englewood Cliffs, NJ: Prentice Hall.

———. 1979. A functional theory of organizational stratification. *Social Forces* 58:128–45.

Babbie, Earl. 1999. *The basics of social research.* Belmont, CA: Wadsworth Publishing.

Bailey, Kenneth D. 2000. Typologies. In *Encyclopedia of Sociology,* ed. Edgar F. Borgatta and Rhonda J. V. Montgomery, 3180–89. 2nd ed. New York: McMillan Reference USA.

Baltzell, E. Digby. 1964. *The protestant establishment: Aristocracy and caste in America.* New York: Vintage Books.

Becker, Howard. 1973. *Outsiders: Studies in the sociology of deviance.* New York: Free Press.

Berger, Joseph, and Morris Zelditch, eds. 2002. *New directions in contemporary sociological theory.* Lanham, MD: Rowman & Littlefield.

Berger, Peter. 1967. *The sacred canopy: Elements of a sociological theory of religion.* Garden City, NY: Doubleday & Company, Inc.

Bergesen, Albert. 2004. Chomsky versus Mead. *Sociological Theory* 22:357–70.

Besnard, Philippe. 2000. Marriage and suicide: Testing the Durkheimian theory of marital regulation a century later. In *Durkheim's* Suicide: *A century of research and debate,* ed. W. S. F. Pickering and G. Walford. London: Routledge.

Best, Joel. 1990. *Threatened children: Rhetoric and concern about child-victims.* Chicago: University of Chicago Press.

Best, Joel, and David Luckenbill. 1994. *Organizing deviance.* 2nd ed. Englewood Cliffs: Prentice Hall.

Black, Donald. 1976. *The behavior of law.* New York: Academic Press.

———. 1993. *The social structure of right and wrong.* San Diego: Academic Press.

———. 2000. Dreams of pure sociology. *Sociological Theory* 18:343–67.

Blau, Peter, and Marshall Meyer. 1987. *Bureaucracy in Modern Society*. 3rd ed. New York: Random House.

Blumberg, Rae. 1978. *Stratification: Socioeconomic and social inequality*. Dubuque, IA: W. C. Brown.

Blumer, Herbert. 1969. *Symbolic interactionism: Perspective and method*. Englewood Cliffs, NJ: Prentice Hall.

Blumstein, Alfred, and Joel Wellman, eds. 2000. *The crime drop in America*. Cambridge: Cambridge University Press.

Bourdieu, Pierre. 1984. *Distinction: A social critique of the judgement of taste*. Trans. R. Nice. Cambridge, MA: Harvard University Press.

———. 1989. Social space and symbolic power. *Sociological Theory* 7:14–25.

Breault, K. D. 1994. Was Durkheim right? A critical survey of the empirical literature on *Le Suicide*. In *Émile Durkheim: Le Suicide 100 Years Later*, ed. D. Lester. Philadelphia: Charles Press.

Breault, K. D., and A. J. Kposowa. 2000. Social integration and marital status: A multi-variate individual level study of 30,157 suicides. In *Durkheim's Suicide: A century of research and debate*, ed. W. S. F. Pickering and G. Walford. London: Routledge.

Brint, Steven. 1994. *In an age of experts: The changing role of professionals in politics*. Princeton, NJ: Princeton University Press.

Brooks, David. 2000. *Bobos in paradise: The new upper class and how they got there*. New York: Simon & Schuster.

Brown, Richard Harvey. 1989(1977). *A poetic for sociology: Toward a logic of discovery for the human sciences*. Chicago: University of Chicago Press.

Bryson, Bethany. 1996. Anything but heavy metal: Symbolic exclusion and musical dislikes. *American Sociological Review* 61:884–99.

Buss, David. 1994. *The evolution of desire: Strategies of human mating*. New York: Basic Books.

———. 2000. *The dangerous passion: Why jealousy is as necessary as love and sex*. New York: Free Press.

Butterfield, Fox. 1995. *All God's children: The Bosket family and the American tradition of violence*. New York: Avon Books.

Camic, Charles. 1980. Charisma: Its varieties, preconditions, and consequences. *Sociological Inquiry* 50:5–23.

Chafetz, Janet. 1984. *Sex and advantage: A comparative macro-structural theory of sex stratification*. Totowa, NJ: Roman & Allenheld.

Charon, Joel. 1995. *Symbolic interactionism: An introduction, an interpretation, an integration*. 5th ed. Englewood Cliffs, NJ: Prentice Hall.

Collins, Randall. 1975. *Conflict sociology: Toward an explanatory science*. New York: Academic Press.

———. 1979. *The credential society: An historical sociology of education and stratification*. New York: Academic Press.

———. 1986. *Weberian sociological theory*. Cambridge: Cambridge University Press.

———. 1988a. *Theoretical sociology*. San Diego, CA: Harcourt Brace Jovanovich.

———. 1988b. Theoretical continuities in Goffman's work. In *Erving Goffman: Exploring the interaction order*, ed. Paul Drew and Anthony Wooten. Oxford: Basil Blackwell.

―――. 1994. *Four sociological traditions.* New York: Oxford University Press.

―――. 2004. *Interaction ritual chains.* Princeton and Oxford: Princeton University Press.

Collins, Randall, Janet S. Chafetz, Rae L. Blumberg, Scott Coltrane, and Jonathan Turner. 1993. Toward an integrated theory of gender stratification. *Sociological Perspectives* 36:185–216.

Conger, Jay, and Rabindra Kanungo. 1987. Toward a behavioral theory of charismatic leadership in organizational settings. *Academy of Management Review* 12:637–47.

Courtwright, David. 1996. *Violent land: Single men and social disorder from the frontier to the inner city.* Cambridge, MA: Harvard University Press.

Daly, Martin, and Margo Wilson. 1988. *Homicide.* Hawthorn, NY: Aldine de Gruyter.

Darnton, Robert. 1984. *The great cat massacre and other episodes in French cultural history.* New York: Basic Books.

Darwin, Charles. 1872. *The expression of the emotions in man and animals.* London: J. Murray.

Davies, Christie, and Mark Neal. 2000. Durkheim's altruistic and fatalistic suicide. In *Durkheim's Suicide: A century of research and debate,* ed. W. S. F. Pickering and G. Walford. London: Routledge.

Davis, Kingsley, and Wilbert Moore. 1945. Some principles of stratification. *American Sociological Review* 10:242–49.

DiMaggio, Paul. 1987. Classification in art. *American Sociological Review* 52:440–55.

―――. 1997. Culture and cognition. *Annual Review of Sociology* 23:263–87.

DiMaggio, Paul, and John Mohr. 1985. Cultural capital, educational attainment, and marital selection. *American Journal of Sociology* 90:1231–61.

DiMaggio, Paul, and Walter Powell. 1983. The iron cage revisited: Institutional isomorphism and collective rationality in organizational fields. *American Sociological Review* 48:147–60.

Dobbin, Frank. 1994. *Forging industrial policy: The United States, Britain, and France.* Cambridge: Cambridge University Press.

Dollard, John. 1949. *Caste and class in a Southern town.* 2nd ed. New York: Harper.

Douglas, Jack. 1967. *The social meanings of suicide.* Princeton, NJ: Princeton University Press.

Douglas, Mary. 1970. *Natural symbols: Explorations in cosmology.* New York: Pantheon.

Drew, Paul, and Anthony Wooten, eds. 1988. *Erving Goffman: Exploring the interaction order.* Oxford: Basil Blackwell.

Durkheim, Emile. 1915. *The elementary forms of the religious life.* Trans. J. W. Swain. London: George Allen & Unwin, 1964.

―――. 1933. *The division of labor in society.* Trans. George Simpson. New York: Free Press.

―――. 1938. *The rules of sociological method.* Trans. S. Solovay and J. Mueller. Ed. G. Catlin. 8th ed. New York: Free Press.

―――. 1951. *Suicide: A study in sociology.* Trans. J. Spaulding and G. Simpson. Ed. G. Simpson. Glencoe, IL: Free Press.

Ehrenreich, Barbara, and Annette Fuentes. 1981. Life on the global assembly line. *Ms. Magazine* (January): 53–59.

Elias, Norbert. 1978. *The civilizing process.* Trans. Edmund Jephcott. New York: Urizen Books/Pantheon Books.

Engels, Friedrich. 1958. *The condition of the working class in England.* Trans. and ed. W. O. Henderson and W. H. Chandler. Oxford: Basil Blackwell.

Erickson, Bonnie. 1996. Culture, class, and connections. *American Journal of Sociology* 102:217–52.

Erikson, Kai. 1966. *Wayward Puritans: A study in the sociology of deviance.* New York: John Wiley & Sons.

Etzioni, Amatai. 2000. Toward a theory of public ritual. *Sociological Theory* 18:44–59.

Evans-Pritchard, E. E. 1965. *Theories of primitive religion.* Oxford: Clarendon Press.

Fine, Gary Alan. 1992. The culture of production: Aesthetic choices and constraints in culinary work. *American Journal of Sociology* 97:1268–94.

Foster, George. 1967. *Tzintzuntzan: Mexican peasants in a changing world.* Boston: Little, Brown.

Fox, Kathryn. 1987. Real punks and pretenders: The social organization of a counter-culture. *Journal of Contemporary Ethnography* 16:344–70.

Freidson, Eliot. 2001. *Professionalism: The third logic.* Chicago: University of Chicago Press.

Friedrich, C. J. 1961. Political leadership and the problem of charismatic power. *Journal of Politics* 23:3–24.

Fuchs, Stephan. 1992. *The professional quest for truth: A social theory of science and knowledge.* Albany: State University of New York Press.

Fuchs, Stephan, and Jonathan Turner. 1986. What makes a science "mature"? Patterns of organizational control in scientific production. *Sociological Theory* 4:143–50.

Gans, Herbert. 1972. The positive functions of poverty. *American Journal of Sociology* 78:275–89.

Garston, Neil. 1993. *Bureaucracy: Three paradigms.* Boston: Kluwer Academic Publishers.

Geertz, Clifford. 1973. *The interpretation of cultures: Selected essays.* New York: Basic Books.

Giddens, Anthony. 1971. *Capitalism and modern social theory: An analysis of the writings of Marx, Durkheim and Max Weber.* Cambridge: Cambridge University Press.

Gieryn, Thomas. 1983. Boundary work and the demarcation of science from non-science. *American Sociological Review* 48:781–95.

———. 1999. *The cultural boundaries of science: Credibility on the line.* Chicago: University of Chicago Press.

Girard, Chris. 1993. Age, gender and suicide: A cross-national analysis. *American Sociological Review* 58:553–74.

Goffman, Erving. 1959. *The presentation of self in everyday life.* Garden City, NJ: Doubleday.

———. 1962. *Asylums: Essays on the social situation of mental patients and other inmates.* Chicago: Aldine Publishing.

———. 1967. *Interaction ritual: Essays in face-to-face behavior.* Chicago: Aldine Publishing.

———. 1971. *Relations in public: Microstudies of the public order.* New York: Basic Books.

Goldstone, Jack. 2000. The rise of the west—or not? A revision to socio-economic history. *Sociological Theory* 18:175–95.

Gould, Roger, ed. 2001. *The rational choice controversy in historical sociology*. Chicago: University of Chicago Press.

Grusky, Oscar, and George Miller. 1970. *The sociology of organizations: Basic studies*. New York: Free Press.

Guttentag, Marcia, and Paul Secord. 1983. *Too many women? The sex ratio question*. Beverly Hills, CA: Sage.

Hamilton, Richard. 1996. *The social misconstruction of reality: Validity and verification in the scholarly community*. New Haven, CT: Yale University Press.

Hannan, Michael, and John Freeman. 1989. *Organizational ecology*. Cambridge, MA: Harvard University Press.

Hanson, Norwood R. 1961. *Patterns of discovery*. Cambridge: Cambridge University Press.

Harris, Marvin. 1964. *The nature of cultural things*. New York: Random House.

———. 1968. *The rise of anthropological theory: A history of theories of culture*. New York: Crowell.

———. 1974. *Cows, pigs, wars and witches: Riddles of culture*. New York: Random House.

———. 1977. *Cannibals and kings: The origins of cultures*. New York: Random House.

———. 1979. *Cultural materialism: The struggle for a science of culture*. New York: Random House.

———. 1999. *Theories of culture in postmodern times*. Walnut Creek, CA: Altamira Press.

Hechter, Michael. 1987. *Principles of group solidarity*. Berkeley: University of California Press.

Hermann, Heinz. 1998. *From biology to sociopolitics: Conceptual continuity in complex systems*. New Haven, CT: Yale University Press.

Hixson, Joseph. 1976. *The patchwork mouse*. Garden City, NY: Anchor Press.

Hobsbawm, Eric, and George Rudé. 1968. *Captain Swing*. New York: Pantheon Books.

Hollis, Martin, and Steven Lukes, eds. 1982. *Rationality and relativism*. Cambridge: Massachusetts Institute of Technology Press.

House, James, Karl Landis, and Debra Umberson. 1988. Social relationships and health. *Science* 241:540–45.

Jaynes, Julian. 1977. *The origins of consciousness in the breakdown of the bicameral mind*. Boston: Houghton Mifflin.

Jensen, Arthur. 1992. Scientific fraud or false accusations? The case of Cyril Burt. In *Research Fraud in the Behavioral and Biomedical Sciences*, ed. David Miller and Michael Hersen. New York: John Wiley & Sons.

Jervis, Robert. 1997. *System effects: Complexity in political and social life*. Princeton, NJ: Princeton University Press.

Johnson, Barclay D. 1965. Durkheim's one cause of suicide. *American Sociological Review* 30:875–86.

Kalberg, Stephen. 1980. Max Weber's types of rationality: Cornerstones for the analysis of rationalization processes in history. *American Journal of Sociology* 85:1145–79.

Kessler, Ronald, and Jane McLeod. 1984. Sex differences in vulnerability to undesirable life events. *American Sociological Review* 49:620–31.

Kitcher, Philip. 1967. *Vaulting ambition*. Cambridge, MA: Massachusetts Institute of Technology Press.

Kuhn, Thomas. 1962. *The structure of scientific revolutions*. Chicago: University of Chicago Press.

Lamont, Michele. 1992. *Money, morals, and manners: The culture of the French and American upper-middle class*. Chicago: University of Chicago Press.

Lamont, Michele, and Annette Lareau. 1988. Cultural capital: Allusions, gaps and glissandos in recent theoretical developments. *Sociological Theory* 6:153–68.

Lamont, Michele, and Marcel Fournier. 1992. *Cultivating differences: Symbolic boundaries and the making of inequality*. Chicago: University of Chicago Press.

Lenski, Gerhard. 1966. *Power and privilege*. New York: McGraw-Hill.

———. 1995. *Human societies: An introduction to macrosociology*. 7th ed. New York: McGraw-Hill.

Lepenies, Wolf. 1988. *Between literature and science: The rise of sociology*. Trans. R. J. Hollingdale. New York: Cambridge University Press; Paris: Editions de la maison des sciences de l'homme.

Lester, D., ed. 1994. *Émile Durkheim: Le Suicide 100 Years Later*. Philadelphia: Charles Press.

Levine, Donald. 1995. *Visions of the sociological tradition*. Chicago: University of Chicago Press.

Lindblom, Charles. 1977. *Politics and markets: The world's political economic systems*. New York: Basic Books.

Lindholm, Charles. 1990. *Charisma*. Cambridge: Basil Blackwell.

Little, David. 1991. *Varieties of social explanation: An introduction to the philosophy of social science*. Boulder, CO: Westview Press.

Lukes, Stephen. 1973. *Émile Durkheim: His life and work, a historical and critical study*. London: Allen Lane, Penguin Press.

Macfarlane, Alan. 1989. *The origins of English individualism: The family, property, and social transition*. Oxford: Basil Blackwell, 1978.

Mackie, Gerry. 1996. Ending footbinding and infibulation: A convention account. *American Sociological Review* 61:999–1017.

MacLeod, Jay. 1995. *Ain't no makin' it: Aspirations and attainment in a low-income neighborhood*. Boulder, CO: Westview Press.

MacNeish, Richard S. 1992. *The origins of agriculture and settled life*. Norman: University of Oklahoma Press.

Madsen, Douglas, and Peter G. Snow. 1991. *The charismatic bond: Political behavior in time of crisis*. Cambridge, MA: Harvard University Press.

Manning, Philip. 1992. *Erving Goffman and modern sociology*. Palo Alto, CA: Stanford University Press.

Marshall, Gordon. 1982. *In search of the spirit of capitalism: An essay on Max Weber's Protestant ethic thesis*. London: Hutchinson.

Mead, George Herbert. 1934. *Mind, self, and society from the standpoint of a social behaviorist*. Ed. Charles W. Morris. Chicago: University of Chicago Press.

Merton, Robert. 1957. *Social theory and social structure*. Rev. enl. ed. Glencoe, IL: Free Press.

Miller, David, and Michael Hersen, eds. 1992. *Research fraud in the behavioral and biomedical sciences.* New York: John Wiley & Sons.

Miller, William. 1993. *Humiliation and other essays on honor, social discomfort, and violence.* Cornell, NY: Cornell University Press.

Mills, C. Wright. 1959. *The sociological imagination.* New York: Oxford University Press.

Milner, Murray. 1994. *Status and sacredness : A general theory of status relations and an analysis of Indian culture.* New York: Oxford University Press.

National Academy of Sciences. 1999. *Science and creationism: A view from the National Academy of Science.* 2nd ed. Washington, DC: National Academy Press.

Nisbet, Robert. 1966. *The sociological tradition.* New York: Basic Books.

———. 1976. *Sociology as an art form.* New York: Oxford University Press.

Nisbett, Richard E., and Dov Cohen. 1996. *Culture of honor: The psychology of violence in the South.* Boulder, CO: Westview Press.

Oppenheimer, Valerie. 1982. *Work and the family: A study in social demography.* New York: Academic Press.

Owens, David. 1992. *Causes and coincidences,* ed. Ernest Sosa. Cambridge Studies in Philosophy. Cambridge, MA: Cambridge University Press.

Paige, Jeffrey. 1975. *Agrarian revolution: Social movements and export agriculture in the underdeveloped world.* New York: Free Press.

Patterson, Orlando. 1982. *Slavery and social death: A comparative study.* Cambridge: Harvard University Press.

Perrow, Charles. 1984. *Normal accidents: Living with high-risk technologies.* New York: Basic Books.

Persico, Nicola, Andrew Postlewaite, and Dan Silverman. 2004. The effect of adolescent experience on labor market outcomes: The case of height. *Journal of Political Economy* 112:1019–53.

Peterson, Richard. 1997. *Creating country music: Fabricating authenticity.* Chicago: University of Chicago Press.

Peterson, Richard, and Roger Kern. 1996. Changing highbrow tastes: From snob to omnivore. *American Sociological Review* 61:900–907.

Pfohl, Stephen. 1977. The "discovery" of child abuse. *Social Problems* 24:310–23.

Piaget, Jean. 1970. *Genetic epistemology.* Trans. Eleanor Duckworth. New York: Columbia University Press.

Pickering, W. S. F., and G. Walford, eds. 2000. *Durkheim's Suicide: A century of research and debate.* London: Routledge.

Polanyi, Karl. 1957. *The great transformation.* Boston: Beacon Press, 1944.

Rappaport, Roy. 1968. *Pigs for the ancestors: Ritual in the ecology of a New Guinea people.* New, enl. ed. New Haven, CT: Yale University Press.

Rawls, John. 1971. *A theory of justice.* Cambridge, MA: Belknap Press.

Richter, William. 1995. *The ABC-CLIO Companion to Transportation in America.* Santa Barbara, CA: ABC-CLIO, Inc.

Rosenfeld, Richard. 2004. The case of the unsolved crime decline. *Scientific American* 290:82–90.

Sahlins, Marshall. 1972. *Stone age economics.* Chicago: Aldine-Atherton.

Samuelsson, Kurt. 1961. *Religion and economic action: A critique of Max Weber.* Trans. E. G. French. Ed. D. C. Coleman.

Schlesinger, Jr., Arthur. 1986. *The cycles of American history.* Boston: Houghton Mifflin.

Schmaus, Warren. 1994. *Durkheim's philosophy of science and the sociology of knowledge: Creating an intellectual niche.* Chicago: University of Chicago Press.

Schneider, Joseph. 1985. Social problems theory: The constructionist view. *Annual Review of Sociology* 11:209–29.

Schneider, Mark. 1993. *Culture and enchantment.* Chicago: University of Chicago Press.

———. 1996. Sacredness, status and bodily violation. *Body and Society* 2:75–92.

Schneider, Mark, and Lewellyn Hendrix. 2000. Olfactory sexual inhibition and the Westermarck effect. *Human Nature* 11:65–91.

Schwartz, Barry. 1981. *Vertical classification: A case study in structuralism and the sociology of knowledge.* Chicago: University of Chicago Press.

Schwarzbach, Martin. 1986. *Alfred Wegener: The father of continental drift.* Trans. Carla Love. Madison, WI: Science Tech.

Shils, Edward. 1965. Charisma, order and status. *American Sociological Review* 30:199–212.

Sjoberg, Gideon, and Roger Nett. 1997. *A methodology for social research: With a new introductory essay.* Prospect Heights, IL: Waveland Press.

Skinner, B. F. 1948. *Walden two.* New York: Macmillan Company.

———. 1972. *Beyond freedom and dignity.* New York: Knopf.

Smith, Adam. 1937. *An inquiry into the nature and causes of the wealth of nations.* Ed. Edwin Cannan. New York: Modern Library.

Smith, Thomas. 1992. *Strong interaction.* Chicago: University of Chicago Press.

Spierenburg, Petrus. 1984. *The spectacle of suffering: Executions and the evolution of repression.* New York: Cambridge University Press.

Spiro, Melford. 1963. *Kibbutz: Venture in utopia.* New York: Schocken Books, 1956.

Spitzer, Steven. 1975. Punishment and social organization: A study of Durkheim's theory of penal evolution. *Law and Society Review* 9:613–38.

Stinchcombe, Arthur. 1959. Bureaucratic and craft administration of production: A comparative study. *Administrative Science Quarterly* 4:168–87.

———. 1963. Some empirical consequences of the Davis-Moore theory of stratification. *American Sociological Review* 28:805–808.

———. 1968. *Constructing social theories.* Chicago: Chicago University Press.

Sudnow, David. 1978. *Ways of the hand: The organization of improvised conduct.* Cambridge, MA: Harvard University Press.

Swanson, Guy. 1960. *The birth of the gods: The origins of primitive beliefs.* Ann Arbor: University of Michigan Press.

Taylor, Charles. 1979. Interpretation and the sciences of man. In *Interpretive social science,* ed. Paul Rabinow and William Sullivan, eds. Berkeley: University of California Press, 1971.

Terkel, Studs. 1974. *Working: People talk about what they do all day and how they feel about what they do.* New York: Pantheon.

Tilly, Charles. 1992. *Coercion, capital and European states.* Cambridge, MA: Blackwell.

Tiryakian, Edward. 1965. Typologies. In *International Encyclopedia of the Social Sciences,* ed. David Sills. Vol. 16, 177–86. New York: Macmillan and Free Press.

Turner, Jonathan. 2003. *The structure of sociological theory*. 7th ed. Belmont, CA: Wadsworth Publishing.

Veblen, Thorstein. 1912. *The theory of the leisure class: An economic study of institutions*. New York: Macmillan Company.

Wagner, David G. 1984. *The growth of sociological theories*. Beverly Hills, CA: Sage Publications.

Wagner, David G., and Joseph Berger. 2002. Expectation states theory: An evolving research program. In *New directions in contemporary sociological theory*, ed. Joseph Berger and Morris Zelditch. Lanham, MD: Rowman & Littlefield.

Walker, Mack. 1971. *German home towns: Community, state and general estate, 1648–1871*. Ithaca, NY: Cornell University Press.

Wallace, Walter. 1971. *The logic of science in sociology*. Chicago: Aldine.

Weber, Max. 1949. *The methodology of the social sciences*. Trans. and ed. Edward Shils and Henry Finch. New York: Free Press.

———. 1958a. *The Protestant ethic and the spirit of capitalism*. Trans. Talcott Parsons. New York: Charles Scribner's & Sons.

———. 1958b. *From Max Weber: Essays in sociology*. Trans. and ed. H. H. Gerth and C. Wright Mills. New York: Oxford University Press.

———. 1964. *Theory of social and economic organization*. Trans. A. M. Henderson. Ed. Talcott Parsons. New York: Free Press.

———. 1975. *Roscher and Knies: The logical problems of historical economics*. Trans. Guy Oakes. New York: Free Press.

———. 1977. *Critique of Stammler*. Trans. Guy Oakes. New York: Free Press.

———. 1978. *Economy and society: An outline of interpretive sociology*. Ed. Guenther Roth and Claus Wittich. Berkeley: University of California Press.

Willis, Paul. 1983. *Learning to labor: How working class kids get working class jobs*. Aldershot, Hampshire, UK: Gower, 1977.

Wilson, Bryan. 1975. *The noble savages: The primitive origins of charisma and its contemporary survival*. Berkeley: University of California Press.

Winch, Peter. 1958. *The idea of a social science and its relation to philosophy*. London: Routledge & Kegan Paul; New York: Humanities Press.

Wright, Erik O. 1997. *Class counts: Comparative studies in class analysis*. Cambridge: Cambridge University Press.

Wright, Erik O., Andrew Levine, and Elliot Sober. 1992. *Reconstructing Marxism: Essays on the explanation and the theory of history*. London: Verso.

Zuckerman, Harriet. 1977. Deviant behavior and social control in science. In *Deviance and social change*, ed. E. Sagarin. Beverly Hills, CA: Sage Publications.

Index

ABOS configuration, 295
adventurer capitalism, 118, 120
affect control theory 272, 294–98, 299
affective action, 176
agency, 140, 261
agrarian society, 43, 53, 59, 62, 64, 68, 73, 78, 85, 89, 90, 104, 205, 222
alienation, 44, 52–56, 58–59, 69–73, 76, 90, 116, 128, 144, 172, 188, 196
altruistic suicide, 210–11, 220, 221, 223, 225, 235
analysis, 4–5, 6, 8, 20, 37, 114, 148, 154–55, 186, 304; by Marx, of capitalism, 73–77; of societal sectors, in historical materialism, 93–95; by Weber, of authority, 155–59; of social action, 175–78; by Mead, of self, 275, 278–79; by Goffman, of social space, 281–82, 284; of total institutions, 287–88
analytic typology, 143, 148–54, 267; of authority, 155–59; of social action, 175–78
analytical sectors of society, Marxian, 93–95; cultural materialist, 102
animism, 257, 269
anomaly, 220, 221, 229
anomic suicide, 213
anomie, 213, 214, 218
antithesis, 83, 84

aristocrat/aristocracy, 55, 67, 68, 76, 85
asceticism, worldly, 124, 126–27, 130, 133
authority, 5, 90, 154, 155, 156, 158, 163, 178, 180, 191, 226, 261; bureaucratic, 157, 158, 159–60, 166–71, 191; charismatic, 139, 157, 161–62, 164–66, 191; professional, 158, 159, 191; traditional, 157, 158, 160, 178

backstage, area of social space, 283–86, 301
behaviorism, 272–73, 281, 299
Black, Donald, 264, 302
boundary work, 185, 240
bourgeoisie, 67, 68, 93
bureaucracy, 157, 166–71, 192, 193; social ecology of, 171–74; functional theory for spread of, 174

calibration, of measurements, 217–18, 228
calling (or vocation), 121, 123, 124–25, 130, 132, 144, 305
Calvin, John, 123, 125, 126, 127, 131, 143, 144, 181, 282
capitalism, 43, 44, 49, 50, 56, 72, 77–78; Weber's analysis of origins, 113, 114–34, 137; Marx's mechanism of, 73–76, 112; Marx's causal narrative of origins, 67–69

Index

About the Author

Mark A. Schneider began teaching sociological theory more than thirty years ago at Colorado College and is currently associate professor at Southern Illinois University–Carbondale. In between, he taught at Yale, Princeton, and the University of Michigan. He has written on topics ranging from the origins of the sacred to olfactory mechanisms of incest avoidance, but his central concern, developed in *Culture and Enchantment* (University of Chicago Press), has been with the social conditions that permit science to flourish. He enjoys jazz, bizarre cinematic dreams, his cats, and dining and dancing with his wife.